Mastering Adobe Captivate 6

Create Professional SCORM-compliant eLearning content with Adobe Captivate

Damien Bruyndonckx

BIRMINGHAM - MUMBAI

Mastering Adobe Captivate 6

First published: August 2012

Production Reference: 1160812

Published by Packt Publishing Ltd.
Livery Place
35 Livery Street
Birmingham B3 2PB, UK.

ISBN 978-1-84969-244-1

www.packtpub.com

Cover Image by Asher Wishkerman (a.wishkerman@mpic.de)

Credits

Author
Damien Bruyndonckx

Reviewers
Michael Givens
Nicole Sell

Acquisition Editor
Wilson D'Souza

Lead Technical Editors
Azharuddin Sheikh
Kartikey Pandey

Technical Editors
Jalasha D'costa
Manasi Poonthottam
Zinal Shah

Copy Editors
Alfida Paiva
Laxmi Subramanian

Project Coordinator
Yashodhan Dere

Proofreader
Stephen Swaney

Indexer
Rekha Nair

Graphics
Manu Joseph

Production Coordinator
Shantanu Zagade

Cover Work
Shantanu Zagade

Foreword

Over the past twenty years, eLearning has become a mainstay in education and training around the world. With the transition from formal classroom education, the ever escalating costs of travel, and face-to-face meetings, along with the increasing ease of communication using the Internet, no responsible organization can afford to invest the extraordinary cost and time required for traditional classrooms when virtual education is so easily accomplished.

While corporate and academic demand continues to escalate for eLearning, there is still very little genuine understanding of how great eLearning courses can be developed. At the core of this requirement is the need for texts that explain how rapid eLearning authoring software can be used to create high quality learning modules.

Adobe Captivate has been the leader in eLearning authoring for many years and its continued popularity is assured with the release of Adobe Captivate 6. It has never been easier or faster to create amazing, engaging, and effective eLearning content. Using Adobe Captivate you'll be able to rapidly build great looking content with little or no programming, and deploy it to an amazing variety of media and locations.

Your journey toward mastery of Adobe Captivate may begin here with this wonderful work from Damien Bruyndonckx. Damien provides a concise, easily understood, and thorough introduction to Adobe Captivate 6. He has illustrated the text well, providing a wealth of examples and links to online resources that lead the reader to a deeper understanding of related concepts should you want to learn more about any topic.

Jack Welch said, "An organization's ability to learn, and translate that learning into action rapidly, is the ultimate competitive advantage." Your journey to both facilitate learning in your organization, and to do so rapidly begins here.

Allen Partridge
eLearning Evangelist
Adobe Systems

About the Author

Damien Bruyndonckx was trained as an Elementary school teacher and began his career in 1998 teaching French in two elementary public schools of Louisiana for three years.

Back in his home country of Belgium in 2001, Damien began his career as an IT trainer and acquired the status of Adobe Certified Instructor on ColdFusion, Dreamweaver, Acrobat, and Captivate. This allowed him to be involved in various eLearning and web development projects for various customers.

Today, Damien teaches multimedia at IHECS, a Brussels-based higher education school of communication where he was recently asked to implement eLearning. He also runs his own software training company that provides training on Adobe Products and eLearning consultancy.

Damien is a big time music lover and sometimes works as a live mixing engineer. He lives in Belgium with his girlfriend and her two children.

Blog: `http://www.dbr-training.eu`

Twitter: `@damienbkx`

Acknowledgement

It was on a Sunday morning, early November 2011. I received an e-mail from a guy called Wilson D'Souza. Wilson is an Acquisition Editor at Pack Publishing and he was looking for someone to author a book on Captivate. Three days later, we agreed on a table of content and less than a week after the first e-mail, we signed the contract. The stage was set for the big adventure to begin!

The first persons I would like to thank are Wilson and all his colleagues at Packt Publishing for trusting me and for giving me the fantastic opportunity to become a published author.

Writing such a book is a milestone in someone's professional career and I would like to acknowledge the help, guidance, and support I received from my colleagues and employers. My deepest thanks to Mr. Benoît Ter Burg from Vision IT and to Mrs. Christel de Maeyer from Howest for introducing me to Captivate back in the early days of Captivate 1.

Being a native French speaker, one of the main obstacles for me during the course of this project was the language barrier, so I asked my friend Baudouin Lernoux to review my drafts before sending them to Packt. Aside from being a great friend and a talented musician, Baudouin teaches English in a Belgian High School. His input on this project has been of critical importance and some of the comments he left in the manuscript were truly hilarious. Thank you my friend, for all this hard work!

Finally, my thanks for the ones who share my life on a daily basis. They had to cope with my insane working hours while writing this book and moving to our new house at the same time. The challenge was theirs too. Céline, Antoine, and Sophie, this book is your book. The book of your support, understanding, and patience for me, the UFO that crossed your life three years ago…

About the Reviewers

Michael Givens is the CTO of U Saw It Enterprises, a web-technology consulting firm based in Spring, TX. As a multi-years experienced web-technology specialist, he is willing to shift gears at a moment's notice to the Client's technology of choice. He is both an Adobe Community Professional and an Adobe Corporate Champion known to share his experience and evangelism of all things Adobe. He is certified both in ColdFusion 5 and as an advanced CFMX developer. He has written Adobe Apollo in Flight (Digital Short Cut), co-written Adobe AIR Programming Unleashed, written Sams Teach Yourself AIR Programming in 24 Hours, numerous articles, and blogs regularly at `www.flexination.info`.

I would like to thank my better-half, Shaira Musni Cunanan and our son, Clark Michael Cunanan Givens, for their patience, support, and understanding during my technical reviewing blocks of time away from them. Ok, Clark, Mommy, let's go motorcycling and play some basketball now. ☺

Nicole Sell is an Adobe Certified Instructor (ACI) and Microsoft Certified Trainer (MCT). She has been training since 2004 across various industries, in multiple countries.

Nicole specializes in eLearning design and development as well as web design and development. She also has a background in working with electronic forms.

Over the years, Nicole has been invited to speak in conferences and user group meetings. She is actively involved in her areas of specialty. She has started and maintained user group meetings to provide knowledge and support in various applications.

Nicole is available for training and consulting. You can contact her from her company's website, `www.redvineconsulting.com`. You can also connect with her on LinkedIn and follow her on Twitter.

Nicole Sell has worked for training centers before starting her own company, Red Vine Consulting. She enjoys training, and consulting, and the ability to work with different people on a variety of different projects.

I'd like to thank my partner, Ben. He understood when I needed to spend evenings reviewing the book. He was very supportive throughout the process.

---

www.PacktPub.com

Support files, eBooks, discount offers and more

You might want to visit `www.PacktPub.com` for support files and downloads related to your book.

Did you know that Packt offers eBook versions of every book published, with PDF and ePub files available? You can upgrade to the eBook version at `www.PacktPub.com` and as a print book customer, you are entitled to a discount on the eBook copy. Get in touch with us at `service@packtpub.com` for more details.

At `www.PacktPub.com`, you can also read a collection of free technical articles, sign up for a range of free newsletters and receive exclusive discounts and offers on Packt books and eBooks.

`http://PacktLib.PacktPub.com`

Do you need instant solutions to your IT questions? PacktLib is Packt's online digital book library. Here, you can access, read and search across Packt's entire library of books.

Why Subscribe?

- Fully searchable across every book published by Packt
- Copy and paste, print and bookmark content
- On demand and accessible via web browser

Free Access for Packt account holders

If you have an account with Packt at `www.PacktPub.com`, you can use this to access PacktLib today and view nine entirely free books. Simply use your login credentials for immediate access.

Table of Contents

Preface

Adobe Captivate is the industry-leading solution for authoring eLearning content. With Adobe Captivate one can capture the onscreen action, enhance your eLearning projects, insert SCORM and AICC-compliant quizzes, and publish your work in various formats for easy deployment on virtually any desktop and mobile device.

Mastering Adobe Captivate 6 is a comprehensive guide to creating SCORM-compliant Demonstrations, Simulations, and quizzes with Adobe Captivate. The sample projects demonstrate each and every feature of Adobe Captivate, giving you the expertise you need to create and deploy your own professional quality eLearning courses.

Mastering Adobe Captivate 6 will guide you through the creation of four eLearning projects including a Demonstration, a Simulation, a Video Demo, and a SCORM-compliant Quiz. The first part of the book will drive you through the main three steps of the Captivate production process. In the first step, we will use the powerful capture engine of Captivate to generate the needed slides and screenshots. In the second step, we will enhance our slides and screenshots using the objects provided by Captivate. These objects include animations, interactions, videos, and more. In the third step, we will make our project available to the outside world by publishing it in various formats including Adobe Flash PDF, video, and even HTML5. The second part of the book will focus on the advanced tools of Captivate. These tools include the Question Slides that make up a Quiz, SCORM and AICC compliance, localization of your eLearning content, and Widgets among others. In the last chapter, we will unleash the true power of Captivate by using the Variables and the Advanced Actions to create a unique eLearning experience.

What this book covers

Chapter 1, Getting Started with Captivate, introduces Captivate as an eLearning solution. It then drives you through the tool icons and panels of the Captivate interface. At the end of Chapter 1, we will view the finished sample applications that we will build during the course of the book.

Chapter 2, Capturing the Slides, tells how we will use the screen capture engine of Captivate to capture the slides of our movies. We will also discuss how to choose the right size for the projects we have to make.

Chapter 3, Working with Standard Objects, tells us how we will use the standard objects of Captivate to enhance the slide shots in the previous chapter. The standard objects discussed in this chapter are the Text Captions, the Highlight Boxes, the Images, and the Mouse movements.

Chapter 4, Working with Interactive Objects and Animations, introduces the objects that bring animation in the project. These objects are the Text Animation, the Animation, the Zoom Area, the Rollover Caption, the Rollover Image, and the Rollover Slidelet. At the end of the chapter, we will discover the three interactive objects of Captivate by converting a demonstration into a simulation.

Chapter 5, Working with Audio, tells how we can add sound effects on objects, voice-over narration on slides, and background music to the entire project. We will use the Text-To-Speech engine of Captivate to generate some of the needed audio clips, and we will add Closed Captions for enhanced accessibility.

Chapter 6, Final Changes and Publishing, in the first part of this chapter, we will make our projects ready for publishing by setting up the options valid for the entire project. One of these options is the Skin Editor that will let us customize the Playback Controls and the Table of Contents of our projects. In the second part of this chapter, we will make our projects available to the outside world by publishing them in various formats including Adobe Flash, HTML5, and PDF.

Chapter 7, Working with Quizzes, discusses the powerful quizzing Engine of Captivate. First, we will review each and every question type of Captivate one by one and see how we can integrate them into Question Pools to generate random quizzes. In the second part of this chapter, we will see how the interactions of the Quiz can be reported to a SCORM or AICC-compliant LMS for easy tracking of your student's performance.

Chapter 8, Templates, Master Slides, and Themes, focuses on the cosmetic part of the project. We will see what Themes are and how we can build our own Theme to ensure visual consistency both within a given project and across projects.

Chapter 9, Using Captivate with Other Applications, in this chapter, we will explore we will explore the relationship between Captivate and other Adobe and third-party applications. First, we will convert a PowerPoint presentation into a Captivate project. We will then export some Captivate data to Microsoft Word in order to localize a Captivate project. We will also import an Adobe Photoshop file and export the project to Adobe Flash.

Chapter 10, Reviewing a Captivate Project, tells how we will make the project available to a team of reviewers. The reviewers will then use the Adobe Captivate Reviewer to comment on our work. Finally, we will import the reviewer's comments into Captivate and address them one by one.

Chapter 11, Variables, Advanced Actions, and Widgets, tells us how to unleash the true power of Captivate. It discusses the Variables, the Advanced Actions, the Widgets, and the Smart Interactions. These features will help you design and develop highly interactive eLearning content that provides a unique experience to each and every learner.

What you need for this book

In order to follow the sections and run the corresponding sample code, you need a test environment with the following items:

- Adobe Captivate 6 (Available as a free 30-day trial on the Adobe website).
- Adobe Media Encoder CS6 (Part of the Captivate 6 download).
- The Adobe Captivate Reviewer and the Adobe Captivate Quiz Result Analyzer. Both these applications are bundled with Captivate and available for free on the Adobe Website.
- Microsoft PowerPoint 2003 or higher (optional).
- Microsoft Word 2003 or higher (optional).
- Adobe Photoshop CS3 or higher (optional).
- Adobe Flash CS5.5 or CS6 (optional).

Who this book is for

If you are:

- A teacher wanting to produce high quality eLearning content for your students.
- Working in a training department and want to implement eLearning in your company.
- Using a SCORM or AICC-compliant LMS and want to produce eLearning content to track your students' performance.
- A webmaster in need of a fun and interactive way to produce an FAQ or a support site.
- Interested in eLearning.

Then, this book is for you! A basic knowledge of your operating system (Mac or Windows) is all it takes to author the next generation of eLearning content with this book.

Conventions

In this book, you will find a number of styles of text that distinguish between different kinds of information. Here are some examples of these styles, and an explanation of their meaning:

New terms and **important words** are shown in bold. Words that you see on the screen, in menus or dialog boxes for example, appear in the text like this: "Click on the word **Classic** in the top right corner of the screen to reveal a list of available workspaces".

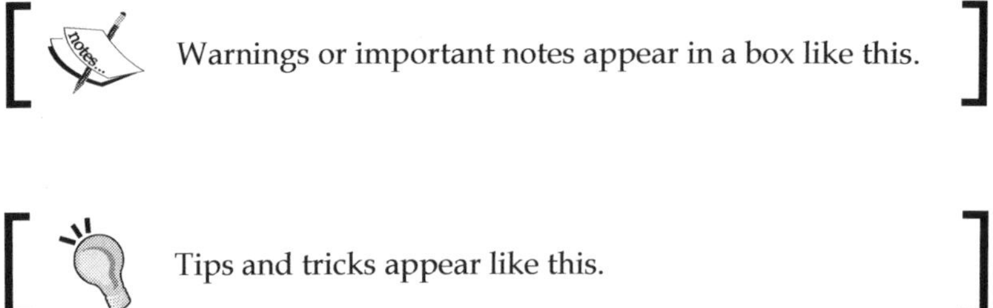

Reader feedback

Feedback from our readers is always welcome. Let us know what you think about this book—what you liked or may have disliked. Reader feedback is important for us to develop titles that you really get the most out of.

Customer support

Now that you are the proud owner of a Packt book, we have a number of things to help you to get the most from your purchase.

Downloading the example code

You can download the example code files for all Packt books you have purchased from your account at `http://www.packtpub.com`. If you purchased this book elsewhere, you can visit `http://www.packtpub.com/support` and register to have the files e-mailed directly to you.

Errata

Although we have taken every care to ensure the accuracy of our content, mistakes do happen. If you find a mistake in one of our books—maybe a mistake in the text or the code—we would be grateful if you would report this to us. By doing so, you can save other readers from frustration and help us improve subsequent versions of this book. If you find any errata, please report them by visiting `http://www.packtpub.com/support`, selecting your book, clicking on the **errata submission form** link, and entering the details of your errata. Once your errata are verified, your submission will be accepted and the errata will be uploaded to our website, or added to any list of existing errata, under the Errata section of that title.

Piracy

Piracy of copyright material on the Internet is an ongoing problem across all media. At Packt, we take the protection of our copyright and licenses very seriously. If you come across any illegal copies of our works, in any form, on the Internet, please provide us with the location address or website name immediately so that we can pursue a remedy.

Please contact us at `copyright@packtpub.com` with a link to the suspected pirated material.

We appreciate your help in protecting our authors, and our ability to bring you valuable content.

Questions

You can contact us at `questions@packtpub.com` if you are having a problem with any aspect of the book, and we will do our best to address it.

1
Getting Started with Captivate

Since its introduction in 2004, Captivate has always been the industry-leading solution for authoring eLearning content. At the beginning, it was a very simple screen-capture utility named *FlashCam*. In 2002, a company named *eHelp* acquired FlashCam and turned it into an eLearning authoring tool named *Robodemo*. In 2004, another company called *Macromedia* acquired eHelp and changed the name of the product one last time. Macromedia *Captivate* was born. A few months later, Adobe acquired Macromedia and, consequently, *Macromedia Captivate* became *Adobe Captivate*.

As the years passed, Adobe released Captivate 2, Captivate 3 and Captivate 4, adding tools, objects, and features along the way. One of the most significant events in the Captivate history took place in July 2010, when Adobe released Captivate 5. For the release of Captivate 5, Adobe engineers have rewritten the code of the entire application from the ground up. As a result, Captivate 5 was the first version to be available on both Mac OS and Windows. Captivate 5 was also equipped with a brand new user interface, similar to the interface of other Adobe Applications, not to mention an impressive array of new and enhanced tools.

As of today, the latest version of Captivate is version 6. Captivate 6 comes with a new improved quiz engine that supports partial scoring and pretests, HTML5 publishing, advanced interactions, new Smart Shapes, a new video capture mode, and tons of other (not so) small enhancements. With all this power sitting one click away, it is easy to overcharge our projects with lots of complicated sound and visual effects, lots of sophisticated interactions that can ultimately drive the user away from the primary objective of every Captivate Project: teaching.

While working with Captivate, one should never forget that Captivate is an eLearning tool. At the most basic level, it simply means that you, the developer of the Project, and your audience are united by a very special kind of relationship: a student to teacher relationship. Therefore, from now on, and for the rest of the book, you, the reader of these pages, will not be called "the developer" or "the programmer", but *the teacher*, and the ones who will view your finished applications will not be the "users" or "the visitors", but will be called *the learners* or *the students*. You will see that it changes everything.

In this chapter, we will:

- Discuss the different editions of Captivate
- Discuss the general steps of the Captivate production process
- Tour the Captivate interface
- Work with panels and workspaces
- View the finished sample applications

The three editions of Captivate

There are three ways to obtain Captivate. Depending on the way you choose to obtain the application, you will not have exactly the same set of features available, so it is important to mention this point right from the start.

Captivate as a standalone product. This is the basic way of obtaining the software. You get all the core features of Captivate and you can start working on your eLearning content right away. This book has been designed to work with the standalone edition of Captivate.

> See the Captivate page on the Adobe website at `http://www.adobe.com/ap/products/captivate.html`.

You can download and use the standalone version of Captivate free of charge for 30 days. It should be more than enough to go through the exercises of this book. Be aware though, that once the trial expires, you will not have access to Captivate anymore unless you convert your trial version to a licensed one.

> Download your Captivate 30 days trial at `http://www.adobe.com/downloads/`.

Captivate in the eLearning Suite. You probably know Adobe Creative Suite, but do you know the **eLearning Suite**? Adobe eLearning Suite is a bundle of applications specially designed for authoring and publishing eLearning content. It includes some of the most popular Adobe applications (like Flash Professional, Photoshop and Dreamweaver) plus, of course, Adobe Captivate. When you get Captivate as part of the eLearning Suite, you'll have extra tools available. Those extra features enable workflows between the applications of the eLearning Suite. Some of these features will be mentioned in this book, but none of them are required to go through the exercises.

As of this writing, Adobe eLearning Suite 6 is the current version.

For more info on the eLearning Suite, visit `http://www.adobe.com/products/elearningsuite.html`.

Captivate in the Technical Communication Suite. The **Technical Communication Suite** (**TCS**) is yet another bundle of applications from Adobe. This one is designed to create technical content such as help files and user guides. The Technical Communication Suite includes applications such as Adobe RoboHelp, Adobe FrameMaker, Adobe Acrobat Professional and, of course, Adobe Captivate.

For more info on the Technical Communication Suite, visit `http://www.adobe.com/products/technicalcommunicationsuite.html`.

The Captivate production process at a glance

Producing content with Captivate is three steps process, or to be exact, four steps process, but only three of these steps take place in Captivate. That's why I like to refer to the first step as *Step zero*!

Step zero: The pre-production phase. This is the only step of the process that does not involve working with the Captivate application. Depending on the project you are planning, it can last from a few minutes to a few months. Step zero is probably the most important one of the entire process as it is where you actually create the scenarios and the storyboards of your teaching project. This is where you develop the pedagogical approach that will drive the entire project. What will you teach the students? In what order will you introduce the topics? How and when will you assess the students' knowledge? and so on. These are some very important questions that need to be answered before you open Captivate for the first time and start building your project. Step zero is where the teacher's skills will fully express themselves.

Blog post - Scenario-based training

Make sure you read these series of posts on the official Adobe Captivate Blog. Dr Pooja Jaisingh shares her experience in creating scenario-based training. These posts clearly stress the importance of "Step zero" and give you a first high-level approach of the Captivate production process. The first post of the series can be found at `http://blogs.adobe.com/captivate/2012/03/my-experience-with-creating-a-scenario-based-course-part-1.html`.

Step one: Capturing the slides. When you know exactly where and how you will lead your students, it is time to open Captivate. During this first phase, you will use one of the most popular Captivate features: the ability to record any action you perform onscreen. You will simply use your mouse to perform actions on your computer. Behind the scenes, Captivate will be watching and will record any action you do using a sophisticated screen capture engine based on screenshots. This first step can be compared to shooting a movie. The goal is to acquire the required images, actions, and sequences. In the movie industry, the raw material that comes out of the shooting is called *the rushes*. It is not uncommon for a movie director to discard lots of *rushes* along the way, so that only the very best sequences are part of the final release.

Step two: The editing phase. This phase is the most time-consuming phase of the process. This is where your project will slowly take shape. In this step, you will arrange the final sequence of actions, record narration, add objects to the slides (such as Text Captions, Buttons, and many more), arrange those objects in the Timeline, add title and ending slides, program the advanced interactions, and so on. At the end of this phase, the project should be ready for publication.

Step three: The publishing phase. This is where you will make your project available to the learners, and this is where Captivate really is awesome! Captivate lets you publish your project in the popular *Adobe Flash* format. This is great since it makes the deployment of our eLearning courses very easy: only the Flash player is needed. The very same Flash player that is used to read Flash-enabled websites or YouTube videos is enough to read our published Captivate projects.

Captivate can also publish our project as standalone applications (`.exe` on Windows and `.app` on Macintosh) or as a video file that can be easily uploaded to YouTube and viewed on a Tablet or Smartphone.

One of the most significant new features of Captivate 6 is the ability to publish our projects in HTML5. By publishing in HTML5 format, *the Flash player plugin is not required anymore to play our content*. Thanks to this new technology, our students are able to take our courses not only using their desktop computers, *but also their tablets* (including the iPad), *their smartphones, or any other internet-enabled device*. The door is open for the next revolution of our industry: **Mobile Learning** (or **mLearning**).

Blog post

Make sure you read this wonderful blog post by Allen Partridge: *The How & Why of iPads, HTML5, & Mobile Devices in eLearning, Training & Education* at `http://blogs.adobe.com/captivate/2011/11/the-how-why-of-ipads-html5-mobile-devices-in-elearning-training-education.html`. Another interesting read is a blog post by former Adobe Evangelist RJ Jacquez where RJ claims that the *m* of *mLearning* means *More* at `http://rjacquez.com/the-m-in-mlearning-means-more/`.

Touring the Captivate interface

In this book, we shall cover the three steps of the process requiring the use of Captivate. You will discover that Captivate has specific tools to handle each of these three steps. Actually, each step requires so many options, tools, and features that Captivate has a very large number of icons, panels, dialog boxes, and controls available. When developing Captivate, Adobe's designers were, therefore, confronted by a very significant issue: how to display all those tools, features, boxes, and controls on a single computer screen?

To address the issue, the designers at Adobe decided the following:

- Depending on the production step you are working on, you do not need the same set of tools at all times.
- Some tools relevant for a given project are useless in another project.
- Each teacher has different working habits, so each teacher should be able to display the tools of Captivate as he/she sees fit.
- While some Captivate users have large screens, others have a much smaller display area available.

These simple considerations helped the Captivate design team create a very flexible user interface.

If you already use other Adobe Applications, you'll be on known ground as the Captivate 6 user interface works the same way as the user interface of the most popular Adobe Applications.

A first look at the Captivate interface

When you open the application for the first time, you'll get a default set of tools available. Let's check it out using the following steps:

1. Open Captivate.
2. On the left-hand side of the Welcome screen, click the **open** icon.
3. Open the `final/drivingInBe.cptx` file situated in the exercises folder that you have downloaded from the Internet.
4. Your screen should look like the following screenshot:

The Captivate user interface is composed of panels laid out around the **stage** (1). The stage is the main area of the screen. It is where we lay out the objects that make up each slide of the project.

At the very top of the screen is the **menu bar** (2). The menu bar gives us access to every single feature of Captivate.

Right below the menu bar, is the **Main Options toolbar** (3). Each icon of the *Main Options* toolbar is a shortcut to a feature that also exists in the menu bar.

A special toolbar spans across the left-hand side of the screen from the top down. It is the **Object toolbar** (4). The Objects toolbar lets you insert new objects on your Captivate slides. This is one of the most important toolbars of Captivate and one that we will use a lot during the course of this book.

The next panel is called the **Filmstrip** (5). It shows the sequence of slides that makes up your Captivate project. The primary use of the **Filmstrip** is to enable navigation between the slides of the project, but the **Filmstrip** can also be used to perform basic operations on the slides such as reordering slides or deleting slides.

At the bottom of the screen is another important panel: the **Timeline** (6). As its name implies, this panel will be used to arrange the objects of the slide in time. This panel is also used to set up the stacking order of the objects.

The right-hand side of the screen shows a group of four panels. The one that is shown by default is the **Properties** panel (7), while the **Library** panel, the **Quiz Properties** panel, and the **Project Info** panel are hidden. The **Properties** panel is a dynamic panel. It means that its content depends on the currently selected item.

Such a set of panels is known as a **workspace**. Depending on the project you are working on, the size of your computer screen, your working habits, and so on, this basic workspace might not be exactly the one you need. The name of the workspace in use is displayed at the top right corner of the screen. Currently, the **Classic** workspace is the one in use.

5. Click on the word **Classic** in the top right corner of the screen to reveal a list of available workspaces.
6. In the workspace switcher, choose the **Quizzing** workspace, as shown in the following screenshot:

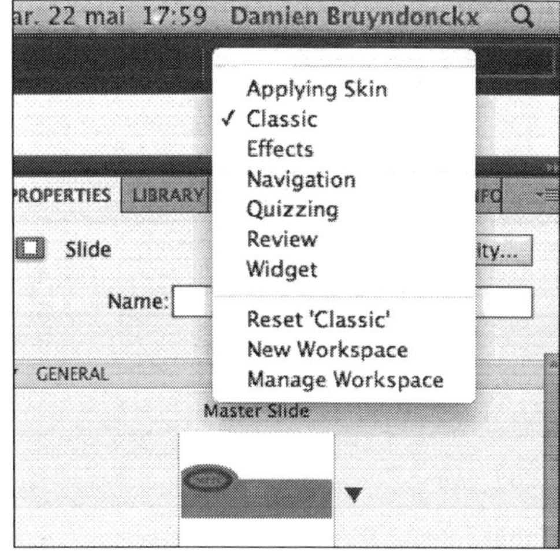

When done, take a close look at the screen. The set of available panels is not exactly the same as before. First of all, the **Filmstrip** is displayed at the bottom of the screen, where the **Timeline** used to be. The **Timeline** panel is still there, but hidden by default, while two new panels (**Master Slide** and **Question Pool**) are shown between the **Filmstrip** and the **Timeline** panels. The left-hand side of the screen has also changed. Right where the **Filmstrip** used to be, a big empty panel called **Quiz Properties** is now displayed.

This example clearly shows what a workspace is: a set of panels arranged in a specific layout. While the **Classic** workspace we explored earlier was perfect to perform some basic tasks, the **Quizzing** workspace currently in use is perfect when developing a Captivate quiz.

7. At the bottom of the screen, click on the **Question Pool** tab to open the **Question Pool** panel.
8. The **Question Pool** panel displays four question slides. Click on each question slide one by one while taking a look at the **Quiz Properties** panel on the left-hand side of the screen.

As you go through each of the question slides listed in the **Question Pool** panel, the **Quiz Properties** panel displays the properties relevant to the currently selected question slide. Notice at the very top of the quiz properties panel, the type of the active question slide (True/False, Sequence, hot spot, and so on), as shown in the following screenshot:

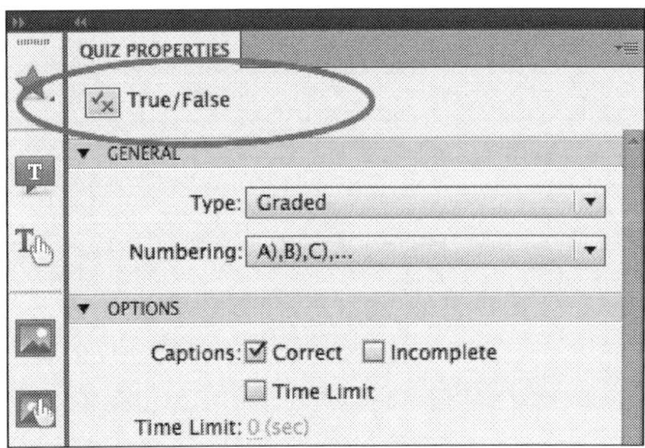

This tells us that the **Quiz Properties** panel of Captivate is a dynamic panel. It works like the **Properties** panel we discussed earlier. It means that it displays information relevant to the current selection. Consequently, as the selection changes, the content of the panel changes as well.

9. Reopen to the Workspace switcher at the top right corner of the screen.
10. In the list of available workspaces, choose **Navigation**.

The **Navigation** workspace is applied, and again the panels are rearranged. This time, the **Branching** panel pops up and covers most of the available screen area. The **Branching** panel is known as a *floating* panel because it floats freely on the screen and is not attached (*docked*) anywhere.

Branching is an important concept in Captivate. When we ask the student to perform an action, he/she might do either the right or the wrong action. Captivate allows the teacher to set up two different reactions when the right or wrong answers are performed so that the student experiences the Captivate application differently (in other words, takes different *branches*) based on his/her actions and answers. The branching view offers a visual representation of this concept.

11. At the top right corner of the screen, reopen to the workspace switcher.
12. Choose the **Classic** workspace to reapply the original default workspace.

These little experiments tell us some important things about the Captivate interface. Before moving on, let's summarize what we have learned so far:

- The Captivate interface is composed of panels laid out around the main editing area called *the stage*.
- A **workspace** shows a selection of panels in a specific arrangement. No workspace shows every available panel, so there are always tools that are not shown on the screen.
- Captivate ships with different workspaces. These workspaces are available in the workspace switcher at the top right corner of the screen.
- When we open Captivate the workspace applied is the last workspace used. When the Captivate application is executed for the first time, the **Classic** workspace is applied by default.

We have rapidly inspected three of the workspaces available in Captivate. Before moving on to the next topic, feel free to inspect the remaining workspaces. You will uncover some more panels along the way. Just make sure you reapply the **Classic** workspace when you are done.

Working with panels

Captivate has a very flexible interface. You can move the panels around, open more panels, or close the ones you don't need. You can enlarge and reduce the panels or even turn them into icons to gain some space on your screen. Perform the following steps to reduce/enlarge the panels:

1. Double-click on the **Filmstrip** tab at the top of the **Filmstrip** panel. This collapses the **Filmstrip** panel.

2. Double-click on the **Filmstrip** tab again to expand the panel, as shown in the following screenshot:

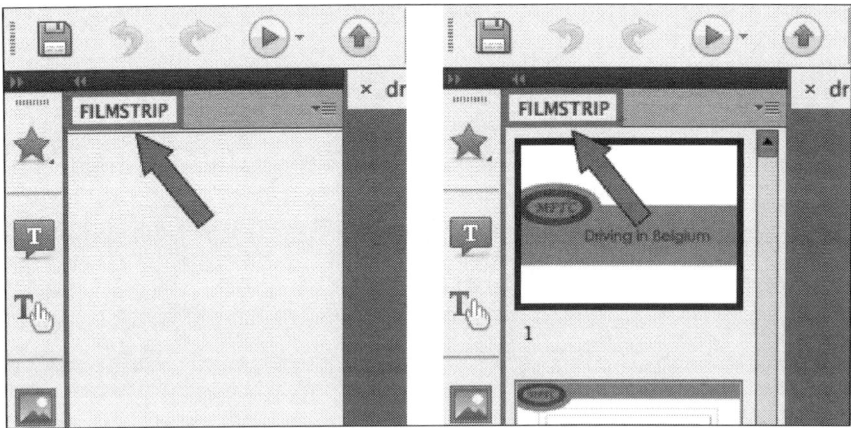

3. Do the same experiment with the other panels of the screen including the **Timeline** (at the bottom) and the **Properties** panel (on the right-hand side).
4. When you are done, reset the **Classic** workspace to its original state by going into the **Window** | **Workspace** | **Reset 'Classic'** menu.

As you can see, collapsing and expanding the panels is very simple and is the first tool at our disposal to customize the Captivate interface. The second tool we will discuss is the very small double arrow icon that is displayed on top of every panel or groups of panels. For the **Properties/Library/Quiz Properties/Project Info** panel group, this very small icon is located at the far right-hand side of the interface, as shown in the following screenshot:

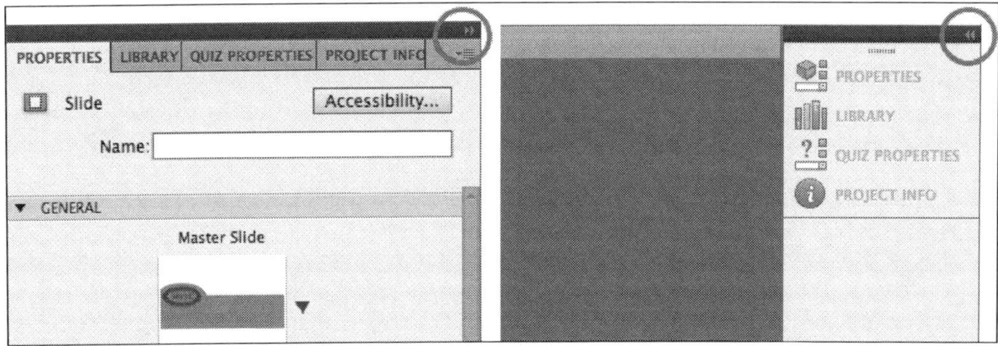

Perform the following steps to expand/collapse the panels:

1. Click on this *very small double arrow* to reduce the **Properties/Library/Quiz Properties/Project Info** panel group to a set of four icons.

2. Click on the **Properties** icon to reveal the **Properties** panel. Click on the same icon again to hide the **Properties** panel.
3. Reveal and hide the **Library**, **Quiz Properties**, and **Project Info** panels by clicking on their respective icons.
4. Click on the double arrow to toggle the panel group back to its original state.

If you have a small screen, you probably want the stage to cover most of the available area. Reducing the panels to icons is a very simple and effective way to gain space on your computer screen, so this *very little double arrow* might be a great tool for you!

Notice that such double arrows are also available at the top of the Objects toolbar. Clicking on that one puts the icons of the Objects toolbar in two columns while a second click on the same icon toggles the Objects toolbar back to a single column display.

Another possible customization is to enlarge/reduce the panels present on the screen. This is particularly interesting when working with the **Filmstrip**. Perform the following steps to reduce/enlarge the **Filmstrip** panel:

5. Place your mouse above the vertical line that separates the **Filmstrip** from the stage until the mouse pointer turns to a double arrow.
6. Click-and-drag the vertical separator to the right until the **Filmstrip** covers more or less half of the screen.

The **Filmstrip** now displays (more or less) all the slides of your Captivate project in columns, as shown in the following screenshot:

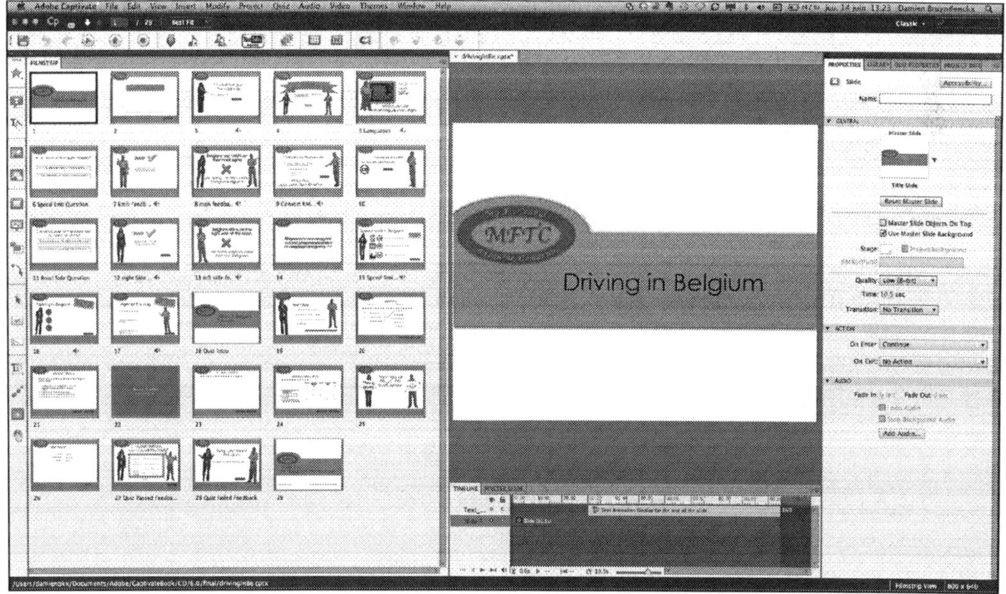

This layout is very practical if you have to work with a large number of slides as it helps you see the "big picture" more efficiently. This view of the **Filmstrip** can be compared to the *Slide sorter* view of Microsoft PowerPoint.

Of course, the other areas of the screen can be resized the same way. Take the **Timeline** for instance. Resizing **Timeline** might be very interesting if you have a large number of objects on a given slide using the following steps:

1. Open the **Window** menu and click on the **Workspace | Reset 'Classic'** command. This resets the current workspace to its default state.
2. In **Filmstrip**, select slide **15**. It should appear on the stage.

Slide 15 contains a large number of objects. If you take a look at **Timeline**, you'll notice that it is not high enough to display every object of the slide and that a vertical scrollbar appears on the right-hand side of the **Timeline** panel. In order to have a clearer view on the objects that compose this slide and of their timing, we will now enlarge the **Timeline** panel.

3. Place your mouse above the horizontal separator that spans between the **Timeline** panel and the stage until the mouse pointer turns into a double arrow.
4. Click-and-drag the horizontal separator towards the top of the screen until the **Timeline** is high enough to display all the objects of the slide, that is, when there is no more vertical scroll bar in the **Timeline** panel.

The **Timeline** panel now displays every object present on the slide and we have a much clearer view of the stack of objects present on slide 15.

Adding and removing panels

So far, the panels that we have manipulated were already displayed in the **Classic** workspace. But what if we need to access tools situated in panels *not* present in the **Classic** workspace? How can we add more panels to the interface and how can those panels be arranged to fit our needs?

The **Window** menu holds the answer. If you open it, you'll see a list of all the panels that exist in Captivate. When a checkmark is displayed in front of a panel name, it means that the corresponding panel is currently displayed on the screen, as shown in the following screenshot:

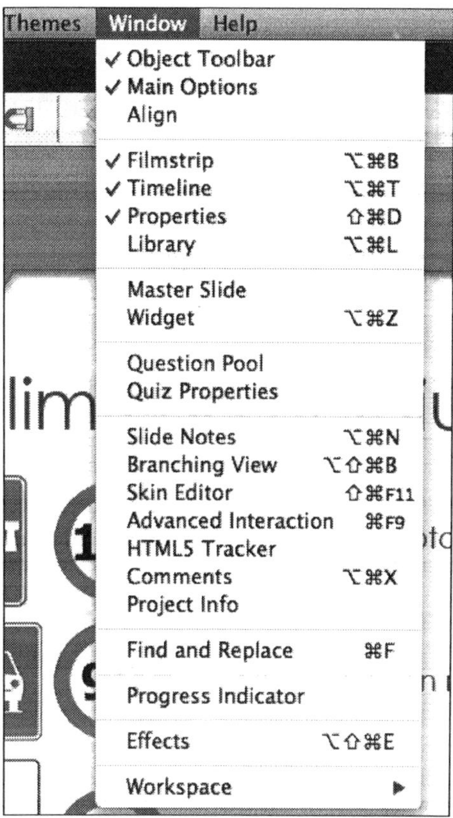

Perform the following steps to add the Slide Notes panel:

1. Open the **Window** menu.
2. Click on the **Slide Notes** to add the **Slide Notes** panel to the workspace. It should appear at the bottom of the interface right next to **Timeline**.

It is the first time we see this panel. This illustrates the fact that some panels are simply hidden from the default workspace unless you explicitly ask Captivate to display them. If you are looking for a tool that you cannot find on the screen, there is a good chance that the tool you are looking for is available in a panel that is currently hidden. In such a case, simply open the **Window** menu and select the panel you want to see.

Of course, the same is true when you want to hide a panel.

3. Open the **Window** menu again.
4. Click on the **Filmstrip** menu item to hide **Filmstrip** from the screen.

The **Filmstrip** panel is now completely gone. To reopen it, the only solution is to go back to the **Window** menu and select the **Filmstrip** entry back on.

Another way to close a panel (or even an entire panel group) is to use the small menu associated with every group of panels.

5. Click on the small icon associated with the **Properties/Library/Quiz Properties/Project Info** panel group.
6. Choose **Close Group** from the available options.

This operation removes the whole group (four panels) from the interface. The following screenshot shows how to close a group:

7. Go in the **Window | Properties** menu item to turn the **Properties** panel back on.

Notice that this operation restores the entire panel group (four panels) back on.

Moving panels around

The last thing we will discuss about the panels is how you can move them around. The **Slide Notes** panel is currently displayed at the bottom of the slide. It is its default-predefined location. Perform the following steps to move the Slide Notes panels:

1. Place your mouse on the **Slide Notes** tab at the top of the **Slide Notes** panel.
2. Click-and-drag the **Slide Notes** panel away from its current location.
3. Release the mouse when the panel floats in the middle of the screen.

Your screen should look like the following screenshot:

Unlike the other panels that are *docked*, the **Slide Notes** panel now *floats* in the middle of the screen. This is known as a floating panel. Captivate allows the panels to be either *docked* or *floating*.

4. Place your mouse on the **Slide Notes** tab again.
5. Click-and-drag the **Slide Notes** panel toward the left-hand side of the screen until you see a blue line spanning across the entire height of the window.
6. When the blue line shows, release the mouse.
7. The **Slide Notes** panel should now be *docked* to the left-hand side of the screen, where the **Filmstrip** used to be.

As you can see, docking a panel is very easy. Feel free to move other panels around before going forward to the next topic. For example, take the **Properties** panel at the right-hand side of the screen and make it float. Then, try to dock it at the bottom of the screen before moving it back to its original location. When a panel is moved above a possible docking location, a blue bar appears on the screen. Releasing the mouse at that moment docks the panel at the location highlighted by the blue bar.

8. When you are done, reset the **Classic** workspace to its original state using the **Window | Workspace | Reset 'Classic'** command.

This concludes our exploration of the Captivate panels. Let's make a quick summary of what has been covered in this topic:

- Double-click on a panel tab to open, expand, or collapse it.
- Use the *very small double arrow* icon to turn a panel or a set of panels into icons. This saves a lot of space on the screen and is especially useful if you have a small screen.
- The **Window** menu shows a list of all the available panels. Use it to display a panel that is not present on the screen, or to completely remove a panel from the interface.
- The panels can be either *docked* or *floating*.
- To dock a panel, move the panel around with the mouse and release the mouse button when a blue line shows.
- If your screen becomes messy, use the **Window | Workspace | Reset 'XXX'** menu item to put the current workspace back to its original state.

Creating a custom workspace

By hiding and showing panels on the interface and by moving them around the screen to lay them out as you see fit, you actually create new workspaces. Captivate allows you to save these new workspaces. So when you come up with a workspace you like, save it, give it a name and you will be able to reapply it later on.

Make sure you have reset the **Classic** workspace to its original state before doing this exercise:

1. Open the **Window** menu and click on **Slide Notes** to display the **Slide Notes** panel. It should appear at the bottom of the screen, right next to the **Timeline**.
2. Click on the **Timeline** tab to make it the active panel of the bottom panel group.
3. Double-click on the same **Timeline** tab to collapse the **Timeline** panel.
4. Click on the *very little double arrow* associated with the **Properties** panel. This will turn the **Properties, Library, Quiz Properties** and **Project Info** panels to icons.
5. In the **Window** Menu, click on **Align**. This will add the *Align* toolbar at the top of the screen.

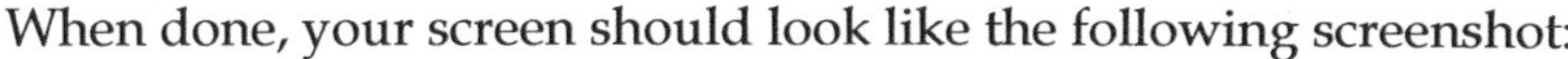

When done, your screen should look like the following screenshot:

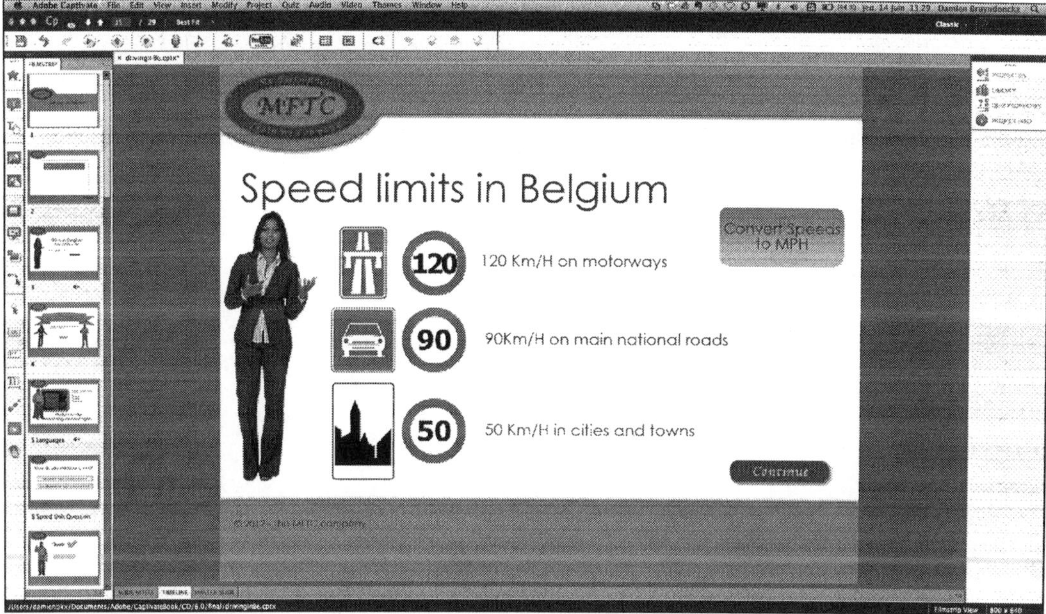

Let's pretend that this new panel layout is something we are very happy with. In such a case, we can save it as a new workspace. Perform the following steps to save the new panel layout:

1. Click on the **Window** | **Workspaces** | **New Workspace** menu item.
2. In the box that pops up, give the workspace your first name and click **OK**.

Once this is done, take a look at the workspace switcher, at the top right corner of your screen. Your name should be written there, indicating that the workspace currently in use is your very own customized workspace!

3. Click on the workspace switcher to reveal the list of available workspaces.
4. In the list, choose any workspace, but the one that bears your name. The chosen workspace is applied and the screen is rearranged.
5. Open the workspace switcher again.
6. Click on your name to reapply your custom workspace.

Awesome! We now have a way to create custom workspaces and make Captivate look exactly the way we want.

If you need to rename or delete a custom workspace, perform the following steps:

1. Go to the **Window** | **Workspace** | **Manage Workspace** menu item.
2. In the box, choose the workspace to delete/rename. In this case, only one workspace is available for renaming/deletion.
3. Click on the **Rename** or **Delete** button. In this example, click on the **OK** button to close the box without doing any changes.
4. Open the workspace switcher one last time to reapply the **Classic** workspace before moving on to the next topic.

Note that there is no menu item to *update* an existing workspace. If you want to update an existing workspace, you must use the **New Workspace** command and give the new workspace the name of the existing workspace you want to update.

Also notice that you cannot delete or rename the default workspaces of Captivate.

Before moving on to the next topic, these are the key points to keep in mind when creating custom workspaces:

- When you make changes to your interface, you actually create new workspaces.
- Use the **Window** | **Workspace** | **New Workspace** menu item to save the current panel layout as a new workspace.
- Use the **Window** | **Workspace** | **Manage Workspace** menu item to rename or delete your custom workspaces.
- To update an existing workspace, use the **New Workspace** command and give the new workspace the same name as the workspace you want to update.
- The default workspaces of Captivate cannot be deleted or renamed.

Exploring the sample applications

Now that we know a bit more about the Captivate interface, we will take a look at the sample applications that we will build together during the course of this book. These applications have been designed to showcase almost every single feature of Captivate. Use them as a reference if there is something unclear during one of the exercises.

Experiencing the Encoder Demonstration

The first application that we will explore is a typical Captivate project. It uses the screen capture engine of Captivate to create a screenshots-based movie. Perform the following steps to view a project:

1. Use the **File | Open** menu item to open the `final/encoderDemo.cptx` file situated in your exercises folder.
2. The file opens as a separate tab in the Captivate interface.
3. In the *Main Options* toolbar, right next to the slide navigator, click on the *Preview* icon.
4. In the drop-down list, choose the **Project** item to preview the entire project as shown in the following screenshot:

Take a closer look at the *Preview* icon (as shown in the previous screenshot). It will be one of the icons we'll use the most during the course of this book. It has five options to control which part of the project we want to preview. Note that each of these options is associated with a keyboard shortcut that depends on the system you work on (Mac or Windows). The options are the following:

- **Play Slide**: This option will play the current slide in the Captivate Interface. It is the only Preview option that does not open the Preview pane. Consequently, this preview option is not able to render all the features of Captivate. Previewing a single slide is a good option to quickly test the timings of the objects.
- **Project**: When choosing this option, Captivate generates a temporary flash file and plays the entire project in the **Preview** pane.
- **From this Slide**: Captivate opens the **Preview** pane and plays the project from the currently selected slide to the end. This option generates a temporary Flash file, so every single feature of Captivate is supported in this preview mode.

- **Next 5 slides**: Captivate opens the **Preview** pane to play a temporary flash file containing five slides starting from the currently selected slide. It is a great option to quickly test a specific sequence in the movie.
- **In Web Browser**: Captivate generates a temporary flash file as well as a temporary HTML file. It then plays the entire project in the default browser. Using this preview option, you will see the project in a context very close to the one that will be used by your learners.
- **HTML5 output in Web Browser**: When using this option, the project is published in HTML5, JavaScript, CSS, and images. It is then played in the default web browser. HTML5 publishing is a brand new feature of Captivate 6 and not every single Captivate feature is supported in HTML5. So it is important to test your projects in HTML5 in addition to testing them in Flash.

Floating and Modal panels

In Captivate, a panel can be *floating* or *docked*. When a panel floats, the tools and switches situated on other panels are still active. But when the **Preview** panel is open, only the buttons of that panel are active, while the tools of the other panels are not active anymore. The Preview pane is said to be a **Modal** floating panel, because it disables every tool situated on other panels. Also, notice that the **Preview** panel *cannot* be docked.

In this case, we clicked on the *Preview Project* option. Captivate generates a temporary Flash file and opens it in the **Preview** pane. Follow the onscreen instructions to go through the project. This puts you in the same situation as a learner viewing the eLearning course for the first time.

This project begins with a **Pretest** of three questions. The Pretest is made to check if the student really needs to take this particular training. If the student fails the pretest, he/she has to take the entire course, but if the Pretest is a success, the student can choose to skip the course or to take it anyway. The pretest feature is one of the new features of Captivate 6. To fully understand this feature, it is necessary to take the course twice. Try to answer the questions of the Pretest correctly the first time and incorrectly the second time and see how you experience the project in both situations.

The second part of this first sample application (after the Pretest) is known as a **Demonstration**. As the name suggests, a demonstration is used to *demonstrate* something to the learner. Consequently, the learner is *passive* and simply watches whatever is going on in the Captivate movie. In a Demonstration, the mouse object is shown. It moves and clicks automatically.

This particular demonstration features some of the most popular Captivate tools. You have seen Text Captions, Highlight Boxes, a Zoom Area, and so on. You have also experienced sound in the Captivate demonstration as well as the ability to close-caption the sound-enabled slides, but the most amazing thing featured in this demonstration is probably the ability to insert video files in the Captivate slides.

Experiencing the Encoder Simulation

We will now open another sample application. Actually, it is not a real *other* application, but another version of the Encoder Demonstration we experienced in the previous topic. Perform the following steps to open the application and to view it:

1. Use the **File | Open** menu item to open the `final/encoderSim.cptx` file situated in your exercise folder.
2. Once the file is open, click on the Preview icon in the *main toolbar* and choose to preview the entire **project**.
3. The **Preview** pane opens and the Encoder Simulation starts to play.

When the animation reaches slide number 4, the play head stops moving, and waits for the learner to *do* an action. This is the main difference between a Demonstration and a Simulation.

In Captivate, a **Simulation** is a project in which the learner is *active*. In a simulation, the mouse object is hidden, as the learner will use his/her own mouse to click around the screen in order to progress towards the end of the movie. The very fact that the user is active implies a whole new level of complexity: the learner can perform either the right or the wrong action. In each case, the application must react accordingly. This concept is known as **branching**, that is, each student experiences the application based on his/her actions.

4. Follow the onscreen instructions and try to perform the *right* actions. The application has been set up to give you two chances to perform each action correctly.

When you are through, close the **Preview** pane.

In order to experience the branching concept hands-on, preview the entire movie again, but this time, give yourself a break and perform the wrong actions at each and every step of the simulation (don't worry, it is *not* graded!). You should see that the application reacts differently and shows you things that were not shown when the right actions were performed! That's *branching* in action!

This particular simulation features pretty much the same Captivate objects as the demonstration we experienced earlier. Only the mouse had to be replaced by the interactive objects of Captivate. An interactive object is an object that has the ability to stop the play head and wait for the learner to interact with the movie. Each of the interactive objects of Captivate can implement the *branching* concept.

The Media Encoder *Demonstration* and the Media Encoder *Simulation* are both based on screenshots. To create these sample applications, the first two steps of the production process described earlier have been used:

- In step one (the capture phase), the actions have been performed for real in the real Adobe Media Encoder as they were recorded by Captivate behind the scenes.
- In step two (the post-production phase), the movie has been edited in Captivate. Sound and closed captions were added, video was imported, the title and ending slides were created, the timing was adjusted, and so on. We even imported a slide created in Microsoft PowerPoint!
- Step three (the publishing phase) has not been performed (yet) on these files.

Experiencing the Driving in Belgium sample application

We will now open and preview the third sample application. Normally it should already be open in Captivate as a tab in the main area. Click on the file tab to make it the active file, as shown in the following screenshot:

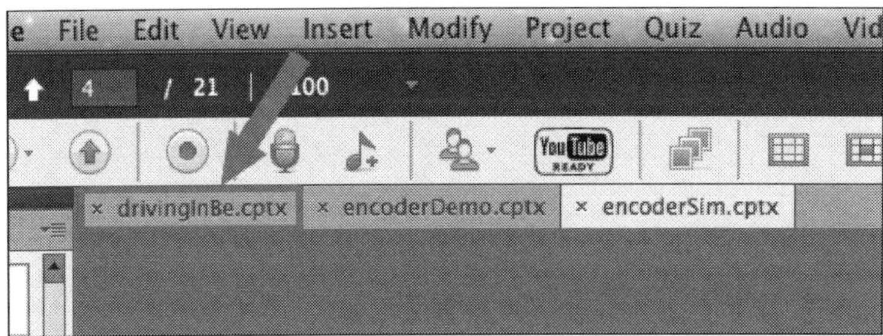

If the file is not open, use the **File | open** menu item to open the `final/drivingInBe.cptx` file situated in the exercises folder you downloaded from the Web.

When the file is open and active, use the Preview icon to preview the entire project. Follow the onscreen instructions as a student would do when viewing this project for the first time. When done, close the **Preview** pane, then, use the Preview icon again to preview the entire project a second time. Answer the question differently from the first time. You will have yet another experience of the *branching* concept.

This third sample application is very different from the previous projects we have seen. It is not really a demonstration, nor a simulation. It is none of it and a bit of both at the same time. As you can see, the borderline between a demonstration and a simulation is sometimes very difficult to spot!

When it comes to sound, this movie makes use of the **Text-to-Speech** engine of Captivate. Text-to-Speech is a great alternative to quickly create the sound clips you need, but the quality of the speech is not as good as when a real human being speaks in front of a good old microphone!

This application is not based on screenshots and does not teach software related skills. Instead, each slide has been created one by one, right in Captivate or imported from an existing PowerPoint presentation.

This application is also much more sophisticated than the Encoder applications. **Advanced actions** and **Variables** are used throughout the project to power the dynamic features, such as the name of the student appearing in a Text Caption. It also features the certificate **Widget** on the last slide (only if you pass the quiz!) and uses the new collection of **Characters** to spice up the training with a human touch! But the most impressive feature of this particular project is probably the **Quiz**, one of the biggest and most appreciated tools of Captivate.

The project contains eight question slides. Four of these are stored in a question pool. Each time the project is viewed, three questions are asked to the student, while a fourth one is randomly chosen from the question pool. That's why, the second time you previewed the application, you did not experience the very same quiz as compared to the first time.

Experiencing the Encoder Video Demo

Video Demo is a brand new feature of Captivate 6. A *Video Demo* generates a `.mp4` video file that can be uploaded to online services such as YouTube, Vimeo, or Daily Motion for playback on any device (including iPad, iPhone, and other Internet-enabled mobile devices). Perform the following steps to view a Video Demo project:

1. Use the **File** | **Open** menu item to open the `final/encoderVideo.cpvc` file situated in your exercises folder.

First of all notice that a Video Demo project does not use the same `.cptx` file extension as a regular Captivate project. It uses the `.cpvc` file extension. For us, it is the first indication that this project is not going to behave as the other ones we have experienced so far.

In addition to a specific file extension, Video Demo projects also have their specific Captivate Interface, as shown in the following screenshot:

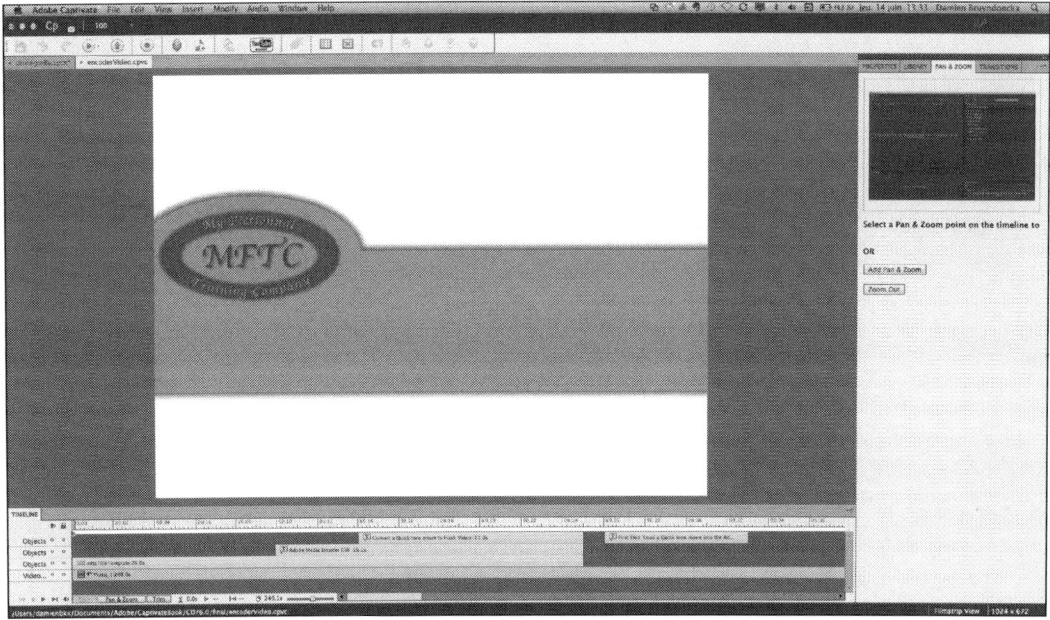

In the previous screenshot, notice the absence of the Filmstrip. A Video Demo project is not based on slides. It actually is a big video file, so the Filmstrip makes no sense in a Video Demo project.

In a video file, branching is not possible. The file can only be experienced from start to finish in the order defined by the teacher. To use proper words, we said that a video file proposes a *linear* experience to the learner while the branch-aware projects we experienced earlier, propose a *non-linear* experience. Consequently, no quiz is possible in a Video Demo project and the Quiz Properties panel has been removed as well.

2. Take some time to inspect the rest of the interface. Try to spot the other differences between the regular Captivate interface and the interface used for Video Demos.
3. When you are ready, click on the **Preview** icon

Surprise! Only two options are available in the Preview icon!

4. In the **Preview** drop-down, choose the **Full Screen** option.
5. Watch the whole movie as if you were viewing it on YouTube!
6. When the movie is finished, click on the **Edit** button situated at the bottom right corner of the screen to return to the Video Demo editing interface.
7. Use the **File | Close All** menu item to close every open file. If prompted to save the changes, make sure you do *not* save the changes to these files.

After viewing these four sample applications, you should have a pretty good idea of the tools and general capabilities of Captivate. Before moving on, let's summarize what we have learned from these movies:

- Captivate is able to capture the actions you do on your computer and turn them into slides using a sophisticated capture engine based on screenshots.
- A **Demonstration** is a project in which the learner is passive and simply watches the onscreen actions
- A **Simulation** is a project in which the user is active.
- PowerPoint slides can be imported into Captivate and converted to Captivate slides.
- Sound and video can be imported in Captivate. The application also features a Text-to-Speech engine and closed captioning.
- Question Slides can be created in Captivate. These question slides can be stored in Question Pools to create random quizzes.
- Other objects that can be included in a Captivate project are the Text Caption, the Highlight Box, and the Zoom Area, among others.
- Captivate supports interactive objects. An interactive object is able to stop the play head and wait for the user to interact with the movie.
- Captivate 6 introduces the **Video Demo** project type. A Video Demo is not based on screenshots, but is a big video file instead.
- Video Demo projects use the `.cpvc` file extension and have a specific user interface.

Discussing the sample apps scenario

In the exercises folder you downloaded from the Web, you'll find the scenarios of these sample apps in PDF format in the `scenarios` folder. Feel free to read those documents and compare them to the finished applications.

When working with Captivate, the scenario is a very important document. Its goal is to guide you during the whole production process. Thanks to the scenario, you'll always have the big picture of the entire project in mind. The scenario will also help you stay within the scope of your project.

That being said, the scenario can, and probably will, evolve during the production process. And this is a good thing! Every teacher knows that his/her own understanding of a given topic increases and changes while teaching it. What is true in a classroom also is true in a Captivate Project. After all, working in Captivate is all about teaching and consequently, your scenario is nothing more than a guide.

Summary

In this chapter, we have introduced the four steps of a typical Captivate production process. We toured the application's interface and learned how to customize it to fit our needs. Thanks to the *workspace* feature, we were able to save our customized interface as a new workspace in order to reapply our custom panel layout anytime we want to. Finally, we toured the sample applications used in this book, which gave us a first look at the rich set of features of Captivate.

In the next chapter, we will concentrate on the first step of the Captivate production process: the *capture* step. We will discuss various techniques used to capture the slides and discover the inner working of Captivates' capture engine. We will also discuss tips and tricks that will help us make a critical choice: choosing the right size for our project.

To see and experience more Captivate applications, visit `http://www.adobe.com/products/captivate/showcase.html`.

Meet the Community

The title of the book you are reading is "Mastering Adobe Captivate 6". In order to truly "Master" a piece of software, I'm convinced that one must be introduced to the community that supports it.

At the end of each chapter, I'll add a *Meet the community* section in which I'll introduce you to a key-member of the community. By the end of the book, you'll know the names, blog addresses, twitter handles, and so on of the most influential members of the Captivate and eLearning community. I hope these resources will jump start your own Captivate career and, who knows, your own involvement in the community.

Dr Allen Partridge

Bio

Dr. Allen Partridge is an eLearning Evangelist for Adobe. In addition to his work for Adobe Systems, he continues to serve on the doctoral faculty in the Communications Media and Instructional Technology program at Indiana University of Pennsylvania.

Allen has written several books and a host of articles on topics ranging from 3D game development to Instructional Design for new technologies. He is active in explorations of Immersive Learning as well as traditional multimedia enhanced eLearning and rapid eLearning. Allen works closely with the eLearning Suite and Captivate teams at Adobe, providing a channel to customer needs and concerns and helping facilitate communication among team members.

Contact details

Blog: `http://blogs.adobe.com/captivate/`

Twitter: `@adobeElearning`

Facebook: `http://www.facebook.com/adobecaptivate`

LinkedIn: `http://www.linkedin.com/in/doctorpartridge`

YouTube: `http://www.youtube.com/adobeelearning/`

My personal note

Allen Partridge is the ultimate key member of the Captivate community. As an Adobe Evangelist for Captivate, he is one of the main contributors of the official Captivate blog and animates the official Captivate page on Facebook. Allen also participates in virtually every Captivate-related event around the world, so chances are that you'll have an opportunity to meet him not far from where you live.

You definitely want to bookmark his blog and follow him on Twitter.

When I asked him to author the foreword of this book, it took Allen exactly 29 minutes to reply to my email and to accept.

Thank you, Allen, for supporting this project and for your outstanding work with the Captivate community.

2
Capturing the Slides

Now that we have a better understanding of the features offered by Captivate, we will move on to the first step of the production process: capturing the slides.

This step can be compared to the filming of a movie. When filming a movie, the director wants to capture all the images, sequences, and shots that he/she needs. In the movie industry, this raw material is called the *rushes*. When the filming is complete, the director goes back to the studio with his/her rushes and starts the post-production process. It is during the post-production process that the final movie will slowly take shape. Only the best rushes will make their way to the movie theatre, while most of them will be discarded along the way. That being said, the post-production phase can only be successful if the filming provides enough material of good quality to create a great movie.

The same basic idea applies to Captivate. When capturing the slide, one should always keep in mind that the post-production phase will follow. Therefore, the goal is not to come up with a perfect movie right away, but to create enough quality slides to ensure the success of the next phase of the process.

At the end of this chapter, we will be far from the final result we want to achieve, but we will have enough slides to start editing our project.

In this chapter, we will:

- Discuss how to choose the right size/resolution for the project
- Discuss the recording preferences and the recording modes
- Record Demonstrations and Simulations
- Discuss and use the Full Motion Recording
- Discuss and experience the new Video Demo mode of Captivate 6
- Use the Manual Panning
- Resize a project

If you are ready, it's almost time to turn the camera on and start the real action!

Choosing the right resolution for the project

Choosing the right resolution for capturing the slides is the first critical decision we have to make. And we have to make it right, because the size of the captured slides will play a critical role in the quality of the final movie.

What exactly the problem is

A typical Captivate project, like the Encoder Demonstration you experienced in the previous chapter, involves taking screenshots of an actual piece of software. At the end of the process, the project will be typically published in Flash or HTML5 format and placed on a web page. Most of the time, that web page has to display lots of other page elements (such as logos, headers, footers, navigation bars, and the like) in addition to the Captivate movie. This can lead to a very delicate situation as shown by the following screenshot:

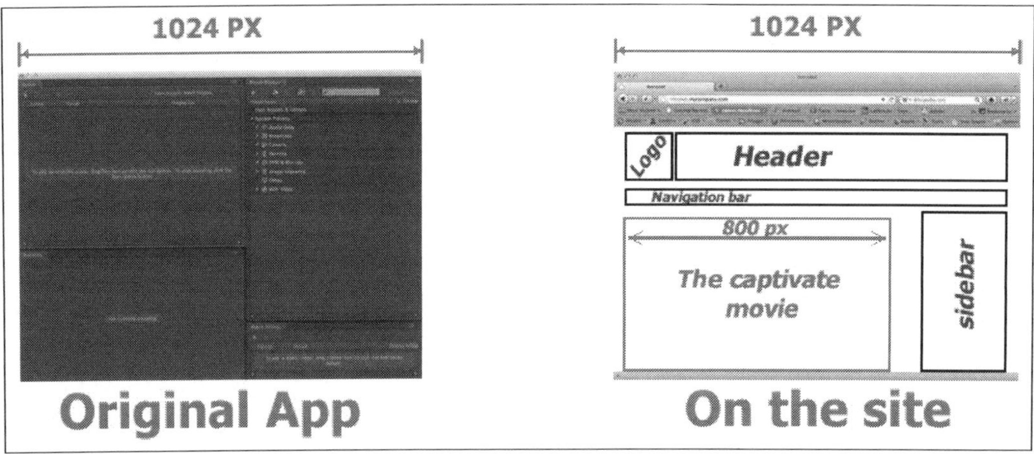

The previous screenshot shows the application we need to capture on the left-hand side of the screenshot. This application requires a minimal width of 1024 pixels to be displayed without horizontal scrollbars. On the right-hand side of the screen, we can see the wireframe of the web page we must put our finished movie on. The page has been designed to fit a 1024 pixels wide screen and has to display lots of elements in addition to the Captivate movie. To cope with the design requirement of the web page, our project should not be wider than 800 pixels.

So here is our problem. **We have to find a way to fit 1024 pixels in 800 pixels!**

Several approaches are possible to address this problem. Each of these approaches has its pros and cons. We will briefly review them one by one.

Resizing the project after the initial shooting

The first approach is a two-step process. The first step is to shoot the movie in a resolution of 1024 pixels and the second step is to use the **Rescale Project** feature of Captivate to downsize the project to 800 pixels.

By shooting with a resolution of 1024 pixels, the minimal requirements of the application to shoot are met, so the screenshots will capture the application in its intended size.

The disadvantage is that this approach requires the project to be resized, and the resize operation always has a cost in terms of quality. Not mentioning that the resulting project may result in a bigger file size. The smaller project size will also reduce the size of the screen elements of the captured application. In the resulting resized screenshots, make sure the font size is still big enough for the learners to read comfortably.

When resizing a project, it is always better to start with a big picture and reduce it rather than to enlarge a picture that is too small, so, as a first general rule, shoot big and eventually reduce the size, not the other way round!

Downsizing the application during the shooting

The second approach is to downsize the application to shoot in order to fit the requirements of the project. In our example, it means the application would be 800 pixels in width instead of 1024 pixels during the filming.

The biggest advantage of this solution is its easiness. Captivate shoots the movie at a width of 800 pixels and the movie is played back at 800 pixels too, so no special processing is required from Captivate.

There are however several disadvantages. Remember that the application that we want to shoot requires a width of 1024 pixels minimum, so by downsizing it to a width of 800 pixels; we will generate a horizontal scrollbar. This horizontal scrollbar will be captured and will be shown in the resulting Captivate movie. It could also hide some potentially important information from the screen.

Using the Panning feature of Captivate

In the movie industry, Panning refers to moving the camera while filming. In Captivate, it means that you can move the recording area while capturing the slides.

This approach tries to cope with both the requirements of the application to shoot and the requirements of the movie to produce.

The idea is to leave the application to its intended width of 1024 pixels and, at the same time, define a capture area of 800 pixels in width. During the shooting, the smaller capture area will be moved over the bigger application as illustrated by the following screenshot:

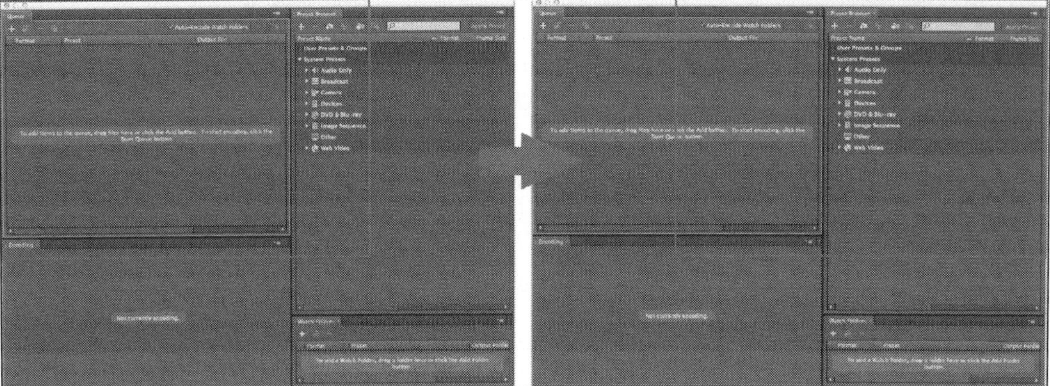

In the previous screenshot, the capture area is the red rectangle. As you can see, the capture area will not always cover the same part of the application during the shooting.

This approach is a good compromise, but it has two major disadvantages. First, moving the recording area while filming will increase the size of your final movie, but more importantly, using this approach, your learner will never see the application entirely, which could compromise the quality of the learning process.

Using the new Scalable HTML content feature

This new feature of Captivate 6 allows the published movie to be resized to fit the screen it is viewed on.

Say we shoot and publish our movie at a size of 1024 pixels, but the movie is viewed on a website where the maximal resolution of our work can only be 800 pixels. In such a case, the Scalable HTML content feature will scale our movie down to 800 pixels so it fits in the available space.

The main advantage of this approach is that it makes our Captivate content ready for the mobile transition. When viewed on a Tablet or a Smartphone, our content will be resized!

The major disadvantage though is that, as a teacher, you lose control over how your content will be *actually* experienced. Only a small percentage of your students (those who have the exact same screen as yours) will see the course as you designed it. The other students will see the course either bigger (which means possibly pixelized) or smaller (which may mean too small to be comfortable).

This option will be covered in the *Scalable HTML content* section in *Chapter 6, Finishing Touches and Publishing*.

Conclusion

No approach is perfect, but you'll have to choose one anyway! The best approach depends on the project, on your learners, and on your personal taste. Here are some general guidelines to help you make the best choice:

- The size of the capture area must match the size of the application to capture whenever possible.
- If you need to resize the project, take a big project and make it smaller. This will help maintain the best possible image quality.
- Use Panning only if you really need it.
- When using panning, move the camera (the red capture area) only when needed, and move it slowly to help the students build a mental picture of the entire application.
- If you use the new Scalable HTML content feature, make sure you test your work on an array of different screens and devices to ensure the best possible student experience in the majority of the scenarios.
- Finally, never forget that you are teaching. Your students don't care about your sizing concerns; they just want to learn something! If the chosen approach compromises the quality of the learning process, then, it is the wrong approach!

Shooting the first movie

It is time to have a first experience of an actual recording session. Shooting a movie is a four-step process, as the following:

- Preparing the application to shoot
- Rehearsing the scenario
- Shooting the movie
- Previewing the rushes

Let's review these four steps one by one.

Preparing the application to shoot

For this exercise, the application we will use is the *Adobe Media Encoder CS6*. This application is used to convert virtually any type of video files to Flash video and HTML5 video. The Adobe Media Encoder CS6 is part of your Captivate or eLearning Suite bundle. Therefore, if you have Captivate (even the trial version), you also have the Adobe Media Encoder CS6!

We will now reset the Captivate workspace and open the Adobe Media Encoder using the following steps:

1. Open Captivate. If Captivate is already opened, close every open file.
2. Make sure the default **Classic** workspace is applied.
3. Open the Adobe Media Encoder Application. On the Mac, it is situated in the `/Applications/Adobe Media Encoder CS6` folder. On Windows, a shortcut to the Adobe Media Encoder is available in the Start menu.

When the *Adobe Media Encoder* opens, make sure it looks like the following screenshot:

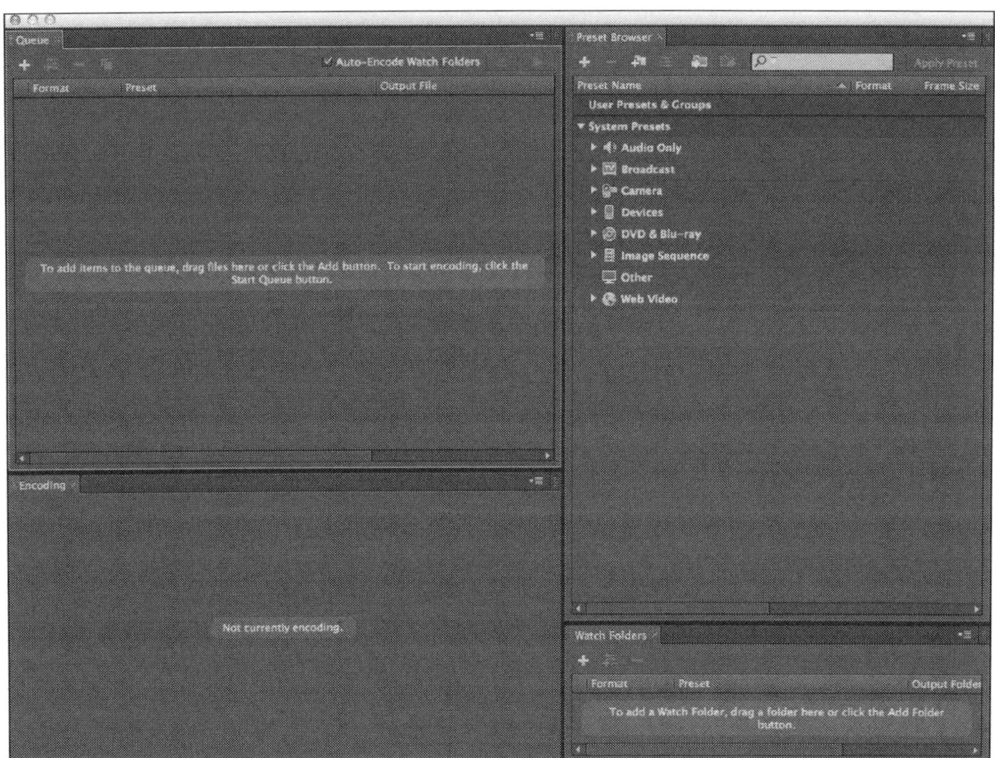

Rehearsing the scenario

The goal of the movie is to teach the students how to use the *Adobe Media Encoder* to convert a QuickTime movie (with a `.mov` extension) to a Flash video (with a `.flv` extension). This scenario follows the exact same steps as the ones we experienced while seeing the Encoder Demonstration and Simulation in the previous chapter. Perform the following steps to convert a `.mov` to `.flv` file:

1. Go to the **Adobe Media Encoder** application.
2. In the top left corner of the application, click on the **+** icon.
3. Browse to the `videos/MOV` folder of the exercises files and load the `demo_en.mov` QuickTime movie into the **Adobe Media Encoder**.
4. Open the **Format** drop-down list and choose the **FLV** format.
5. Open the **Preset** drop-down list and apply the 4 x 3 preset (the second to last item in the list).
6. Click on the preset name to open the **Export Settings** dialog.
7. In the lower-right area of the **Export Settings** dialog, open the **Video** tab (if needed).
8. Scroll down the **Video** tab until you see the **Resize Video** section.
9. Make sure the **Maintain Aspect Ratio** icon (the chain icon) is active and change the **Width** of the video to `400` pixels. Normally, the new **Height** of the video is automatically set to **300** pixels.
10. Click on the **OK** button to validate the new **Export Settings**.
11. Click on the **Start Queue** button (the green play icon) to start the actual encoding.

The encoding process begins. In the **Encoding** panel, at the bottom of the screen, a yellowish bar shows the progression of this operation.

Make sure you master these steps, and make sure the *Adobe Media Encoder CS6* behaves as expected before moving on. If you need more practice, feel free to rehearse this scenario a few more times before the shooting. After all, on a real movie set, even the most famous actors rehearse their scenes before the director finally decides to turn the camera on!

When you are ready to shoot the scene, don't forget to reset the *Adobe Media Encoder* application to its original state. The best way to do it is to close the application, and restart it. Perform the following steps to reset the application:

1. Close the **Adobe Media Encoder CS6**.
2. When the application is closed, reopen it.
3. When the application reopens, make sure it looks like the previous screenshot.

Also delete the `.flv` file(s) you generated during the rehearsal(s):

4. Open the Finder (Mac) or the Windows Explorer (Windows) and browse to the `videos/MOV` folder of the exercise files.
5. Delete all the `.flv` files present in this folder.

Shooting the movie

We know the scenario and the application is ready to be captured. It's time to return to Captivate and start the actual shooting process.

[Mac users only] – Enable access to assistive devices

If you work on Macintosh, there is one preliminary step to take before Captivate can shoot the movie. This action can be done by performing the following steps:

1. Open the **System Preferences** application.
2. In the **Personal** section of **System preferences**, click on the **Universal Access** icon.
3. At the bottom of the **Universal Access** preference pane, select the **Enable access for assistive devices** checkbox.
4. Close the **System Preferences** application and return to Captivate.

Without this step, Mac OS does not broadcast the events that Captivate uses to capture user interactivity (such as clicking a button, typing into a text entry, and so on).

Preparing Captivate to shoot

For this firsthand experience, we will use the default options of Captivate by performing the following steps to shoot the movie:

1. Close every open file, so that the Captivate Welcome screen is displayed.
2. In the right column of the Welcome screen, click on the **Create New Software Simulation** link. You can also use the **File | Record new Software Simulation** menu item to achieve the same result.

The Captivate interface disappears and a red rectangle is displayed on the screen. This red rectangle is the recording area.

3. In the recording window, choose **Application** to record an application.
4. In the **Select the window to record** drop-down list, choose to record the **Adobe Media Encoder CS6** application.

Adobe Media Encoder opens and the red recording area snaps to the application window.

5. In the **Snap to** section of the box, choose to record at a **Custom Size**.
6. Choose a size of **1024 x 768** in the drop-down list. The red recording area and the **Adobe Media Encoder CS6** application are both resized to the chosen size.
7. Leave the remaining options at their default settings. The recording window should look like the following screenshot:

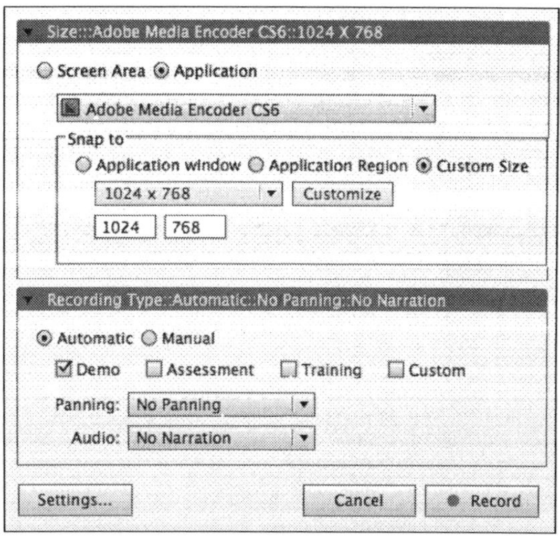

In the previous screenshot, notice the **Demo** checkbox in the lower part of the window. Make sure this checkbox is the only one selected.

The stage is set and the actors are in place. Everyone is waiting for the director's signal to get started!

And... Action!

The signal is the red **Record** button at the bottom of the recording window. Once you click on it, all your actions will be recorded by Captivate until you stop the capture.

If you have a problem while doing this exercise, refer to the `Chapter02/final/encoderDemo_1024.cptx` file of your exercises folder.

Perform the following steps to record a video:

1. Click on the red **Record** button at the bottom of the recording window. After a short countdown, you'll be in the recording mode.
2. In the **Adobe Media Encoder**, perform the actions as written in the scenario that we rehearsed earlier in this chapter in the *Rehearsing the Scenario* section.
    - Each time you click, you should hear a camera shutter sound.
    - When you type in the **Width** field, you should hear keystrokes.
    - Perform the actions slowly enough to allow captivate to capture all the required images and actions.
    - After clicking on the **Start Queue** icon, hit the *Print Screen* key (Windows) or the *cmd* + *Fn* + *F6* shortcut (Mac) three or four times to manually capture a few screenshots of the yellowish bar as it progresses to the right edge of the **Encoding** panel.
3. When done, hit the *End* key (Windows) or do the *cmd* + *Fn* + *Enter* Shortcut (Mac). Captivate generates the slides.
4. When the project has finished loading in Captivate, save it as `Chapter02/encoderDemo_1024.cptx`.
5. Close the **Adobe Media Encoder** application.

The shooting phase of the movie is now finished. If you don't get it right the first time, don't worry, you can simply discard your sequence and start over. On a real movie set, even the most famous actors are granted many chances to do it right!

Previewing the rushes

The project should be open in Captivate. To launch the preview, we will use the same Preview icon as in the previous chapter by performing the following steps:

1. On the *Main Options* toolbar, click on the *Preview* icon.
2. In the drop-down list, choose **Project** to preview the entire project.
3. Captivate generates the slides and opens the **Preview** pane.

Captivate has already generated lots of objects on the slides. Remember that in the recording window, the **Demo** mode was selected by default. The **Demo** mode automatically adds Text Captions, Highlight Boxes, and Mouse movements to the slides.

Of course, some of the content of the Text Captions must be corrected, the size and position of the Highlight Boxes must be fine-tuned and the overall rhythm of the project is probably too fast, but this is an acceptable starting point to begin with.

4. Close the **Preview** pane when done.

Exploring the recording preferences

Our first shooting experience was based on the default preferences of Captivate. In order to take full control of the situation, we will explore and fine-tune the recording preferences using the following steps before we make a second try:

1. Use the **Edit | Preferences** (Windows) or the **Adobe Captivate | Preferences** (Mac) menu item to open the **Preferences** window.
2. On the left-hand side of the **Preferences** window, click on the **Modes** category in the **Recording** section.
3. At the top of the **Preferences** window, make sure the **Mode** drop-down list is set to **Demonstration**, as shown in the following screenshot:

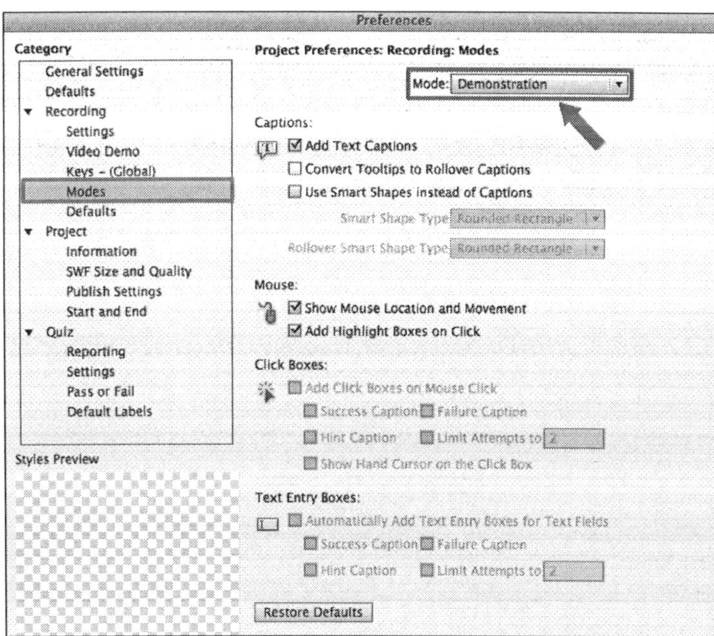

The **Preferences** window currently shows the settings of the **Demonstration** recording mode we used to shoot our first movie. As expected, this recording mode adds Text Captions on the slides. It also features the Mouse and adds an Highlight Box each time the mouse is clicked during the capture. These settings reflect what we have seen when previewing the rushes of our first movie.

4. At the top of the **Preferences** window, open the **Modes** drop-down list. It is currently set to **Demonstration**.
5. Choose the **Assessment Simulation** mode option of the drop-down list.

The **Assessment Simulation** mode is the second automatic recording mode of Captivate. As discussed in the previous chapter, a *Simulation* is a project in which the user is *active*, so the **Show Mouse Location and Movement** option is, logically, not selected. Instead, each time a mouse click occurs during the filming, a **Click Box** is automatically added to the slide.

A *Click Box* is one of the three interactive objects of Captivate. Remember that such an object is able to pause the movie and wait for an interaction from the student. Notice that the *Failure Caption* option is selected. It simply means that a failure notice will be displayed in case the student does not perform the intended action.

If the keyboard is used during the filming, Captivate will generate a **Text Entry Box.** The *Text Entry Box* is the second interactive object of Captivate.

6. Open the **Modes** drop-down list again.
7. In the list, choose the **Training Simulation** mode.

The **Training Simulation** mode is very similar to the **Assessment Simulation** mode. The only difference is the **Hint Caption** option that is selected for both the *Click Box* object and the *Text Entry Box* object. A *Hint Caption* is a piece of text that will show when the student passes his/her mouse over the hit area of the *Click Box/Text Entry Box*.

8. Open the **Modes** drop-down one last time.
9. In the drop-down list, choose the **Custom** mode.

Surprise! When choosing the **Custom** mode, no option is selected by default! In fact, the **Custom** mode is ours to create, so let's go:

10. In the **Caption** section, select the **Add Text Captions** box.
11. In the **Click Boxes** section, select the **Add Click Boxes on Mouse Click** option. Also select the **Failure Caption** and the **Hint Caption** boxes.
12. Finally, in the **Text Entry Boxes** section, select the **Automatically Add Text Entry Boxes for Text Fields** with a **Failure Caption** and a **Hint Caption**.

Depending on the recording mode (Custom, Demonstration, and so on), *Text Captions*, *Failure Captions*, and/or *Hint Captions* will be added to the slides.

13. Open the **Recording: Settings** category by clicking on **Settings** in the left column of the **Preferences** window, as shown in the following screenshot:

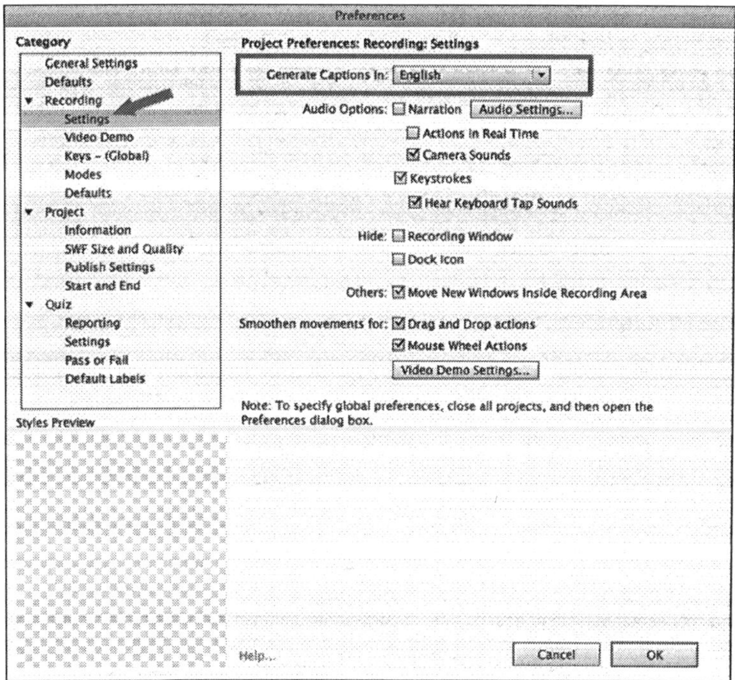

The first available option at the top of the recording settings preference pane is the **Generate Captions In** drop-down list. Use it to choose the language used by Captivate to generate the various types of captions.

Other options available on this pane include the following:

- The **Camera Sounds** checkbox. Make sure this option is selected. It turns on the camera shutter sounds during the filming, which helps us control the count of screenshots taken by Captivate.
- The **Keystrokes** and **Hear Keyboard Tap Sounds** checkboxes. These options are responsible for recording the Keystrokes and for the Keystrokes sound during the filming of the project. It is best to leave these options as selected.
- The **Move New Windows Inside Recording Area** checkbox. This option is used during the capture when the application you record opens a new window or a dialog box. It prevents the new window from opening outside, or partially outside of the recording area. This option should be selected at all times.

- [Windows only] The **Hides System Tray Icon** and **Hide Task Icon** checkboxes are great when you record in full screen. It hides the Captivate button from the taskbar and the Captivate icon from the notification area.
- [Mac only] The **Hide Dock Icon** checkbox is used to remove the Captivate icon from the Dock during the filming. This option is very useful when shooting full screen.

14. Open the *Recording: Keys* preferences by clicking on **Keys - (Global)** in the left column of the **Preferences** window.

This page of the *Recording* preferences is very important to understand.

Both Windows and Mac OS are *multi-tasks* operating systems. This means they can handle multiple applications running at the same time. That being said, only *one* of the running applications is the *Active* application. In normal situations, there can be only one *Active* application at any given time. For example, both Word and Outlook can *run* at the same time but you use either Word *or* Outlook at any given time.

The Active application is the one you currently interact with, and consequently, is the one that currently listens to the keyboard, the mouse, and other input devices.

When recording with Captivate, there are *two* Active applications: the application you capture and Captivate itself. You should be able to interact with both applications, so both applications must share the same mouse and the same keyboard *at the same time*.

By default, the mouse and the keyboard will send their data to the application you record, except for a few keys and shortcuts that will be wired to Captivate. These keys and shortcuts are the ones listed on the **Keys - (Global)** preferences.

If you need to assign another set of keys to Captivate, you can do so in this window using the following steps:

1. Click on the field where the key used to stop recording is defined (*End* on Windows and *cmd* + *Enter* on the Mac).
2. Type the *Ctrl* + *E* shortcut on your keyboard, as shown in the following screenshot:

3. The *Ctrl* + *E* shortcut is now the one to use to stop the recording.
4. At the bottom of the window, click on the **Restore Defaults** button to return to the default settings.
5. Take some time to inspect the other keys and shortcuts available.

One of the other available shortcuts is the *Print Screen* key (Windows) or the *cmd* + *F6* shortcut (Mac) we used during the filming of our movie to take some extra screenshots of the yellow progression bar.

6. Click on **OK** to close the **Preferences** window.

Shortcut keys and the Mac

On the Mac, the functions key, at the top of the keyboard, are used by default for some system-specific operations like adjusting the brightness of the screen or adjusting the sound volume. For these keys to behave as function keys, we must add the *Fn* key into the mix. So to take a screenshot, the *cmd* + *F6* shortcut actually is *cmd* + *Fn* + *F6*. The funny thing is that the *Fn* key must be added to stop the recording. So the stop recording shortcut is not *cmd* + *Enter*, but *cmd* + *Fn* + *Enter*.

Shooting the other versions of the project

Now that we have a better understanding of the automatic recording modes of Captivate, we will use them to shoot the other versions of the project.

If you have a problem while doing this exercise, refer to the `Chapter02/final/encoderAssessment_1024.cptx`, `Chapter02/final/encoderTraining_1024.cptx`, and `Chapter02/final/encoderCustom_1024.cptx` files of your exercises folder.

Perform the following steps to shoot other versions of the project:

1. Reopen the Adobe Media Encoder application. When the application appears in the screen, make sure it looks like the image in *Preparing the application to shoot* section mentioned previously.
2. Delete all the `.flv` files situated in the `videos/MOV` folder of the exercise files you downloaded from the Internet.

These first two steps are used to reset our system to the way it was before the first shooting. On a real movie set, this is the work of the script girl!

3. In Captivate, create a new project by using the **File | Record new Software Simulation** menu item. The Captivate interface disappears. The red recording area and the recording window are displayed.
4. In the recording window, choose to record the **Adobe Media Encoder** application. The **Adobe Media Encoder** application opens and the red recording area snaps to it.
5. Use a **Custom Size** of **1024 x 768** pixels to shoot your application.
6. In the recording modes section of the recording window, select the **Assessment**, **Training**, and **Custom** modes, but uncheck the **Demo** mode.
7. Leave the other options at their current value.
8. Make sure your recording window looks like the following screenshot:

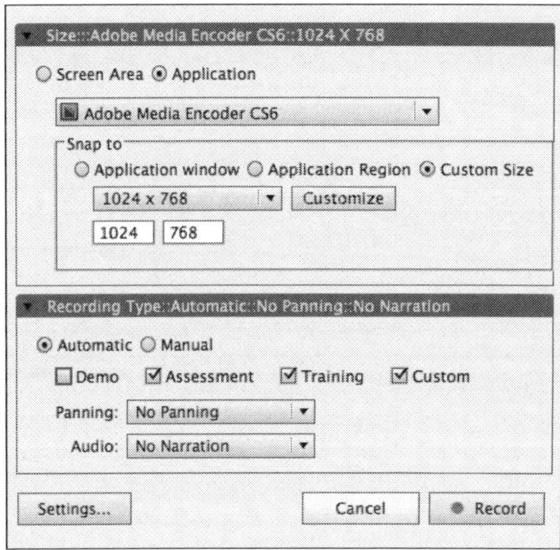

9. When you are ready, click on the red **Record** button. After a short countdown, you'll be back in recording mode.
10. In **Adobe Media Encoder**, perform the actions as rehearsed earlier in *Shooting the movie* section. Behind the scenes, Captivate is recording!

You should hear the sound of a camera shutter each time you click and a keystroke sound each time you use the keyboard. Notice that, even though two applications are currently active, the mouse and the keyboard are used to interact with *Adobe Media Encoder*, not with Captivate.

11. When done, stop the recording by using the *End* key (Windows) or the *cmd + Fn + Enter* shortcut (Mac). As discussed in the **Keys - (Global)** section of the Preferences pane, this particular shortcut is intercepted by Captivate.
12. Captivate generates the slides and opens the projects.

Alternate way to stop a Captivate recording

In addition to the keyboard shortcuts discussed previously, you can also use your mouse to stop a Captivate recording. On Windows, click on the Captivate icon situated in the taskbar, at the bottom of the screen. On the Mac, the same icon is situated in the notification area at the top right corner of the screen.

Again, don't worry if you don't get it right the first time. You are granted as many chances as needed!

This time, after Captivate has finished generating the slides, three files are added to the interface, as mentioned in the following list:

- **untitled_assessment1.cptx** has been generated based on the *Assessment Simulation* mode. Save it in your exercises folder as `Chapter02/encoderAssessment_1024.cptx`.
- **untitled_training1.cptx** has been generated based on the *Training Simulation* mode. Save it in your exercises folder as `Chapter02/encoderTraining_1024.cptx`.
- **untitled_custom.cptx** has been generated with the settings of our very own *Custom* mode. Save it in your exercises folder as `Chapter02/encoderCustom_1024.cptx`.

Once these three files are saved, return to the `Chapter02/encoderAssessment_1024.cptx` file and use the *Preview* icon to preview the entire project. Captivate generates the slides and opens the **Preview** pane.

As described in the *Assessment Simulation* recording mode (step 5 of the *Exploring the recording preferences* section), the mouse pointer does not show in this version of the project and no Text Captions have been added to the slides. The project is simply waiting for us to click on the right icon. If we click on the right icon, the project moves on to the next slide and pauses again waiting for our second action. If we do not perform the right action, a red *Failure Caption* is shown. When you are through the entire project, close the **Preview** pane.

We will now preview the `encoderTraining_1024.cptx` version of the project. As expected, this version of the project is very similar to the previous one. The only difference is the orange *Hint Caption* that shows when the mouse is over the hit area of the *Click Boxes* and *Text Entry Boxes*.

Finally, preview the `encoderCustom_1024.cptx` version of the project. Our Custom recording mode has added *Text Captions* to the slides, as well as *Click Boxes* and *Text Entry Boxes*.

The Full Motion Recording

In the projects we have shot so far, you might have noticed that one slide does not behave exactly like the other slides. This is especially noticeable in the Simulation modes where the student is active. (See slide 10 of the `Chapter02/final/encoderdemo_1024.cptx` project). In Captivate, this slide can easily be spotted thanks to the small video camera icon that appears below the slide in the **Filmstrip**. Let's see what makes this slide different. The following screenshot shows the location of small video camera icon:

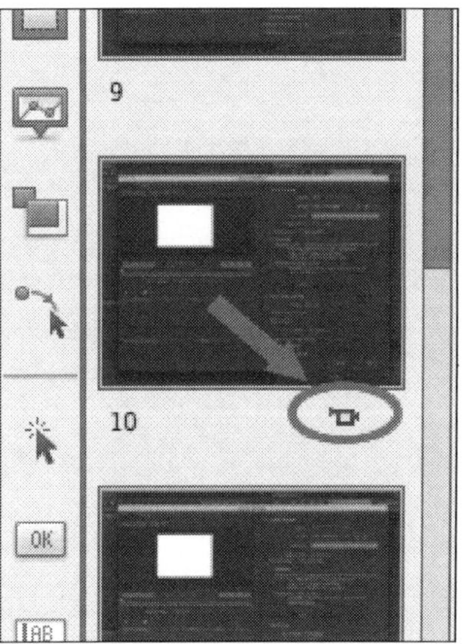

The inner working of the Captivate capture engine

The Captivate capture engine is based on screenshots. Going back to our Adobe Media Encoder project, we will try to understand what exactly happened when we clicked on our mouse during the capture using the following steps:

1. Open the `Chapter02/final/encoderDemo_1024.cptx` file.
2. When the project opens, make sure slide 1 is selected in the **Filmstrip**.

Slide 1 shows the initial state of the application. When filming, we used our mouse to click on the *Add Source* icon. When we clicked on this icon, Captivate launched a sequence of actions behind the scenes:

- Captivate recorded the position of the mouse at the time of the click (using X, Y coordinates).
- Adobe Media Encoder executed the action.
- When Adobe Media Encoder completed its action, Captivate took a static screenshot of the new state of the application.

We then used our mouse a second time to double-click on the `demo_en.mov` file. When this second click occurred, Captivate has launched the same sequence of actions and took a third screenshot.

When the movie is played back, the static screen shot of slide 1 (a `.bmp` image) is displayed. Captivate *recreates a movement* from the top left corner of the slide to the position of the click as recorded during the filming. Just after the click, Captivate displays the static (`.bmp`) screenshot of slide 2.

When it is time to move the mouse on slide 2, the Captivate *recreates a movement* from where the click occurred on slide 1 to the location of the click on slide 2 as recorded during the filming. Right after the second click, the Captivate displays the third static screenshot. This process repeats itself till the end of the movie.

It may sound very simple and logical, but the way this process works has lots of implications, as mentioned in the following list:

- Only the starting points and the ending points of the mouse movements are recorded by Captivate. During the playback, a movement is recreated between these points.
- Every Mouse movement made during the filming *between* two clicks is *not* recorded.
- The Timeline of the generated movie is *independent* of the time that has passed during the filming.

This system creates a very lightweight animation. A bunch of images and a few coordinates are enough to reproduce an entire movie.

That being said, this system is limited, as some mouse actions cannot be reproduced that way. These actions are: the *drag and drop* actions, actions involving the *scrollbar* and actions involving the *mouse wheel*.

These three types of actions require an actual video shooting to be played back correctly. Such a frame-by-frame animation is known as **Full Motion Recording,** or to make it short an **FMR**.

To make sure we understand this concept, we will return to the Captivate preferences. There are a few options that should make more sense now. Perform the following steps to understand Full Motion Recording:

1. In Captivate, use the **Edit** | **Preferences** (Windows) or the **Adobe Captivate** | **Preferences** (Mac) menu item to return to the **Preferences** window.
2. Once the **Preferences** window opens, click on the **Settings** category in the **Recording** group.

Notice at the end of the **Preferences** window two options that we did not discuss earlier. They are **Smoothen movements for Drag and Drop actions** and **Smoothen movements for Mouse Wheel Actions**.

These two options are checked by default, and you should not tamper with them unless you have a good reason to do so. Thanks to those two boxes, Captivate automatically switches to *Full Motion Recording* mode when a drag and drop or a mouse wheel action occurs during the filming.

3. Click on the **Keys - (Global)** category to return to the Keys Preferences pane.

Take another look at the keys available during the recording. Notice that you can use keyboard shortcuts to manually start and stop a *Full Motion Recording* if you need it.

4. Click on the **Video Demo** category to open the **Video Demo** Preferences pane.

The **Video Demo** preferences pane shows options to optimize the conversion of a *Full Motion Recording* into a Flash or HTML5 video format. Normally, the default options should work fine in almost every situation, so there is no need to change anything on this page right now.

5. Click on **Cancel** to close the preferences window without making any changes.

We have our answer! Slide 10 is different from the other slides of the project because it uses a *Full Motion Recording* to reproduce the scrolling action we made in the **Video** tab of the **Export Settings** dialog during the filming. One of the limitations of a Full Motion Recording is that it does not allow any kind of interaction (during the playback, such a scrolling movement cannot be done by the student as a click action or a typing action). That's why it is not suitable in Simulations as we just experienced when previewing our rushes.

The Video Demo

Video Demo is a brand new feature of Captivate 6. It allows us to create a video file by shooting our onscreen actions. A Video Demo recording project can be seen as a big Full Motion Recording.

A Video Demo project is very different from the other projects we have worked on so far in this chapter. Because it is a video file, no interactive objects are possible in such a project. In other words, a Video Demo can only be a *Demonstration*. A Video Demo project is based on a single big video file. It means that there are no slides and no Filmstrip in a Video Demo project.

When it comes to publishing, a Video Demo project can only be published as an `.mp4` video file. This makes Video Demo project particularly suitable for upload to an online video hosting service such as YouTube, Vimeo, or Daily Motion.

In the next exercise, we will create a Video Demo version of our Encoder Demonstration. The first operation to do is to reset our system.

If you have a problem while doing this exercise, refer to the `Chapter02/final/encoderVideo.cpvc` file of your exercises folder.

Perform the following steps to initialise the system and record a new Video Demo project:

1. If the **Adobe Media Encoder** application is still open, close it.
2. Reopen the **Adobe Media Encoder**.

Closing and reopening the Adobe Media Encoder resets the application, so it has its default look when we start the shooting.

3. Delete all the `.flv` files present in the `videos/MOV` folder of the exercise files.

Now that our system is ready, let's create a new Video Demo project.

4. Use the **File | Record new Video Demo** menu item to start a new Video Demo project.

A link to this option is also available on the Welcome screen of Captivate when no file is open. The following screenshot shows the Record new Video Demo path:

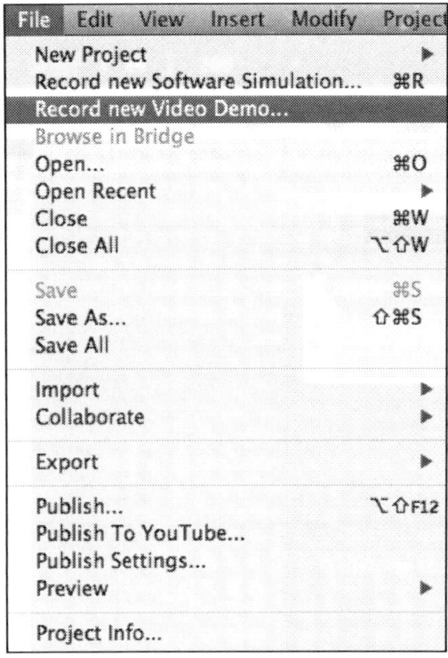

5. In the drop-down list at the top of the recording window, choose to record the **Adobe Media Encoder CS6** application.
6. In the **Snap to** section, choose to record at a **Custom Size** of **1024 x 768** pixels.

Most of the time, narration is added to such a video project. If you have a microphone available, you'll record your voice as the audio track of the video! If you don't have a microphone available, just read through these steps.

7. [If microphone available] Open the **Audio** drop-down list and choose your microphone in the list of entries. (The actual content of the list depends on the configuration of your system. In my case, I chose **Built-in Microphone** to use the built-in mike of my laptop)
8. [Everyone] Click on the red **Record** button to start the recording, as shown in the following screenshot:

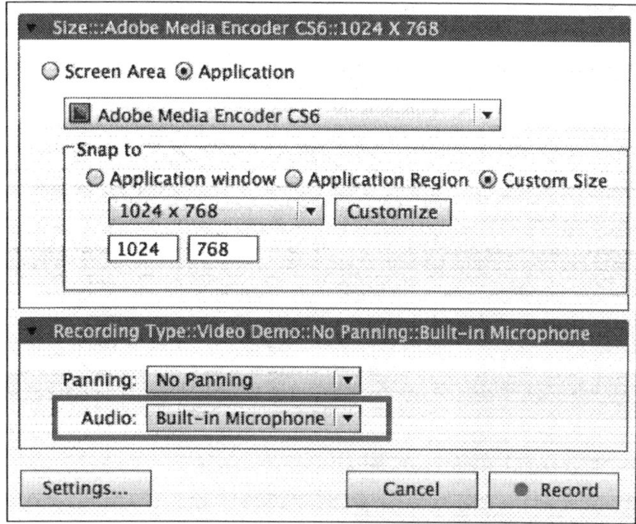

If it is the first time you record sound with your Captivate installation, you'll have to calibrate the sensitivity of your microphone.

9. [Optional] In the **Calibrate Audio Input** dialog, click on the **Auto Calibrate** button. Speak normally in the microphone until the **Input level OK** message appears on the screen. Click on **OK** to validate the sensitivity settings and to discard the box.
10. [Everyone] After a short countdown, the recording begins.
11. [Everyone] In **Adobe Media Encoder**, perform the actions as rehearsed earlier in this chapter. If you have a microphone, speak as you go through the steps of the scenario.
12. When done, hit the *End* key (Windows) or the *cmd* + *Fn* + *Enter* shortcut (Mac).

Captivate now finalizes the video capture. When the finalization process is finished, your entire recorded video is played back! Enjoy the show!

13. When the video has finished playing, click on the **Edit** button at the far right side of the play bar in the lower right area of the screen.

By clicking on the **Edit** button, leave the preview mode of our Video Demo project for the editing mode.

14. Save your file as `Chapter02/encoderVideo.cpvc`.

Remember that a Video Demo project does not use the standard `.cptx` file extension, but uses the `.cpvc` file extension instead.

Automatic and Manual Panning

In the movie industry, *Panning* is moving the camera during the filming. In Captivate, our camera is the red recording area. When *Panning* is turned on in Captivate, it simply means that the red recording area can be moved during the shooting. This will enable us to shoot a bigger application with a smaller recording area.

In the *Choosing the right resolution for the project* section mentioned earlier, we had a discussion on how to solve the project sizing problem. Panning was one of the possible approaches. Let's take a closer look at it.

> If you have a problem while doing this exercise, refer to the `Chapter02/final/encoderDemo_panning.cptx` file of your exercises folder.

Perform the following steps to use Panning feature:

1. Close and reopen the Adobe Media Encoder application to reset the user interface.
2. Delete all the `.flv` files present in the `videos/MOV` folder of the exercises files.
3. Return to Captivate and go to the **File | Record new Software Simulation** menu item. The Captivate interface disappears and the red recording area shows up.
4. In the recording window, choose to record a **Screen Area** (and not an **Application** as before). Give the area a **Custom Size** of **800 x 600** pixels.

Normally the size of the **Adobe Media Encoder** application should still be 1024 x 768 pixels from the previous filming sessions.

5. Move the red recording area so its top left corner corresponds to the top left corner of the **Adobe Media Encoder** application window.

In this configuration, the **Adobe Media Encoder** application and the red recording area do not have the same size. The recording area should be smaller than the Adobe Media Encoder.

6. In the bottom part of the recording window, make sure the **Demo** mode is the only one selected.
7. In the **Panning** drop-down list, choose **Manual Panning**. Set the **Audio** drop-down to **No Narration**. Your computer screen should look like the following screenshot:

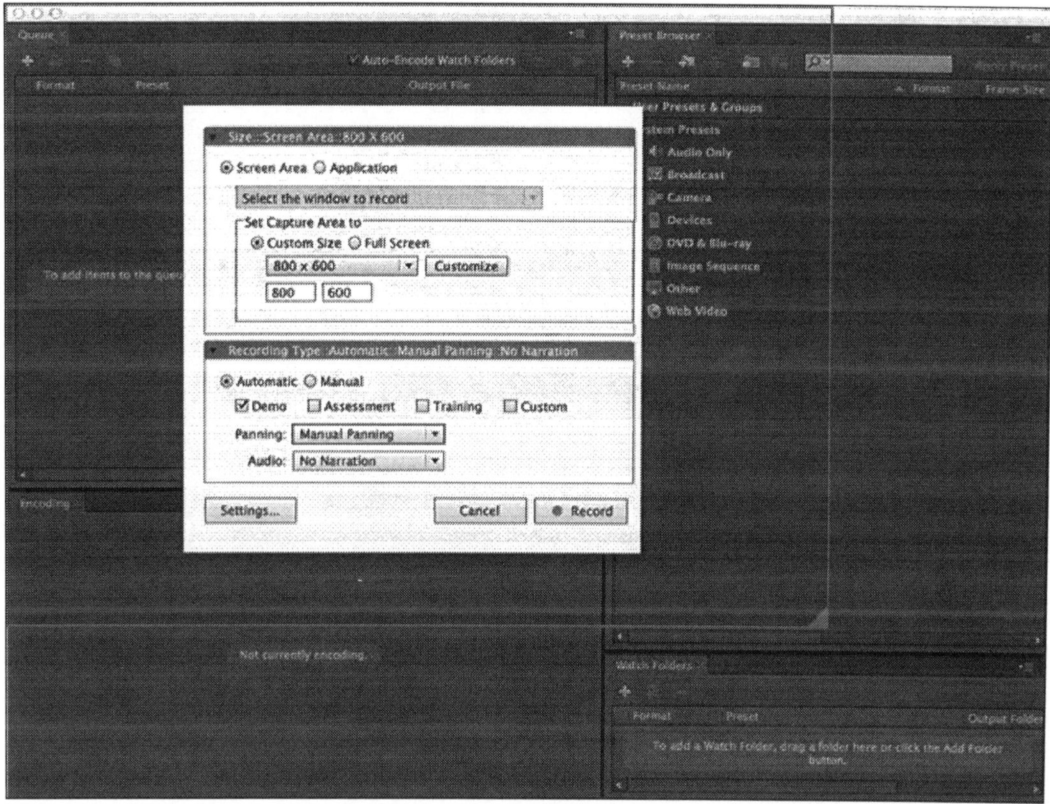

8. When ready, click on the red **Record** button to switch to recording mode.
9. After the countdown, use the Adobe media Encoder to perform the first few steps of the scenario from *Rehearsing the Scenario* section mentioned earlier.
10. When the **Export Settings** window opens, place your mouse above the red line of the recording area until the mouse turns to a grabbing hand. Then, *slowly* move the red recording area until it covers more or less the lower-right part of the **Export Settings** window.
11. Modify the size of the video as defined in the scenario discussed in the *Rehearsing the scenario* section mentioned earlier.
12. When the **Export Settings** dialog closes after you clicked on the **OK** button, move the red recording area back to its original position.
13. Click on the **Start Queue** icon (the green *play* button) as defined in the scenario.
14. Use the *Print Screen* key (Windows) or the *cmd* + *Fn* + *F6* shortcut (Mac) three or four times to capture the progression of the yellow bar.

15. When done, hit *End* (Windows) or *cmd* + *Fn* + *Enter* (Mac) to return to Captivate.
16. When the project loads in Captivate, use the Preview icon to preview the entire project. Can you see the Panning movements in the **Preview** pane?
17. When the movie is finished, close the **Preview** pane and save the file as `Chapter02/encoderDemo_panning.cptx`.

Back in Captivate; take a look at the **Filmstrip**. Beneath some of the slides' thumbnails, you should see the camera icon indicating that there are some *Full Motion Recording* slides in the project. *Full Motion Recording* is used to reproduce the panning movements made during the capture.

In this example, we have used the *Manual Panning*. When using *Automatic Panning*, Captivate places the mouse at the center of the red recording area. During the filming, the red recording area automatically follows any mouse movement. Automatic Panning produces a lot of unnecessary movements and, consequently, a lot of extra *Full Motion Recording* slides.

Rescaling a project

This chapter opened with a discussion on choosing the right size for the project. Our discussion led to four possible approaches to manage the size difference between the application to capture and the movie to produce.

The first approach was to shoot big then downsize. The first step of this approach has been done when we used a resolution of 1024 x 768 pixels to shoot our very first movie. We will now take care of the second step: resizing the movie to 800 by 600 pixels.

Note that resizing a movie always results in data and quality loss! Use this feature if you have no other solution, but if you have another valid solution to solve your sizing concern, then go for it! It will almost always be better than resizing your project. Perform the following steps to resize the project:

1. In Captivate, open the `chapter02/encoderDemo_1024.cptx` file.

If you did not successfully save this file, you can use the one saved in the `chapter02/final` folder.

If you have a problem while doing this exercise, refer to the `Chapter02/final/encoderDemo_800.cptx` file of your exercises folder.

Rescaling a Captivate project is a one-way operation. In other words, it cannot be undone! So we will use the Save As command to create a backup copy of the original project before we rescale it.

2. Use the **File | Save As** menu item to save the file as `Chapter02/encoderDemo_800.cptx`.
3. When the project is saved, go to the **Modify | Rescale Project** menu item.

The **Rescale Project** window opens. This window is divided into three parts. The top part allows you to define the new size of the project. It is the only part available at the moment.

4. Make sure the **Maintain Aspect Ratio** box is selected, and reduce the **Width** of the project from **1024** to **800** pixels. The new **Height** of **600** pixels should be calculated automatically.

As the new size is smaller than the original size, the lower right part of the box becomes available. It is titled as **If new size is smaller**. The lower-left part of the box is still inactive. It would activate if the new size of the project had been larger than the original size.

5. Take some time to review the available options, but leave the default unchanged. When ready, click on **Finish**.
6. A dialog box informs you that resizing a project cannot be undone. Click on **OK** to confirm you want to resize the project anyway.
7. Captivate resizes each slide, one by one.
8. Save the file when the resize process is complete.

Summary

In this second chapter, we have completed the first step of the Captivate production process: capturing the slides. Throughout this chapter, our main concern was to manage the size of the project as compared to the size of the application to capture.

Several approaches are possible to address this sizing issue. While experiencing each of these approaches we uncovered two important features of Captivate: *Full Motion Recording* and *Panning*.

Shooting a Captivate movie is a four-step process. First we have to prepare the application to shoot and reset our system to default. Then, we rehearse the script as many times as needed to fully master all the actions. The third step is to shoot the movie, and the last one is to preview the *rushes*. If you decide that the rushes are not good enough, just start over until you get it right. Remember that the success of the editing phase that follows depends on the quality of the shooting

We also discovered that Captivate has four automatic recording modes that are *Demonstration*, *Assessment Simulation*, *Training Simulation*, and a *Custom* mode that is ours to create. Each of these automatic recording modes adds *Text Captions* and other objects to our slides.

Captivate 6 also introduces the **Video Demo** project type. A Video Demo is like a big Full Motion Recording. It is used to create a `.mp4` video file that can be easily uploaded to an online video hosting service such as YouTube, Vimeo, DailyMotion, or else.

Of course, we are far away from the final result we want to achieve, but that was not our goal anyway. The project now has to go through the editing phase to reach its final aspect.

To wrap up this chapter, these are some tips and tricks for successful recordings:

- Use the automatic recording modes whenever possible.
- If you have to shoot full screen, reset your desktop to its default appearance, that is: remove your custom wallpaper, turn off any custom color scheme, or mouse-pointers-sets. Your computer should look like *any* computer.
- Turn off your screen saver.
- Turn on the sound, so you can hear the camera shutter and the keystrokes. This will help you have a better control over the recording process.
- If you are not sure whether or not Captivate took a given screenshot, don't hesitate to take one manually by using the *Print Screen* key (Windows) or the *cmd* + *Fn* + *F6* shortcut (Mac OS). During the editing phase that follows, it is much easier to delete an extra slide than to generate a missing slide.
- Perform the actions slowly, especially the text typing actions and the actions that require a *Full Motion Recording*. You'll be able to set up the timing of each slide with great precision during the editing phase.
- Rehearse your scripts before shooting.

With these tips and tricks and a bit of practice, you'll soon be producing high quality eLearning content!

In the next chapter, we will begin the editing phase of our work. The editing phase is the most time-consuming phase of the entire process. There are so many options and tools to discover that one chapter will not be enough to cover it all. Consequently, the editing phase will span in the few upcoming chapters.

In the next chapter, we will cover Text Captions, Mouse movements, Highlight Boxes, Images, Zoom Areas, and their formatting options. We will also use the Timeline to arrange our objects in time and the alignment toolbar to arrange our objects in space.

Meet the Community

Anita Horsley

Bio

Anita Horsley is a hard working, ambitious leader who possesses high energy and is a motivator about education and eLearning. Horsley has a Masters degree in Education. She is an Adobe Certified Expert in Captivate 5.5 and coordinates the Oregon State Captivate User Group. Horsley was a firefighter and officer for ten years in Atlanta and has worked for the Oregon Office of State Fire Marshal as a Training and Development Specialist since 2009.

Contact details

Blogs: `http://captivatecrazy.blogspot.com/` and `http://captivatecrazy.posterous.com/`

LinkedIn: `http://tinyurl.com/AnitaHorsleyLinkedIn`

Twitter: `@captivatecrazy`

My personal note

What an impressive blog is Anita's Captivate Crazy! At the time of this writing, her blog was four months old, but already contained tons of very interesting content. Just make sure you follow Anita on Twitter, as she is very active and very good at sharing great content with the community.

3
Working with Standard Objects

When the filming is complete, the director takes the rushes and heads to the post-production studio to begin the most time-consuming phase of the project. While in the studio, the director arranges the sequences shot during the filming in the correct order, adds sound effects, arranges transitions, fine-tunes visual and special effects, adds subtitles, re-records narration, and so on. When the director leaves the post-production studio, the motion picture is complete and ready for publishing.

The same basic principle applies to our Captivate projects. During the post-production phase, we will revisit each of our slides one by one to arrange, reorder, synchronize, add, modify, align, delete, and so on. To help us turn our rushes into a great eLearning experience, Captivate provides an extensive array of tools, features, and objects. In the next few chapters, we will take a deep look at each of them one by one.

The first thing we can do to enhance our projects is to add some basic objects to the slides of our movie. In this particular chapter, we will focus on five basic objects. We will also discuss the formatting tools and the Timeline.

In this chapter, we will:

- Learn how to work with the Properties panel
- Take a deep look at five basic objects of Captivate (Text Captions, Highlight Boxes, Mouse movements, Images, and Smart Shapes)
- Add basic formatting to these objects
- Use the styles and the Object Style Manager to achieve formatting consistency within the project
- Use the Timeline panel to organize the sequence of events

Preparing your work

Before we get started, we will make Captivate ready by opening the required files and by resetting the **Classic** workspace to its default appearance using the following steps:

1. Open Captivate.
2. Use the **File** | **Open** menu to open the `Chapter03/encoderDemo_800.cptx` file situated in your exercises folder.
3. Also open the `Chapter03/drivingInBe.cptx` file situated in your exercises folder.
4. When both files are open, make sure the **Classic** workspace is applied.
5. Use the **Window** | **Workspace** | **Reset 'Classic'** to reset the **Classic** workspace to its default look.

To ensure maximum accuracy between the files you work with and the exercises as described in this book, make sure you use the files of the `Chapter03` folder and not the ones you created in the previous chapter. During the exercises, feel free to experiment with the files. You'll have a fresh set of files to work with at the beginning of each chapter.

Each of the open files has its own tab in the Captivate interface. When doing the exercises of this chapter, make sure you are using the right file.

The `Chapter03/final` folder contains the files as they are supposed to be at the end of this chapter. Use these files as references if you get confused by any of the exercises.

Working with the Properties panel

For this first topic, use the `encoderDemo_800.cptx` file (1).

In the **Classic** workspace, the **Properties** panel is situated on the right-hand side of the interface (2). It is one of the most important panels of Captivate and certainly one of the most useful, as shown in the following screenshot:

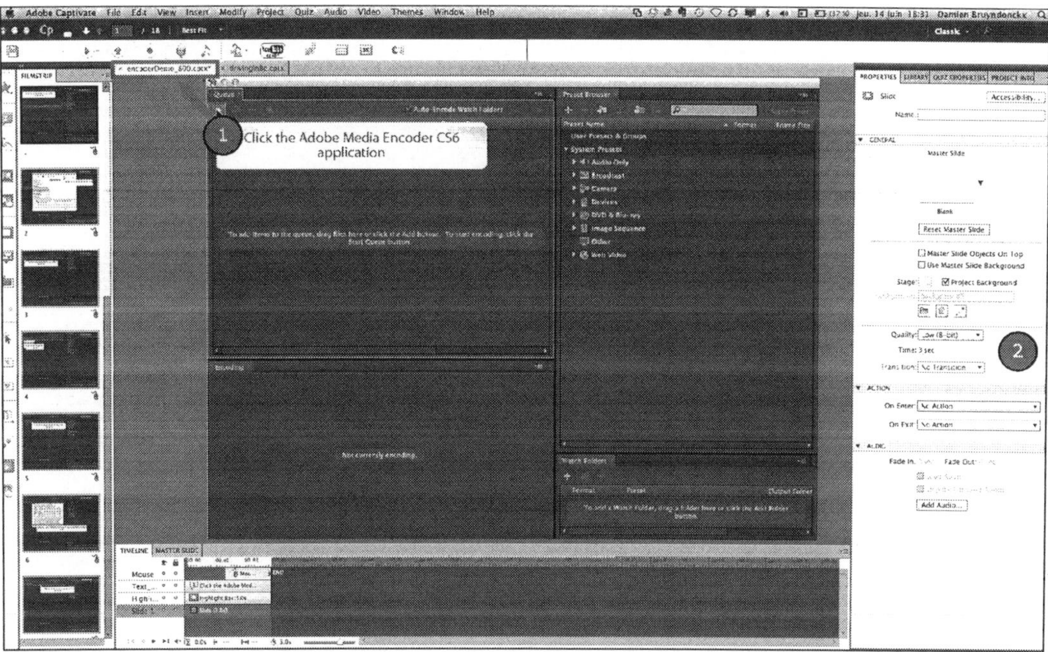

The **Properties** panel (2), as shown in the previous screenshot is a dynamic panel. This means that the content of this panel changes depending on the selected object. Let's make a simple experiment with the **Properties** panel using the following steps:

1. On the **Filmstrip**, click on the first slide to make it the active slide.

The word **Slide** should be displayed at the very top of the **Properties** panel. This tells us that the active item is currently the **Slide** itself. Take some time to inspect the content of the **Properties** panel, but leave all the options at their current settings.

The first slide contains three objects: a *Text Caption*, the *Mouse* object, and a blue *Highlight Box* next to the mouse pointer. These three objects have been automatically generated by the *Demo* recording mode we used during the capture.

2. Click on the Text Caption object on slide 1 to make it the active object.

At the very top of the **Properties** panel, you should see that the **Text Caption** is now the active object. Consequently, the panel shows the properties relevant to an object of type Text Caption, as shown in the following screenshot:

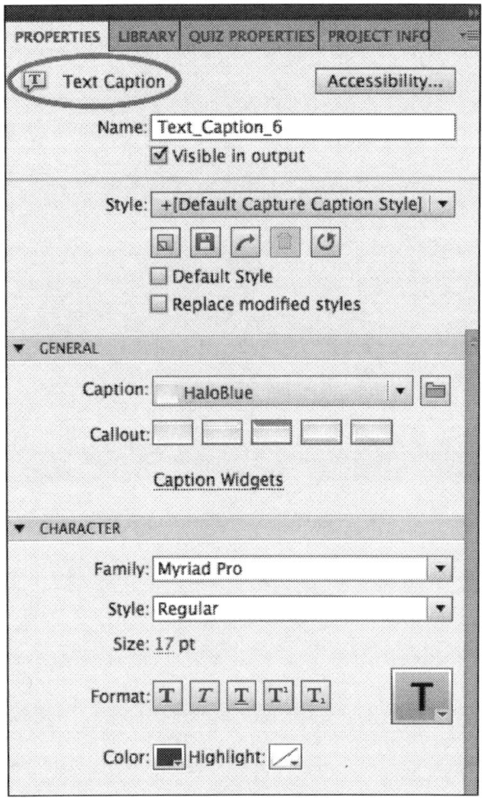

In the panel, the properties of the **Text Caption** are divided into sections. These sections are often called **accordions** because they can be expanded and collapsed by clicking on their respective title bars. For an object of type Text Caption, there should be eight accordions available in the **Properties** panel.

3. Click on the word **Character** to collapse the **Character** accordion in the **Properties** panel.
4. Click on the **Character** word again to expand the accordion.

Before moving on, take a look at the other accordions of the **Properties** panel, but leave all the options at their current settings.

5. Still on slide 1, select the blue *Highlight Box* next to the mouse pointer.

> Because all three objects share the same area of the slide, selecting the Highlight Box might be tricky. To make it easier to select the right object, you can use the **Timeline** panel (at the bottom of the screen).

6. **Highlight Box** is now written at the very top of the **Properties** panel, which displays the properties relevant to an object of type Highlight Box.

With the Highlight Box selected, take a close look at the accordions of the **Properties** panel. Most of the accordions available for an object of type Highlight Box are the same as the accordions available for an object of type Text Caption.

Usually, the accordions situated at the top of the stack (here the **Fill & Stroke** accordion) contain properties that are specific to the selected object. The accordions at the bottom of the stack (such as the **Timing** or the **Transition** accordions) contain properties relevant to many (if not every) types of objects.

To work with the **Properties** panel, remember the following points:

- In the default **Classic** workspace, the **Properties** panel is displayed at the right-hand side of the screen.
- The **Properties** panel is a *dynamic* panel. It means it shows the properties relevant to the *active* object. Consequently, selecting another object updates the content of the **Properties** panel.
- The **Properties** panel is divided into **accordions** that can be expanded and collapsed at will.
- Some *accordions* are specific to a certain type of objects.
- Other *accordions* are common to many (and sometimes to *every*) types of objects.

Now that we know how the **Properties** panel works, we will start the tour of the basic objects of Captivate.

Exploring the basic objects

Captivate offers more than a dozen objects to enhance the slides of our projects. In this chapter, we will explore five of those objects. We will start with the most basic of them: the **Text Caption**.

The Text Caption object

The **Text Caption** is one of the most basic and popular objects of Captivate. It is used in many different situations where we need to display text to the learners. In its most basic form, the *Text Caption* is just a piece of text that appears and disappears from the screen according to its position on the **Timeline**.

The *Demo* auto-recording mode we used during the filming in the previous chapter has already added lots of Text Captions to our slides. Some of these might be just right, but most of them, if not all of them, need some extra work.

Modifying the content of a Text Caption

When working with Text Captions, you can be in either one of two modes.

First, you can consider the Text Caption as *an object*. In this case, eight white squares appear around the Text Caption (1), as shown in the following screenshot. These white squares are the *handles* used to resize the Text Caption. Perform the following steps to modify the contents of Text Caption:

1. In the `encoderDemo_800.cptx` file, click on the Text Caption of slide 1 to make it the active object.
2. *Double-click* in the Text Caption object or press the *F2* shortcut key.

The eight white handles disappear and a blinking cursor shows up in the Text Caption (2), as shown in the following screenshot:

By double-clicking on a Text Caption, you switch to *text editing* mode where you can easily modify the content of a Text Caption.

3. *Triple-click* in the Text Caption to select its current content entirely.

4. In the Text Caption, type `The Mouse will now click on the Add files icon.`
5. Hit the *ESC* key to toggle the Text Caption back to *object* mode.

As you can see, modifying the content of a Text Caption is very easy. Before moving on to the next topic, we will update the content of the remaining Text Captions of the movie according to the following table. Don't hesitate to resize the Text Captions as appropriate after updating the slides with following content:

Slide number	Content of Text Caption
Slide 2	`The mouse will now double-click on the demo_en.mov video file.`
Slide 3	`The mouse will now click on the Format drop down menu.`
Slide 4	`The mouse will now click on the FLV menu item.`
Slide 5	`The mouse will now click on the Preset drop down menu.`
Slide 6	`The mouse will now click on the WEB-640x480, 4x3... preset.`
Slide 7	`The mouse will now click on the preset's name to open the Export Settings dialog.`
Slide 8	`The mouse will now click on the Video tab to access the video options.`
Slide 11	`The mouse will now click the current Width of the video.`
Slide 12	`Type the desired width (in this case 400 pixels) and hit the Enter key.`
Slide 13	`The mouse will now click on the OK button to validate the changes and close the Export Settings dialog.`
Slide 14	`The mouse will now click on the Play button to start the actual conversion to Flash video.`

These simple edits already made the project much easier to understand for the learners.

6. Save the file (*Ctrl* + *S* on Windows or *cmd* + *S* on Mac).
7. Use the Preview icon to test the entire project.

Of course, we still have to fine-tune the formatting and the timing of the objects, but the content of the Text Captions should be correct.

8. Close the **Preview** pane when finished.

Creating new Text Captions

So far, we have modified Text Captions that were automatically generated during the filming. We will now create and modify *brand new* Text Captions using the following steps:

1. Use the **Filmstrip** to return to slide 1.

Slide 1 already holds one Text Caption. We will add a second one.

2. Use the **Insert | Standard Object | Text Caption** menu item to create a new Text Caption.

By default, a new Text Caption appears in the middle of the slide in *text editing* mode.

3. Type `Welcome to the Adobe Media Encoder` in the new Text Caption.
4. Hit the *Esc* key to leave the *text editing* mode. The new Text Caption should still be selected.

In this particular project, the default formatting of a new Text Caption does not allow for a comfortable reading.

5. With the Text Caption still selected, take a look at the **General** accordion of the **Properties** panel. Note that the **Caption** drop-down list is set to **Transparent**.
6. Open the **Caption** drop-down list and choose **Adobe Blue** in the list of available Caption types.

There is another Text Caption to add on slide 4.

7. Use the **Filmstrip**, to select slide 4.
8. Use the second icon of the Objects toolbar to create a new Text Caption. Type `The H.264 options generate a .mp4 video file` [Press *Enter* to type the next sentence in a new line] `The MP3 option is for sound only!`
9. Hit the *Esc* key to leave the *text editing* mode while keeping the Text Caption selected.
10. In the **General** accordion of the **Properties** panel, apply the **Adobe Blue** Caption type to the new Text Caption.
11. Use the **Filmstrip** to go to slide 5.
12. Use the *Ctrl* + *Shift* + *C* (Windows) or the *cmd* + *Shift* + *C* (Mac) shortcut to add a second Text Caption to the slide.

13. Type `The conversion settings will be different depending on the intended purpose of your video file.` in the Text Caption.
14. Apply the **Adobe Blue** Caption type to the new Text Caption.

To insert a new Text Caption, you can use either the **Insert | Standard Object | Text Caption** menu item, the second icon of the *Objects* toolbar or the *Ctrl* + *Shift* + *C* (Windows) or *cmd* + *Shift* + *C* (Mac) shortcut. Remember that the Objects toolbar is the set of icons that spans across the left-hand side of the screen. Actually, the icons of the *Objects* toolbar reflect more or less the content of the **Insert | Standard Objects** menu.

Add the remaining Text Captions in the project according to the following table. Make sure you apply the **Adobe Blue** Caption type to each new Text Caption:

Slide	Text Caption	# of TC on slide.
Slide 5	`The Adobe Media Encoder contains a list of presets to help us make the right choice.`	3
Slide 7	`The chosen preset needs some adjustments to perfectly match our needs.`	2
Slide 8	`The chosen preset already adjusted most of these options correctly` `Only the size of the generated video must be changed.`	3
Slide13	`Notice that The Adobe Media Encoder automatically calculates the new Height of the video` `This is because the Maintain aspect ratio icon is currently selected.`	3
Slide 14	`When we modify existing presets, we actually create new ones.`	2
Slide 15	`The encoding panel contains information about how the conversion is progressing.`	1
Slide 18	`Done!`	1

Formatting a Text Caption

Captivate offers many tools and features to format a Text Caption. Most of them are available through the accordions of the **Properties** panel. Some of these properties are obvious and self-explanatory, others need additional explanation. Let's review some of these properties together.

Resizing and moving Text Captions

The first option we will cover is how a Text Caption object can be resized and moved around the slide using the following steps:

1. Still on the `encoderDemo_800.cptx` file, use the **Filmstrip** to select slide 1.
2. Click on the **Welcome to the Adobe Media Encoder** Text Caption to make it the active object.
3. In the **Properties** panel, expand the **Transform** accordion.

In the **Transform** accordion, take a look at the size of the selected Text Caption. **W** indicates the *Width* of the object, while **H** stands for the *Height*. Both dimensions are expressed in *pixels*. Actual values may differ from the following screenshot:

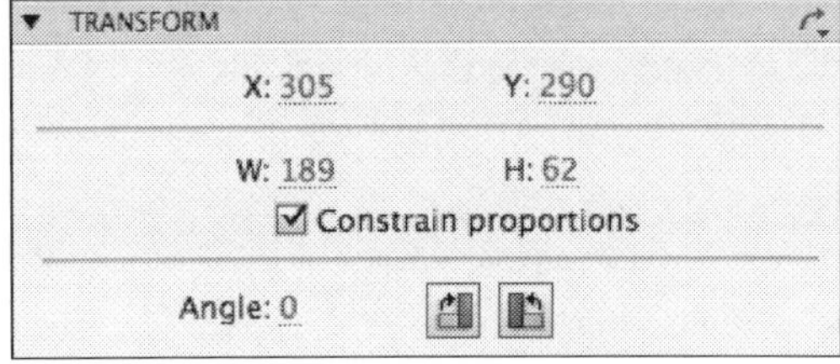

4. On the stage, use the white handles to make the Text Caption a bit bigger.
5. Take another look at the **Properties** panel. The new size of the object should be written in the **Transform** accordion.

If you want to give your objects a specific size, you can enter the *Height* and the *Width* in the **Properties** panel directly. If the **Constrain proportions** checkbox is selected, Captivate automatically calculates the new **Height** of the object when you modify the **Width** (and vice versa) so that the Height/Width ratio of the object does not change.

6. With the Text Caption still selected, take look at the **X** and the **Y** values in the **Transform** accordion.
7. Use your mouse to move the Text Caption around the slide.

See how the **X** and the **Y** values of the **Transform** panels change as you move the Text Caption. The **X** coordinate is the distance (in pixels) between the left edge of the selected object and the left edge of the slide. The **Y** coordinate is the distance (in pixels) between the top edge of the selected object and the top of the slide. You can manually enter the **X** and the **Y** coordinates in the **Transform** panel to give the selected object a pixel-precise location on the slide.

Changing the Callout and the Caption type

You probably noticed that a Text Caption has the shape of a callout. Captivate proposes five **Callout Types** for each Text Caption. Perform the following steps to change the Callout type:

1. Use the **Filmstrip** to go to slide 5 of the `encoderDemo_800.cptx` file.
2. Select the Text Caption that starts with **The Adobe Media Encoder contains....**
3. Resize this Text Caption so the entire text nicely fits on two lines.
4. Take a look at the **General** accordion of the **Properties** Panel.
5. In the **Callout** section, choose the second callout type, as shown in the following screenshot:

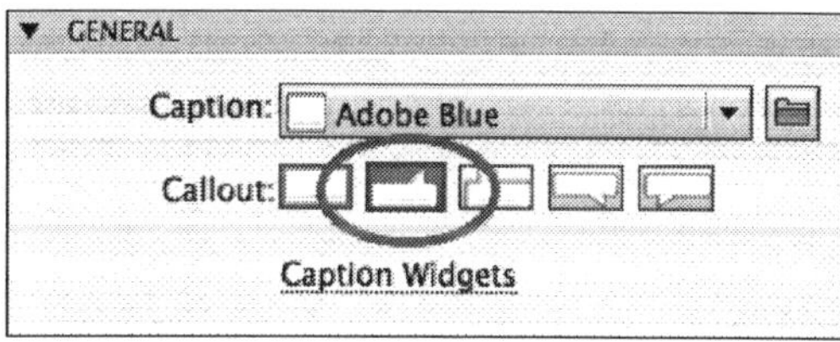

Captivate applies the new callout to the Text Caption **and recalculates the size of the object**. Since we carefully resized the Text Caption just before changing the **Callout** type, we do *not* appreciate that Captivate resizes this object on its own. To avoid this from happening in the future, we will modify two of the preferences of Captivate.

6. Use the **Edit | Preferences** (Windows) or **Adobe Captivate | Preferences** (Mac OS) menu item to open the **Preferences** dialog.
7. On the left-hand side of the **Preferences** dialog, click on the **Defaults** category.
8. At the end of the **Preferences** dialog, uncheck both the **Autosize Buttons** and the **Autosize Captions** check boxes and click on **OK**.
9. On slide 5, resize the selected Text Caption until the text fits nicely in the object again.

From now on, the objects will keep their assigned size when we change their Callout Type. Notice that this preference applies to the **currently active file only**.

Changing the preferences globally

If you want to change the preferences globally for the entire application, you should close any open files and modify the preferences while no file is open.

10. In the **General** accordion of the **Properties** panel, open the **Caption** drop-down list.
11. In the list, choose the **Business Yellow** Caption Type.

The **Business Yellow** Caption Type is applied to the object. Notice that the size of the Text Caption is *not* recalculated anymore.

Character and paragraph formatting

To finalize the formatting of this Text Caption we will use options of the **Character** and the **Format** accordions. Perform the following steps to format the Text Caption:

1. Still on slide 5, make sure that the **The Adobe Media Encoder contains...** Text Caption is still selected.
2. In the **Character** accordion of the **Properties** panel, change the font **Family** to **Century Gothic**.
3. Also change the font **Size** to `19` points.
4. In the **Align** section of the **Format** accordion, use the **Align Center** and the **Align Middle** icons to position the text in the middle of the Text Caption.
5. Make sure the Text Caption looks like the following screenshot before moving on:

Later in this chapter, we will see how we can quickly apply the formatting of this Text Caption to all the other Text Captions of the project.

Working with Text Effects

The new Text Effects feature of Captivate 6 lets us create and apply some sophisticated visual effects on our Text Captions. If you are a Photoshop user, you'll be in known ground as the Text Effects feature of Captivate 6 shares most of its functionalities with the effects of Photoshop. Let's take a closer look at this brand new feature of Captivate.

To experiment with Text Effects, we will use the Driving in Belgium project and performing the following steps:

1. Open the `chapter03/drivingInBe.cptx` file from your exercises folder. If the project is already open, just switch to the right tab in Captivate.
2. Use the **Filmstrip** to go to slide 5 of this project.

Slide 5 should contain two Text Captions.

3. Select the Text Caption that reads **Good** to make it the active object.
4. In the **General** accordion of the **Properties** panel, change the **Caption** type to **Transparent**.
5. In the **Character** accordion, change the font **Family** to **Century Gothic** and the font **Size** to `49`.
6. Still in the **Character** accordion of the **Properties** panel, click on the Text Effects (1) icon. (It is the big **T** icon.)

The Text Effects menu opens. In the topmost area of the menu, eight predefined effects are ready to use (2). The last four effects are ours to create (3), as shown in the following screenshot:

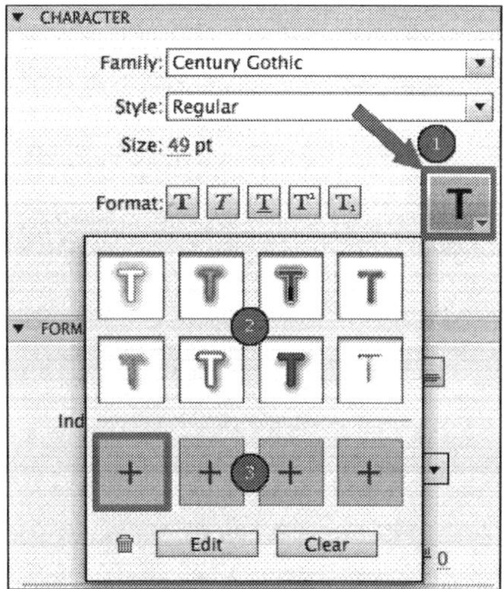

7. Click on the first empty effect available (shown as the red rectangle in the previous screenshot).

The **Text Effects** window opens. The left-hand side of the window contains nine effects. We can easily turn these effects on and off by clicking on their respective checkbox. The right-hand side of the window displays the options of the effect selected on the left-hand side of the window. At this moment, no effect is applied.

8. In the left column of the **Text Effects** window, select the **Drop Shadow** checkbox to turn the **Drop Shadow** effect on.

A Drop Shadow effect is applied to the **Good** Text Caption. For this example, we will accept the default settings of the Drop Shadow effect.

9. In the left column of the **Text Effects** window, select the **Outer Glow** checkbox to turn the **Outer Glow** effect on.

The **Outer Glow** effect is applied to the Text Caption and the options of the **Outer Glow** effect are displayed in the right hand side of the **Text Effects** window. To make our effect more attractive and visible, we will modify the color of the Outer Glow effect.

10. In the right-hand side of the **Text Effects** window, click on the **Color** option of the **Outer Glow** effect.
11. In the color picker, choose any bright green color.

Hey! It looks like we just came up with a very nice effect. Let's save it for future use.

12. At the bottom of the **Text Effects** window, click on the **Save** button.

The Text Effects window closes and our effect is applied to the selected Text Caption. Because we have saved our nice effect, it will be very easy to apply it to another Text Caption of the project.

13. Still in the `drivingInBe.cptx` file, use the **Filmstrip** to go to slide 9.
14. Once on slide 9, select the Text Caption that reads **Good**.
15. In the **General** accordion, change the **Caption** type to **Transparent**.
16. In the **Character** accordion, change the font **Family** to **Century Gothic** and the font **Size** to `49`.
17. Still in the **Character** accordion of the **Properties** panel, open the **Text Effects** menu (use the big T icon as we did in the previous screenshot).

Surprise! A ninth effect is now available in the **Text Effects** icon! It is the effect that we just saved a few lines ago.

18. Click on this new effect to apply it to the selected Text Caption.

Great! We can now create some sophisticated visual effect and easily apply them to the Text Captions of our movie.

19. Still in the `drivingInBe.cptx` file, use the **Filmstrip** to go to slide 6.
20. Once on slide 6, select the Text Caption that begins with **Belgian use…**.
21. In the **General** accordion, change the **Caption** type to **Transparent**.
22. In the **Character** accordion, change the font **Family** to **Century Gothic** and the font **Size** to `49`.
23. Still in the **Character** accordion of the **Properties** panel, open the **Text Effect** icon one more time.
24. Apply our new effect to the selected Text Caption.

Our effect is applied to the **Belgian use…** Text Caption as well. We will now modify the color of the Outer Glow effect. By doing so, we will come up with a new Text Effect that we will save and apply to another Text Caption of the project.

25. Make sure the **Text Effects** icon is still open in the **Character** accordion of the **Properties** panel.
26. Click on the **Edit** button.

This action reopens the Text Effects window we used earlier to create our special effect.

27. On the left-hand side of the **Text Effects** window, click on the **Outer Glow** effect (make sure you click on the name of the effect, not on the checkbox).
28. On the right-hand side of the window, open the **Color** option of the **Outer Glow** effect.
29. In the color picker, choose any bright red color. The new **Outer Glow** color is automatically applied to the selected Text Caption.
30. At the bottom of the **Text Effects** window, click on the **Save** button to save this as a new effect.

Make sure the Text Caption looks like the following screenshot:

Finally, we will apply this second effect to another Text Caption of the project.

31. Use the **Filmstrip** to go to slide 10.
32. Once on slide 10, select the Text Caption that begins with **Belgian drive....**
33. In the **General** accordion, change the **Caption** type to **Transparent**.
34. In the **Character** accordion, change the font **Family** to **Century Gothic** and the font **Size** to `49`.
35. Still in the **Character** accordion of the **Properties** panel, open the **Text Effects** icon.
36. Apply our new *red* effect to the selected Text Caption.
37. Save the `drivingInBe.cptx` file when done.

This exercise concludes our first exploration of the Text Caption object. Before moving on to the next topic, let's summarize what we have learned about the Text Caption object:

- The Text Caption object is used to display text to the learner.
- The *Demo* recording mode automatically adds lots of Text Captions to the slides.
- When inserting or updating a Text Caption, Captivate automatically calculates the size of the object according to the amount of text it contains.
- To prevent Captivate from automatically calculating the size of a Text Caption, modify the **Defaults** category of the **Properties** dialog.
- Changing the size or the position of an object with the mouse also changes the corresponding values in the **Transform** accordion of the **Properties** panel and vice versa.
- Apply a **Caption Type** to the object to quickly format it.
- Captivate provides 5 **Callout Types** for each **Caption Type**.
- The new Text Effects feature of Captivate 6 lets us create and apply sophisticated visual effect on our Text Captions.

There still is some work to be done on the other Text Captions of our projects, but, for now, we will leave them as they are and explore another object.

The Highlight Box object

The second object we will focus on is the **Highlight Box**. As its name implies, a Highlight Box is used to highlight a specific area of the screen. A Highlight Box simply is a semi-transparent rectangle that appears and disappears from the screen according to its position on the Timeline.

When using the default *Demo* recording mode during the capture, Captivate adds one Highlight Box for each mouse click. Perform the following steps to format the Highlight Box:

1. Return to the `Chapter03/EncoderDemo_800.cptx` project.
2. In the **Filmstrip**, click on slide 1.

Slide 1 should contain four objects: two *Text Captions*, the *Mouse*, and a small blue *Highlight Box* below to the mouse pointer. This Highlight Box has been automatically added by Captivate during the filming.

3. Click on the Highlight Box to make it the active object.

Selecting the Highlight Box updates the **Properties** panel. At the top of the **Properties** panel, the **Fill & Stroke** accordion is the only one that is specific to this type of object. It provides the main formatting options of the Highlight Box object.

- The first setting is the **Fill**. The **Fill** is the *inside* of the object.
- Next to the fill is the Alpha parameter. It is used to control the opacity of the Highlight Box. When the Alpha is set to `0` %, the object is completely transparent. When the Alpha is set to `100` %, the object is completely opaque.
- The third setting is the **Stroke**. The **Stroke** is the **border** *around* the object. The **Stroke** option manages the color of the border.
- The last setting is the **Width**. This option manages the **Width** of the stroke. Setting this option to `0` removes the stroke from the object.

Now that we have a better idea of the available formatting options, we will change the formatting of the selected Highlight Box:

4. In the **Fill & Stroke** accordion of the **Properties** panel, click on **Fill**.
5. In the color picker, choose a dark orange as the fill color of the Highlight Box.
6. Leave the Alpha value at **20** %.
7. Click on **Stroke**.
8. In the Color picker, choose the same orange color as the one you chose for the Fill.
9. In the **Width** section, choose a stroke width of **2** pixels.

Make sure your **Fill & Stroke** accordion looks like the following screenshot:

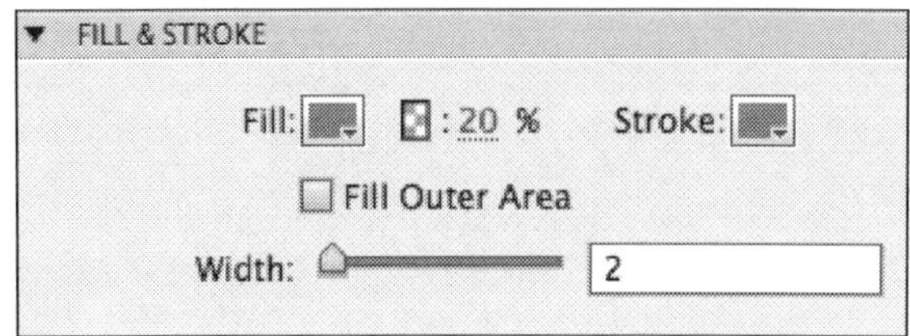

Finally, we will use the **Transform** accordion to modify the size and the position of the Highlight Box.

10. Still on Slide 1 of the `encoderDemo_800.cptx` file, make sure the Highlight Box is the selected object.
11. In the **Properties** panel, open the **Transform** accordion.
12. For the size, give the Highlight Box a Width of `24` pixels and a Height of `20` pixels (To be able to modify the **Height** independently from the **Width**, make sure the **Constrain proportions** box is *deselected*).
13. For the position, give the Highlight Box a **X** coordinate of `4` pixels and a **Y** coordinate of `32` pixels.

The Highlight Box should precisely cover the **Add Files (+)** icon.

14. Use the Preview icon to preview the **Next 5 slides**.

Captivate generates the slides and opens the **Preview** pane. Take a close look at the Highlight Box of slide 1. The timing and the formatting of the objects are of no importance at this time.

When the preview is finished, close the **Preview** pane to return to Captivate. There is one last option to experiment with.

15. Return on Slide 1 of the `encoderDemo_800.cptx` file and select the orange Highlight Box.
16. In the **Fill & Stroke** accordion of the **Properties** panel, select the **Fill Outer Area** box.

With this box selected, the fill color of the Highlight Box will be applied to the area *outside* of the object. The only part of the slide that will *not* be covered by the fill color will be the *inside* of the Highlight Box, as shown in the following screenshot:

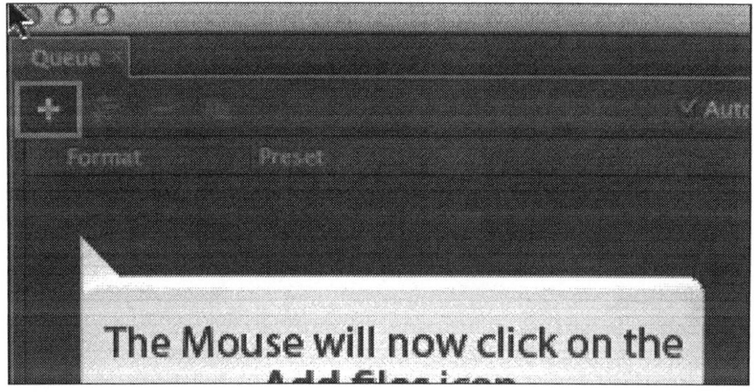

To experiment with it, save the file and use the Preview icon to test the **Next 5 slides** again. While previewing slide 1, pay close attention to the Highlight Box object. When the preview is finished, close the **Preview** pane to return to Captivate.

17. Return on Slide 1 of the `encoderDemo_800.cptx` file and select the orange Highlight Box one last time.
18. In this particular case, we want the Highlight Box to behave normally, so, in the **Fill & Stroke** accordion of the **Properties** panel, uncheck the **Fill Outer Area** box.
19. Save the file when done.

This last experiment concludes our discussion on Highlight Boxes. Here is a summary of what we have learned:

- A Highlight Box is a semi-transparent rectangle used to highlight a particular spot on the slide.
- The **Fill** is the *inside* of the Highlight Box object. The **Fill & Stroke** accordion of the **Properties** panel lets you choose the *color* and the *opacity* of the fill.
- The **Stroke** is the *border* around the Highlight Box object. You can choose the *color* and the *width* of the stroke in the **Properties** panel.
- Select the **Fill Outer Area** box to apply the fill color to the *outside* of the Highlight Box rather than to the *inside*.

Working with the Mouse

The third object we will study is the **Mouse**. Remember that during the filming, only the *coordinates* of the mouse clicks have been recorded and that the Mouse movements are recreated during the playback.

Understanding the Mouse movements

We will start our study of the Mouse object by discussing the continuity of the Mouse movements between the Captivate slides using the following steps:

1. Return on Slide 1 of the `encoderDemo_800.cptx` file.

On this slide, you should see four red dots in the top-left corner of the slide. These four dots mark the starting point of the mouse.

2. Use your mouse to move the four red dots anywhere on the slide.

By moving the four red dots, you change the starting point of the mouse on slide 1, as shown in the following screenshot:

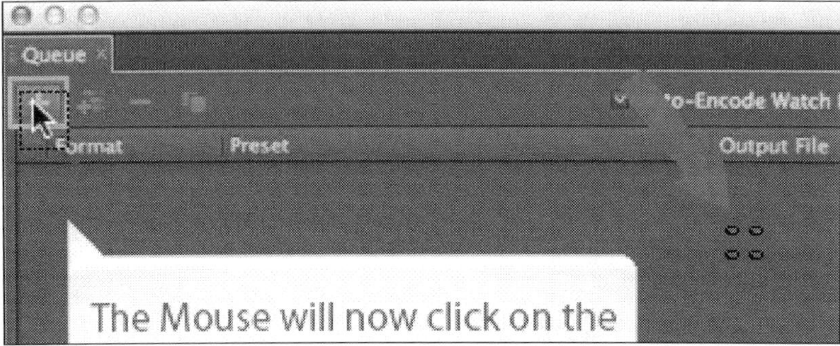

From the chosen spot, a curved blue line shows the Mouse movement, as shown in the previous screenshot. The line ends with the mouse pointer.

3. Click on the mouse pointer at the end of the curved blue line to select the Mouse object. The **Properties** panel updates.
4. In the **Options** accordion of the **Properties** panel, select the **Straight Pointer Path** box.

By clicking this box, we generate a straight line between the starting and the ending points of the Mouse movement.

5. In the **Options** accordion of the **Properties** panel, uncheck the **Straight Pointer Path** checkbox.
6. Use the **Filmstrip** to select Slide 2.

On the second slide, the four red dots visible on slide 1 do *not* show. It means that we cannot move the starting point of the mouse on slide 2. This is because **the starting point of the mouse on slide 2 corresponds to the ending point of the mouse on slide 1**.

7. Use the **Filmstrip** to browse the remaining slides of the project.

When browsing the slides of the project, you should notice that the first slide is the only one where the starting point of the Mouse movement can be moved. No other slides display the four red dots at the beginning of the curved blue line.

8. When done, return to slide 1.
9. Take the mouse pointer and move it to a random location.
10. Use the **Filmstrip** to select slide 2.

On slide 2, you should notice that the starting point of the curved blue line has changed and corresponds to the random location you chose on slide 1.

11. On the **Filmstrip**, click on slide 1 to make it the active slide.
12. Move the mouse pointer back to its original location.
13. Use the **Filmstrip** to go to the last slide of the project (slide 18).

On slide 18, the mouse makes a long movement. Slide 18 being the last one of the project, this movement is unnecessary. What we want to do is to move the mouse pointer so its position corresponds to the position of the mouse pointer on the previous slide.

14. On slide 18, right-click the mouse pointer at the end of the blue line.
15. In the contextual menu, click on the **Align to Previous Slide** item.

By clicking on the **Align to Previous Slide** item, the mouse pointer on slide 18 will be aligned to the mouse pointer on slide 17. Consequently, the starting and ending points of the Mouse movement on slide 18 have the same coordinates and the mouse will no longer move on slide 18.

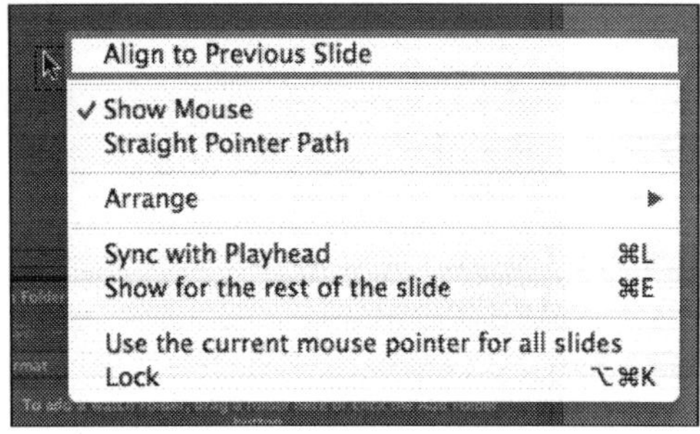

16. Use the Preview icon to preview the entire movie.
17. In the **Preview** pane, pay close attention to the Mouse movements. Make sure each click occurs at the right place.
18. When the preview is complete, close the **Preview** pane.
19. If needed, adjust the position of the mouse on the slides where the click is not well positioned.
20. Save the file when done.

Formatting the Mouse object

During the preview, you probably noticed that a blue circle and a *click* sound highlight each mouse click, except on slide 3 where these options have been removed from the Mouse object. Perform the following steps to format the Mouse object on slide 3:

1. Use the **Filmstrip** to activate slide 3.
2. Once on slide 3, select the mouse pointer to make it the active object.
3. In the **Options** accordion of the **Properties** panel, select the **Mouse Click Sound** box.
4. Also select the **Show Mouse Click** box.

Before moving on, take some time to inspect the remaining settings of the **Options** accordion. Notice the two drop-down lists that let us chose the sound to use and the shape of the visual click. We can also choose the color of the visual click if needed.

The topmost part of the **Options** accordion lets us choose the most appropriate mouse pointer. In our case, the default pointer suits our needs perfectly, so we will not change it in this project.

Choosing the right mouse pointer

My very first big eLearning project was to build an online course on SAP for a big multinational company. SAP uses custom mouse pointers that I wanted to reproduce in Captivate. A mouse pointer is a `.cur` file, so I clicked on the **Browse** button situated right below the collection of mouse pointers in the **Properties** panel and searched for the appropriate `.cur` file in the `C:\Program files` folder of Windows. Eventually, I found the `.cur` file I was looking for and I could import it in Captivate. If you work on Mac, you can inspect the content of an `.app` file by right-clicking on the file and choose **Show Package Contents**. You might find the `.cur` file you are looking for in the package. The bottom line is, your Captivate project should reproduce the behavior of the actual application as close as possible.

Let's make a quick summary of what we have learned:

- During the filming, only the position of the mouse at each click is recorded. A Mouse movement is recreated between these positions at runtime.
- By default, the Mouse movement uses a curved line, but we can make it a straight line in the **Options** accordion of the **Properties** panel.
- The first slide of the project is the only slide where we can move both the starting and the ending points of the Mouse movement.
- To prevent the mouse from moving on a given slide, right-click on the mouse pointer and choose **Align to Previous Slide** in the contextual menu.
- Moving the mouse pointer on a slide also moves the origin of the Mouse movement on the next slide.
- We can add a visual click as well as a click sound in the **Options** accordion of the **Properties** panel.

Working with images

The next object we will focus on is the **Image** object. Captivate lets us insert various types of images in any slide of the project. Once an image is inserted, we are able to modify and format the image using the image editing tools of Captivate. Keep in mind though that Captivate is *not* an image editing application. To guarantee the best possible result, you should always prepare your images in a real image editing application (such as Adobe Photoshop or Adobe Fireworks) *before* inserting the image in Captivate.

Before inserting an image in our project, we will insert one extra slide in the **Filmstrip** using the following steps:

1. Open the `Chapter03/videoInCaptivate.cptx` file from your exercises folder.

This project is a one-slide Captivate movie. That single slide contains four Text Captions. In order to accelerate our work, we will simply copy-paste this slide in the `encoderDemo.cptx` file.

2. Still in the `videoInCaptivate.cptx` file, right-click on the slide's thumbnail in the **Filmstrip**.
3. In the contextual menu, select the **Copy** item.
4. Return to the `encoderDemo_800.cptx` file.
5. In the **Filmstrip**, right-click on the first slide and select the **Paste** menu item.

When we insert a new slide in a Captivate project, it gets inserted *after* the selected slide. There is *no way* to insert a new slide as the first slide directly. However, the **Filmstrip** lets us reorder the slides easily using a simple drag-and-drop action.

6. Use the **Filmstrip** to drag the new slide up so it becomes the first slide of the movie.

Now that the stage is set, let's move to what *really* is the subject of this particular topic: inserting pictures.

7. Make sure you are still on the first slide of the `encoderDemo_800.cptx` file.
8. Use the **Insert | image** menu item.
9. Browse to the `images/AMELogo.png` file stored in your exercises folder.
10. Click on **Open** to insert the picture.

The image is inserted in the middle of the slide. Obviously, it is way too big for this slide. Our next operation will be to resize and position this image so it integrates nicely with the other elements of the slide.

11. Make sure the image is the selected object.
12. Use your mouse to change the size of the image. This will most likely *distort* the image.

Note that you can avoid distortion by pressing and holding the *Shift* key on your keyboard while using a corner handle to resize (scale) the image.

13. In the **Image** accordion of the **Properties** panel, click on the **Reset To Original Size** button for the image to restore to its original aspect.

In this case, the **Transform** accordion of the **Properties** panel probably is the most appropriate way to resize this picture.

14. If needed, expand the **Transform** accordion of the **Properties** panel.
15. Make sure the **Constrain proportions** checkbox is selected, and change the Width (**W**)of the picture to `180` pixels. Captivate calculates the new Height (**H**)of the image (176 pixels) so its Height/Width ratio does not change.
16. Move the image to the lower left area of the slide next to the Text Captions

Your slide should now look like the following screenshot:

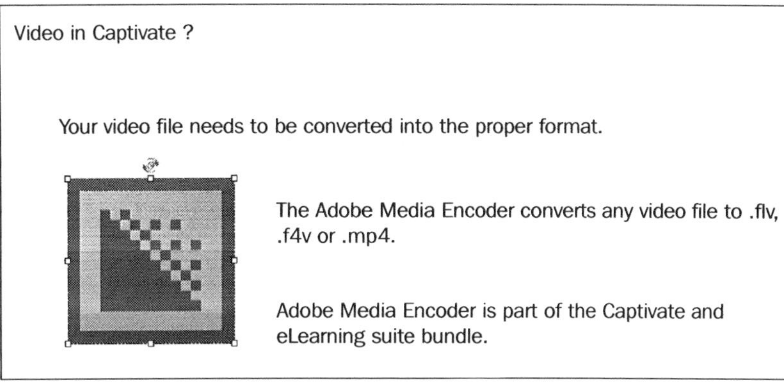

Using the image editing tools

Inserting an image in Captivate is *that* easy! We will now explore some of the image editing tools using the following steps:

1. Make sure the newly imported image is selected, and take a look at the **Properties** panel.

It shows properties relevant to an Image object. The first two accordions (**Image** and **Image Edit**) should be expanded. The remaining accordions are more or less the same as for the Text Captions and the Highlight Box objects and should be collapsed by default.

2. Move the sliders of the **Image Edit** accordion to see how each affects the selected image.
3. When done, click on the **Reset All** button to return every slider to its original position.

To finish off with this first image, we will now add a nice finishing touch thanks to a new feature of Captivate 6.

4. Make sure the image is still selected.
5. In the **Properties** panel, expand the **Shadow & Reflection** accordion.
6. Select the **Reflection** checkbox and choose the preset you like the most.

Great! This little effect adds a whole new dimension and impact to our picture! Our students will certainly enjoy this level of details in their visual experience.

Inserting a picture slide

We will now insert yet another slide in our project. This new slide will be based on a `.png` file. We could insert a blank slide in the project and import the `.png` picture on that slide. But we will use another method that streamlines this workflow. Perform the following steps to insert a picture slide:

1. Make sure you are still on the first slide of the `encoderDemo_800.cptx` file.
2. Use the **Insert** | **Image Slide** menu item, as shown in the following screenshot:

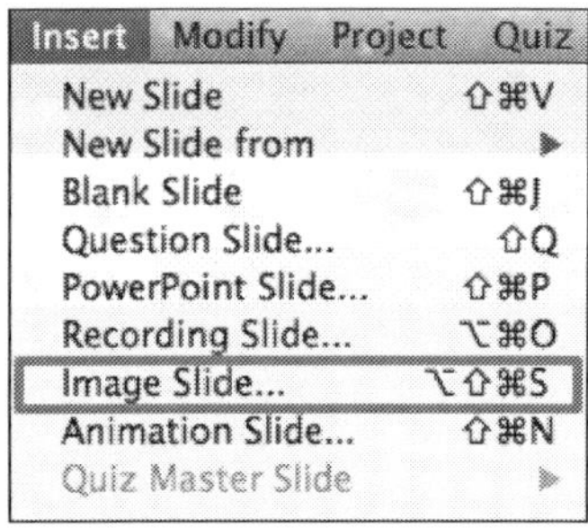

3. Browse to the `images/mftcTitleTemplate.jpg` file stored in your exercises folder.
4. Click on the **Open** button.

The new picture is inserted as a new slide. Notice that the picture we used has a Width of 800 pixels and a Height of 600 pixels, which is the exact same size as the project itself. It is not a coincidence. Remember that the images must be prepared *before* being inserted in Captivate. In this case, preparing the image was making sure it had the right size.

5. In the **Filmstrip**, drag-and-drop the new slide up so it is the first slide of the project.
6. Save the file when done.

Extra credit: working with Characters

Characters are a new feature of Captivate 6. It is a collection of images that you can insert in your Captivate projects. These images represent male and female characters in various postures. Inserting such pictures in your eLearning projects brings in a very welcome human and humoristic touch.

These images are *not* installed with the rest of Captivate. The installation of an extra-package is required to be able to use these characters. This extra-installer can be found on your Captivate installation disk or it can be downloaded from the Adobe website at the following address:

[Windows] - `http://www.adobe.com/go/captivate_assets_installer`
[Mac] - `http://www.adobe.com/go/captivate_assets_installer_mac`

In this extra credit section, you'll install the characters collection of images and insert some of these characters in the `drivingInBe.cptx` file:

- Download the Characters from the Adobe website or locate the installer on your Captivate or eLearning suite installation disk.
- Run the installer to install the characters.
- Open the `drivingInBe.cptx` file and use the **Filmstrip** to go to slide 1.
- Use the new **Insert | Characters** menu item to open the **Characters** dialog, as shown in the following screenshot:

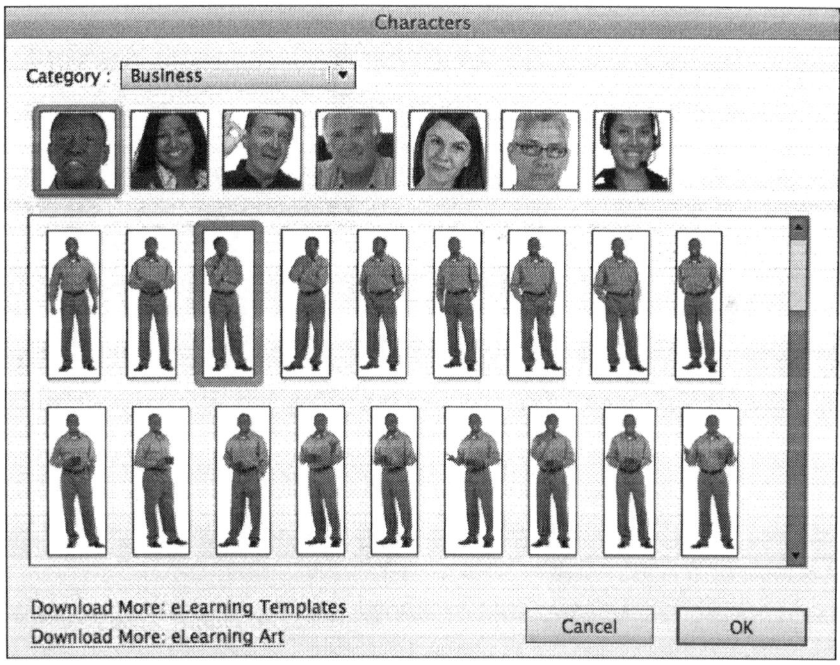

- Insert the character of your choice on the slide.
- Repeat this operation anywhere you feel like a character may enhance the learning experience.

Refer to the `final/drivingInBe.cptx` file for inspiration. In this case, we have used two characters, a male and a female. Their presence on the slides is synchronized to the audio (we will cover audio in *Chapter 5, Working with Audio*). We have also used the tools of the **Properties** panel to adapt the imported image to the project (especially the **Flip image horizontal** icon at the end of the **Image Edit** accordion).

This last exercise concludes our first overview of the image object. Here is a summary of what we have learned:

- We can easily insert many types of images in Captivate.
- Captivate provides some image editing capabilities in the **Properties** panel.
- It is best to prepare the image in a real image editing application *before* inserting it in Captivate.
- If needed, use the **Reset To Original Size** and the **Reset All** buttons to reset the picture to its original state.
- By using the **Insert | Image Slide** menu item, we can create new slides that are based on images.
- Captivate 6 introduces the **Characters** feature. The Characters are a collection of pictures that can be used in our eLearning project. Characters add a human and humoristic touch to our online courses.
- The installation of an extra-package is required to use the Characters.

We will now study the fifth and last object of this chapter.

Working with Smart Shapes

Captivate 6 introduces a brand new object type: the **Smart Shapes**. Captivate contains a predefined collection of Smart Shapes including rectangles, circles, banners, stars, arrows, and many more. In the following exercise, we will draw a Smart Shape and explore how it can be modified using the tools of Captivate 6. Perform the following steps to work with Smart Shapes:

1. Return to the `drivingInBe.cptx` project.
2. Use the **Filmstrip** to go to slide 3.

At this moment, slide 3 should contain three objects: two Text Captions and one Image. We will use the Smart Shapes feature to draw a rounded rectangle on the slide. We will use that shape as a background frame for the image.

3. Click on the first icon of the Objects toolbar or use the **Insert | Standard Objects | Smart Shape** menu item to open the **Smart Shapes** panel.

The Smart Shapes panel displays the collection of shapes available in Captivate 6. All these shapes can be edited and transformed using the tools of Captivate.

4. Click on the Rounded Rectangle shape to activate the Rounded Rectangle tool, as shown in the following screenshot:

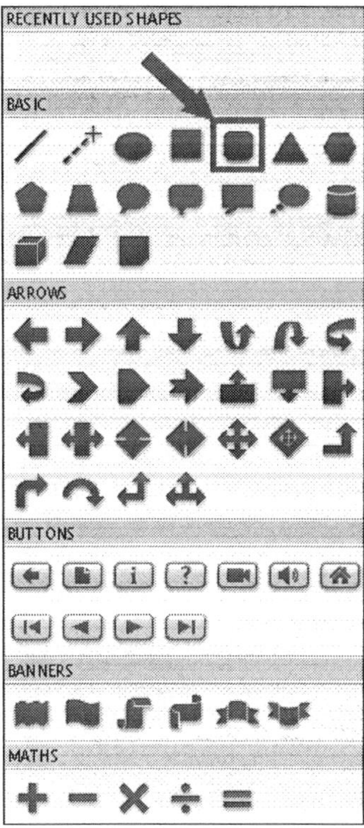

The Smart Shape panel disappears and the mouse pointer turns to a small cross.

5. Use your mouse to draw a Rounded Rectangle shape that entirely covers the image present on slide 3. Don't hesitate to resize and move the shape if needed.

In the top left area of the shape, you should see a yellow handle in addition to the eight white handles that surrounds the shape. This yellow handle is what makes a Smart Shape… smart. It is used to modify the shape. In the case of the rounded rectangle, this yellow handle is used to adjust the roundness of the shape's stroke.

6. Use the yellow handle to adjust the roundness of the rectangle to your taste.

Formatting a Smart Shape

The Smart Shape is in place. We will now adjust the look and feel of the shape using the following steps so it integrates nicely in the slide:

1. Use the **Send Selected Object Behind** icon of the main toolbar to place the rounded rectangle behind the image, as shown in the following screenshot:

2. Click on the **Fill** icon situated in the **Fill & Stroke** accordion of the **Properties** panel.

By default the Fill of a Smart Shape is a Linear Gradient. As you can see, this particular gradient uses different shades of blue and white to achieve the current look and feel of the rounded rectangle (1). In this exercise, we want to use a solid color as the fill of the rounded rectangle.

3. Click on the **Solid Color** (2) icon at the top of the **Fill** window, as shown in the following screenshot:

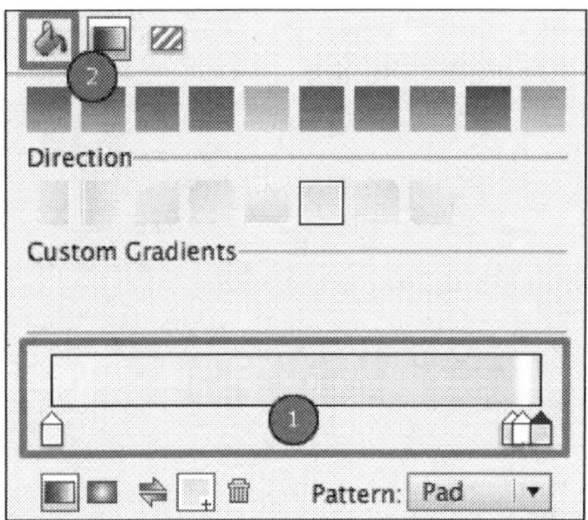

4. Type color code `#AB8F1D` in the Fill window. It is a somewhat light brown color.
5. Still in the **Fill & Stroke** accordion, change the Alpha to `100` % (entirely opaque).
6. Click on the **Stroke** icon and type color code `#4C421D` as the color of the stroke. It is a dark brown color.
7. Increase the stroke **Width** to `2` pixels.

8. Make sure your **Fill & Stroke** accordion looks like the following screenshot:

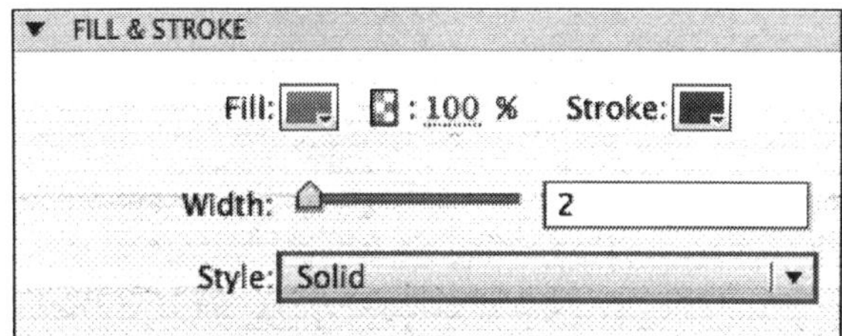

Using the Align toolbar

The Align toolbar contains the tools necessary to align, distribute, and resize the objects of our slides. Thanks to these tools it will be very easy for us to precisely align the image with the rounded corner and achieve the background frame effect we are trying to generate.

By default, the Align toolbar is not present on the screen, so our first task will be to turn it on using the following steps:

1. Use the **Window | Align** menu item to turn the Align toolbar on. By default, it appears in the top left area of the screen.
2. Click on the Rounded Rectangle to make it the active object. Eight white handles appear around the shape.
3. Maintain the *Shift* key of the keyboard down and click on the image to add the image to the current selection. Eight black handles appear around the image.

When selecting multiple objects, white handles surround the first selected object. Black handles surround the other objects of the selection. The tools of the Align toolbar will always use the first selected object (the one with the white handles) as the master object for alignment.

4. Click on the **Align Center** and **Align Middle** icons of the Align toolbar one at a time, as shown in the following screenshot:

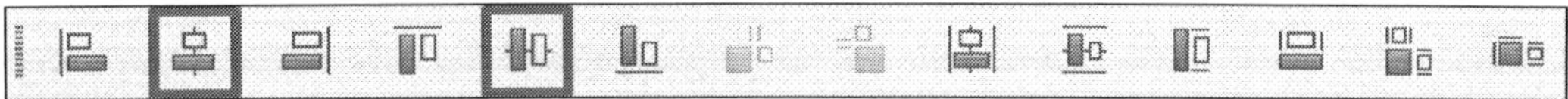

The Rounded Rectangle and the image should now be perfectly aligned! To avoid any accidental movement that would break this perfect alignment, we will now group these objects together. Grouping objects is yet another new feature of Captivate 6.

5. Make sure the Rounded Rectangle and the image are still selected.
6. Right-click on any of the two objects. In the contextual menu, click on **Group**.
7. Save the file when done.

At the end of this exercise, your slide should look like the following screenshot (the screenshot does not include the eventual Character you have added in the previous *Extra Credit: working with Characters* section mentioned previously):

Converting Smart Shapes to freeform

A Smart Shape is a **vector object** similar to those you can draw in Adobe Fireworks or Adobe Illustrator. To draw these shapes, designers use the *Pen tool* of Illustrator or Fireworks to draw Bezier points and Bezier curves. If you know how to use these points and curves Captivate offers you the possibility to further customize your Smart Shapes. Simply right-click a Smart Shape and choose **Convert to freeform** in the contextual menu.

This concludes our exploration of five basic objects of Captivate. We will explore some more objects in the next chapter, but right now, we will discuss a powerful formatting tool that will make your life as an eLearning developer a lot easier.

Working with styles

When working on an eLearning project, it is very important to precisely format the various objects of the movie. Never forget that we are actually *teaching* something to *students*. In such a situation, most students will try to make sense out of every single formatting anomaly. Inconsistent formatting will most likely mislead and confuse the students.

Consistent formatting on eLearning

In my first eLearning project with Captivate, I used blue Text Captions to *explain* things to the learners and black captions when I wanted them to *do* something. After a short while, the learners knew that when seeing a blue Caption, they just had to *read* through the text, and when seeing a black Caption, they made themselves ready to *do* something. Learners have reported that this formatting consistency helped them structure their learning.

A **Style** enables us to save the formatting properties of an object and to reapply them on the other objects of the same type. This system helps us achieve the high-level of consistency that the *teaching* situation requires.

Captivate ships with lots of predefined styles. We can, of course, modify these default styles and even create our own custom styles.

Managing styles with the Properties panel

For the next exercise, we will return to the `encoderDemo_800.cptx` project. Perform the following steps to experiment the styles:

1. Return to the `encoderDemo_800.cptx` project.
2. Use the **Filmstrip** to go to slide 7.

Slide 7 contains three Text Captions. Normally, each of these Text Captions should have a different formatting.

3. Select the Text Caption that begins with **The mouse will now click...**.

The **Style** drop-down list (1) is situated in the topmost area of the **Properties** panel. It should mention that the style currently applied to the selected Text Caption is the **[Default Capture Caption Style]**, as shown in the following screenshot:

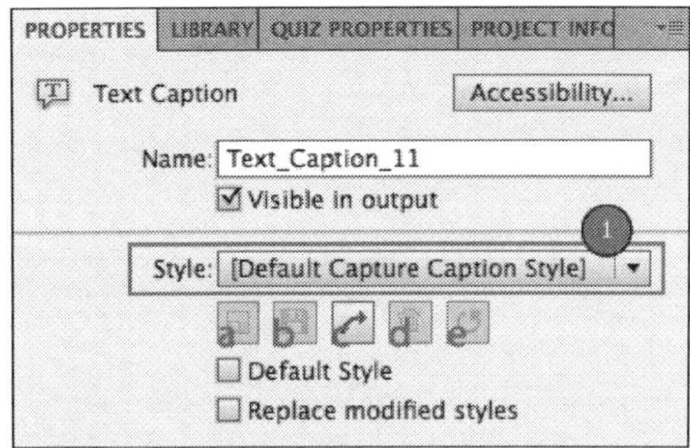

Just below the **Style** drop-down are five icons, identified by the letters *a* to *e* in the above screenshot. These icons are used to *create*, *update*, *apply*, *delete*, and *reset* the styles. I'll refer to these icons by their letter in the next few exercises.

4. Select the Text Caption that begins with **The conversion settings will...**.

Take a look at the topmost area of the **Properties** Panel. The **Style** drop-down list informs us that the **+[Default Caption Style]** is in use.

Resetting a style

Resetting a style is the first operation that can be done with the icons of the **Properties** panel.

The little + sign that precedes the name of the style in the **Style** drop-down, means that some formatting properties have been *added* to the original **[Default Caption Style]**. Remember that, earlier in this chapter, we decided that the default styling was not appropriate for this project, so we changed the **Caption** type to **Adobe Blue**. Perform the following steps to reset a style:

1. Below the **Style** drop-down, click on the **last** icon (e) to *reset* the style.
2. The original **[Default Caption Style]** is reapplied to the selected caption and the little + sign disappears.

The *Reset Style* icon (e) is very practical when you want to reset the format of the selected object back to default.

3. Make sure the Text Caption is still selected.
4. In the **General** accordion of the **Properties** panel, change the **Caption** type back to **Adobe Blue**. In the Style drop-down, the little + sign reappears.

Creating new styles

Creating a new style is the second operation that can be done with the icons of the **Properties** panel. In the next exercise, we will save the current formatting of the Text Caption that begins with **The Adobe Media Encoder....** Perform the following steps to create new styles:

1. Click on the Text Caption that begins with **The Adobe Media Encoder...** to make it the active object.
2. In the **Style** drop-down list of the **Properties** panel, notice the little + sign in front of the **[Default Caption Style].**
3. Right below the **Style** drop-down, click on the **first** icon (a) to create a new style.
4. In the **Save New Object Style** dialog box, name the new style **MFTC-Caption** and click on **OK**.

Take another look at the **Style** drop-down list of the **Properties** panel. It tells us that the new **MFTC-Caption** style is applied to the selected object. This style can now be applied to any other Text Caption of the project.

5. Reselect the Text Caption that begins with **The Adobe Media Encoder....**
6. At the top of the **Properties** panel, open the **Style** drop-down list.
7. In the list, select the **MFTC-Caption** style.

This last action applies the **MFTC-Caption** style to the selected Text Caption. The Text Captions of slide 7 should now look like the following screenshot:

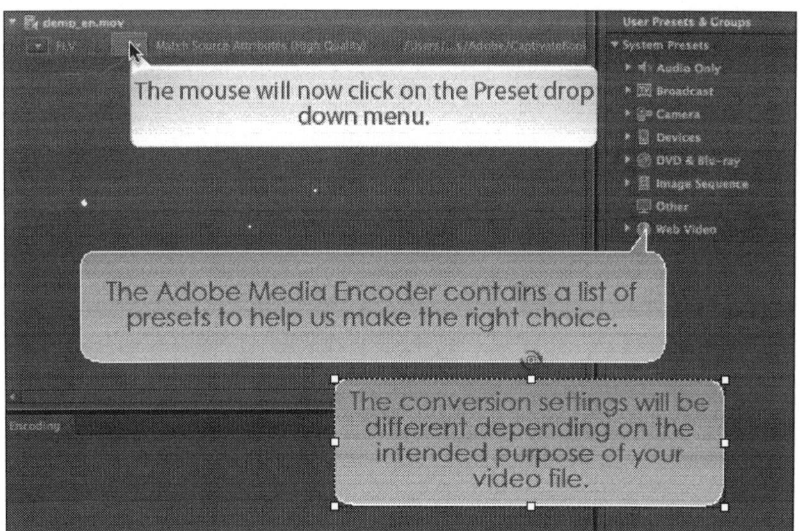

Modifying a style

Modifying a style is yet another action that can be done with the icons of the **Properties** panel. Currently, two of the three Text Captions of slide 7 share the same style. In this section, we will slightly modify the formatting of one of these two Text Captions. We will then update the **MFTC-Caption** style to the new formatting and see how the other Text Captions reacts. Perform the following steps to modify a style:

1. Make sure that the Text Caption that begins with **The conversion settings...** is still selected.
2. In the **Characters** accordion of the **Properties** panel, change the font **Size** to `20`.

Because we have made a formatting change, the little **+** sign appears in the **Style** drop down list.

3. In the topmost area of the **Properties** panel, click on the **second** icon (b) to *save the changes to the existing style.*

The little **+** sign disappears from the **Styles** drop down list.

4. Select the Text Caption that begins with **The Adobe Media Encoder....**
5. In the **Characters** accordion of the **Properties** panel, confirm that the new **font Size** of **20** is applied to this Text Caption as well.

By updating the **MFTC-Caption** style, we have updated the formatting of every Text Caption of the project this style is applied to.

Applying styles automatically

The style currently applied to the Text Captions of slide 7 is the one we want for every Text Captions of the project. We could browse each slide one by one to manually apply the new style to each and every Text Caption, but there is another, more automated, way using the following steps:

1. Use the **Filmstrip** to go to slide 3.

Slide 3 currently has two Text Captions with different styles applied.

2. Select Text Caption that begins with **The mouse will now click on...** Confirm that the **[Default Capture Caption Style]** is the style in use.

What we want to do is to apply our custom **MFTC-Caption** style to all the Text Captions of the project that currently use the **[Default Capture Caption Style]**.

3. Use the **Filmstrip** to return to slide 7.
4. Select any of the two Text Captions that currently use our **MFTC-Caption** style.
5. Right below the **Style** drop-down, click on the **third** icon (c).
6. In the **Apply Object Style** box that pops up, select the **[Default Capture Caption Style]** in the drop-down list, and click on **OK**.

This operation applies the **MFTC-Caption** style to every Text Caption of the project that was using the **[Default Capture Caption Style]**.

7. Use the **Filmstrip** to browse the slides one by one and confirm that all the Text Captions of the project that were using the **[Default Capture Caption Style]** now use our custom **MFTC-Caption** style.

Let's try the same operation with the Text Captions of the project that are using the **[Default Caption Style]**.

8. Make sure that a Text Caption using the **MFTC-Caption** style is still selected.
9. In the **Properties** Panel, click on the third icon (c) again.
10. In the **Apply Object Style** box that pops up, select the **[Default Caption Style]** in the drop-down list, and click on **OK**.
11. Use the **Filmstrip** to return to slide 3.

Well, it looks like our last operation didn't work as expected! **The Welcome to the Adobe Media Encoder** Text Caption still has the same formatting as before.

12. Click on the **Welcome to...** Text Caption to make it the active object.
13. Take a close look at the **Style** drop-down list situated at the top of the **Properties** panel.

The Style drop-down list should say that the **MFTC-Caption** style has indeed been applied to this Text Caption. But a little **+** sign tells us that what we are seeing now is not the genuine **MFTC-Caption** style. Actually, the manual edit that we did earlier on this Text Caption (change the **Caption** type to **Adobe Blue**) is still applied and overrides our custom style.

14. In the **Properties** panel, click on the last icon (e) to reset the style to its default look.
15. Repeat the same operation for all the remaining Text Captions starting from slide 3 till the end of the project.

Extra credit

What is true for the Text Captions also applies to the other objects. In this Extra credit section, you will format one of the Highlight Boxes of the project, save the new formatting as a new style and apply it to every single Highlight Box of the project.

These are the general steps to follow:

- Use the **Filmstrip** to return to slide 3 and select the orange Highlight Box we formatted earlier in this chapter.
- Save the current formatting of the Text Caption as a new style named `MFTC-HighlightBox`.
- Use the icons of the **Properties** panel to apply the new **MFTC-HighlightBox** style to the remaining Highlight Boxes of the project. (Hint: by default the Highlight Boxes use the [Default Blue Highlight Box Style]).
- Browse the slides of the project and confirm that every Highlight Box now shares the same orange look and feel. If needed, move and resize the Highlight Boxes so they integrate nicely into the slides.

This concludes our explorations of the styles in Captivate. By using the styles, it has been easy and fast to format every Text Captions and every Highlight Boxes of our project the *exact same* way. It helped us achieve the high degree of formatting consistency our students need to learn in the best possible conditions.

Before we move on to the next topic, let's summarize what we have learned:

- The styles help us create and maintain consistent formatting throughout the entire project.
- In the topmost section of the **Properties** panel, the **Style** drop-down list is used to apply a style to the selected object.
- When some additional formatting is applied on an object, a little + sign appears in front of the style name.
- When you modify a style, you change the formatting of all the objects using that particular style.
- Right below the **Style** drop-down, five icons are used to manage the style applied to the selected object.

Working with the Object Style manager

So far, we have used the icons of the **Properties** panel to apply and manage the styles. These icons give us a quick and easy access to the main styling features of Captivate. But behind the scenes, a much more sophisticated engine is at work!

This engine is the **Object Style Manager**. The icons of the **Properties** panel are just a *remote control* to the actual Object Style Manager. Everything these icons made possible is also possible through the Object Style Manager itself, but the Object Style Manager has much more to offer.

Exporting a style

One of the extra features offered by the Object Style manager is the ability to export styles. Make sure you are still in the `encoderDemo_800.cptx` project. Perform the following steps to export a style:

1. Use the **Edit | Object Style Manger** menu to open the Object Style Manager window, as shown in the following screenshot:

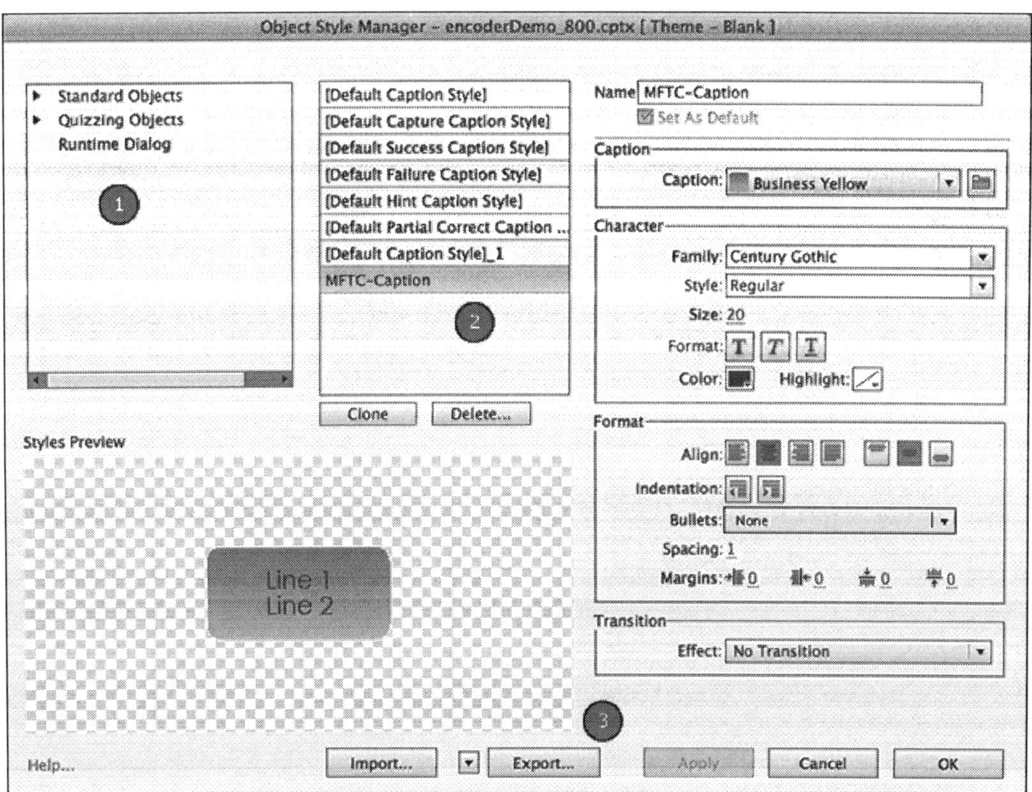

The left-hand side of the Object Style Manager (1) contains a list of all the objects of Captivate.

2. In the left column of the Object Style Manager, expand the **Standard Objects** section.
3. In the **Standard Objects** section, expand the **Captions** subsection.

The **Captions** subsection shows a list of all the caption types of Captivate.

4. Click on the **Text Caption**.

The middle column (2) shows a list of the styles that can be applied to the object selected in the first column. In our case, the styles listed in the middle column can be applied to the Text Caption object. Among them is our custom **MFTC-Caption** style.

5. In the middle column, select our **MFTC-Caption** style.
6. At the bottom of the **Object Style Manager**, click on the **Export** button (3).
7. Save the style in your exercises folder as `Chapter03/MFTC-Caption.cps`.
8. Click on **OK** to close the Object Style Manager.
9. Save the `encoderDemo_800.cptx` file.

Exporting a style creates a `.cps` file. This file will be used to import the style in another project.

Importing a style

In order to use our custom *MFTC-Caption* style in another project, we will now use the Object Style Manager to import the `.cps` file created in the previous topic. Perform the following steps to import a style:

1. Return to the `drivingInBe.cptx` project.
2. Open Object Style Manger by using the **Edit | Object Style Manager** menu item.
3. In the **Object Style Manager**, expand the **Standard Objects** section.
4. In the **Standard Objects** section, expand the **Captions** section.
5. Select the **Text Caption** object.

In the middle column of the Object Style Manager, notice that our *MFTC-Caption* style is *not* listed. This tells us that the styles listed in the Object Style Manager are specific to the active file. **Each project has its own list of styles**.

Adding styles globally

If you want to add styles to the Object Style Manager and make them available to every projects of your Captivate installation, close every open files and go to the **Edit | Object Style Manager** menu while no file is open.

6. At the bottom of the Object Style Manager, click on the **Import** button.
7. Browse to the `Chapter03/MFTC-Caption.cps` file and click on **Open**.
8. Read the message that pops up and click on **OK** to discard it.
9. Close **Object Style Manager** by clicking on the **OK** button.

After this operation, we should be able to apply our custom style to the Text Captions of this project as well.

10. In the **Filmstrip**, select slide 11.
11. Select the Text Caption containing the text **Convert Speeds to MPH**.
12. Use the **Style** drop down list in the topmost area of the **Properties** panel to apply the **MFTC-Caption** style to the selected Text Caption.
13. Follow the same procedure to apply the **MFTC-Caption** style to the following Text Captions:
    - On slide 12, on the Text Caption beginning with **pass your mouse on these road signs .....**
    - On slide 13, on the Text Caption beginning with **pass your mouse on the sentences to .....**
14. Return to slide 12 and reselect the caption you applied the style to.
15. In the **Properties** panel, open the **Shadow & Reflection** accordion, the select the **Enable** check box of the **Shadow** section. This applies a drop shadow effect to the selected Text Caption.
16. In the **Properties** panel, open the **Transform** accordion, type **10** in the **Angle** section. This applies a 10 degrees *rotation* to the selected object.
17. Apply the same drop shadow and rotation to the styled Text Caption of slide 13.

Thanks to the Object Style Manager, we have been able to exchange styles between projects. This will help us achieve formatting consistency not only within each project, but also *between different projects*.

Creating a style in the Object Style Manager

To create the **MFTC-Caption** style, we have used the icons situated in the topmost area of the **Properties** panel. We will now create another style from within the Object Style Manager directly using the following steps:

1. Make sure you are in the `drivingInBe.cptx` file.
2. Use the *Shift* + *F7* shortcut (Win and Mac) to reopen the Object Style Manager window.
3. In the middle column, select the **[Default Caption Style]**.
4. Right below the middle column, click on the **Clone** button.

Captivate duplicates the **[Default Caption Style]** and saves the clone as **[Default Caption Style] 1**.

5. In the rightmost column of the Object Style Manager, rename the new style **Transparent Title**.
6. Still in the rightmost column, change the **Caption Type** from **Halo Blue** to **transparent**.
7. Change the font **Family** to **Century Gothic**.
8. Change the **Character Size** from **20** to `49`.
9. Leave the other options to their default values and click on **OK** to close the Object Style Manager.
10. Use the **Filmstrip** to return to slide 1.
11. On slide 1, select the Text Caption containing **Drive in Belgium the safe way**.
12. Use the **Style** drop-down list of the **Properties** panel to apply the new **Transparent Title** style to the selected caption.
13. With the caption still selected, click on the **Apply this style to** icon (c).
14. In the box that pops up, choose to apply the **Transparent Title** style to every Text Caption currently using the **[Default Caption Style]** and click on **OK**.
15. Use the **Filmstrip** to browse the slides of your project one by one. There should be no more Text Captions with the default styling.
16. Save the `drivingInBe.cptx` file.

This exercise concludes our overview of the Object Style Manager. Before moving on, let's summarize what we have learned:

- The five styling icons of the **Properties** panel act as a *remote control* to the Object Style Manager.
- The Object Style Manager provides extra tools as compared to the five styling icons of the **Properties** panel.
- The leftmost column of the Object Style Manager contains a list of all the objects of Captivate.
- Using the Object Style Manager, styles can be exported from a movie and imported in another one.
- It is possible to create a style in the Object Style Manager directly.

Extra credit

The `drivingInBe.cptx` file contains some interesting styles that are not present in the `encoderDemo_800.cptx` project. Let's make those styles available in all our projects. Here are the general steps to follow:

- In the `drivingInBe.cptx` file open the **Object Style Manager**.
- Export the **WatchOut** ,the **transparentCaption** and the **Transparent Title** styles to the `chapter03` folder of your exercises.
- Return to the `encoderDemo_800.cptx` file and use the **Object Style Manager** to import those 3 styles in the project.
- Go to slide 2 of the `encoderDemo_800.cptx` file. Use the **transparentTitle** and **transparentCaption** styles to format the Text Captions of this slide.
- Save both files when done.

If you use the Preview icon to test the movies, you'll notice that we've already come a long way since the original rushes we had at the beginning of this chapter. There is still a lot of work to be done though! One of the main problems that remain is the timing of the objects. This is what we will fix by studying the **Timeline** panel in the next and last section of this chapter.

Working with the Timeline

The **Timeline** panel is situated at the bottom of the interface. The primary purpose of the **Timeline** is to organize the sequence of events on each slide, but the **Timeline** panel can be used for other purposes as well.

Using the Timeline to select objects

When resizing the Highlight Boxes earlier in this chapter, you probably had a hard time selecting the right object and you ended up moving or resizing the Mouse or a Text Caption instead of the Highlight Box. Using the **Timeline** panel, you can make sure that the object you select is the one you actually want to select! Perform the following steps to select an object using the Timeline panel:

1. Return to the slide 3 of the `encoderDemo_800.cptx` file.

This slide contains four objects: two Text Captions, one Highlight Box, and the Mouse movement.

2. In the **Timeline** panel, click on the line that represents the **Highlight Box**.

Notice that eight white handles now surround the Highlight Box on the stage. Selecting an object on the **Timeline** panel also selects it on the stage, as shown in the following screenshot:

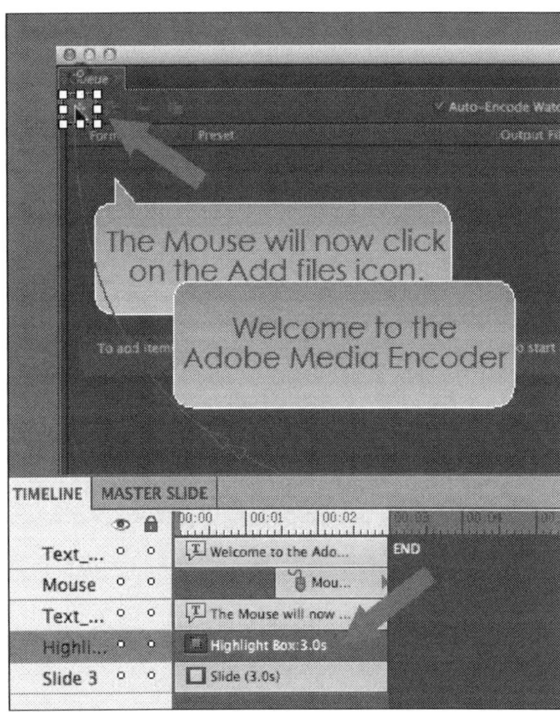

Hiding and locking objects with the Timeline

Hiding and locking objects is another feature that will help us make the right selection. It will also prevent us from accidentally modifying finished objects. Perform the following steps to hide or lock certain objects in the Timeline panel:

1. Make sure you are still on slide 3 of the `encoderDemo_800.cptx` file.

On slide 3, the Highlight Box and the mouse pointer share the same area of the slide. If we try to click on one of these two objects on the stage, chances are we'll end up clicking on the other one! For this exercise, imagine that we want to select the orange Highlight Box.

2. In the **Timeline**, click on the *Lock/Unlock All Items* icon (1).
3. Click on the *lock* icon situated in front of the Highlight Box object (2), as shown in the following screenshot:

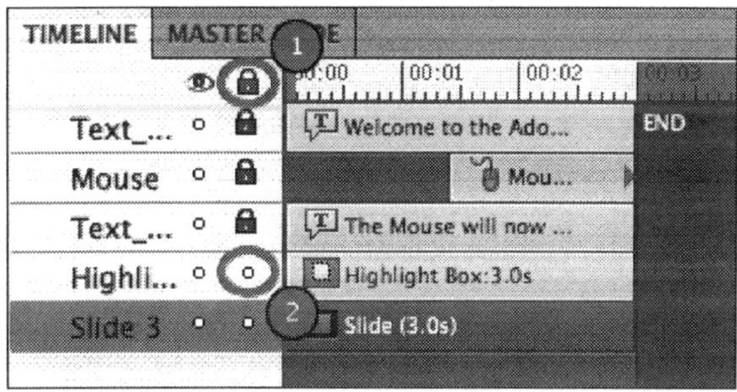

The Highlight Box is now the only object on the slide that is *not* locked. Consequently, it is the only one that can be selected and modified.

4. On the slide, try to select one of the Text Captions or the mouse pointer. The application should *not* let you do it!
5. But if you try to select the Highlight Box, the application reacts normally.
6. In the **Timeline**, unlock both Text Captions and the Mouse.

All the objects of the slide should now be unlocked and we should be back to the original situation.

In the **Timeline** panel, next to the *Lock/Unlock All Items* icons, is the *Show/Hide All Items* icons (the eye icons). We can use them to hide objects from the slide. When the slide holds a large number of objects, it can help us select and work with the right one. Note that hiding an object with this tool hides it **from the Captivate interface only**, not from the movie as viewed by the students.

Using the Timeline to change the stacking order of the objects

The stacking order decides which object goes *in front of* or *behind* which object. In the **Timeline** panel, the topmost object is in front of any other objects. It means that in case the objects overlap, the topmost object will cover the ones below it. The *slide* always is at the very bottom of the stack as it is used as the background on which the objects are placed. Perform the following steps to change the stacking order of the objects:

1. Make sure you are still on slide 3 of the `encoderDemo_800.cptx` file.

Notice that the **Welcome to the Adobe Media Encoder** Text Caption is on top of the stack.

2. In the **Timeline** panel, take the **Welcome to...** Text Caption and drag it down two levels.

The **Welcome to...** Text Caption is now *behind* the **The mouse will now...** Text Caption.

3. Right-click on the **Welcome To...** Text Caption.
4. In the contextual menu, choose the **Arrange | Bring to Front** menu item

This last operation brings the **Welcome To...** Text Caption back to the top of the stack both on the stage and in the **Timeline** panel.

Use the Timeline to set the timing of the objects.

The primary purpose of the **Timeline** is to let you control the timing of the objects. For each object, you can choose when it appears on the stage and how long it stays visible. By carefully and precisely arranging the objects on the **Timeline**, you'll be able to achieve great visual effects very easily. Perform the following steps to set timings to the objects:

1. Make sure you are still on slide 3 of the `encoderDemo_800.cptx` file.
2. Take a look at the **Timeline** panel and notice how the four objects of the slide are organized.
3. Click on an empty area of the slide to make it the active item. The **Properties** panel updates and displays the properties of the slide.
4. In the **General** accordion of the **Properties** panel, change the **Display Time** of the slide to **10** sec. This change is reflected in the **Timeline** panel.

5. In the **Timeline** panel, take the right edge of the slide and drag it to the **15** sec mark. This change is reflected in the **Display Time** property of the **General** accordion of the **Properties** panel.

The changes made in the **Timeline** panel are reflected in the various accordions of the **Properties** panel and vice versa. This gives us two methods to organize the timing of our objects.

6. Click on the **Welcome to...** Text Caption to make it the active object. The **Properties** panel updates and shows the properties of the Text Caption.
7. In the **Properties** panel, open the **Timing** accordion.

The Timing accordion states that the Text Caption **Appears After: 0 sec** and stays visible for a **specific time** of **3 sec**. The **Timeline** panel is a visual representation of this situation. In this particular case, the default timing is exactly the one we need!

Adjusting the default timing of the objects

When a new object is added to the stage, its timing is set to three seconds by default. In Captivate 6, this default timing can be adjusted for each type of object separately. Simply go to the **Defaults** page of the **Preferences**, choose an object in the **Select** drop-down list and adjust the default timing of the selected object type.

8. Select the **The mouse will now...** Text Caption to make it the active object.
9. In the **Timeline** panel, place your mouse in the middle of the selected Text Caption until the mouse pointer turns to a grabbing hand.
10. Move the Text Caption seven seconds to the right.
11. Still in the **Timeline** panel, place your mouse on the right edge of the selected Text Caption until the mouse pointer turns into a double arrow.
12. Use the mouse to extend the duration of the **The mouse will now...** Text Caption to the 13 seconds mark.
13. In the **Timing** accordion of the **Properties** panel, confirm that the selected Text Caption is set to **Appear After 7 sec** and to **Display For** a **specific time** of **6 sec**.
14. In the **Properties** panel, open the **Transition** accordion.

By default, Captivate applies a *Fade In* and a *Fade Out* effect of half a second on every object. It means that if a Text Caption is set to stay a specific time of 3 seconds on the stage, the first half a second will be used for the *Fade In* effect and the last half a second will be used for the *Fade Out* effect. It leaves two seconds to the learner to read the text contained in the Caption!

15. Still on slide 3, use the **Timeline** panel or the **Timing** accordion to change the timing of the Highlight Box. Make it appear at 8 seconds into the slide and stay visible for a specific time of 6 seconds.
16. Also change the Timing of the Mouse movement so it begins at 13 seconds into the slide and lasts for 2 seconds

The **Timeline** of slide 3 is now correct. Make sure it looks like the following screenshot:

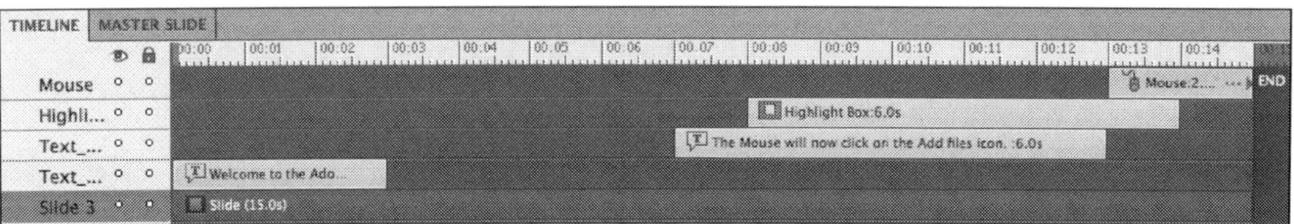

To test the new timing of the objects, use the preview icon and choose to preview the **Next 5 slides**. If you feel that the current timing is not exactly right, don't hesitate to adjust the position of the objects on the **Timeline** to your liking. After all, you're the teacher!

Extra credit

Now that you know the tools and techniques used to set the timing and the stacking order of the objects, browse the other slides of the `encoderDemo_800.cptx` project and adjust the timing of the various Text Captions, Images, Highlight Boxes, and Mouse movements contained in the project. Refer to the `Chapter03/final/encoderDemo_800.cptx` file of your exercises folders for examples and inspiration. Just a few tips before you get started:

- Use the **Timeline** whenever possible. It is the fastest and easiest way to adjust the timing of the objects.
- If you require super-precise timing, then use the **Timing** accordion of the **Properties** panel.
- Don't hesitate to use the tools of the **Align** toolbar to resize and relocate the objects on the slide. Proper size/location combined with precise timing can lead to strong yet easy to achieve visual effects.

Not too fast and not too slow

When creating an online course with Captivate, you'll quickly discover that one of the most difficult things is to find the right pace. For the Text Caption object, there is an easy trick. Use the stopwatch function of your cell phone and *slowly* read the content of the Text Caption aloud, then round up the timing to the upper half a second. For example, if it takes you 5.7 seconds to read a Text Caption aloud, make that Text Caption stay on the stage for a specific time of 6 seconds. If your audience is multi-lingual, add up to 1.5 seconds to the timing so that the students taking the course in a language other than their native language will be allowed some more time to read and understand your Text Captions.

Here is a quick summary of what we have learned:

- The primary purpose of the **Timeline** panel is to let us arrange the timing of the objects.
- The **Timeline** can also be used to select the objects and to modify their stacking order.
- The **Timeline** is a visual representation of the **Timing** accordion of the **Properties** panel.
- Changing the objects on the **Timeline** updates the **Timing** accordion and vice versa.
- By default, Captivate applies a Fade In and a Fade Out effect of half a second on every object. This can be modified in the **Transition** accordion.

Summary

The post-production phase of our projects is now well on its way! We have already come a long way since we entered the studio with our rushes.

The five objects we have studied in this chapter have already made a very big difference.

The **Text Caption** allows us to display text to the students. It is one of the most widely used objects of Captivate. The **Highlight Boxes** are used to attract the student's attention to a specific spot of the slide. Various types of **Images** can be imported in our projects and can be used as background image for the slides. Captivate 6 ships with a collection of **Characters** images that we can use in our projects. Captivate 6 also introduced the all-new **Smart Shape** object that allows us to insert highly customizable shapes on the slides of our project. Finally, the **Mouse** object can be customized and fine-tuned in a lot of ways!

To make these objects look the way we want, Captivate provides a very large array of formatting options. These options are arranged in the various accordions of the **Properties** panel.

While formatting the objects of our eLearning courses, we should not forget that we are *teachers* involved in a *pedagogical* process. To learn in the best possible conditions, our students need the formatting of our objects to be extremely *consistent* throughout the entire project. Luckily, the **Styles** and the **Object Style Manager** help us achieve this consistency while speeding up the formatting part of our work!

Finally, the **Timeline** panel allows us to arrange the timing of each object. It also provides an easy way to *select* objects as well as the ability to change the *stacking order* of the objects.

In the next chapter, we will introduce some more tools and objects. First, we will concentrate on the various types of *animations* that can be added in a Captivate movie. These include *Text Animations*, *Flash animations*, and *video* files. Then, we will focus on the *interactive objects* of Captivate. These objects will allow us to convert our *Demonstration* into a *Simulation* and to introduce the *Branching* concept.

As you can see, there is lots of exciting stuff ahead. See you in Chapter 4!

Meet the Community

RJ Jacquez

Bio

My name is RJ Jacquez, Mobile Learning Analyst and Consultant, helping companies understand the potential of Mobile and make a successful transition from eLearning to mLearning in their organizations. Also a Mobile Learning Evangelist, Podcasting and Blogging the Mobile Learning Revolution as it happens. Before that, I worked for Adobe Systems and Macromedia as a Senior Evangelist.

I'm now running a consulting firm focused on helping companies understand the potential of Mobile and helping them make a successful transition from eLearning to mLearning.

I'm honored to be among great company in the following lists and articles:

1. Top 25 Most Influential Bloggers in Technical Communications available at `http://bit.ly/a8ooZC`.
2. *Top 20 most influential tweeters in eLearning, training and HR* available at `http://bit.ly/KCOjqf`.
3. I was also mentioned in this article on *Why Every Company Needs a Robert Scoble (infographic)* for my work as an Adobe Evangelist available at `http://bit.ly/v0IMHs`.

Contact details

Blog: `http://rjacquez.com/`

Twitter: `@rjacquez`

My personal note

The bio says it all. RJ is one of the most influential bloggers, not only in the Captivate community, but also for the entire eLearning industry. His blog and his tweets are one of my primary sources of information to stay current on the rapidly evolving world of eLearning and mLearning.

His interviews on eLearn chat is a must see and are available at `http://vimeo.com/channels/elearnchat/36028732` and `http://vimeo.com/channels/elearnchat/40598579`.

4

Working with Animations and Interactive Objects

In this chapter, we will continue the post-production phase of our project by adding animation and interactivity to our Captivate movies. This will make our projects even more interesting, sophisticated, and fun to use.

This interactivity is made possible by three interactive objects. These objects have the ability to stop the playhead and wait for the user to *do* or to *type* something. This introduces a whole new level of complexity, as the student shall receive feedback that depends on whatever action he/she performed. Therefore, we will have to analyze the clicks and answers of the students and act accordingly. This concept is known as **branching**.

Before exploring these interactive objects and converting our *Demonstration* into a *Simulation*, we will continue to explore the basic objects of Captivate by introducing different kinds of animations to our slides. These animations can either be created directly in Captivate or in an external application (such as Adobe Flash) and imported in the project afterwards.

Some smaller tools, such as the *Align* toolbar, the *Find And Replace* feature, the *Library* or the custom *Effects* will be unveiled along the way.

At the end of this chapter, we will take a second look at our Video Demo project. As discussed in *Chapter 1, Getting Started with Captivate*, Video Demo is a brand new type of project introduced by Captivate 6. We will discuss the objects that can be inserted in a Video Demo and cover some specific Video Demo features.

In this chapter, we will:

- Insert text animations, Flash animations, and videos in our projects
- Arrange the objects on the slide using the alignment toolbar
- Insert Rollover Captions, Rollover Images, and Rollover Slidelet for enhanced interactivity
- Add text into a Smart Shape and convert it into a Rollover Smart Shape
- Use the Library to manage the assets of the project and to share assets between different Captivate files
- Let the student control the timing of the project by inserting *Buttons*
- Convert a Demonstration into a Simulation by replacing the Mouse with *Click Boxes* and *Text Entry Boxes*
- Discuss the objects that can be added to a Video Demo project
- Use the Pan and Zoom feature of the Video Demo

Preparing our work

For the exercises of this chapter, we will need to work with three files. A fourth one will be created later on.

1. Open Captivate and make sure the **Classic** workspace is applied.
2. Use **Window | Workspace | Reset 'Classic'** to return to the default **Classic** workspace.
3. Open the `Chapter04/encoderDemo_800.cptx` file situated in your exercises folder.
4. Also open the `Chapter04/drivingInBe.cptx` files stored at the same location.
5. At the end of the chapter, we will use the `Chapter04/encoderVideo.cpvc` Video Demo project.

All three files should be open in the Captivate interface. Make sure you use the right one when doing an exercise!

Discovering the animated objects

In the last chapter, we learned about the basic objects of Captivate. To make our eLearning content even more interesting and fun for the students, we will now introduce four more objects. These four objects are used to add animation and movement to our course.

Using the Text Animation

The first one is the **Text Animation**. A Text Animation is an object that can be created and managed entirely from within Captivate.

In the next exercise, we will create the front slide and the final slide of the project and add a Text Animation on both these slides.

1. Go to the `encoderDemo_800.cptx` file.
2. Use the **Filmstrip** to go to the first slide of the movie.

The first slide of the `encoderDemo_800.cptx` file has been created in the previous chapter using the **Insert | Image Slide** feature of Captivate 6 (see *Inserting an Image slide* discussed in *Chapter 3, Working with Standard Objects*). There are currently no objects on this slide. Let's add a **Text Animation** onto it.

3. Use the **Insert | Text Animation** menu or the corresponding icon of the Objects toolbar.
4. In the **Text Animation Properties** box type *Adobe Media Encoder The Demonstration*.
5. Change the **Font** to **Century Gothic** and the **Size** to **52**.
6. Click on the **OK** button. The new object appears on the slide.

With the new Text Animation selected, take some time to inspect the accordions of the **Properties** panel. At the top of the stack, the **General** accordion contains options that are specific to a Text Animation. The other accordions are the same as for the objects we have already covered.

The new Text Animation is too wide to fit on the slide. If this situation happens with a regular Text Caption, we would use the white resize handles or the **Transform** accordion of the **Properties** panel to resize the object.

7. Make sure the Text Animation is the selected item.
8. If needed, expand the **Transform** accordion of the **Properties** panel.

As usual, the **X** and the **Y** coordinates as well as the rotation **Angle** are available in the **Transform** accordion. But, where are the Width and the Height properties?

Actually, Captivate automatically calculates the size of a Text Animation based on the text content and on the font size. So our only options to modify the size of a Text Animation are to modify its text content and/or its font size. In our case, we will add a line break just before the **The Demonstration** part of the content.

9. Make sure the Text Animation is still selected.
10. In the **General** accordion of the **Properties** panel, click on the **Properties** button.

This action reopens the **Text Animation Properties** box where we can change both the text content and the font size of our Text Animation object.

11. In the upper area of the **Text Animation Properties** box, use your mouse to place the cursor between **Encoder** and **The Demonstration**.
12. Hit the *Enter* key to create a line break at the location of the cursor.

The **Text Animation Properties** box closes and the Text Animation object is updated.

13. Use your mouse to move the Text Animation in the middle of the Brown area.
14. In the **General** accordion of the **Properties** panel, choose an effect in the **Effect** drop-down list.

Use the preview at the top of the **Properties** panel to have an idea of how the chosen effect will render. In the *final* application that you experienced in *Chapter 1, Getting Started with Captivate*, we used the **Waltz** effect.

15. Use the **Timeline** panel or the **Timing** accordion of the **Properties** panel to:
    - make the Text Animation **Appear After 1sec**
    - make the Text Animation **Display For** a **Specific Time** of **6 sec**
    - set the **Display Time** of the entire slide to **7 sec**
16. Make sure your **Timeline** panel looks like the following screenshot:

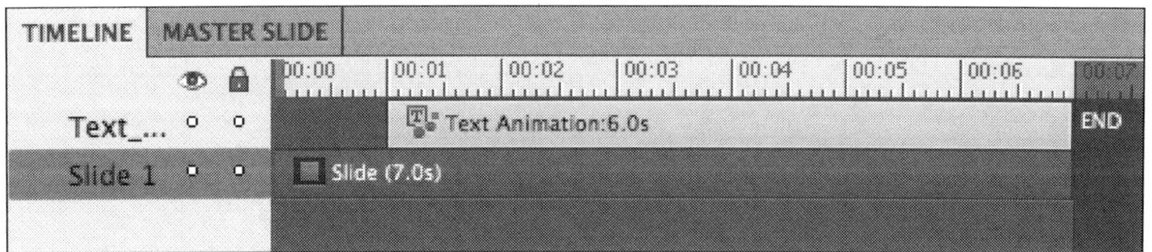

17. In order to test the new slide, save the file and use the preview icon to preview the **Next 5 Slides**.

Now that the front slide of the project is finished, we will create the closing slide. It will be very similar to the front slide, so instead of repeating the whole procedure a second time, we will simply copy/paste the first slide and change the content of the Text Animation.

18. In the **Filmstrip**, right-click on the first slide of the project and choose **Copy** in the contextual menu.
19. Right-click on the last slide (slide 20) and click on **Paste**. A copy of the first slide is added at the end of the movie.

Remember that new slides get inserted *after* the currently selected slide.

20. Go to the last slide (slide 21) and select the Text Animation.
21. In the **General** accordion of the **Properties** panel, click on the **Properties** button.
22. In the **Text Animation Properties** dialog, change the Text to **Thank you for viewing this Demonstration**! Leave the other properties unchanged and click on the **OK** button.

The Text Animation is updated and is too large to fit on the slide.

23. Make sure the Text Animation is selected and click on the **Properties** button of the **General** accordion again.
24. In the **Text Animation Properties** box, place your cursor between **viewing** and **this** and then press *Enter* to force the text on two lines.
25. Save the file when done.

To test the new slide, use the **Filmstrip** to select the slide just before the last one, then, use the preview icon to preview **From this Slide**.

Use the Text Animation with care

The Text Animation object must be used with care. It is a great effect if we use it every once in a while, but if we use it too often, it overcharges our projects, which give a non-professional impression.

Converting a typing object into a Text Animation

In Captivate, a Typing object is a very special type of object. It appears only in Demonstrations and it is created during the initial filming of the project when text is typed in the captured application. During the filming of our Encoder Demo project, we typed some text in the **Width** field of the **Video** tab. Consequently, a Typing object has been generated.

1. Still in the `encoderDemo_800.cptx` file, use the **Filmstrip** to go to slide 14.

Once on slide 14, take a look at the **Timeline**. It contains three layers in addition to the slide itself, indicating that the slide contains three objects. One of these objects is labeled **Typing Text**. It represents the text that is typed in the **Width** field during the filming. This object was *automatically* generated when the slide was captured back in *Chapter 2, Capturing the Slides.*

2. Click anywhere on an empty spot of slide 14. Make sure the **Properties** panel displays the properties of the **Slide**.
3. In the **Timeline**, click on the **Text Typing** object to select it. Notice that the **Properties** panel is *not* updated and still shows the properties of the **Slide**.

The **Text Typing** object is the *only* object of Captivate that does *not* update the **Properties** panel. This unexpected behavior tells us that this object is very special indeed, and that it has no properties that we can adjust. One of the only available options is to control the typing speed by modifying the object's timing in the **Timeline**, but there is no solution to modify the text itself, its font, its font size, or its color.

Hopefully, Captivate lets us convert the Text Typing objects into Text Animations. Once converted, the Text Typing object has the same editing capabilities as any other Text Animation.

4. In the **Timeline**, right-click on the **Text Typing** object.
5. In the contextual menu, choose **Replace with Text Animation**. Note that this operation cannot be undone.

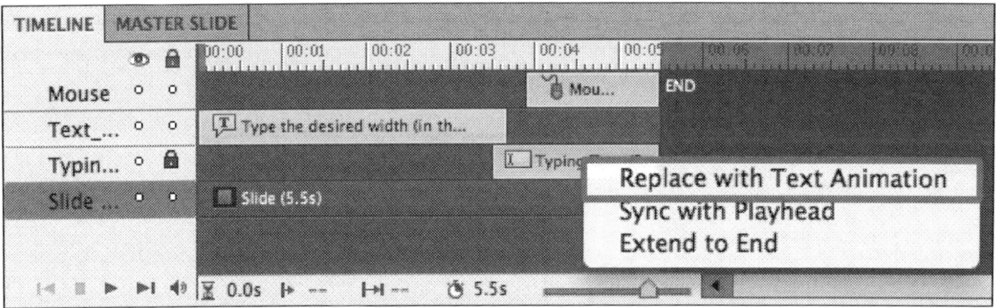

6. Use the **Timeline** to adjust the timing of the newly created Text Animation so it stays on the stage until the end of the slide.
7. If necessary, adjust the other properties of the Text Animation, such as the spelling of the text or the font size.
8. Don't forget to save the file when done.

This little option can be very handy in many situations, especially when you need to modify the text that was typed during the capture. Note that the effect applied to the converted Text Typing object is the **Typing Text With Sound** effect. If needed, you can use another effect, but I strongly recommend you stick to this one as it has been specifically designed to mimic the typing of a text.

The Text Animation object has no Fill property. In other words, it is transparent, which causes us a small problem in this case. To solve this problem, I've used a gray Highlight Box with an **Alpha** set to **100%** (to make it completely opaque). I adjusted the size of the Highlight Box so it is exactly the same size as the **Width** field. I then used the **Timeline** to send this Highlight Box at the bottom of the stack. Finally, I used the **Timing** accordion to make the Highlight Box display for the entire duration of the slide and the **Transition** accordion to remove the default Fade In and Fade Out effect. Look for this Highlight Box on slide 14 of the `Chapter04/final/encoderDemo_800.cptx` file. Can you implement it in your file as well?

Extra credit

Now that we have inserted the front slide and the ending slide in the Encoder Demo project, why don't you try to do the same in the *Driving in Belgium* project? The following are the general steps:

- Switch to the `drivingInBe.cptx` file.
- Use **Insert | Image Slide** to create a new slide based on the `image/mftcTitleTemplate.jpg` image. Make the new slide the first one of the movie.
- Insert a new text animation on the new slide. Type **Driving in Belgium** and use the **Century Gothic** font with a size of **52**.
- Choose an effect for your Text Animation. In the *final* version of the application, we used the **Waltz** effect.
- Place your new Text Animation on the slide and adjust its timing on the **Timeline** panel. Use the preview feature to test your changes.
- Once you are satisfied with slide 1, copy it and paste it as the last slide of the movie.
- Change the text to **Thank you for taking this online course!** It might be necessary to insert a line break to make the Text Animation fit on the slide.
- Adjust the position of the updated Text Animation.
- Don't forget to preview your changes along the way.

This extra credit section concludes our study of the Text Animation object. Let's make a quick summary of what we have learned.

- The Text Animation object can be created entirely in Captivate. No need of an external application (such as Adobe Flash) to create it!
- This object is typically used on the first and on the last slide of the project.
- Use this object wisely. If you use it too often, you will overcharge your Captivate file with lots of unnecessary and distracting animations.
- To resize a Text Animation, change its content, add a line break into the text, or change the font size.
- When text is typed during the capture, a Text Typing object is generated. Convert this object to a Text Animation for enhanced editing capabilities.

Inserting external animations in the project

The second type of object of this chapter is the **animation**. This object lets us insert an *external* animation into our Captivate Project. Typically, the external application used to generate these animations is *Adobe Flash* and the file imported in Captivate is the compiled `.swf` file, but Captivate lets us import an animated `.gif` as well.

The file extensions of Adobe Flash Professional

When saving a file with Adobe Flash professional, the file extension used is `.fla`. The `.fla` file contains every objects, animations, filters, and so on, needed for the flash animation to work properly. Consequently, it can be a very large file. Once the `.fla` file is finished, it is necessary to export it (the proper word is to *compile* it) in the `.swf` format. The `.swf` file is the *compiled* version of the `.fla` file and is the one that can be read by the Flash Player plugin. Converting a `.swf` file back to `.fla` (an operation known as *reverse engineering*) is not possible. (Well actually, it is with specialized software, but you never get back to the *original* `.fla` file!)

In the next exercise, we will import a Flash animation in our Encoder Demo project.

1. Return to the `encoderDemo_800.cptx` file.
2. Use the **Filmstrip** to select slide 4.

It is the slide where we double-click on the `demo_en.mov` file. Before the mouse moves and clicks on the file, we want to insist on the amazing list of file types shown in the **enable** drop down.

3. Insert a new Highlight Box into the slide. Resize it so it covers the entire **Enable** drop down. Make sure it uses the **MFTC-HighlightBox** style.
4. Use the **Insert | Animation** menu to insert a new animation on the current slide.

The **Open** dialog box pops up in order to let us locate the animation to insert.

If you do not have Adobe Flash Professional or if you do not know how to use it, don't worry! To get you started, Captivate ships with a *gallery* containing many objects that we can insert in our project. This gallery is situated at:

- **Windows**: In the `C:\Program Files\Adobe\Captivate 6\Gallery` folder.
- **Mac OS**: In the `Applications/Adobe Captivate 6/Gallery` folder

The `Gallery` folder itself is divided into several subfolders, containing various types of objects that we can use in our projects. One of these folders is the `SWF Animations` folder.

5. Browse to `SWF Animations/Arrows/Orange arrow/down.swf` of the Gallery and click on the **Open** button.

The animation is imported and appears on slide 4. Note that only `.swf` and `.gif` files can be inserted as animations in Captivate.

6. Place the new object as shown in the following screenshot:

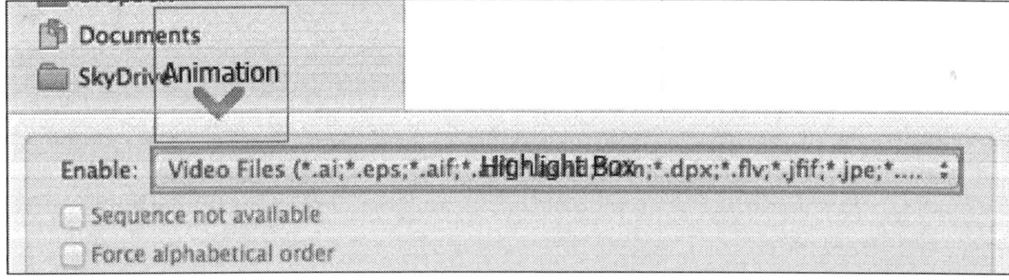

7. Use the **Timeline** or the **Timing** accordion of the **Properties** panel to:
   - Make the animation **Appear After 1** sec
   - Make it **Display For** a **specific time** of **6** sec
   - If needed, extend the duration of the slide
   - Apply the same timing properties to the Highlight Box
8. To test the changes, use the **Filmstrip** to select slide 13 and use the preview icon to preview the **Next 5 slides**.

Inserting animations in the project is *that* easy! Later in this chapter, we will return to this slide and use the **Library** panel, as well as the *Alignment* toolbar to further enhance the animations, but for now, we will quickly summarize what we have learned and move on to the next object.

- Captivate lets us insert external `.swf` and `.gif` animations in our projects.
- These animations are typically created in Adobe Flash Professional.
- Captivate ships with an extensive Gallery containing various types of objects that we can use in our projects.

Working with the Zoom Area

The third object of this chapter is the **Zoom Area**. This object was introduced in October 2006 as a cool new feature of Captivate 2. It is used to highlight a specific spot of the slide by zooming on it.

We will use it in our Encoder Demo project to zoom on the **Video** tab of the **Export Settings** dialog in order to emphasize the **Maintain Aspect Ratio** icon.

1. Still in the `encoderDemo_800.cptx` file, use the **Filmstrip** to select slide 15.
2. Use the **Insert | Standard Objects | Zoom Area** or the corresponding icon on the Objects toolbar to create a new Zoom Area.

The Zoom Area inserts *two* new objects on the slide. The first one is the **Zoom Source** and the second one is the **Zoom Destination**. As both of these objects are necessary to make the Zoom area work, removing one of them automatically removes the other one.

3. Click on the **Zoom Source** to make it the active object. The **Properties** panel is updated and shows the properties of the **Zoom Source**.
4. In the **Fill & Stroke** accordion, set the stroke **Width** to *0*. This removes the yellow stroke from the **Zoom Source** object.
5. In the **Transform** accordion, enter the following values:
    - a **Width** of *311* pixels.
    - a **Height** of *85* pixels. (It may be necessary to un-tick the **Constrain proportions** checkbox to modify the **Height** and the **Width** independently).
    - a **X** coordinate of *426* pixels.
    - a **Y** coordinate of *341* pixels.

The **Zoom Source** should cover more or less the **Height**, **Width**, and **Maintain Aspect ratio** controls of the **Video** tab.

> If you feel like the other objects of the slide are in the way, don't hesitate to use the eye icons of the **Timeline** to temporarily turn the visibility of those objects off while you are working with the Zoom Area.

6. Select the **Zoom Destination**. The **Properties** panel is updated.
7. With the Zoom Destination selected, enter the following values in the **Transform** accordion:
    - A **Width** of *382* pixels
    - A **Height** of *98* pixels
    - An **X** coordinate of *141* pixels
    - And a **Y** coordinate of *411* pixels

The **Zoom Destination** should be positioned over the lower left area of the **Export Settings** dialog.

8. Make sure the Zoom Destination is still selected.
9. In the **Fill & Stroke** accordion of the **Properties** panel, give the **Stroke** the same bright orange color as for the Highlight Boxes.
10. Also increase the **Width** of the Stroke to 2 pixels.

This additional formatting makes the Zoom Destination more visible. Make sure your Zoom Destination and your Zoom Source look like the following screenshot (The Text Captions has been hidden in the screenshot—the blue stroke on the Zoom Destination marks the selection, but does not show in the resulting project).

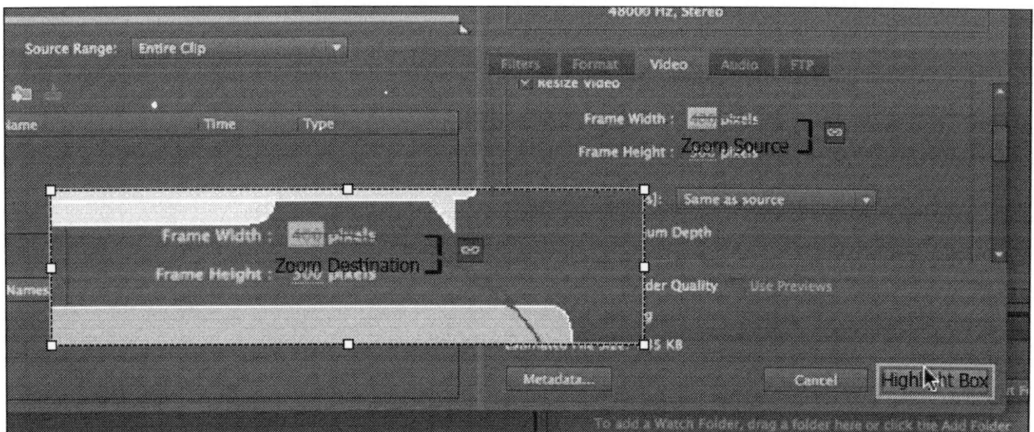

With both the **Zoom Source** and the **Zoom Destination** correctly positioned, we will now focus on the **Timeline** to arrange the timing on the Zoom Area.

In the **Timeline**, the Zoom Area object is separated in two zones. The first zone is called **Zoom Source** and it represents the length of the *Zooming animation* going from the Zoom Source to the Zoom Destination. The second zone represents the duration of the static Zoom Destination on the stage after the zooming animation is finished.

11. Select the **Zoom Source** object.
12. Open the **Timing** accordion of the **Properties** panel.

The **Timing** accordion shows an extra field called **Zoom for** in addition to the normal fields used on any objects.

13. Use the **Timeline** Panel *or* the **Timing** Accordion to:
    - make the Zoom Source **Appear After 1 sec**
    - make it **Zoom For 4 sec**
    - after zooming, make it **Display For** the **rest of the slide**
14. Also, adjust the timing of the other objects so that the **Timeline** panel looks like the following screenshot:

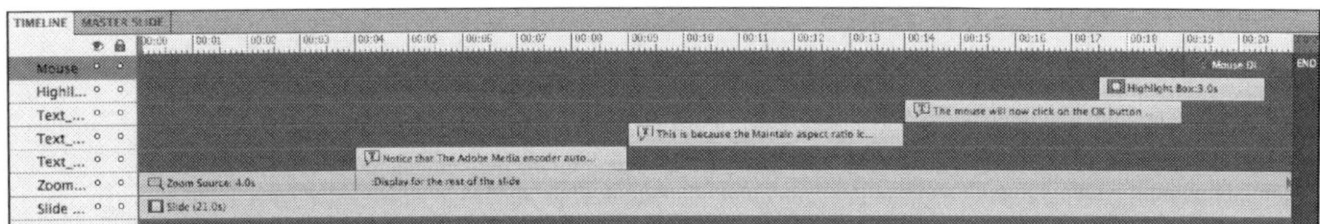

15. When done, test the new sequence by selecting the previous slide (slide 14) and use the preview icon to preview the **Next 5 Slides**.

As you can see when previewing your sequence, the Zoom Area is another great way to focus the learner's attention to a specific spot of the slide.

The blurry Zoom Destination

When creating Zoom Areas, you will inevitably run into the *blurry Zoom Destination* issue. As the Zoom Destination grows bigger and bigger, the image it contains becomes more and more blurry. Kevin Siegel details a cure for this problem on his blog `http://iconlogic.blogs.com/weblog/2009/09/adobe-captivate-4-the-cure-for-the-blurry-zoom-destination.html`.

In the next section, we will insert a video file in our project, but before doing that, here is a quick summary of what we have learned about the Zoom Area.

- A Zoom Area is composed of two different objects: the **Zoom Source** and the **Zoom Destination**.
- Both objects are necessary to make the Zoom Area work. Deleting one of them automatically deletes the other one.
- In the **Timeline** panel, the Zoom area is divided into two zones. The first zone describes the length of the zooming animation while the second zone shows the duration of the static Zoom Destination on the stage after the zooming animation is finished.
- This situation is reflected in the **Timeline** and in the **Timing** accordion of the **Properties** panel with the addition of the **Zoom For** field.

Inserting a video file

Remember that Captivate was originally designed to create Adobe Flash (`.swf`) files that can be played back by the Adobe Flash Player plugin. In 2006, Adobe (formerly Macromedia) added video support to Flash. At that time, the Flash Player supported only a specific Flash video format: the `.flv` format (flv stands for **F**lash **V**ideo). In 2007, some restrictions of the `.flv` format led to the development by Adobe of the `.f4v` Flash video format. Today, the Flash Player supports both the `.flv` and `.f4v` video formats. The Adobe Media Encoder is used to convert any kind of video to the `.flv` or `.f4v` file format.

With the arrival of HTML 5, it is now possible for a web browser to play a video (or audio) file natively, without the help of an external plugin such as the Flash Player. Unfortunately, the industry has not yet decided what video format/codec should be used for HTML 5 video playback. As of today, it looks like two formats are emerging, the `.mp4` format and the `.webm` format. To embrace this futuristic technology, the Adobe Media Encoder supports the `.mp4` video format in addition to the `.flv` and `.f4v` formats.

> More on Flash video can be found at `http://en.wikipedia.org/wiki/Flash_Video`.
>
> More on the Adobe Media Encoder can be found at `http://www.adobe.com/products/premiere/features.html - categorylens_c972_featureset_62f1`.

In the next exercise, we will insert a new slide in the Encoder Demo project.

1. Return to the `Chapter04/encoderDemo_800.cptx` file.
2. Use the **Filmstrip** to go to slide 1.
3. Go to **Insert | Image slide** to create a new slide based on the `images/mftcContentTemplate.jpg` file situated in your exercises folder.

The new slide is inserted as slide 2. Remember that new slides are always inserted *after* the active slide.

4. Add a new Text Caption to the slide. Write **Welcome!!** in the Text Caption.
5. With the new Text Caption selected, use the **Properties** panel to apply the **TransparentTitle** style to the Text Caption.
6. If necessary, enlarge the Text Caption so that the text fits comfortably in the object, then position it in the upper-left corner of the slide
7. In the **Timeline** or in the **Timing** accordion, make the Text Caption **Appear After 0** sec and **display for** the **rest of** the **slide**.

The new slide is now ready to receive its video file. Make sure it looks like the following screenshot before moving on to the next step:

8. Go to the **Video | Insert Video** menu.

The **Insert Video** dialog opens. At the top of the **Insert Video** dialog, we have to choose between an **Event video** or a **Multi-Slide synchronized video**. The following table lists some of the differences between these two options:

	Event Video	Multi-Slide synchronized video.
Sync	Cannot be distributed over several slides.	Can be distributed over several slides or not
Timeline	The Timeline of the video is independent from the Timeline of the project.	The video is synced with the slide or slides it appears on.
Playback controls	Event video can have its own playback controls.	Have no specific playback controls associated.
Closed Captions	Cannot be closed captioned	Can be closed captioned

In our case, we want the video to show on slide 2 only, something that both the **Event Video** and the **Multi-Slide Synchronized Video** can do. However, in *Chapter 5, Working with Audio*, we'll also want to add closed captions to our video. So, in our case, a **Multi-Slide Synchronized Video** is the solution.

9. Make sure the **Multi-Slide Synchronized Video** option is the one in use.
10. Click on the **Browse** button, browse to the `videos/flv/demo_en.flv` file of your exercises folder, and click on **open**.
11. In the lower area of the **Insert Video** dialog, tick the **Modify slide duration to accommodate video** option.
12. Make sure the **Insert Video** dialog looks like the following screenshot and click on the **OK** button:

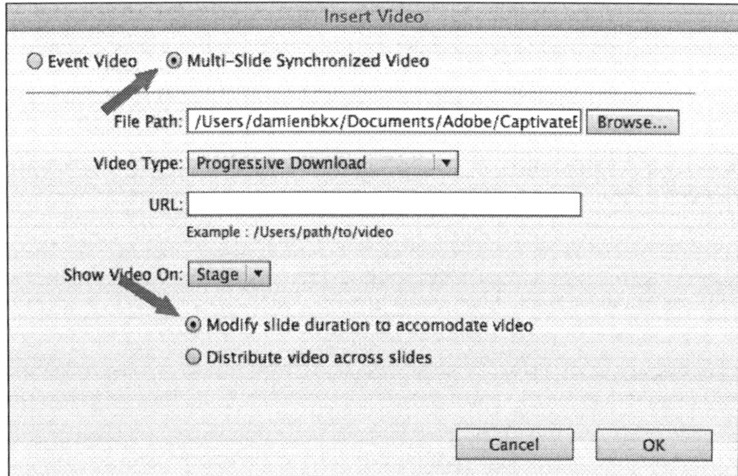

The video is inserted into the slide. Since the first frame of the video is white, it may be necessary to click on the video to reveal its boundaries.

13. Make sure the video is still selected and take a look at the **Transform** accordion of the **Properties** panel.

Notice the message **Proportions are locked**. It means that we *cannot* change the **Width** of the Video independently from its **Height**. This is made to ensure that the *proportions* of the video are respected when the *size* is changed. In our case, the size of the video has been set in the Adobe Media Encoder while converting the video from `.mov` to `.flv`.

14. For the position, set the **X** and the **Y** coordinates both at *200*.
15. In the **Timeline** or in **Timing** accordion, make the video **Appear After 1** sec. Consequently, the duration of the slide is extended to 9 sec.

While working in the **Timeline**, notice that the duration of the video cannot be changed. In the **Timing** accordion, we only have access to the **Appear After** parameter.

16. Save the file and use the Preview Icon to preview the **Next 5 slides**.
17. When the preview is finished, close the **Preview** pane.

Here is a summary of what we have learned about inserting Videos in Captivate:

- There are two options available to insert videos in Captivate: **Event Video** and **Multi-Slide Synchronized Video**.
- If you want to publish your Captivate movie in Flash format, it is necessary to use the `.flv` or the `.f4v` video file format.
- If you want to publish your project in HTML 5, use the `.mp4` video format.
- The *Adobe Media Encoder* is an external application. It is bundled with every Creative Suite editions as well as with the eLearning suite and the standalone version of Captivate.
- The *Adobe Media Encoder* is used to convert any video file to `.flv`, `.f4v`, or `.mp4`, so it can be used in Captivate.

Adding effects to objects

The ability to add effects to any object was a new and long-awaited feature of Captivate 5.

In the next exercise, we will animate the Adobe Media encoder logo we inserted on slide 3 in the previous chapter.

1. Return to the `Chapter04/encoderDemo_800.cptx` file.
2. Use the **Filmstrip** to go to slide 2.
3. Use the preview icon to preview the **Next 5 Slides**.

When the preview reaches slide 3, pay particular attention to how the Adobe Media Encoder logo enters and leaves the stage. Besides the Fade In and Fade Out, no particular effect is applied. Close the **Preview** pane when finished.

4. Back in the `Chapter04/encoderDemo_800.cptx` file, go to slide 3 and select the Adobe Media Encoder logo.
5. In the **Transition** accordion of the **Properties** panel, open the **Effect** drop-down list and choose **No Transition**.

We remove the **Fade In and Out** transition because we want to replace it with a much more sophisticated effect.

6. Use the **Window | Effects** menu to open the **Effects** panel.

By default, the **Effects** panel appears at the bottom of the screen next to the **Timeline**.

The **Effects** panel also displays a timeline, but, unlike the **Timeline** panel that displays the timeline of the entire slide, the **Effects** panel displays the timeline of the selected object only. In this case, the **Effects** panel displays the timeline of the Adobe Media encoder Logo (1).

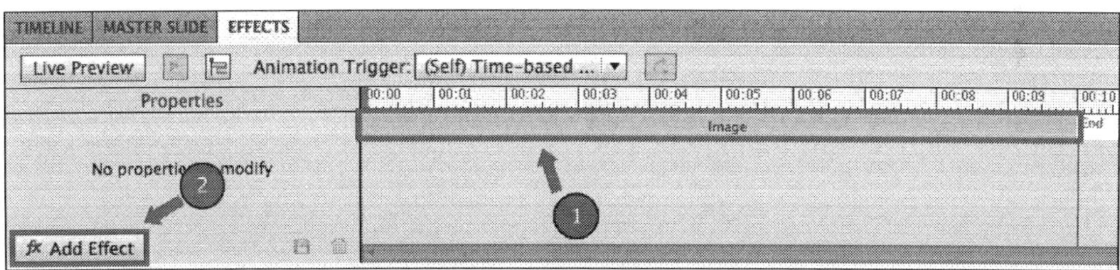

7. Click on the **Add Effect** icon (2) situated at the bottom left corner of the **Effects** panel.
8. In the menu that pops up, choose **Emphasis | Flip | Flip from center**.
9. In the **Effects** panel, reduce the length of the **FlipFromCenter** effect to the first half-second of the Adobe Media Encoder image timeline.

10.. Save your file.

11. Use the preview icon to preview the **Next 5 Slides**.

Pay particular attention to the way the Adobe Media Encoder logo enters the stage. Thanks to the **Effects** panel, we have applied a nice effect to the image. This adds another great touch of design, professionalism, and dynamism to this eLearning project!

Combining effects

In the next exercise, we will import an image and animate it using a combination of two effects.

1. Return to the `drivingInBe.cptx` file.
2. Use the **Filmstrip** to go to slide 6.

This slide already contains two transparent text Captions and one image.

3. Use **Insert | Image** to insert the `images/check.png` file situated in your exercises folder.
4. Use the **Transform** accordion to position the new image at **X 450** and **Y 115**. The image should be positioned on the right-hand side of the Text Caption that reads **Good!**
5. In the **Timeline** Panel or in the **Timing** accordion, make the image **Appear After 1.5 sec** and **Display For** the **rest of** the **slide**.
6. With the image still selected, open the **Effects** panel at the bottom of the screen.
7. Use the **Add Effect** icon to add the **Entrance | Spiral In** effect to the picture. Make the effect last for 1.5 sec.
8. Return to slide 5 and use the Preview icon to Preview the **Next 5 Slides**.

When the preview reaches slide 6, pay close attention to the way the green checkmark image enters the stage. Close the **Preview** pane when the preview is finished.

We will now add a second effect to the same object to make it look even more engaging.

9. Return to slide 6, select the green checkmark image and open the **Effects** panel.
10. Use the **Add Effect** button to add the **Emphasis | Clockwise Rotate** effect. Make it last the same 1.5 sec as the **Spiral In** effect we added earlier.

11. Make sure the **Effects** panel looks like the following screenshot and use the preview icon to test your sequence. When the preview is complete, close the **Preview** pane.

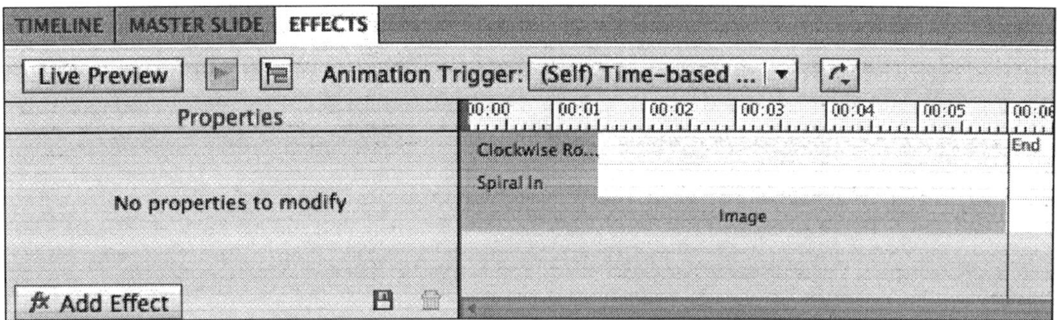

12. Still on slide 6, select the green checkmark image and copy it (*Ctrl*+*c* on Windows/*cmd* +*c* on Mac).
13. Go to slide 10 and paste (*Ctrl*+*V* on Windows/*cmd* +*V* on Mac) the image.
14. Save the file when done.

When you copy and paste an object, you also copy-paste the *properties* of the object including its size, its position and its effects.

Extra credit

Now that we have inserted an image and added effects onto it, why don't you try it on your own on another image? The general steps we need to follow are:

- You will be working with the `drivingInBe.cptx` file
- Add the `images/redCross.png` on slide 7
- Position the *red cross* image in the middle of the slide, between the two Text Captions
- On the **Timeline**, make the red cross **appear after 1 sec** and **display for** the **rest of** the **slide**
- Use the **Effects** panel to add the **Spiral In** and the **Clockwise Rotate** effects
- Make both effects last 1.5 seconds as we did for the green Checkmark
- Use the preview **Next 5 slides** feature to test your sequence
- If everything is fine, copy-paste the red cross image on slide 11

Finishing touches

To wrap up this topic on animating objects, we will inspect another slide of the project and see how the **Effects** and the **Timeline** panels can work together to produce a great visual experience.

1. Use the **Filmstrip** to go to slide 12 of the `drivingInBe.cptx` file.

This slide contains five Text Captions, seven images, and one button.

2. Take a look at the **Timeline** panel to see how the objects of this slide are organized. Notice that some images appear two-tenths of a second from one another.
3. Select any of the road sign images and open the **Effects** panel. The **FlipFromCenter** effect is applied to each and every image.
4. Use the preview **Next 5 Slides** feature to test the slide.
5. If necessary, adjust the timing of the objects as well as the timing of the animations to your liking.
6. Don't forget to save the file when done.

This little experiment concludes our coverage of the animations in Captivate. Feel free to experiment further by applying other effects to other objects or by modifying the effects we applied together during the last few pages. The possibilities are endless and this book only shows a few examples of what is possible.

Before moving on to the next topic, the following is a list of what we have learned about effects:

- It is possible to add effects to any object of Captivate.
- By Default, the **Effects** panel is not a part of the **Classic** workspace. Use the **Window | Effects** menu item to turn it on.
- In the bottom-left corner of the **Effects** panel, the **Add Effect** icon contains a large collection of effects to choose from.
- Different effects can be combined to create sophisticated animations.

Working with Buttons

The Button is the first interactive object of Captivate we will focus on. Remember that an interactive object can stop the playhead and wait for the student to *do* something.

In the case of a button, a simple click is enough to trigger an action. Despite its apparent simplicity, the Button object is an essential part of every Captivate project as it lets the student control the timing of his/her online course.

In the next exercise, we will add a simple button below the video file we inserted earlier in this chapter.

1. Return to the `encoderDemo_800.cptx` file.
2. Use the **Filmstrip** to go to slide 2. It is the slide on which we added the video file earlier in this chapter.
3. Use the **Insert | Standard Objects | Button** or the corresponding icon in the Objects toolbar to insert a new button on the slide.
4. With the new button selected, inspect the **Properties** panel.

When a button is selected on the stage, the **Properties** panel shows the properties that are relevant to a button. If you take a look at the available accordions, you'll notice three accordions that were *not* present for the other objects we have used so far.

- The **Action** accordion is used to determine what happens when the student clicks on the button
- The **Options** accordion gives us more options to manage the interaction with the student
- The **Reporting** accordion is used to report the interaction to an LMS server (see *Chapter 7, Working with Quizzes*)

These three accordions only appear when an interactive object is selected.

5. Position the new button in the bottom-right corner of the slide.
6. In the **General** accordion of the **Properties** panel, change the button **Caption** to continue.
7. Increase the width of the button so the new text fits comfortably in the object.
8. In the **Action** accordion, open the **On Success** drop-down list.
9. Take some time to inspect the options provided by the drop-down list. When done, choose the **Go to Next Slide** option.

Now that the button has the right look and performs the right action, our next task will be to arrange it on the **Timeline**. As the button is an interactive object that stops the playhead, we have a few more options than usual to take care of.

On the **Timeline**, the button object is separated in two areas. The separator between the two areas (see the following screenshot) is a *pause* symbol. It represents the exact moment when the button will stop the playhead and wait for the student to click.

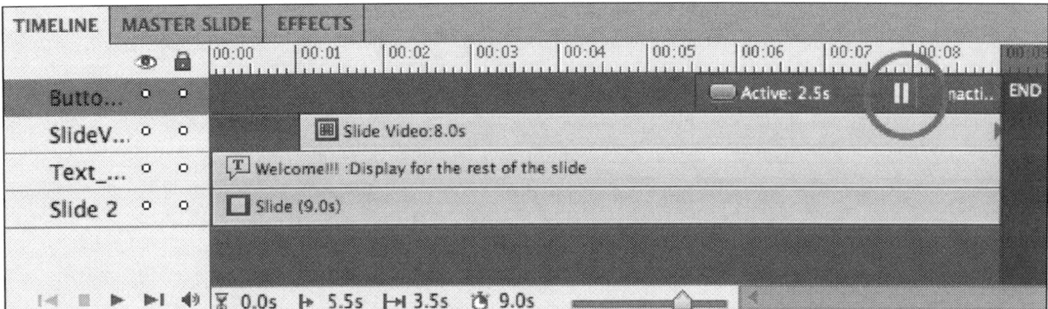

When the button is clicked, the action set in the **Action** accordion occurs. In our case, the action is **Go to Next Slide**. It means that when the student will click on the button, the playhead will jump from the *pause* symbol *directly to the first frame of the next slide*. Consequently, the frames of slide 2 situated after the pause symbol of the button *will not be played*.

10. Use the **Timeline** or the **Timing** accordion to:
    - Make the button **appear after 5.5 sec**
    - **Pause After 2.5 sec**
    - **Display for** the **rest of** the **slide**
11. Make sure the **Timeline** panel looks like the preceding screenshot.
12. Use the preview **Next 5 slides** feature to test the new button. Close the **Preview** pane when done.

This concludes our first approach of the button object. During the course of this book, we will add some more buttons in our projects and discover other options along the way, but for now, let's make a quick listing of what we have learned.

- The Button object is one of the three interactive objects of Captivate.
- As such, the Button object is able to pause the playhead and wait for the student to click on it.
- When an interactive object is selected, the **Properties** panel shows three additional accordions as compared to the accordions we are used to with non-interactive objects.
- One of these accordions is the **Action** accordion used to define what happens when the button is clicked.

- Since the button stops the playhead, it is separated in two areas on the **Timeline** panel. The separator represents the exact moment when the playhead is stopped.

The button object and the pedagogy

Two of the most important things to keep in mind while teaching are:

1. To keep the students focused
2. To adapt your teaching to each student (the latter is known as *differentiated instruction*)

Basically, it means that it is the course that has to adapt to the student and not the other way around (see `http://en.wikipedia.org/wiki/Differentiated_instruction` for more information). The Button object helps us in both these concerns. While watching a long Demonstration, your students' attention will inevitably drift away from the course. Each time you add a button, you make the students active, which helps in refreshing their attention. Another benefit of the button is that it lets each student manage the timing of the course. If you have a slide with a lot of text, it is a good idea to pause the playhead with a button and let each student read the slide at his/her own pace.

Discovering the Rollover objects

In this section, we will introduce three more objects. These objects are known as the *rollover objects*, because they are originally hidden and show only when the user *rolls over* a specific area of the slide. We will also uncover two more features of the Smart Shape object we covered in the previous chapter.

The first rollover object we will focus on is the Rollover Caption.

Working with Rollover Captions

A **Rollover Caption** is a Text Caption that appears when the user places his/her mouse over a specific spot on the slide known as the **Rollover Area**.

In the next exercise, we will add a Rollover Caption in the Driving in Belgium project.

1. Return to the `chapter04/drinvinInBe.cptx` file.
2. Use the **Filmstrip** to go to slide 13.

Slide 13 holds two Text Captions, four Images, and a Button that pauses the playhead at 2.5 seconds into the slide. The Text Caption in the top-right corner of the slide explains what we will try to achieve in this exercise.

3. Use the **Insert | Standard Objects | Rollover Caption** or the corresponding icon in the Objects toolbar to insert a new Rollover Caption.

A Rollover Caption inserts *two objects* on the slide. The first object is a basic Text Caption. The second object is the **Rollover Area**. The Text Caption will show only *if* and *when* the student passes his/her mouse on the Rollover Area.

4. Change the text of the Rollover Caption to **No parking is allowed at any time!**.
5. Use the **Properties** panel to apply the **transparentCaption** style to the Rollover Caption.
6. Resize the Caption and position it to the right of the first road sign.
7. Select the Rollover Area and position it more or less over the first road sign. Don't hesitate to resize the Rollover Area if necessary.
8. In the **Fill & Stroke** accordion, set the stroke **Width** to **0** to remove the Stroke of the Rollover Area.
9. Use the **Timeline** or the **Timing** accordion to make the rollover area **Appear After 1 sec** and **Display For** the **rest of** the **slide**.

When done, the slide should look like the following screenshot:

10. Save the file and use the preview **Next 5 Slides** feature to test the rollover Caption.

The Text Caption should be hidden by default and displays only *if* and *when* you pass your mouse over the Rollover Area.

11. Close the **Preview** pane when done.

Working with Rollover Smart Shapes

In the previous chapter, we have introduced the all-new Smart Shape object type. We used it to draw a rounded rectangle that we used as a picture frame. We will now cover two more features offered by the new Smart Shapes object type.

Writing text into a Smart Shape

The first of these two features is the possibility to write text into a Smart Shape, thus converting it into yet another type of Text Caption.

1. Return to slide 13 of the `drivingInBe.cptx` file.
2. Select either the Rollover Area or the Rollover Caption that we added in the previous topic.
3. Delete the selected object.

Notice that both the Rollover Area and the Text Captions are deleted even though only one of these two objects was selected.

4. Click on the first icon of the Objects toolbar to open the Smart Shape menu.
5. In the **Arrows** section, choose the **Left Arrow Callout** shape.

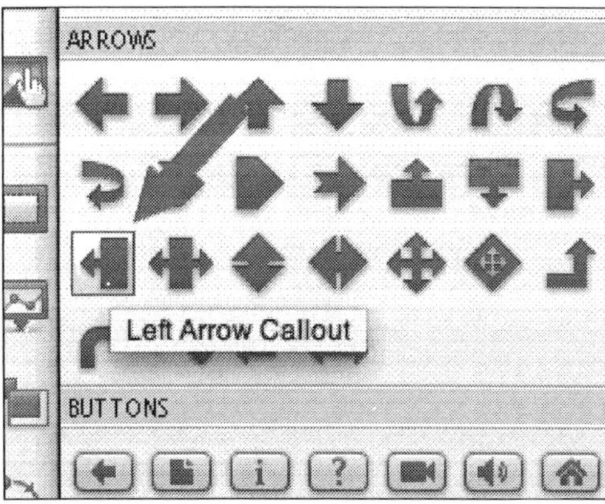

6. Draw a **Left Arrow Callout** to replace the Text Caption you deleted in step 3.

Notice that there are three yellow squares around that particular Smart Shape. Each one of these yellow squares can be used to modify the Smart Shape in a specific way.

7. Use the yellow squares to make your Smart Shape look like the one in the following screenshot:

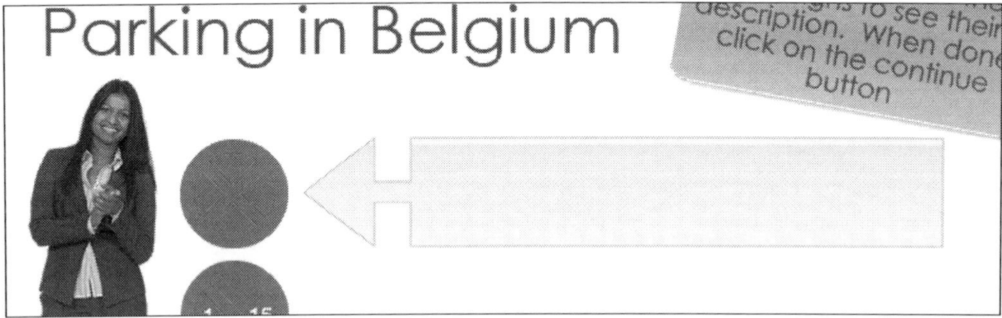

8. Make sure the Smart Shape is the selected object.
9. In the **Fill & Stroke** accordion of the **Properties** panel:
   - Change the **Fill** of the Smart Shape to the solid color *#AB8F1D*
   - Set **Alpha** to **100%** to make the Smart Shape completely opaque
   - Change the **Stroke** color to *#4C421D*
   - Change the stoke **Width** to *3* pixels

The smart shape should now look like the following screenshot:

10. Make sure the Smart Shape is the selected object.
11. Use the **Create New Style** icon of the **Properties** panel to save the current formatting of the Smart Shape as a new style called *MFTC-SmartShape*.

Before we move on to the next step, it is important that you take a close look at the accordions of the **Properties** panel when the Smart Shape is selected. There should be only six accordions in the **Properties** panel.

12. Double-click on the Smart Shape.

A small blinking cursor should appear in the top-left corner of the Smart Shape. After this operation, take another look at the **Properties** panel. There should be two extra accordions in the **Properties** panel. These are the **Character** and the **Format** accordion. Usually, these two panels are associated with a Text Caption.

13. Type `No parking is allowed at any time` in the Smart shape.
14. Use the Format and the Character accordion to:
    - Change the font **Family** to **Century Gothic**
    - Change the font **Size** to *20* points
    - Change the **Alignment** to left center

After these simple operations, the text in the Smart shape should be pretty much final. There is one more detail to take care of. Notice that the text touches the left edge of the Smart Shape (which is not very beautiful).

15. With the Smart Shape still selected, use the **Margins** option of the **Format** accordion to create a left margin of *10* pixels in the Smart Shape.
16. The Smart shape should now look like the following screenshot:

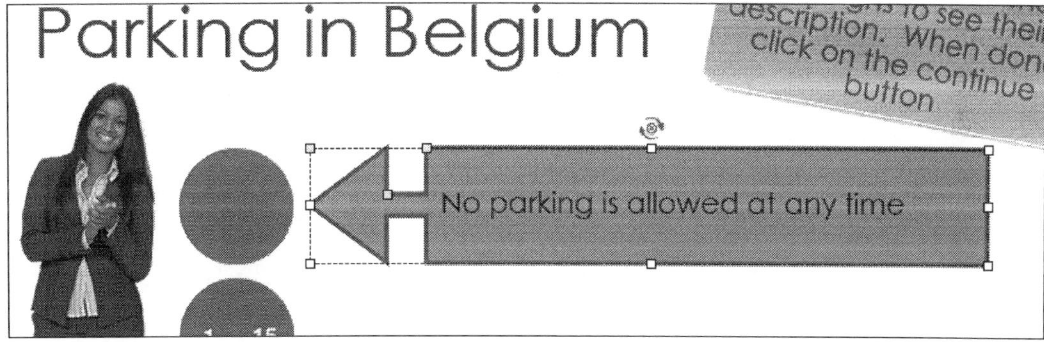

17. Use the **Save changes to Existing Style** icon at the top of the **Properties** panel to update the **MFTC-SmartShape** style to the current formatting of the Smart Shape.
18. Copy/paste the Smart Shape two times so you have three identical Smart Shapes on the Slide.

19. Roughly position the Smart Shapes to the right of each road sign image.
20. Change the text of the middle Smart Shape to **No parking allowed between the 1st and the 15th of the month**.
21. Change the text of the bottom Smart Shape to **No parking allowed between the 16th and the 31st of the month**.
22. Save the file when done.

Working with Rollover Smart Shapes

In the previous exercise, we have seen how to add text into a Smart Shape, which turns the Smart Shape into a Text Caption. Let's go one step further by turning these Smart Shapes into Rollover Smart Shapes.

The idea is very simple. We will associate a Rollover Area to each Smart Shape of slide 13. At runtime, the Smart Shapes will be hidden by default. It will become visible only *if* and *when* the student passes his/her mouse into the corresponding rollover area.

1. Make sure you are still in slide 13 of the `drivingInBe.cptx` file.
2. Right-click on the topmost Smart Shape.
3. Choose the **Convert to Rollover Smart Shape** command in the contextual menu.

The Smart Shape is converted into a Rollover Smart Shape and a corresponding Rollover Area appears on the slide.

4. Move and resize the Rollover Area so it roughly covers the topmost road sign.
5. In the **Fill & Stroke** accordion of the **Properties** panel, set the stroke **Width** to 0.
6. Repeat this sequence of actions with the remaining two Smart Shapes. Place the Rollover Areas over the corresponding road signs.
7. Save the file when done.

Now that three Rollover Smart Shapes are in place on the same slide, we will use the alignment toolbar to adjust their size and their position.

Using the Align toolbar to adjust the size and the position of objects

By Default, the Align toolbar is *not* displayed on the screen, so our first task will be to turn it on.

1. Use the **Window | Align** menu to turn the Align toolbar on.
2. The Align toolbar is a set of 14 icons appearing in the top-left corner of the screen.

Notice that the icons of the Align toolbar are all grayed out. The alignment tools will not work unless two (and sometimes three) objects are selected at the same time.

3. Select the *topmost* rollover Caption.
4. Keep the *Shift* key down and click on the other two Captions to add them to the selection.

Now that three objects are selected, notice that the icons of the Align toolbar are *not* grayed out anymore, indicating that every tool is available for use.

More importantly, you should see that:

- The first caption you selected is surrounded by *white* handles. We will call it the *White Object*.
- The other two objects are surrounded by *black* handles. We will call them the *Black Objects*.

This is very important to understand in order to work with the Alignment tools. **The white object (the first one you selected) is the object of reference**. The Alignment tools will be used to apply some properties of the white object to the black objects.

5. On the Align toolbar, click on the **Resize to same size icon**.

It is the next to last icon. By clicking on it, the two *Black* objects will be resized to have the exact same Width and the exact same Height as the *White* (first selected) object.

6. With the very same selection active, click on the very first icon of the Align toolbar.

This first icon is called **Align Left**. When you click on this icon, all the *Black* objects will share the same X coordinate as the *White* object. In other words, the left edge of the objects will be aligned. In our case, the three text Captions now have the very same size *and* the very same X coordinate.

7. Finally, with the same selection active, click on the eighth icon of the Align toolbar.

The eighth icon is the **Distribute Vertically** icon. When clicking on this icon, the topmost object and the bottommost object of the selection *won't* move, but all the Y coordinate of the objects in between (in our case, the middle Caption only) will be adjusted so that the vertical space between all the objects of the selection is the same.

When done, the three Rollover Captions should have the very same size and should be properly aligned on the slide.

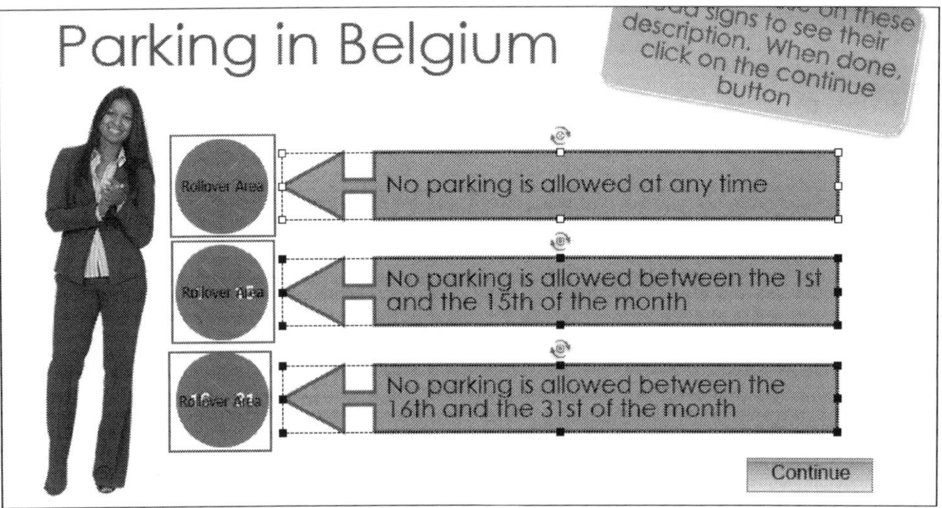

Before moving on to the next object, let's make a quick summary of what we have learned.

- Inserting a Rollover Caption adds two objects to the Slide.
- The first object is a regular Text Caption. The second object is a corresponding Rollover Area.
- At runtime, the Text Caption appears when the learner puts his/her mouse in the Rollover Area.
- The Align toolbar is not displayed by default. Use the **Window | Align** menu to turn it on.

- Text can be added in a Smart Shape. In this case, two extra accordions appear in the **Properties** panel. Use them to adjust the formatting of the text.
- A Smart Shape can be converted to a Rollover Smart Shape. A Rollover Smart Shape is not displayed by default. At runtime, it shows only *if* and *when* the student put his/her mouse over the corresponding Rollover Area.
- The icons of the Align toolbar only work if two or more objects are selected.
- To select multiple objects, select the first object, and then add other objects to the selection by clicking on them while holding down the *Shift* key.
- White handles surround the first selected object. It is used as the object of reference by the alignment tools. Black handles surround the other objects of the selection.

Now that we know how the Rollover Captions and Rollover Smart Shapes work, the next object will be very easy to understand.

Working with Rollover Images

A **Rollover Image** is an image that shows only if the learner puts his/her mouse in the corresponding Rollover Area.

In the next exercise, we will add three rollover images to the `drivingInBe.cptx` file.

1. If needed, return to the `chapter04/drinvinInBe.cptx` file.
2. Use the **Filmstrip** to go to slide 14.

Slide 14 contains five text Captions, one image, and a button that pauses the playhead at 7.5 seconds into the slide. The Text Caption in the top-right corner tells it all!

3. Use the **Insert | Standard Objects | Rollover Image** to insert a new Rollover Image.
4. Browse to the `images/priority.png` file and click on **open** to insert it onto the slide.

A Rollover Image inserts *two objects* on the slide: an *Image* and a corresponding *Rollover Area*. At runtime, the Image will be displayed only *if* and *when* the learner places his/her mouse in the Rollover Area.

5. Place the Image to the right of the Text Caption that says **I have the right of the way**.
6. Move and resize the Rollover Area so it covers more or less of the **I have the right of the way** Text Caption.

7. With the Rollover Area selected, use the **Fill & Stroke** accordion to remove its stroke (Set the stroke **Width** to **0**).
8. Use the **Timeline** or the **Timing** accordion to make the Rollover Area **Appear After 6 sec** and **Display For** the **rest of** the **slide**.
9. Add two more Rollover Images with the same formatting and timing properties.
    - Use the `images/noPriority.png` image for the first one. Position it on the right of the **I do not have the right of the way**. Text Caption. Move and resize the Rollover Area appropriately.
    - Use the `images/PriorityRight.png` image for the second one. Position it on the right of the **Those coming from the right hand side have the right of the way** Text Caption. Move and resize the Rollover Area appropriately.
10. If needed, use the tools of the Align toolbar to size and position the Rollover Images. Make sure slide 14 looks like the following screenshot:

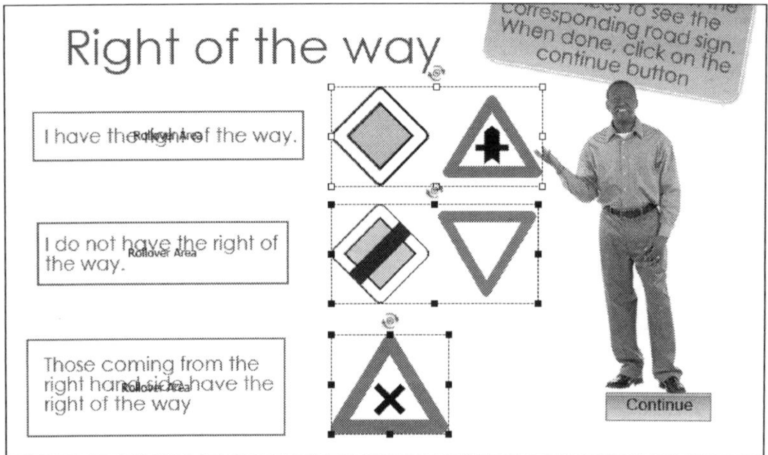

11. Save the file when done.
12. Use the **Filmstrip** to return to slide 13. Use the preview **Next 5 Sides** feature to test your Rollover Smart Shapes and your Rollover images.

On these two slides (13 and 14), the role of the button is critical in making the rollover system work. It stops the playhead and lets each student go through each Rollover object at his/her own pace and in the order he/she wants. This is yet another example of the *Differentiated Instruction* concept.

Before moving on to the last rollover object, this is a quick summary of what we have learned:

- The Rollover Image adds two objects to the slide: an *image* and a corresponding *Rollover Area*
- When the project is played back, the image shows only *if* and *when* the student puts his/her mouse in the corresponding Rollover Area

Working with Rollover Slidelets

The last rollover object of Captivate is the **Rollover Slidelet**. This object was a new feature of Captivate 3 released in July 2007.

As with every other rollover objects of Captivate, the Rollover Slidelet adds *two objects* to the slide: the *slidelet* and a corresponding *rollover area*.

Inserting and formatting a Rollover Slidelet

In the next exercise, we will add a **Rollover Slidelet** to the Driving in Belgium project.

1. If needed, return to the `chapter04/drinvinInBe.cptx` file.
2. Use the **Filmstrip** to go to slide 12.
3. Use **Insert | Standard Objects | Rollover Slidelet**. This adds the two objects that compose the Rollover Slidelet system to the slide.
4. Click on an empty area of the slide to deselect the Rollover Slidelet.
5. Click on the object with the blue border to select the Rollover Slidelet.

Make sure that **Rollover Slidelet Area** is written at the top of the **Properties** panel. If *Slidelet* is written instead, it means that *you did not select the right object*.

The selected object is used as the *Rollover Area* of the Rollover Slidelet. We will position it on top of the **Convert Speeds to MPH** Text Caption and turn off its stroke.

6. Move and resize the selected object so it covers more or less the **Convert Speeds to MPH** text Caption.
7. In the **Fill & Stroke** accordion of the **Properties** panel, deselect **Show Border** and the **Show Runtime Border** checkboxes.
8. In the **Timeline** panel or in the **Timing** accordion, make the Rollover Slidelet **Appear After 15 sec** and **Display For** the **rest of** the **slide**.

Notice that, as expected, the **Timeline** panel shows a list of all the objects that are present on the slide. There should be 14 objects in addition to the slide itself.

9. Click on the other object of the Rollover Slidelet system to make it the active object. The word **Slidelet** should be written at the top of the **Properties** panel.

Take another look at the **Timeline** and notice that the objects of the slide are *not* listed anymore. This is because the **Timeline** we are viewing at the moment is not the **Timeline** of the slide, but *the Timeline of the Rollover Slidelet*. This helps us understand what a Rollover Slidelet really is.

A Rollover Slidelet is *a slide within a slide*. Consequently, objects (such as Text Captions, Images, and so on) can be inserted inside the Rollover Slidelet and arranged on its **Timeline**. At runtime, the Slidelet will appear and play its **Timeline** only *if* and *when* the student passes his/her mouse over the corresponding Rollover Area (called **Rollover Slidelet Area** in this case).

We will now give the Slidelet the correct size, position, and format. Make sure the Slidelet is selected to perform the following actions:

10. In the **Transform** accordion, deselect the **Constrain proportions** box
11. Give the slidelet a **Width** of **630** pixels and a **Height** of **260** pixels

With the slidelet selected, take a look at the Align toolbar. Only two icons should be available. These icons are called **Center horizontally on the slide / Slidelet** and **Center Vertically on the Slide / Slidelet**.

12. Click on both these icons to position the slidelet *exactly in center of the stage*.
13. In the **Fill & Stroke** accordion:
    - Choose color *#AB8F1D* (light brown) as the **Fill** Color
    - Set **Alpha** to **90 %**
    - Set the **Width** of the Stroke to **3** pixels
    - Choose **#4C421E** (Dark Brown) as the **stroke** color
14. Make sure your slidelet looks like the following screenshot:

Inserting objects in a Rollover Slidelet

Now that the Rollover Slidelet has the proper format, the proper position, and the proper size, we will insert three Text Captions in the Slidelet and organize them on its **Timeline**.

1. To make sure the Slidelet is the active object, take a look at the **Timeline** panel and confirm it shows the **Timeline** of the slidelet, not the **Timeline** of the slide (No objects should appear on the **Timeline**).
2. Use **Insert | Standard Objects | Text Caption** to insert a new Text Caption in the slidelet.

While inserting the new Text Caption in the slidelet, notice that some of the objects of the **Insert | Standard Objects** menu are dimmed. It means that these objects *cannot* be inserted in a slidelet. These objects are the interactive objects of Captivate, the mouse and, of course, the Rollover Slidelet itself!

3. Type `Motorways - 120 km/H is approx. 80 MPH` in the new Text Caption and apply the **Transparent Caption** style.
4. Resize the Text Caption and position it in the upper area of the Slidelet.
5. Use the same procedure to add two more Text Captions in the slidelet. Apply the **Transparent Caption** style to both Captions.
    - Type `National roads - 90 Km/h is approx. 60 MPH` in the second Caption
    - And `Cities and towns - 50 Km/h is approx. 30 MPH` in the third caption.

6. Use the tools of the Align toolbar to position the three Text Captions properly in the Slidelet.
7. In the **Timeline** panel or in the **Timing** accordion, extend the duration of the slidelet to **15 sec**.
8. Arrange the three Text Captions using the following properties:
    - The topmost Caption **Appears After 0 sec** and displays for the **rest of** the **slidelet**
    - The middle Caption **Appears After 2 sec** and displays for the **rest of** the **slidelet**
    - The bottom Caption **Appears After 4** sec and displays for the **rest of** the **slidelet**
9. Save the file and use the Preview **Next 5 slides feature** to test the Rollover Slidelet.

When the preview is finished, close the **Preview** pane.

This exercise concludes our exploration of the Rollover Slidelet. In the next section we will focus on the **Library** panel, but for now, let's summarize what we have learned in this section.

- Like every other rollover object, the Rollover Slidelet adds *two* objects to the slide: the *slidelet* and a corresponding *Rollover Area*.
- During the playback, the slidelet will show *if* and *when* the student passes his/her mouse over the associated rollover area.
- A Rollover Slidelet is *a slide within a slide*. As such, it has its own **Timeline**.
- Most of the objects that can be inserted on a regular slide can be inserted in a Rollover Slidelet.
- However, some objects *cannot* be inserted in a slidelet. These are the interactive objects, the Mouse and, of course, the Rollover Slidelet itself.

Working with the Library

The **Library** panel was a new feature of Captivate 2 released in October 2006. When using the **Classic** workspace, the **Library** panel appears as a tab next to the **Properties** panel at the right-hand side of the screen.

1. Return to the `encoderDemo_800.cptx` file.
2. To open the **Library** panel, click on the **Library** tab situated next to the **Properties** panel. Alternatively, use the **Window | library** menu.

The **Library** holds a list of all the assets of the current file. These assets include the background pictures captured during the filming of the project, all the external files imported into the movie (images, video, sounds, and so on), as well as the Full Motion Recording clips, and the sound recordings made with Captivate.

- At the very top of the **Library** panel, we can see the name of the file the **Library** belongs to (1).
- The preview area (2) lets us take a quick look at the selected item. In the preceding screenshot, the `AMELogo.png` image is selected (see the red arrow) and shows in the preview area.

- Just below the preview area, the Library *toolbar* (3) displays a row of icons. These are the tools we will use to manage the assets present in the **Library**.
- The main area of the **Library** panel (4) lists the assets of the project organized by type.

As you can see, the **Library** contains one folder for each type of assets it can contain.

3. In the **Library** panel, select the **mftcTitleTemplate.jpg** file in the **Backgounds** folder.
4. Click on the *Sixth* icon of the **Library** toolbar. This icon is called **Usage**.
5. A box pops up and informs us that this particular image is used as the background of both slide 1 and slide 22.
6. Click on **OK** to close the **Usage** dialog box.

The only purpose of the **Usage** dialog box is to inform us about where the selected asset is used in the project.

Reusing library items

When an external file (like an image or a Flash animation) is inserted in the project, it is *automatically* added to the project's **Library**. That is why the `down.swf` file is listed in the **Media** section of the **Library**.

1. Still in the `encoderDemo_800.cptx` file, use the **Filmstrip** to go to slide 5.

This is the slide where we inserted the orange `down.swf` Flash animation earlier in this chapter. If we want to use the same file again, there is no need to import it a second time. It can be taken directly from the **Library** and reused as many times as needed throughout the entire project. Using many instances of the same file helps in keeping the resulting file size as low as possible.

We will now use the **Library** panel to insert two more instances of this Flash animation on the slide.

2. Drag two more instances of the `down.swf` animation from the **Library** panel to the middle slide.
3. *Roughly*, distribute the three orange arrows along the top edge of the orange Highlight Box.
4. Select all three orange arrows starting by the leftmost one.
5. Use the tools of the Align toolbar to properly position the arrows on the slide.
6. In the **Timeline** panel, all three animations should **Appear After 1 sec** and **Display For a specific time** of **6 sec**.

7. Save the file and use the preview icon to test the sequence.

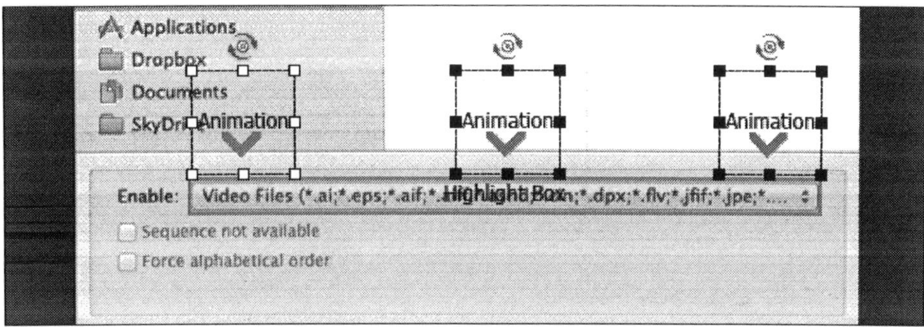

Importing objects from another library

Another great feature of the **Library** panel is the ability to open *the Library of another file*. This makes it easy to share assets between different Captivate projects.

In the next exercise, we will open the Library of another Captivate file in order to insert another image in the Encoder Demonstration project.

1. Still in the `encoderDemo_800.cptx` file, use the **Filmstrip** to go to slide 2.
2. In the **Library** panel, click on the *first* icon of the Library Toolbar to open the Library of another file.
3. Browse to the exercises folder and open the `Chapter04/library.cptx` file. The **Library** panel of this file appears as an extra floating panel.
4. Enlarge the **Library** panel of the other file. It contains one image called `inAmsterdam.jpg`.
5. Drag the `inAmsterdam.jpg` image from the external Library to the middle of slide 2.
6. Close the External Library once done.

Oops, wrong image! Sorry folks, this is an image of me in Amsterdam a few hours before the show of AC/DC during their Black Ice world tour! Well, even though, this is not the intended picture, I've made my point: the **Library** can be used to share assets between Captivate files. Notice that the `inAmsterdam.jpg` image is now present in the **Images** folder of the **Library** of the `encoderDemo_800.cptx` file.

7. Select the newly inserted image and delete it.

Take another look at the **Library** panel *after* you deleted the image. Notice that, even though it is *not* used in the project anymore, the image still appears in the **Images** folder of the **Library**.

Deleting unused assets from the library

The unused items are the assets that are present in the **Library**, but are *not* used in the project. In order to control the size of the `.cptx` file, we will use the **Library** panel to quickly identify and delete these unused items.

1. In the **Library** panel, click on the *eighth* icon of the Library Toolbar. This icon is called **Select Unused Item**.

The **inAmsterdam.jpg** image and the **Slide 16 background** item should be selected in the **Library**.

2. Click on the *last* icon of the Library Toolbar (the trash can icon) to *delete* the selected assets.
3. Click on **Yes** to confirm the deletion.

That's it! Thanks to the **Library** panel, it has been quick and easy to identify and delete the unused assets. This will help us keep the size of our *cptx* file as low as possible.

Be careful when deleting background images (like the Slide 16 background item we just deleted) because you can't get those back if needed!

We will discover a few more goodies of the **Library** panel later in the book, but for now, let's make a quick list of what we already know about it.

- The **Library** panel appears on the right-hand side of the screen, next to the **Properties** panel.
- The primary purpose of the **Library** is to list the assets present in the active project. These assets are the background pictures and the Full Motion Recordings captured during the filming, the external files imported in the project, and the audio clips recorded with Captivate.
- The **Library** panel provides the necessary tools to let us manage the various assets used in the project.
- We can use the **Library** panel to insert multiple instances of the same file in the project. This helps in keeping the project size as low as possible.
- It is possible to share assets among various projects by opening the Library of other files and importing the assets they contain in the current project.
- When you delete an asset from a slide, it is *not* deleted from the **Library**. As a result, the **Library** panel can contain many unused items.
- We can easily select and delete the unused items with the tools of the **Library** panel.

Creating a Simulation

In this section, we will convert the `encoderDemo_800.cptx` *Demonstration* into a *Simulation*. Remember that when viewing a Demonstration, the student is *passive* and only *watches* whatever happens on the screen. When viewing a Simulation however, the student is active and has to *do* things.

Now, as far as objects are concerned, the difference between a Demonstration and a Simulation is to be found elsewhere. The object associated with a Demonstration is the *Mouse* object. Remember that the Mouse object lets us show the mouse on the screen and controls its movements. In order to convert the Demonstration to a Simulation, we'll have to remove the mouse from the project.

Hiding the mouse is one thing, but we'll have to replace it with something else. If we think about it, there are two kinds of actions that we need to be able to simulate, and that's why Captivate provides two interactive objects to let us replace the mouse in a Simulation. The first object is the **Click Box**. It is used each time we need to make the student *click* somewhere. The second object is the **Text Entry Box**. We will use it when we need the student to *type* something. Those two objects are interactive, which means that they can stop the playhead and wait for the learner to interact.

Before we get started, we will create the Simulation file and save it in our exercises folder.

1. Return to the `encoderDemo_800.cptx` file.
2. Use the **File | Save As** menu item to create another version of this file.
3. Name the file `encoderSim_800.cptx` and save it in the `Chapter04` subfolder of your exercises folder.

Hiding the mouse

Now that the Simulation file exists, the first step in converting this Demonstration to a Simulation is to remove the mouse object.

Normally, there should be 22 slides in the project. In the **Filmstrip**, a Mouse icon at the bottom-right corner of the slides' thumbnails indicates that the Mouse object shows on slides 4 to 21.

For the following procedure, feel free to enlarge the **Filmstrip** as described in the *Working with panels* section of *Chapter 1, Getting Started with Captivate.*

1. In the **Filmstrip**, select slide 4. It is the first slide of the project where the mouse shows.

2. Hold down the *Shift* key and select slide 21. This operation selects 18 slides from slide 4 to slide 21.
3. Hold down the *cmd* (Mac) or the *Ctrl* (Windows) key and click on slide 13 to remove it from the current selection

Slide 13 is the Full Motion Recording slide that shows the scroll down action on the Video tab. The mouse does not show on this slide, so we can safely remove it from the selection.

4. To remove the mouse from the selected slides, use the **Modify | Mouse | Show Mouse** menu item to *deselect* the **Show Mouse** option.
5. Go through the slides of the project to confirm that the Mouse object has been removed.

Our project is not yet a Simulation, but with the removal of the mouse, it is not a Demonstration anymore. The conversion is underway! Before we move on, there are a few more objects to remove/modify in the file.

The first slide to modify is slide 2 where we will replace the video file by another one.

6. Go to slide 2 and remove the Video file.
7. Use **Video | Insert Slide Video** to insert a **Multi-Slide Synchronized Video**.
8. Use the `video/flv/sim_en.flv` file situated in the exercises folder.
9. At the bottom of the **Insert Video** dialog, make sure to select the **Modify slide duration to accommodate video** option.
10. In the **Transform** accordion, position the video at **X** = 200 and **Y** = 196.
11. Change the **Timeline** so that the video **Appears After 1 sec**. Make the button pause the playhead just before the end of the video. The overall duration of the slide should be reduced to 5 seconds.

We will now remove the Zoom Area from slide 16 and the animations from slide 5.

12. Use the **Filmstrip** to go to slide 16.
13. Select the Zoom Area and delete it.

To delete the Zoom area entirely, you can delete either the Zoom Destination or the Zoom Source.

14. Go to slide 5 and remove the three instances of the `down.swf` orange arrow animations that we added earlier in this chapter.
15. Save the file when done.

Finally, we will update the text animation on the very last slide of the project.

16. Use the **Filmstrip** to go to slide 22.
17. Select the text animation and click on the **Properties** button situated in the **General** accordion. The **Text Animation Properties** box opens.
18. In the box, change the word **Demonstration** to **Simulation** so that the sentence becomes **Thank you for viewing this Simulation**.
19. Use the same procedure to update the Text Animation on slide 1.
20. Save the file when done.

With these small updates done, we are now well on our way to convert this Demonstration into a Simulation. In the next section, we will change the necessary Text Captions to give the students precise instructions on what they have to *do* in the Simulation.

Using Find and Replace

When developing a Simulation, never forget that our students will be *active* and will have to *do* things on their own. As we do not want to mislead, and possibly to lose, our students, it is critical to give them precise instructions on what they have to do at each step of the Simulation. For the teacher, coming up with the proper instructions is not an easy thing to achieve, but it is very important for the pedagogical approach to be successful, so **don't hesitate to spend the necessary time to come up with the proper instruction**.

1. Use the **Filmstrip** to go to slide 4 of the `encoderSim_800.cptx` file.

Notice the message contained in the Text Caption of this slide. It says **The mouse will now click on the Add files icon**. This message was right when in a Demonstration, but in a Simulation, we should change it in order to give the user the precise instruction to *click* on the item.

2. One by one, browse the remaining slides of the project.

Notice that on most of the remaining slides, the message contained in the Text Caption follows the same pattern as the message of slide 4. In the next exercise, we will use the *Find and Replace* feature to change the **The mouse will now click** part of the sentence into **Click**.

3. Use the **Edit | Find and Replace** menu to open the **Find And Replace** panel.

By default, the **Find And Replace** panel appears at the bottom-right corner of the screen right below the **Properties** panel.

4. Type `The Mouse will now click` in the **Find** field.
5. Type `Click` (with a capital C) in the **Replace** field.

It is a good idea to take a look at the other options provided by the **Find And Replace** Panel.

6. Leave all the other options at their default and click on **Replace All**.
7. You should get a message saying that ten instances have been replaced. Click on **OK** to discard the confirmation box.
8. Use the **Filmstrip** to browse the remaining slides of the project.

Confirm that the text displayed in the Text Captions has changed as expected. While browsing the slides, notice that the Text Caption of slide 5 uses a slightly different pattern as the Text Captions of the other slides.

9. Use the **Filmstrip** to go to slide 5 and select the Text Caption.
10. Manually modify the text contained in the caption so it reads **Double-click on the demo_en.mov video file**.

At each step of the Simulation, the student now has a Text Caption explaining precisely what he/she has to do. This is a great thing, but it is not enough! To give the student complete information about the purpose of the Simulation, we should provide some extra information at the beginning of the project.

11. In the **Filmstrip**, right-click on slide 3.
12. In the contextual menu, click on the **Delete** command.
13. Read the message and click on **OK** to confirm the deletion of the slide.

We will now replace the deleted slide by another one.

14. Open the `Chapter04/instructions.cptx` file situated in your exercises folder.

This project contains a single slide that we will import in the `encoderSim_800.cptx` file using a simple copy/paste.

15. In the **Filmstrip** of the `instructions.cptx` file, right-click on the first (and only) slide.
16. In the contextual menu, click on **Copy**.
17. Return to the `encoderSim_800.cptx` file.

18. In the **Filmstrip**, right-click on slide 2.
19. In the contextual menu, click on **Paste**.

Remember that when inserting a new slide in a project, the new slide gets inserted *after* the currently selected slide.

Take some time to examine the content of the slide we just inserted. It is a very important introduction slide. After reading this slide, the student will have all the information he/she needs to experience the Simulation in the best possible conditions.

Let them be in charge!

The button placed on the new slide 3 has *two* purposes. First, it pauses the playhead to let the learners read through the slide at their own pace. The second purpose of this button has to do with psychology. When doing a Simulation, you confront the students with something they have to *do* for the first time. For some of them, this uncomfortable situation generates a lot of stress and anxiety. The button gives them time to put their thoughts together and take a deep breath before they give the go to the Simulation *themselves*. The button gives them the illusion that *they* are in charge. This helps them manage their anxiety. I have used this method successfully in many projects with great feedback from the students.

Working with Click Boxes

Our Simulation is slowly taking shape but it still misses the object that will definitely make the whole difference. This object is what will replace the Mouse we removed earlier. This object is the **Click Box**.

Like the Button we studied earlier, the Click Box is an interactive object. It is used to define an area of the screen in which the student has to click. If the learner clicks inside the Click Box, the right action is performed and the Simulation can move on to the next step. If the student clicks outside the box, the wrong action is performed and the appropriate feedback should be displayed.

In the next exercise, we will add the required Click Boxes to the Encoder Simulation project.

1. Use the **Filmstrip** to go to slide 4 of `encoderSim_800.cptx`.
2. Hide the Highlight Box by clicking on its eye icon in the **Timeline** panel.

We need to add the Click Box at the same spot where the Highlight Box is located. By hiding the Highlight Box, we clear the way for the Click Box to be added in the best possible conditions. Remember that when using the eye icon as we have just done, we hide the corresponding object in Captivate only, not in the resulting animation.

3. Use **Insert | Standard Objects | Click Box** or the corresponding icon in the Objects toolbar to add the Click Box to the slide.

By default, adding a Click Box adds four objects to the slide. The first object is the Click Box itself. The three other objects are:

- The **Success Caption** that will show if the student performs the right action.
- The **Failure Caption** that will show if the student does not perform the right action.
- The **Hint Caption** that will show when the student puts his/her mouse on the Click Box. It behaves like a Rollover Caption using the Click Box as its rollover area.

We will now set up the Click Box so that it looks the right way.

4. With the Click Box selected, take a look at the **Options** accordion of the **Properties** panel. In the **Captions** section, deselect the **Success** and **Hint** checkboxes. Leave only the **Failure** option selected.

By deselecting the **Success** and **Hint** options, the corresponding captions disappear from the slide. There are two objects left: the Click Box and the Failure Caption.

5. Move and resize the Click Box so that it covers more or less the **Add file** icon of the background image.
6. Type `Sorry, you did not perform the right action` in the Failure Caption.
7. Select the Failure Caption object.
8. In the **Character** accordion of the **Properties** panel, change its font **Family**, to **Century Gothic.**
9. At the top of the **Properties** panel, click on the **Create new Style** icon and save the current formatting of the Failure Caption as *MFTC-Failure*.
10. If needed, resize the Failure Caption so the text fits comfortably in the Caption and move it somewhere in the middle of the slide.

Sizing the Click Boxes

When sizing the Click Boxes, don't hesitate to make them a bit bigger than what is actually needed. The extra space will make it easier for your students to find the Click Box and perform the right action. Don't forget that you are *teaching*. You want your students to concentrate on the *concepts* to learn and so, the *exact* location of a mouse click is a secondary concern.

With the Click Box and the Failure Caption at the right location, we will now set up the actions that have to occur when the student performs the right or the wrong action.

11. Select the Click Box.
12. In the **Action** accordion of the **Properties** panel, confirm that the **On Success** action is set to **Go to the next slide**.
13. Deselect the **Infinite** option and set the number of **Attempts** to **2**. This means that we will let the student two chances to perform the right action.
14. Confirm the **Last Attempt** drop-down list is set to **Continue**.

The **Continue** action simply releases the playhead, while the **Go to the next slide** action directly moves the playhead to the next slide. This setup will help us do some *branching* without adding an extra slide to the project.

To finish with this slide, we will now organize the objects on the **Timeline**.

15. Use the eye icon of the **Timeline** to reveal the Highlight box we hid earlier.
16. Make the Click Box **Appear After 3 sec** and pause the slide 1 sec later.
17. Apply the same timing to the **Click on the Add files icon** Text Caption.
18. With the Text Caption selected, open the **Transition** accordion and change the transition to **Fade In Only**.
19. Insert a new Text Caption on the slide. Type `The correct spot is currently highlighted. The Simulation will now continue as if you performed the right action` in the new Text Caption.
20. Resize the new Caption and move it somewhere in the middle of the slide.
21. In the **Timeline** Panel or in the **Timing** accordion, make the new Text Caption **Appear After 4.5 sec** and **Display For** a **specific time** of **6.5 sec**. Consequently, the duration of the slide has to be extended to 8 seconds.
22. Select the Highlight Box and give it the same timing.
23. Reduce the length of the slide to 11 seconds.

Make sure the **Timeline** panel of slide 4 looks like the following screenshot:

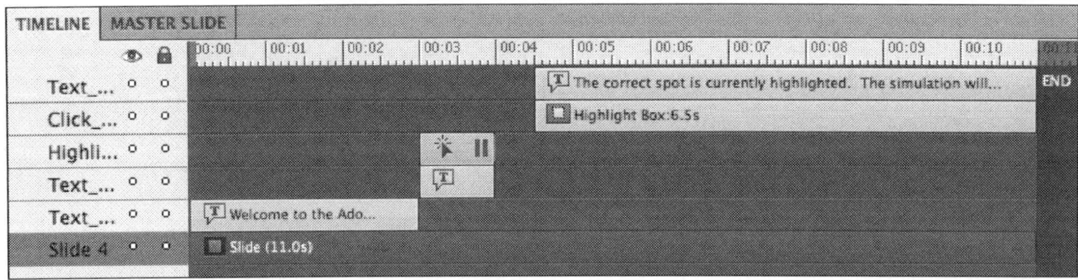

The Click box will stop the playhead at 4 seconds into slide 4 and wait for the student to perform an action. If the student performs the right action, the playhead directly jumps to slide 5 without playing the second part of slide 4. If the student performs the wrong action, then, the playhead is simply released and plays the Highlight Box and the Text Caption before moving on to slide 5. This is a first example of the *Branching* concept *without* adding any extra slides to the project.

24. Save the file and use the Preview **Next 5 slides** feature to test your sequence.

It is necessary to test it twice. The first time, perform the right actions and confirm that the playhead moves to the next slide. The second time, perform the wrong actions twice and confirm that the feedback messages and the Highlight Boxes are displayed before the Simulation moves on to the next slide.

If everything works as expected, you can use the same procedure to add a Click Box and a failure message on slides 5, 6, 7, 8, 9, 10, 11, 14, 16, and 17. Use the `chapter04/final/encoderSim_800.cptx` file as reference. To help you out, these are the basic steps of the procedure to perform on each slide.

- Hide the Highlight Box using the eye icon of the **Timeline**.
- Insert a Click Box and make it cover the same spot as the Highlight Box.
- Set the Click Box so it accepts two attempts. It should *Jump to the next slide* on success and *Continue* after the last attempt.
- Make sure that the transition of the Text Caption is set to **Fade In Only**.
- Write a failure message in the Failure Caption.
- Apply the **MFTC-Failure** style to the Failure Caption.
- Create a Text Caption with extra Feedback on the same model that what we did on slide 4.
- Arrange the objects on the **Timeline**.
- Delete the unneeded objects (extra Text Captions, Highlight Boxes, and so on)

When done, don't forget to save the file and preview your movie. In order to fully test the Click Boxes, it is necessary to preview the movie twice. The first time, perform the right actions and confirm that the Simulation always jumps to the next slide. The second time, perform the wrong actions and confirm that the Simulation displays the appropriate feedback messages.

Working with Text Entry Boxes

There is one more action to take care of on slide 15. Currently, the slide holds a Text Animation that automatically types the desired Width of the video. In a Simulation, we want the student to type in this information, so we will delete the current text animation and replace it with a **Text Entry Box**.

After the Button and the Click Box, the Text Entry Box is the third and last interactive object of Captivate. It is used to simulate a text typing action.

1. Use the **Filmstrip** to go to slide 15 of the `encoderSim_800.cptx` file.
2. *Select* the Text Animation that writes **400** in the **Width** field and *delete* it.
3. Use **Insert | Standard Objects | Text Entry Box** or the corresponding icon in the Objects toolbar to insert a new Text Entry Box.

The Text Entry Box system can add up to *5 objects* to the slide:

- The Text Entry Box itself
- A Success Caption
- A Failure Caption
- A Hint Caption
- A Submit button (The Submit button is often hidden below the Success Caption)

We will now set up the Text Entry Box so it looks the right way and behaves as we want it to behave.

4. Move and resize the Text Entry Box object so it covers the **Width** field of the Background image.

Don't hesitate to use the Zoom feature of Captivate to help you precisely size and position the Text Entry Box.

5. With the Text Entry Box selected, take a look at the **General** accordion of the **Properties** panel and confirm that the **Validate User Input** checkbox *is* selected.
6. In the **Correct Entries** box, click on the + sign and type **400**. Do not tick the **Case Sensitive** option.

This last action enables the Text Entry Box to tell the right answer apart from the wrong answers. You can add as many correct entries as needed by clicking on the + sign. To remove an entry from the list, select it and click on the - icon.

7. With the Text Entry Box selected, go to the **General** Accordion of the **Properties** panel and deselect the **Show Text Box Frame** option.
8. In the **Options** accordion, deselect the **Success** and **Hint** captions. Leave only the **Failure** caption selected.
9. In the **Others** section of the **Options** accordion, deselect the **Show Button** option to hide the **Submit** button.
10. In the **Transition** accordion, set the effect to **No transition** (if needed).
11. Type `Sorry you did not perform the right action!` in the failure Caption. When done, resize the failure Caption so the text fits comfortably in it and move it somewhere in the middle of the slide.
12. Apply the **MFTC-Failure** style to the Failure Caption.
13. Select the Text Entry Box object again.
14. In the **Action** accordion, open the **On Success** drop-down list and choose **Go to the next slide**.
15. Deselect the **Infinite** option and set the **Attempts** to **2**.
16. Make sure the **Last Attempt** drop down is set to **Continue**.
17. Confirm that the **Shortcut** option is set to **Enter**.
18. In the **Character** accordion, set the font **Family** to **Courier** and the text **Size** to **10**. This sets the formatting properties of the text that the student will type in the Text Entry Box.

Now that the Text Entry Box looks the right way and performs the right actions, we will move to the final step of this exercise: arranging the objects on the **Timeline** and providing the necessary feedback.

19. Select the Text entry Box and use the **Timeline** panel or the **Timing** accordion to:
    - Make the object **Appear After 0 sec**
    - Make it **Display For a specific time** of **1 sec**
    - Make it **Pause After 1 sec**

20. Select the Text Caption and apply the same timing as for the Text Entry Box. In the **Transition** accordion, change **Effect** to **Fade In Only**.
21. Insert a new Text Caption on the slide. Type `The Simulation will now continue as if you performed the right action`. Resize the Text Caption so the text fits comfortably in the object and place it somewhere in the middle of the slide.
22. In the **Timeline** panel or in the **Timing** accordion, make the new Text Caption **Appear After 1.5 sec** and **Display For** a **Specific time** of **5.5 sec**.
23. Reduce the duration of the slide to 7 sec. When done, make sure the **Timeline** panel looks like the following screenshot:

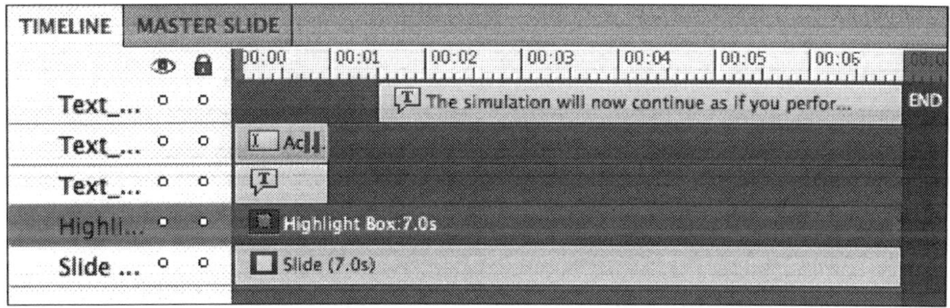

Don't forget to save the file and to test the new Text Entry Box in the **Preview** pane to make sure it works as expected.

Fine tuning the Simulation

There are a few more things to fine tune in order to finalize our Encoder Simulation.

The first fine tuning has to do with a limitation of Captivate 6. In a Captivate Simulation, we have the Click Box object to simulate a mouse click and the Text Entry Box object to simulate a typing action, but **there is no interactive object to simulate a drag-and-drop or a scrolling action**.

Due to this limitation, we will now delete slide 12 and 13 of our Simulation.

1. In the **Filmstrip** right-click on slide 12.
2. In the contextual menu, click on **Delete**. Confirm the deletion of the slide in the warning message.
3. Repeat this procedure with slide 13 (that is now slide 12 since you deleted the previous slide 12!!!).

The second thing to fine tune is the double-click action on slide 5.

4. Use the **Filmstrip** to return to slide 5.
5. Use the **Timeline** panel to select the Click Box object.
6. In the **Options** accordion of the **Properties** panel, select the **Double-click** checkbox.

The last fine-tuning option takes place on slide 10. To better simulate the click over a link, we will turn the standard mouse pointer to a Hand pointer over the Click Box.

7. Use the **Filmstrip** to return to slide 10.
8. Use the **Timeline** panel to select the Click Box object.
9. In the **Options** accordion of the **Properties** panel, select the **Hand Cursor** checkbox.

The conversion of our Encoder Demonstration into its Simulation counterpart is now finished. To reach this milestone, we have used many objects and features of Captivate. Let's quickly summarize them.

- The main object of a Demonstration is the **Mouse**. The main objects of a Simulation are the **Click Boxes** and the **Text Entry Boxes**.
- To convert a Demonstration to a Simulation, we must first remove the mouse from the Demonstration and then, replace it with Click Boxes and Text Entry Boxes.
- It is very important to provide specific and precise instruction to the learners at each and every step of the Simulation.
- The **Find and Replace** feature is very useful to quickly modify the text contained in the Text Captions throughout the entire project.
- The three interactive objects of Captivate are the *Button*, the *Click Box*, and the *Text Entry Box*.
- When using Text Entry Boxes, we can provide more than one good answer in the Correct Entries box.
- Each of these objects implements the *Branching* concept.
- Failure Captions, Hint Captions, and Success Captions can be added to these interactive objects.
- Captivate is not able to simulate drag-and-drop and scrolling actions in a Simulation.

Branching with Click Boxes

We will now use the Click Box object in a completely different situation and have yet another approach of the *Branching* concept.

1. Return to the `Chapter04/drivingInBe.cptx` file. Use the **Filmstrip** to go to slide 5.

This slide asks a question to the student and provides two possible answers. In the next exercise, we will add a Click Box on top of each of the possible answers. If the user clicks on the first answer, slide 7 and 8 should appear with feedback specific to the first answer, then the user should be taken to slide 9 where a second question is asked. If the user clicks on the second answer, slide 6 should be displayed followed by slide 9 where a second question is asked.

2. Use **Insert | Standard Objects | Click Box** or the corresponding icon in the Objects toolbar to add a first Click Box to the slide.
3. In the **Options** accordion, *deselect* the **Success**, **Failure**, and **Hint** captions. The only remaining object is the Click Box itself.
4. Move and resize the Click Box so it covers more or less the first possible answer.
5. In the **Action** accordion, open the **On Success** drop-down list and choose the **Jump to slide** action. In the **Slide** drop down that appears below, choose **Slide 7 mph Feedback**.
6. Leave the **Infinite** option selected.
7. Insert a second Click Box using either the Insert menu or the Object toolbar.

Notice that the properties set for the last inserted Click Box apply by default to the subsequent Click Boxes.

8. Move and resize the second Click Box so it covers the second answer.
9. In the **Action** accordion, set the **On Success** action of the second Click Box to **Jump to slide - 6 kmh feedback**. Leave the **infinite** option selected.
10. In the **Timeline** panel or in the **Timing** accordion, make both Click Boxes **Appear After 0 sec** and **Display For** a **specific time** of **1.5 seconds**. Also, reduce the duration of the slide to **1.5 sec**.
11. Use the **Filmstrip** to go to slide 6.
12. Make sure the **Properties** panel displays the properties of the slide. In the **Action** accordion, change the **On Exit** action to **Jump to slide – 9 Road Side Question**.

13. Go to slide 9 and insert two Click Boxes. Move and resize them so that a Click Box covers each possible answer.
14. In the **Timeline** panel or in the **Timing** accordion, make both Click Boxes **Appear After 0 sec** and **Display For** a **specific time** of **1 seconds**. Also, reduce the duration of the slide to **1 sec**.
15. Select the Click Box that sits on top of the first answer. In the **Action** accordion, set its **On Success** action to **Jump to slide - 10 right Side Feedback**.
16. Select the Click Box that covers the second answer. In the **Action** accordion, set its **On Success** action to **Jump to slide - 11 left side feedback**.
17. Go to slide 10. Make sure the **Properties** panel displays the properties of the slide and set the **On Exit** action to **Jump to Slide - 12**.
18. Use the **Window | Branching View** menu to open the floating **Branching** panel.

The **Branching** panel provides a visual representation of the all the possible itineraries that the student can take in the project. Make sure it looks like the following screenshot. If needed, adjust the Zoom level at the top-right corner of the floating **Branching** panel.

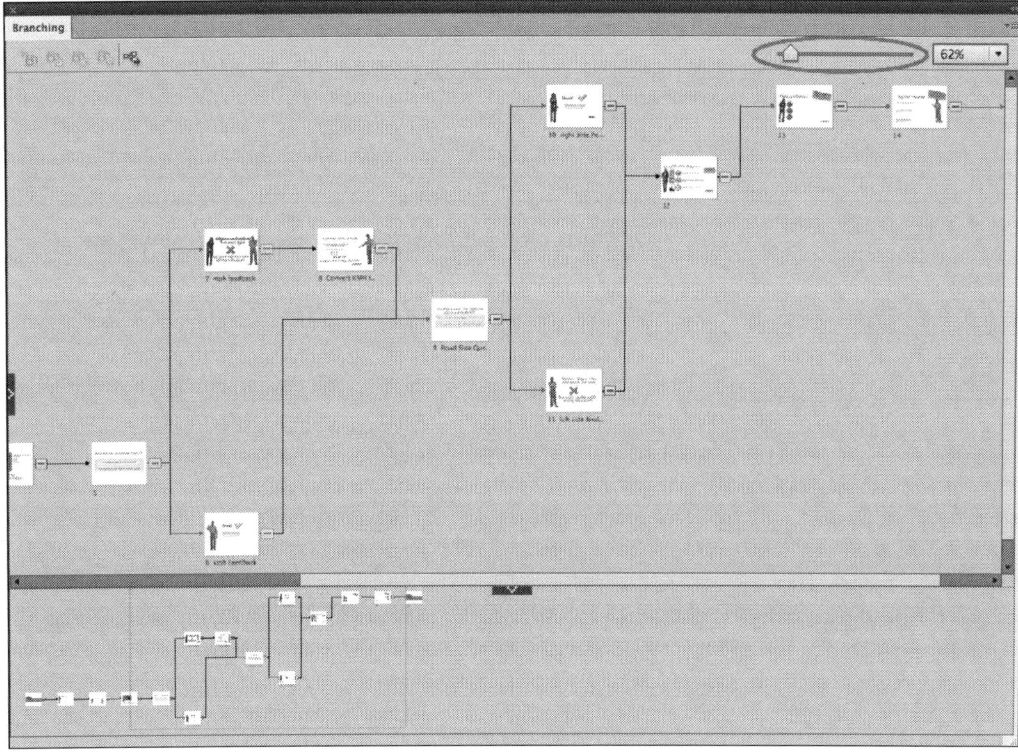

19. When done, close the floating **Branching** panel.
20. Use the preview feature at least two times to test the sequence. In order to test the branching, click on different answers at each preview.

Objects and animations in Video Demo projects

We already discussed the all new Video Demo recording mode and project type in *Chapter 1, Getting Started with Captivate*, and *Chapter 2, Capturing the Slides*. We discovered that Video Demo projects are much different from the standard Demonstrations and Simulations. In fact, they are so different that they use a specific file extension. However, how different are they as far as objects, animations, and interactivity are concerned? This is what we will discover in this section.

Interactivity in Video Demo projects

Let's begin with the easiest and shortest topic.

Remember that a Video Demo project is a big Full Motion Recording and that it can only be published as an `.mp4` video file. To make it short, a Video Demo can only propose a linear video-like experience to the Students.

Consequently, **there is no interactivity in a Video Project**. In other words, the interactive objects (Buttons, Click Boxes, and Text Entry Boxes) as well as the Rollover objects of Captivate are *not* supported in Video Demo projects.

Standard objects in Video Demo projects

However, most of the other standard objects of Captivate are supported in Video Demo projects.

1. Open the `Chapter04/encoderVideo.cpvc` file from your exercises folder.
2. Open the **Insert** menu to have a list of the objects that can be inserted in a Video Demo.

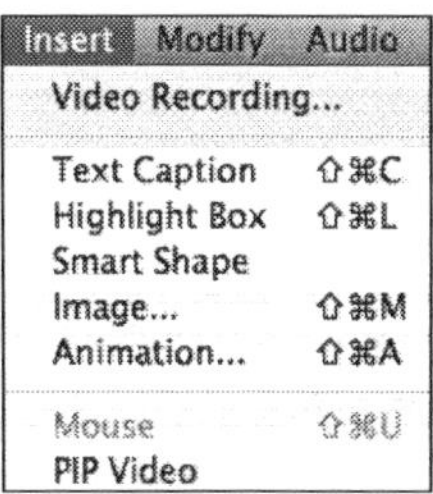

The **Insert** menu of a Video Demo project is much smaller than the **Insert** menu of a standard Captivate 6 project. Take good note of the objects that are supported in a Video Demo. They all work the exact same way as the standard object we studied in the previous two chapters, so these objects have already been added to the project for you.

3. Browse the **Timeline** of the Video Demo to see how these objects have been inserted in this particular project. Don't hesitate to select them and inspect their properties in the **Properties** panel.

Animations in Video Demo projects

When it comes to animations, there are two interesting features that are specific to Video Demo projects.

Using Pan and Zoom

The first one of these features is called **Pan and Zoom**. It allows us to zoom to a specific area of the video and to move the camera during the movie. In the next exercise, we will add two Pan and Zoom animations into this particular project.

1. In the **Timeline** panel, move the playhead more or less to the 02:25 mark.
2. Use the **Window | Pan & Zoom** menu item to turn the **Pan & Zoom** panel on.
3. In the **Pan & Zoom** panel, click on the **Add Pan & Zoom** button.

The **Pan & Zoom** panel updates and shows the available **Pan & Zoom** controls along with a thumbnail image of our video in the topmost area of the panel. This thumbnail image is surrounded by a blue bounding box with eight handles.

4. Resize and move the blue bounding box so it covers only the **Video** tab part of the thumbnail (1).
5. Increase the **Speed** of the **Pan & Zoom** animation to 1 sec (2).

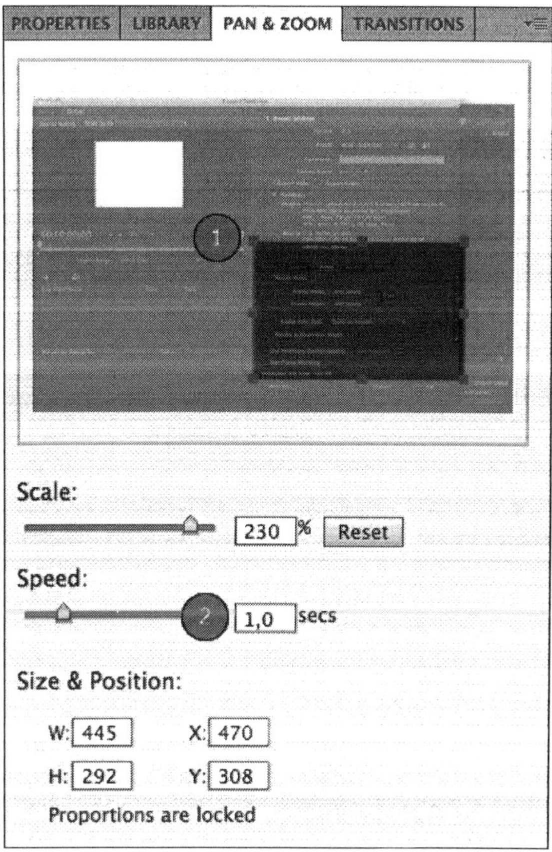

After this procedure, notice that a **Pan & Zoom** icon appears in the **Timeline** panel. Click on this icon to load the properties of this **Pan & Zoom** animation in the **Pan & Zoom** panel should you modify or delete this **Pan & Zoom** animation later on.

We will now move our playhead ahead on the **Timeline** and add a corresponding *Zoom Out* animation to our Video Demo project.

6. In the **Timeline** panel, move the playhead more or less to the 2:50 mark.
7. In the **Pan & Zoom** panel, click on the **Zoom Out** button to restore the view.

This last action adds a second **Pan & Zoom** animation in the project as indicated by the second **Pan & Zoom** icon in the **Timeline** at the 2:50 mark.

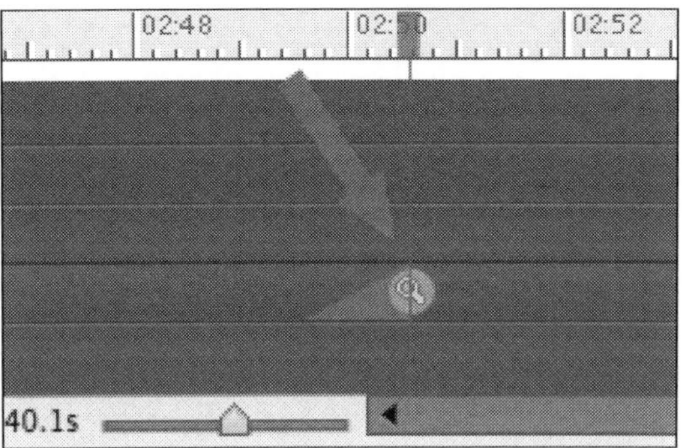

8. In the **Pan & Zoom** panel, increase the **Speed** of this animation to 1 second.

Adding Transitions in Video Demos

Another way of adding some kind of animations to a Video Demo project is by adding transitions. A **Transition** defines how the Video moves from one video clip to the next.

In our case, we only have a single big video clip in our project, so it is not possible to add transitions to our project at the moment. To make it possible, we first have to *split* our video into smaller sequences. We will then be able to add transitions between these sequences. Let's check it out!

1. In the **Timeline**, move the playhead to the 00:25 mark, where the front title of the video finishes (1).
2. At the bottom of the **Timeline** panel, click on the **Split** button (2).

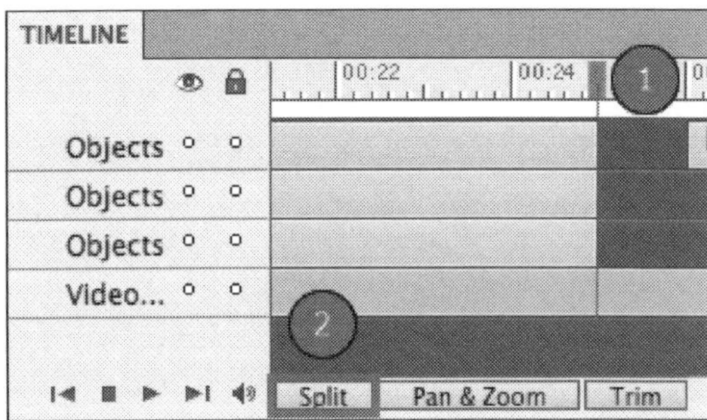

This effectively splits our video file into two separate sequences as indicated by the small diamond that appears in the **Timeline** at the exact location of the split. Since we now have two video clips in our project, it is possible to add a transition between these two sequences.

3. Use the **Window | Transitions** menu item to open the **Transitions** panel.
4. In the **Timeline**, click on the diamond situated between the two sequences that we have split.
5. In the **Transitions** panel, choose any nice Transition.
6. Repeat the same sequence of actions at the end of the project (more or less at the 03:52 mark of the **Timeline**).
7. When done, click on the preview icon and choose to preview the video **Full Screen**.

During the preview, pay particular attention to our newly added **Pan & Zoom** animations and **Transitions**.

8. When the preview is finished, click on the **Edit** button at the bottom-right corner of the screen to return in edit mode.
9. Save and close the file when done.

This last exercise concludes this big chapter on animations and interactive objects.

Summary

We are now deep into the post-production phase of our Captivate movie. Our projects are very different from the original rushes. They have also become fully interactive and animated. To achieve these things, it has been necessary to add different kinds of objects to our slides and to use a lot of tools and features of Captivate.

In this particular chapter, we focused on the three objects that can bring animation to our slides.

- The **Text Animation** that can be created entirely in Captivate
- The **Animation** that let us import external `.swf` or `.gif` files in the project
- The **Zoom Area** that we used to highlight a specific spot on a slide by zooming on it

We have also added some multimedia content to the slides by discussing the insertion of video files in Captivate.

In the second part of the chapter, we focused on the four rollover objects of Captivate.

- The **Rollover Caption** is a Text Caption that appears only *if* and *when* the student passes his/her mouse in a corresponding *rollover area*.
- The **Rollover image** is an image that appears only *if* and *when* the student passes his/her mouse in a corresponding *rollover area*.
- The **Rollover slidelet** is a slide within a slide. It has its own Timeline and appears only *if* and *when* the student passes his/her mouse in a corresponding *rollover area*.
- Finally, a standard Smart Shape can easily be converted to a rollover object to become a **Rollover Smart Shape**.

In the third section of this chapter, we introduced the three Interactive objects of Captivate.

- The **Click Box**: Used to simulate a mouse click
- The **Text Entry Box**: Used to simulate the typing of a piece of text.
- The **Button**: Used to stop the playhead and let the student experience the movie in a personalized fashion

It is these four rollover objects and the three interactive objects that make our projects interactive and fun to use.

In the final section of this chapter, we discussed the insertion of objects and animations in a Video Demo project. We discovered that only the standard objects of Captivate are supported in a Video Demo. We also discovered the **Pan & Zoom** and the **Transitions**. These two features are specific to the Video Demo project type.

While discovering all these objects, we discovered some very useful tools and features of Captivate.

- The **Effects** panel lets us apply single or multiple effects to any objects of Captivate
- The **Align** toolbar holds the tools that help us position, resize, and align the objects inserted on the slide.
- The **Library** panel helps us manage the assets of the file and share these assets with other Captivate projects.

The Captivate developer that we are becoming now has a lot of tools in his/her toolbox!

In the next chapter, we will focus on *sound*. We will add sound effects to objects, background music to the project and narration to the slides. We will see how we can use Captivate to record a new sound clip and how we can import a sound clip created in an external audio application into the project. We will also use the new Text-To-Speech engine to generate the narrations and we will add subtitles.

As you can see, there are still some very cool things to discover in Captivate! (And yes, the AC/DC concert in Amsterdam was absolutely awesome!)

Meet the Community

Dr Pooja Jaisingh

Bio

Pooja Jaisingh has worked for more than 10 years as a Teacher Trainer, eLearning Instructional Designer, and, currently, as an eLearning Evangelist with Adobe Systems. Pooja's core strengths are communication and innovation. In all her roles, she has promoted eLearning as a mode of delivery and has created a host of eLearning courses. In her current role, she conducts numerous seminars and workshops, educating training folks on the features of Adobe Systems' eLearning products. She regularly blogs, initiating creative discussions on multiple opportunities in eLearning. Pooja holds a master's degree in Education and Economics and a doctorate degree in Educational Technology.

Contact info

Blog: `http://blogs.adobe.com/captivate`

Twitter: `@poojajaisingh`

Facebook: `http://www.facebook.com/adobecaptivate`

My personal note

Pooja is one of the three Adobe eLearning evangelists. As such, she is one of the main contributors of the official Adobe Captivate blog and of the Captivate page on Facebook. Recently, she wrote a very nice series of blog posts in which she shares her experience in creating scenario-based trainings using Captivate. These posts are a must-read if you want to know more about eLearning and instructional design.

`http://blogs.adobe.com/captivate/2012/03/my-experience-with-creating-a-scenario-based-course-part-1.html`

5
Working with Audio

In this chapter, the post-production phase of our projects will continue with the addition of audio files. In Captivate, we can add sound at three different levels:

- At **object level**: The sound associated with an object plays when the object appears on the screen. This is a great place to add small *sound effects* (whoosh, clings, bangs, tones, and so on) to the project.
- At **slide level**: The audio clip plays in sync with the slide. Most of the time, this option is used to add *voice-over narration*.
- At **project level**: The audio clip is used to add *background music* to the entire project.

In this chapter, we will review these three options one by one. The one that we will focus most of our attention on is the *slide level* audio. Slide level audio can either be recorded (with Captivate or with an external audio application) or generated by the *Text-to-Speech* engine of Captivate. *Closed Captioning* can also be added to the slide level audio.

In this chapter, we will:

- Add *sound effects* to some of the objects of Captivate
- Record *narration* to the slides
- *Import* external sound files in Captivate
- *Edit* a sound clip in Captivate
- Generate narration with the *Text-to-Speech* engine
- Use the **Slide Notes** panel to convert Slide Notes to Closed Captions and Text-to-Speech
- Synchronize the Closed Captions with the corresponding sound clip
- Add *background music* to the project

Preparing our work

For the exercises of this chapter, we will need to reset the Captivate interface and open two files using the following steps:

1. Open Captivate. Make sure the **Classic** workspace is applied.
2. Use the **Window** | **Workspace** | **Reset 'Classic'** to put the workspace back to default.
3. Open the `Chapter05/encoderDemo_800.cptx` file situated in your exercises folder.
4. Also, open the `Chapter05/drivingInBe.cptx` file.

In addition to these two files, one of the exercises requires a microphone. A simple microphone like those found in any computer store is more than enough. If you have a built-in microphone in your computer, you're ready to go! If you do not have a microphone, don't worry, just read through the *Recording narration with Captivate* section mentioned later. It has been designed to be optional, so that the absence of a microphone will not compromise your progress.

Adding audio to objects

Sound can be added on each and every object of Captivate. The audio clip associated with an object plays when the object it belongs to appears on the stage. Even though nothing prevents us from adding narration or music at the object level, most of the time, the object level audio is used to add *sound effects* to the movie.

In the next exercise, we will add a sound effect to the Adobe Media Encoder logo in the Encoder Demonstration project using the following steps:

1. Go to slide 3 of the `encoderDemo_800.cptx` file.
2. Select the Adobe Media Encoder logo to make it the active object. The **Properties** panel is updated.
3. Open the **Audio** accordion of the **Properties** panel and click on the **Add Audio** button.
4. At the bottom of the **Object Audio** dialog, click on the **Import** button. The **Import Audio** box opens.

By default, the **Import Audio** dialog shows the content of the *Sound* directory of the *Gallery*. Remember that the *Gallery* is a collection of assets that ships with Captivate. In the previous chapter, we used the *Gallery* to import the animated orange arrow.

> If the Import Audio dialog does not show the content of the Sound directory, remember that the Gallery is located in the `C:\Program Files\Adobe\Captivate 6\Gallery` folder (Win) or in the `Applications/Adobe Captivate 6/Gallery` folder (Mac).

5. At the end of the list, choose the `Whoosh 2.mp3` file and click on **Open**.

The sound clip is imported into the project and the sound wave appears in the **Object Audio** dialog.

6. Click on the **Play** button situated in the top left corner of the **Object Audio** dialog to control the imported sound.
7. Click on the **Save** button at the bottom right corner of the box.
8. Click on the **Close** button to close the **Object Audio** box.

In the **Timeline**, a loudspeaker icon is added to the AMELogo indicating that an audio clip is associated with this particular object.

9. Use the Preview icon to preview the **Next 5 slides** and test the sound effect. Close the **Preview** pane when done.
10. In the top right corner of the screen, click on the **Library** tab to open the **Library** panel.

Notice that the **Whoosh 2** sound clip has been added to the **Audio** section of the **Library**. It means that if we want to use the same sound effect elsewhere in the project, there is no need to import the file a second time.

> **Supported audio formats**
>
> Only `.wav` and `.mp3` sound clips can be imported in Captivate. When inserting `.mp3` clip, Captivate automatically converts it in the `.wav` format. So you end up with two versions of the same audio clip: a `.mp3` version and a `.wav` version. Internally, Captivate uses the `.wav` format because this uncompressed format maintains the highest possible sound quality while working with the file. You can safely delete the `.mp3` version from the **Library** panel. When you publish the movie to Flash or HTML5, Captivate converts the `.wav` file back to a `.mp3` file and uses that `.mp3` file in the published movie.

11. Use the **Filmstrip** to go to slide 16.
12. Select the **Zoom Source** to make it the active object.
13. Click on the **Properties** tab to open the **Properties** panel. Confirm that **Zoom Source** is written in the top left corner of the panel.
14. Open the **Audio** accordion and click on the **Add Audio** button.
15. To add an audio file from the **Library**, click on the **Library** button at the bottom of the **Object Audio** dialog.
16. Select the **(Clip) Whoosh 2.wav** sound clip and click on **OK**.
17. Click on the **Save** button to save the changes and then on the **Close** button to close the **Object Audio** dialog.

We can also drag-and-drop the sound clip from the **Library** to the object to do the same thing.

Extra credit

In this extra credit section, we will add a sound effect to the *Rollover Captions* and to the *Rollover Images* of the Driving in Belgium Project. These are the general steps to follow:

- Go to slide 13 of the `drivingInBe.cptx` file.
- Select the Rollover Caption that reads **No parking is allowed at any time!** Make sure you select the **Rollover Caption** and *not* the corresponding Rollover Area.
- Open the **Audio** accordion and click on the **Add Audio** button.
- Click on **Import** and select the **Electronic Beeping.mp3** sound file. **Save** and **Close** the box.
- Open the **Library** tab. The *Electronic Beeping* sound clip should have been added to the **Audio** section of the **Library**.
- Drag-and-drop the Electronic Beeping sound clip from the **Library** to the remaining Rollover Captions of the slide (Make sure you use the Captions and not their corresponding Rollover Areas).
- Go to slide 14 and associate the *same* sound clip to the three Rollover Images of the slide. Make sure you use the Rollover Images and *not* the corresponding Rollover Areas.
- Save the file and use the preview feature to test the added sound clips.

If you take a look at the **Timeline** panel while on slide 13 or 14 of the `drivingInBe.cptx` file, you'll notice that there are *no* objects showing the loudspeaker icon. This is because the objects listed in the **Timeline** are the Rollover Areas and not the corresponding Rollover Captions or Rollover Images we added sound to.

This concludes our overview of object level audio. Let's make a quick summary of what we have learned:

- In Captivate, we can associate a sound clip with any object. The sound plays when the object appears on the screen.
- Usually, object level audio is used to add *sound effects* to the movie.
- Only sound clips in `.wav` or `.mp3` format can be imported into Captivate.
- When inserting a `.mp3` file, Captivate automatically converts it into a `.wav` file and uses that `.wav` file internally. The `.mp3` clip is used in the published movie.
- When an audio file is imported to the movie, it is automatically added to the *Audio* section of the **Library**.
- It is possible to re-use a sound clip stored in the **Library** elsewhere in the project.
- When a sound clip is added to an object, a loudspeaker icon appears in the corresponding layer of the **Timeline**.

Adding background music to the entire project

In this section, we will associate an audio clip to the entire project. Usually, project level audio is used to add background music. To make sure that the music plays during the entire project, we will use a 15 to 30 seconds sound clip and make it loop for the duration of the movie.

In the following exercise, we will add background music to the Encoder Demonstration using the following steps:

1. Return to the `encoderDemo_800.cptx` file.
2. Use the **Audio** | **Import To** | **Background** menu item.

3. Choose the `Loop Acoustic.mp3` file from the `/sound` directory of the Captivate `Gallery` and click on **Open**.
4. The **Background Audio** dialog box opens.

The **Background Audio** dialog informs us that the `loop Acoustic.mp3` sound clip lasts for 16 seconds, as shown (by the arrow) in the following screenshot:

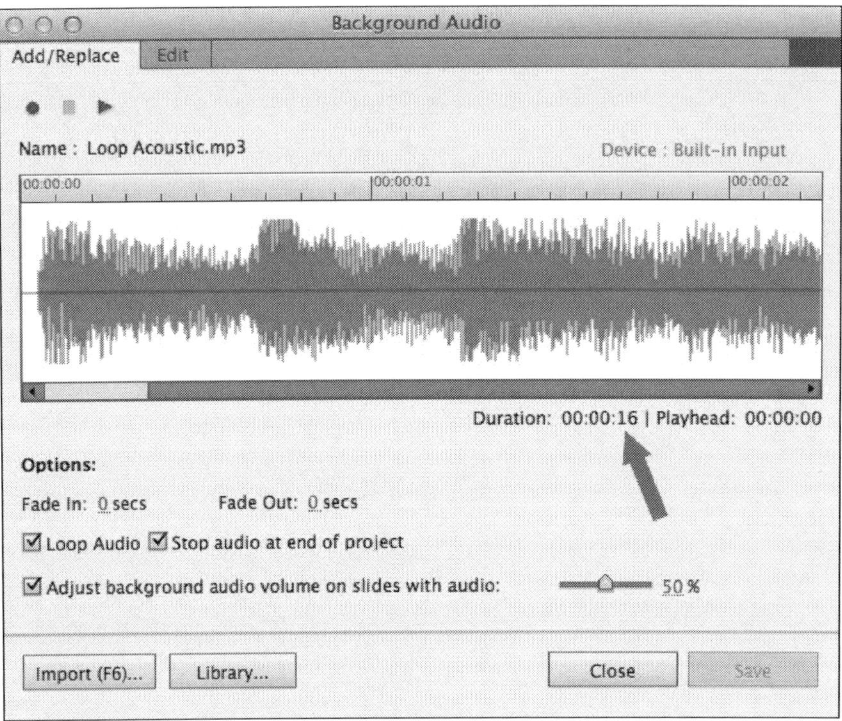

Some interesting options are situated in the lower part of the **Background Audio** dialog. They are as follows:

- When the audio clip is finished, the **Loop Audio** option makes it start over, so the sound clip plays for the entire project.
- The **Stop audio at end of project** option should be selected at all times. If it is not selected, the Background Audio *will keep playing* even *after* the end of the project.
- The **Adjust background audio volume on slides with audio** option will automatically lower the volume of the background music on the slides containing the individual audio files. This option ensures that the slide audio is always *louder* than the Background Audio.

Most of the time, leaving these options to the default values works just fine.

5. Accept the default settings and click on **Close** to close the **Background Audio** dialog.
6. Use the Preview icon to preview the entire **Project**.

During the preview, notice that the Background Audio volume is *not* reduced when the video file plays on slide 2. The volume reduction of the background audio only works when an audio file is added at *slide level*, which does *not* include the audio track of a video file.

If you need to modify the Background Audio or one of its associated options, use the **Audio | Edit | Background** menu item to reopen the **Background Audio** dialog. Use the **Add/Replace** tab of the **Background Audio** dialog to use another sound clip and the **Edit** tab to modify the current sound clip.

When to use Background Audio?

To be honest, I have never used Background Audio in a Captivate project! I find it annoying and distracting. It drives the student away from what I want them to focus on. That being said, there are probably some use cases for which Background Audio would be useful. If you run into one of these use cases, don't hesitate to use the feature. There is only one thing to keep in mind: *you are teaching*, so the background music you use, as well as all the other features of your Captivate project, *should serve the student's learning*.

We will now remove the Background Audio we have added to the project.

7. Use the **Audio | Remove | Background** to remove the project level audio.
8. Confirm you want to remove the audio clip.

Before moving on to the next section, this is a quick list of what we have learned about Background Audio:

- Audio can be added at the project level. Most of the time, this feature is used to add background music to the project.
- Use the **Audio** menu to *add*, *edit*, and *delete* the Background Audio.
- To make sure the background music plays for the entire duration of the movie, use a short sample of music and make it loop.
- Captivate has an option to lower the volume of the Background Audio when a slide with an associated sound clip plays.
- Use Background Audio with care! It should not distract your students!

Adding audio to the slides

Adding audio to the slides is, by far, the most interesting place to use audio in Captivate. Most of the time, slide level audio is used to add *voice-over narration*.

Narration can be added directly during the filming, but most of the time, it is recorded later in the process and carefully synchronized with the rest of the slides content. If you have an external audio application available, it is best to record the voice-over narration using that external application, but Captivate can do the job if needed.

Adobe Audition

Adobe Audition is the audio application from Adobe. It is bundled in the eLearning Suite 6 and in the Creative Suite CS6 Production Premium. It is also available on the Creative Cloud. Adobe Audition (formerly Cool Edit) is an awesome and easy to use audio application. If Audition is available on your computer, use it to record and edit your audio clips instead of using Captivate. If you have the eLearning Suite 6, you can invoke Adobe Audition directly from within Captivate and edit the audio clips. See `http://blogs.adobe.com/captivate/2011/06/audition-roundtripping-with-adobe-captivate-5-5.html` for more information.

Recording narration with Captivate

In this section, we will use Captivate to record an audio clip. To achieve this, our first concern will be to carry the sound data from the microphone to Captivate by using the audio interface of the computer.

The following exercise requires a microphone. If you do not have a microphone available, just read through the steps. You'll have a chance to catch up on a subsequent exercise.

Setting up the sound system

The exact procedure depends on your audio equipment and on your operating system, but basically, setting up the sound system can be divided into these three phases.

- Plug the microphone in the audio input port of your computer (usually it is the red plug of your sound card).

- Check out the audio options of your operating system:
    - [Mac OS]: In **System Preferences**, use the **Input** tab of the **Sound** section
    - [Windows 7]: Use the **Manage Audio Devices** link in the Sound section of the **Hardware and Sound** section of the **Control Panel**, as shown in the following screenshot

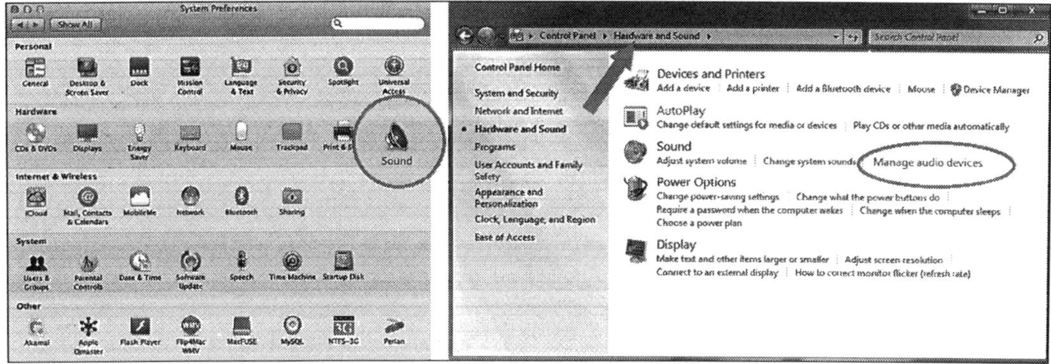

- Check out the audio options of Captivate.

Once the audio options of the operating system are properly set up, we can move on to Captivate. Perform the following steps to make settings for the audio in Captivate:

1. Return to the `encoderDemo_800.cptx` file.
2. Use the **Audio** | **Settings** menu item to open the **Audio Settings** dialog box.
3. Open the **Audio Devices** drop-down list and select the audio device on which the microphone is attached.

If your computer has multiple audio input devices (like a *microphone-in* and a *line-in*), this drop-down list instructs Captivate on which device it has to listen to. This is the single most important part of the procedure. If the wrong device is selected, the audio data will *never* reach Captivate.

For the **Bitrate** options, the default should be OK. If you decide that the default audio quality is not good enough, you can test a new recording with a higher **Bitrate**. Be aware that the higher the **Bitrate**, the bigger the file. When choosing the **Bitrate**, you have to find the most appropriate balance between the quality of the sound and the weight of the resulting file.

4. Leave the **Bitrate** option at its default and click on the **Calibrate Input** button.

Calibrating the input is finding the right *sensitivity* for the microphone. If it is set too high, you'll have a saturated sound with lots of clipping, but if it is set too low, the recorded narration will be lost in the background noise.

To help us out, Captivate provides an auto-calibrating feature. All we need to do is to say a few words in the microphone to let Captivate evaluate the input sensitivity and find the right value.

5. In the **Calibrate Audio Input** dialog box, click on the **Auto Calibrate** button.
6. Speak normally in your microphone until you have a message saying that the microphone has been calibrated. (If you don't know what to say, just tell a joke! Don't worry it is not recorded!)
7. Click on the **OK** button to validate the sensitivity value and to close the **Calibrate Audio Input** dialog.
8. Close the **Audio Settings** dialog box as well.

Recording the narration

Now that the sound system is properly set up, we can move on to the actual recording of the voice-over narration using the following steps:

1. Still in the `encoderDemo_800.cptx` file, use the **Filmstrip** to go to slide 3.
2. Make sure the **Properties** panel displays the properties of the **Slide**. In the **Audio** accordion, click on the **Add Audio** button.
3. In the **Slide Audio** dialog, select the **SWF Preview** option. It will help us sync the narration with the rest of the slide during the recording.

The next step of the exercise is the actual recording of the sound clip! Before we press the *Record* button, it is necessary to take some time to rehearse the narration.

The following text is what we want to record:

Want to insert a video in Captivate? Great! Video will make your eLearning content much more engaging and fun! But before you can import a video file in Captivate, you must convert it into a video format that the Flash player can read! The Adobe Media Encoder is an application that has been designed to convert virtually any video file to the .flv, .f4v, or .mp4 video file format for playback in the Flash player. The good news is, the Adobe Media Encoder is part of your Captivate or eLearning Suite bundle at no extra cost! Want to know how it works? Just click on the Continue button.

Read that sentence aloud a few times. When you feel ready, we'll move on to our first audio take!

4. Click on the red **Record Audio** button at the top left corner of the **Slide Audio** dialog. After a short countdown, read the above sentence aloud at a normal speed and with a normal voice.
5. When the recording is complete, click on the **Stop** button.
6. Control the quality of your take by clicking on the **Play** button. If you are not satisfied, start over with another take.
7. When you are satisfied with the result, click on the **Save** button and **Close** the **Slide Audio** dialog.

If the recorded sound clip is longer than the slide, you will be prompted to extend the duration of the slide to the length of the sound clip. Click on **Yes** to finalize the integration of the new sound clip into the slide, as shown in the following screenshot:

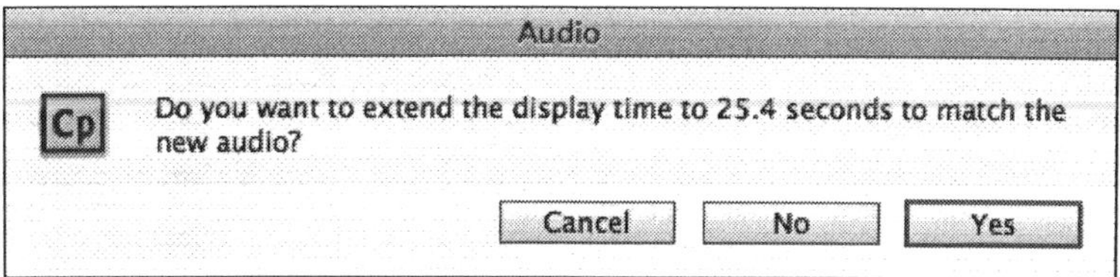

In the **Timeline** panel, the new sound clip is displayed as an additional layer situated *below* the slide. If needed, we can *move* the sound clip on the **Timeline** to synchronize it better with the rest of the slide, but we cannot use the **Timeline** to change the *duration* of the sound clip.

To quickly test the slide, use the **Play** button situated at the bottom left corner of the **Timeline** panel. This button plays only the current slide *without* opening the **Preview** pane. This preview option does *not* let us test every single feature of the slide, but it is a quick and easy way to do some basic testing and synchronization.

Recording narration is not an easy task, especially if you are not used to speaking into a microphone. Here are some basic tips and tricks to help you out:

- Write down the text that needs to be recorded and rehearse it a few times before the recording.
- Keep in mind that you don't have to make it right the first time. Try as many times as needed.
- Speak slowly, especially if you have an international audience where all the students do not speak the same language.

- Have a glass of water ready to avoid the *dry mouth* effect. Remember that lots of student will hear the narration through a headset.
- Position the microphone within 4 to 6 inches of your mouth and slightly to the side to avoid pops and hisses on the letters S and P.
- If you have an external audio application available, use it to record your sound clips and import them in Captivate when they are ready.

With these simple tips and tricks and a basic computer microphone, you should be able to record some pretty good audio clips right away!

Whose voice should be recorded?

If you have the money, it is best to hire a narrator, but most of the time you will be recording your own voice or the voice of a colleague or a friend. When choosing the person that will read the lines, *always* have your students in mind. For my very first big Captivate project, I had to develop a course in English, but most of the students were *not* native English speakers. We met with the customer and agreed to record the voice of a non-native English speaker. (It was an employee from the next-door office who was into theater). The recorded English was not perfect, the accent was a bit strange, but it was not important because *it was adapted to the audience.*

Importing an external sound clip

When using an external audio application, the audio clips will be entirely produced in the external application and imported into Captivate when finished.

In the following exercise, we will import sound clips produced in Adobe Audition into the Captivate project using the following steps:

1. Return to the `encoderDemo_800.cptx` file and use the **Filmstrip** to go to slide 3. Make sure the **Properties** panel displays the properties of the slide.
2. [Optional] If you have made the previous exercise, remove the recorded sound clip by clicking on the **Remove Audio** button situated in the **Audio** accordion.
3. In the **Audio** accordion, click on the **Add Audio** button. The **Slide Audio** dialog box opens.
4. Click on the **Import** button situated in the bottom left corner of the box.
5. Browse your computer to select the `audio/slide03.mp3` file situated in your exercises folder.

6. Click on **Open**. The selected file is imported into the project.
7. Click on the **Play** button to test the imported audio.

Some extra work is needed to make this sound clip final. We will solve this issue by editing the sound clip in the next section.

8. Save the changes by clicking on the **Save** button situated in the bottom right corner of the **Slide Audio** dialog.
9. It is possible that the duration of the slide has to be increased to match the duration of the new audio file. Click on **Yes** if prompted to do so.
10. Close the **Slide Audio** dialog box.
11. Use the very same procedure to import the remaining sound clips of the `audio/` folder to the corresponding slides. Refer to the following table for detailed instructions:
12. If the imported audio file is longer than the duration of the slide it is imported to, always use the **Show the slide for the same amount of time as the length of the audio file** option, as shown in the following screenshot:

Slide #	Audio clip	Slide #	Audio clip
4	`audio/slide04.mp3`	10	`audio/slide10.mp3`
5	`audio/slide05.mp3`	11	`audio/slide11.mp3`
6	`audio/slide06.mp3`	17	`audio/slide17.mp3`
7	`audio/slide07.mp3`	21	`audio/slide21.mp3`
8	`audio/slide08.mp3`		

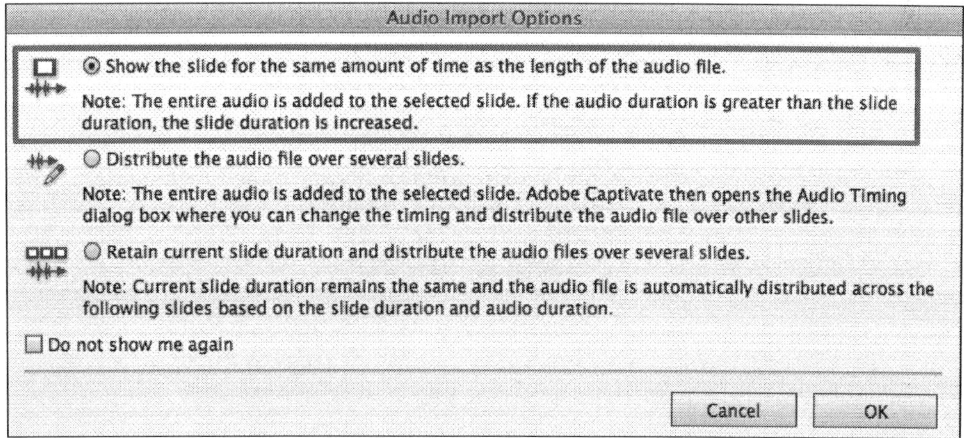

Yes, it is *that* easy to import external sound clips into Captivate! If you take a look at **Filmstrip**, you'll notice a loudspeaker icon next to the slides you have added audio to, as shown in the following screenshot:

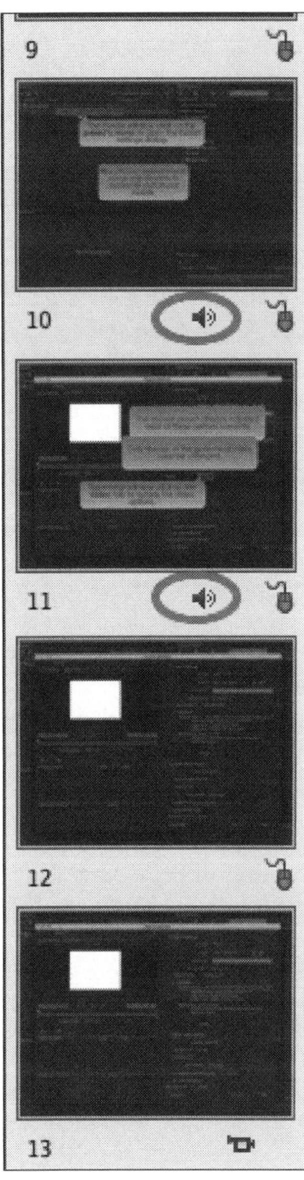

Editing a sound clip in Captivate

Even though Captivate is *not* an audio editing application, it does have some *basic* audio editing capabilities.

In the following exercise, we will explore the audio editing features of Captivate by fine-tuning the sound clip we have imported on slide 3 using the following steps:

1. If needed, return to the `encoderDemo_800.cptx` file and use **Filmstrip** to go to slide 3.
2. Make sure the **Properties** panel shows the properties of the slide.
3. Click on the **Edit Audio** button situated in the **Audio** accordion. Alternatively, you can also use the **Audio | Edit | Slide** menu to do the same thing.
4. The **Slide Audio** dialog box opens on the **Edit** tab (1), as shown in the following screenshot:

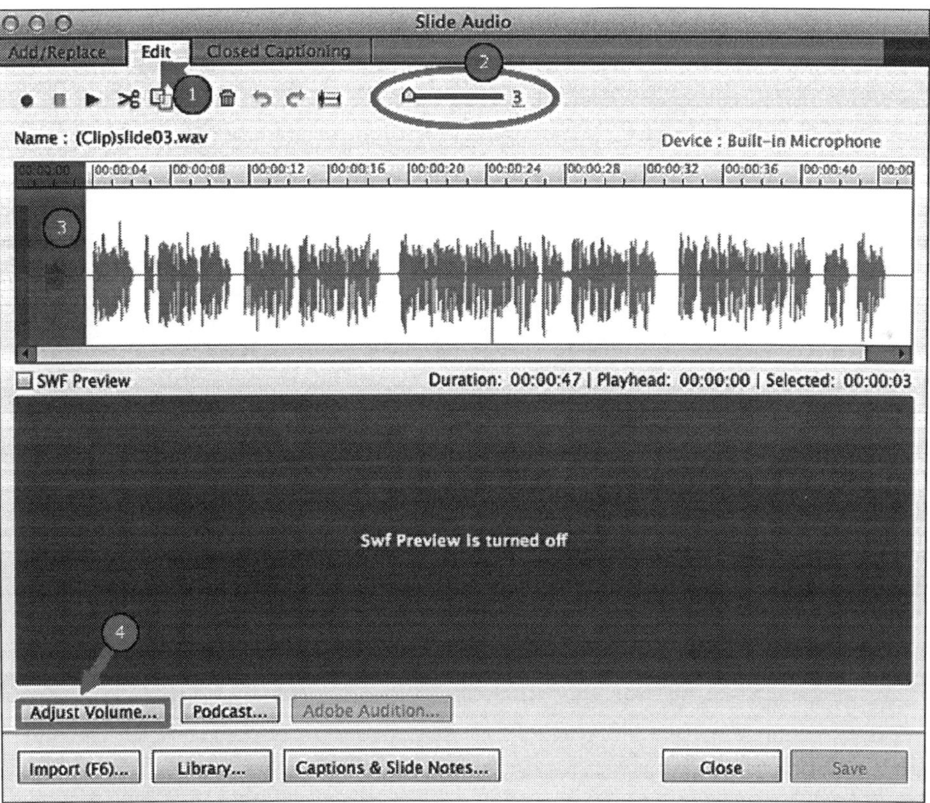

5. Use the Zoom slider (2) to reduce the Zoom level so that the entire sound clip is visible.
6. Click on the Play button and listen to the audio clip.

During the first few seconds of this audio clip, some microphone sensitivity checks are performed. They probably have been recorded by mistake and must be removed. While listening to the audio clip, keep an eye on the red vertical Playhead and spot the beginning of the actual narration (the **third** time the narrator says *Want to insert...*).

7. Use your mouse to select from the spotted location to the beginning of the audio clip (shown as number 3 in the previous screenshot).
8. Click on the Trash Can (**Delete**) icon or hit the *Delete* key of your keyboard.
9. Click the **Play** button to test the new version of the sound clip.

The beginning of the sound clip should be okay, but we still have a small problem at the *end* of the clip.

There are a few seconds of silence at the very end of the sound clip that needs to be taken out as well.

10. Select the silence at the end of the clip and delete it.
11. Click on the **Play** button to test the new version of the clip.

Keep in mind that in an audio clip, *the silence takes up as much space as the sound itself*. Deleting the silence at the beginning and at the end of a sound clip is an operation that should be done systematically for every sound clip, as it will help us keep the size of the resulting movie as low as possible.

We will now use the **Adjust Volume** feature to further fine-tune the audio clip of slide 3.

12. Click on the **Adjust Volume** icon situated in the bottom left corner of the **Slide Audio** dialog (4), as shown in the previous screenshot.
13. Take some time to review the options of the **Adjust Volume** box that pops up, but do not change any of them at this time.
14. In the **Audio Processing** section of the **Adjust Volume** dialog box, select the **Normalize** option and click on the **OK** button.

Normalizing an audio clip is finding the best audio level for that particular sound clip. It is another operation that should be done on each and every audio clip of the project.

15. Click on the **Save** icon to save the changes made to the audio clip and **Close** the **Slide Audio** dialog.

The last step of this exercise is to adjust the **Timeline** panel to synchronize the objects of the slide with the updated sound clip:

16. Use the **Timeline** panel or the **Timing** accordion to synchronize the objects of the slide with the sound clip.
    - The title (Video in Captivate?) should **Appear After: 0 sec**.
    - Make the other Text Caption appear when relevant as compared to the narration.
    - The AMELogo should appear at the same time as the **The Adobe Media Encoder converts...** Text Caption.
    - All the objects of the slide should stay visible for the **rest of slide**.
17. Insert a new Button and position it in the lower-right area of the slide.
    - Change the **Caption** of the Button to `Continue`.
    - Make it appear when the narration starts saying... *click on the Continue button....*
    - Make it pause the Playhead when the audio clip is finished.
    - Make it stay visible for the **rest of the slide**.
    - Make sure its action is set to **Go to the next slide**.
18. The duration of the slide should be around **42** seconds.
19. Use the preview **Next 5 slides** feature to test the sequence in the **Preview** pane.
20. Close the **Preview** pane and save the file when done.

Extra credit

Browse the remaining audio-enabled slides of the project and adjust the timing of the objects they contain so that they appear in sync with the narration.

Refer to the `Chapter05/final/encoderDemo_800.cptx` file for examples and inspiration.

This exercise concludes the first part of our exploration of audio added at the slide level. Before we move on here is a quick summary of what we have learned:

- Most of the time, the audio added at slide level is used to add voice-over narration to the project.
- To insert a sound clip, we can either record it entirely from within Captivate or import it from our hard disk.

- We must check the audio options of our operating system before recording the first sound clip.
- Captivate has an auto calibrating feature to help us find the right sensitivity for the microphone.
- When an audio clip is associated with a slide, the **Timeline** panel shows it as an extra layer situated *below* the slide.
- Captivate provides some basic sound editing capabilities.
- The silence present at the beginning and at the end of an audio clip takes up as much disk space as the actual sound. It should be removed on every single sound clip used in Captivate.
- Normalizing an audio file is finding the right volume for that particular file. This operation should be done on every sound clip used in the project. (Note that it can be done in an external audio application *before* the clip is inserted in Captivate).
- When inserting an audio clip onto a slide, the **Timeline** of that slide must be reorganized in order to make the audio and the objects of the slide play in sync.
- Use the Play button of the **Timeline** to quickly and easily test the synchronization between the audio and the objects of the slide.

Using Text-to-Speech to generate narration

Text-to-Speech was a new feature of Captivate 4. The idea is to *type* the voice-over narration in the **Slide Notes** panel and have Captivate convert it to a sound clip. To convert typed text to sound clips, Captivate uses some preinstalled voices called **Speech Agents**.

Installing the Captivate Speech Agents

Due to their very large size, Adobe decided to make the installation of the Text-to-Speech Agents optional. Captivate 6 ships with one voice package. This package installs five Speech Agents.

If you have access to the original Captivate installation DVD, the additional voices are located in the `Add-ons` folder of the DVD.

If you do not have an installation DVD available, you can download the Speech Agents from the Adobe website:

Windows 32 bits :http://www.adobe.com/go/captivate6_voices_installer

Windows 64 bits :http://www.adobe.com/go/captivate_voices_installer_win64

Mac :http://www.adobe.com/go/captivate_voices_installer_mac

It is required to install the Text-to-Speech Agents to do the exercises that will follow from the next section.

As of Captivate 5, additional third-party Speech Agents can be added to the system. See this blog post from the official Captivate blog for more info. http://blogs.adobe.com/captivate/2010/07/text_to_speech_in_adobe_captiv.html.

Working with the Slide Notes panel

The basic idea of Text-to-Speech is to transform a piece of typed text into a sound clip. In Captivate, we use the **Slide Notes** panel to type the text that we want to convert to speech.

By default, the **Slide Notes** panel is *not* part of the **Classic** workspace, so our first task will be to turn it on using the following steps:

1. Go to the Chapter05/drivingInBe.cptx file. Use **Filmstrip** to go to slide 2.
2. Use the **Window | Slide Notes** menu item to turn the **Slide Notes** panel on.

By default, the **Slide Notes** panel appears at the bottom of the screen, next to the **Timeline** panel.

At the far right-hand side of the panel, the **+** icon is used to create a new Slide Note, as shown in the following screenshot:

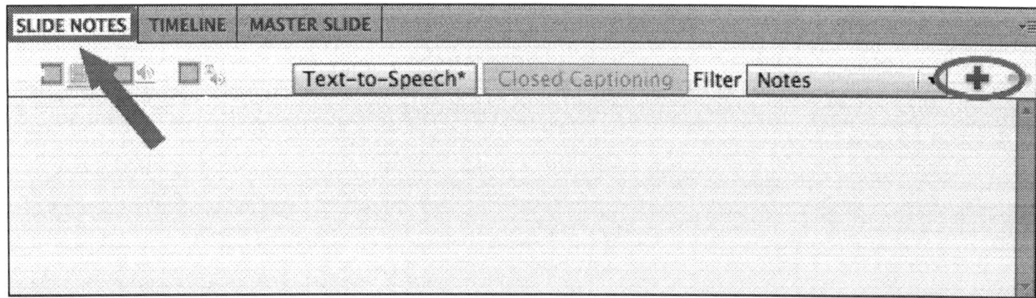

3. Click on the **+** icon to add a new Slide Note.

4. Type `So, you've decided to take a trip to Belgium!` in the new Slide Note.
5. Click on the + icon to add a second Slide Note after the first one.

This part is a bit tricky! Do *not* hit the *Enter* key when you have typed the first Slide Note. The *Enter* key *does not validate* the new Slide Note, but *creates a new paragraph* in the Slide Note. Also, before adding a second Slide Note, make sure that your cursor is still *within the first one*, otherwise, the second Slide Note appears *before* the first one. If the second Note(s) appears before the first, you can use the – icon to delete the topmost Note or you can drag-and-drop the Notes to reorder them.

6. Type `With the tricks and tips provided in this video, you'll soon be on your way to discover Belgium's treasure on a safely fashion.` in the second note.
7. Add a third note to the **Slide Notes** panel and type `Type your name in the box to get started!` in it.
8. If needed, drag-and-drop the Notes within the **Slide Notes** panel to reorder them.

When typing the text in the **Slide Notes** panel, keep in mind that a machine will soon convert it to a sound clip. This machine will not work right if the spelling is not perfect, so double-check (and even *triple-check*) your spelling. If the spelling is wrong, you'll get unexpected (and sometimes hilarious) results.

9. Use the **Filmstrip** to browse the remaining slides of the project. Notice that Slide Notes have already been added where needed.

Now that the Slide Notes have been correctly typed and carefully ordered, we can safely convert them to audio using the Text-to-Speech feature of Captivate.

Converting text to speech

Converting the text typed in the Slide Notes panel to speech is not difficult. All we need to do is to choose the Note(s) to be converted, assign a Speech Agent to each note, and generate the audio file. These actions can be performed using the following steps:

1. Still in the `Chapter05/drivingInBe.cptx` file, use the **Filmstrip** to return to slide 2.
2. At the top of the **Slide Notes** panel, click on the **TTS** checkbox to select all three notes, as shown in the following screenshot:

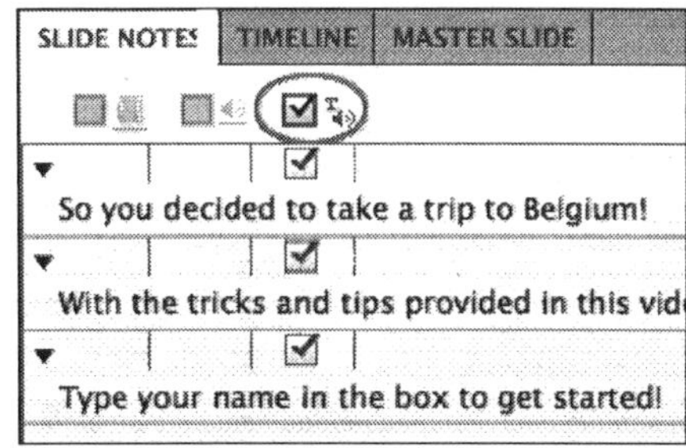

Most of the time, we want to convert every single Slide Note to speech. But, if needed, we can deselect the notes that would not need to be converted to speech.

3. Click on the **Text-to-Speech** button situated at the top of the **Slide Notes** panel. The **Speech Management** box opens.

The **Speech Management** box is where we assign a Speech Agent to the Slide Notes we selected for Text-to-Speech conversion. The number of available Speech Agents depends on the voice packs installed on the system. See the *Installing Captivate Speech Agents* section mentioned earlier for more details. Captivate can also pick up third-party Speech Agents installed on the system.

For this exercise, we will use two Speech Agents: Kate and Paul. These Speech Agents are designed to be used with *English text only* and are installed with the Neo Speech voice pack provided by Captivate.

4. In the **Speech Management** box, select all three Slide Notes (if needed). Open the **Speech Agent** drop-down and choose **Kate**.

For this first experience with Text-to-Speech, we will assign the same Speech Agent to every note.

5. Click on the **Generate Audio** button situated at the bottom left corner of the box. A progress bar appears on the screen while the audio is generated.
6. When the progress bar disappears, click on the **Close** button to close the **Speech Management** dialog.
7. Return to the **Timeline** panel.

Surprise! The **Timeline** panel now shows a sound clip layer under the slide layer.

8. Move the sound clip half a second to the right.
9. Use the Play button of the **Timeline** panel to test the audio clip and the slide timing.

Normally, the timing of the slide should pretty much be fine, but if you want to adjust it, feel free to reorganize the objects on the **Timeline**.

10. Open the **Library** panel. In the **Audio** section, you should see an audio clip named **Text to Audio 1**. (It could be a different number if you did not get it right on the first time when generating the audio clip).
11. Right-click on the **Text to Audio 1** in the **Library** and choose the **Rename** command in the contextual menu.
12. Change the name of the audio clip to `TTS-Slide2` and hit the *Enter* key to validate.

The ability to change the name of an item in the **Library** is yet another feature that helps us better manage the assets of the project.

13. Use the **Filmstrip** to go to slide 4 and open the **Slide Notes** panel.
14. In the **Slide Notes** panel, select all the three slide notes for Text-to-Speech conversion and click on the **Text-to-Speech** button.
15. The **Speech Management** dialog opens.
16. Select the three notes. In the **Speech Agent** drop-down, choose **Paul** and hit the **Generate Audio** button.
17. When the audio generation is complete, close the **Speech Management** dialog and return to the **Timeline** panel.

Again, an audio layer containing the generated sound clip has been added to the slide. Adjust the timing of the objects and of the audio so that everything plays in sync.

Text-to-Speech versus manual voice-over recording

Is Text-to-Speech better than an actual recording? A few years ago, I worked on a project where some Captivate files were using Text-to-Speech while a real recording was made for other files. A few weeks later, my customer contacted me to replace the Text-to-Speech voices with an actual recording because the feedback of the students was bad. A real recording takes a lot of time and, consequently, costs a lot more money, but the result is perfect and can be tailored to fit your particular needs. The Text-to-Speech is fast, easy and cheap, but the result sounds like an old Game Boy. The choice is yours.

Using the Speech Management window

To generate the remaining audio files of the project we will use the **Speech Management** window. This feature will speed us up and make our job a little bit easier.

The idea is to mark the Slide Notes for Text-to-Speech conversion through the entire project and generate all the audio clips at once at the end. Perform the following steps for Text-to-Speech conversion throughout the project:

1. Browse the slides of the project one by one. In the **Slide Notes** panel, confirm that every Slide Notes is marked for Text-to-Speech conversion.
2. When the Slide Notes of the entire project are marked, use the **Audio | Speech Management** menu item to open the **Speech Management** window.

The window that has just opened is very similar to the one we used to generate the audio files of slide 2 and slide 4, except that this window shows the Slide Notes of the *entire project* rather than those of the active slide.

3. In the **Speech Management** window, select the Slide Notes of slide 2 and slide 4.
4. Click on the **-** icon to remove the selected notes.

This action does not delete the Slide Notes, it only clears the checkbox that marks the notes for Text-to-Speech conversion. We have to do it because the audio for slide 2 and slide 4 has already been generated.

5. Assign a **Speech Agent** to each note. It is possible to assign a different Speech Agent to the different notes of the same slide. Use only **Kate** and **Paul** as those two particular agents are designed to convert English text.

If possible, try to match the Character's images, which we inserted in *Chapter 3, Working with Standard Objects*. Use Paul for slides where the male Character is required and Kate for slides when the female Character is required.

6. When done, click on the **Generate Audio** button situated in the bottom left corner of the Speech Management dialog.

Captivate generates all the required audio files, assigns them to the correct slide and adds them to the Library. When it is done, close the **Speech Management** window.

7. Review every slide of the project and make the necessary adjustments in the **Timeline** panel.
8. When done, save the file and use the Preview icon to preview the entire **Project** in the **Preview** pane.

This exercise concludes our study of the Text-to-Speech feature of Captivate. Here follows a quick summary of what we have learned:

- The basic idea of Text-to-Speech is to convert a piece of text into an audio clip.
- To do it, Captivate uses Speech Agents.
- A pack of five Speech Agents can be installed from the Captivate DVD or can be downloaded from the Adobe website.
- Each Speech Agent can be used with a specific language. The Speech Agents provided by Captivate are designed for US English.
- The **Slide Notes** panel is used to type the text to be converted to speech.
- We can choose to convert every Slide Note to speech or just some of them.
- A different Speech Agent can be assigned to the different notes of the same slide.
- The generated sound clips appear in the **Audio** section of the **Library** where their properties can be modified.
- The **Speech Management** window provides a quick and easy way to convert all the Slide Notes of the project to speech at once.

Adding Closed Captions to the slides

Closed Captions make our eLearning content more accessible and more interesting for the learners. There are many situations where the Closed Captions are useful:

- They make our Captivate projects accessible for the hearing impaired students.
- They make the project easier to understand for the foreign students.
- They are useful for the learners who have to take the online course in an office and don't want to bother their colleagues with the voice-over narrations.

For the previous reasons (plus the ones *not* listed here), it is a good idea to use Closed Captions *each time* we add voice-over narration to a slide.

In Captivate, Closed Captions are always associated with a slide level audio clip or with a **Multi-Slide Synchronized Video** inserted with the **Video | Insert Video** feature.

As for the Text-to-Speech narration, the text of the Closed Captions is found in the **Slide Notes** Panel.

In the following exercise, we will add Closed Captions to the Encoder Demonstration using the following steps:

1. Return to the `Chapter05/EncoderDemo_800.cptx` file. Use the **Filmstrip** to go to slide 3.
2. At the bottom of the screen, click on the **Slide Notes** tab to open the **Slide Notes** panel.

Slide 3 is the first slide of the movie we added narration to. There are six notes in the Slide Notes panel that reflect exactly what is said in the audio file associated with the slide.

3. At the top of the **Slide Notes** panel, click on the **Audio CC** checkbox situated right next to the Text-to-Speech checkbox.

This action selects all the Slide Notes for Closed Captioning. Note that the **Audio CC** checkbox is available only if an audio file is associated with the slide.

4. In the top right corner of the **Slide Notes** panel, click on the **Closed Captioning** button.

The **Slide Audio** box opens again, but this time, it shows the **Closed Captioning** tab (1), as shown in the following screenshot:

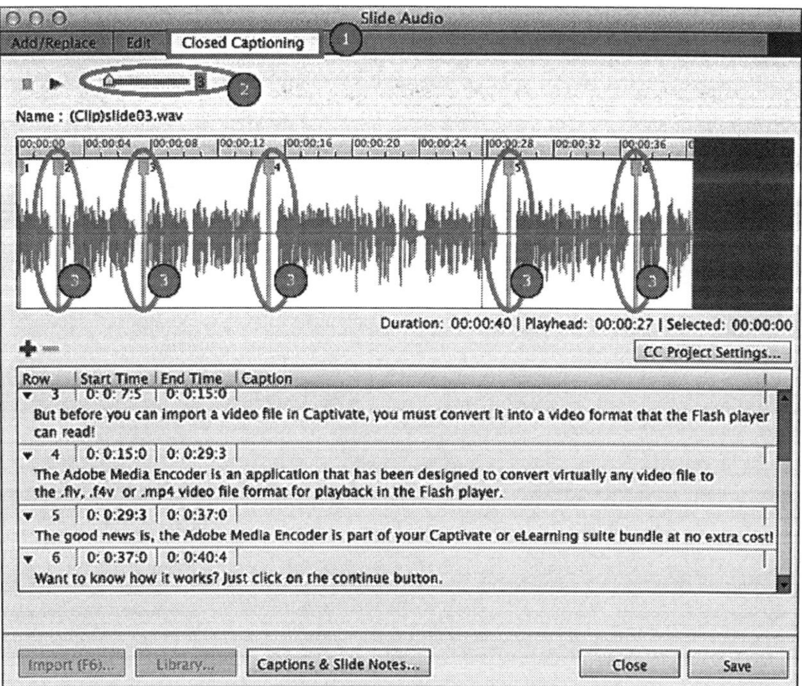

5. Use the Zoom slider (2) (as shown in the previous screenshot) to reduce the Zoom level so you can see the entire sound clip.

Each of the vertical bars (3) represent one of the **Slide Notes** we marked for Closed Captioning.

6. Click on the Play button. While the audio is playing, note the current position of the yellow vertical bars as compared to the audio file.
7. If needed, adjust the position of the vertical bars and test again until all the Closed Captions are in sync with the audio.
8. When you are satisfied with the result, click on the **Save** button at the bottom right corner of the **Slide Audio** dialog.
9. Close the **Slide Audio** dialog.
10. Repeat the procedure on each slide that has an associated audio file.

Don't forget to save the file when you are done!

Viewing the Closed Captions

Now that Closed Captions have been added to every slide with associated audio, we will use the Preview icon to test the entire project using the following steps:

1. Use the Preview icon to test the entire **Project**.
2. When the preview reaches the third slide (the first one with Closed Captions) notice that the Closed Captions do *not* appear.

By default, the Closed Captions do *not* appear in the resulting Captivate movie. It is the student that has to turn them on and off while watching the movie.

To turn them on, we need to add a Closed Captioning button on the Playbar that appears at the bottom of the movie while in the **Preview** pane. To add this button, we have to use the **Skin Editor**.

This chapter only shows how to use the Skin Editor to add a Closed Captioning button to the Playbar. We will study the other features of the Skin Editor in the next chapter.

3. Close the **Preview** pane.
4. Use the **Project | Skin Editor** menu to open the floating **Skin Editor** panel.
5. On the left-hand side of the Skin Editor, select the **Closed Captioning** box to add a CC button on the Playbar.

6. Click on the **Settings** button situated right below. The **CC Project Settings** dialog box pops up.

The **CC Project Settings** dialog box lets us fine-tune the formatting of the Closed Captions.

7. Choose the **Century Gothic** font **Family** and a **Font Size** of `14` points.
8. Click on the **OK** button to validate your choices and to close the **CC Projects Settings** dialog.
9. Click on the top left corner of the floating **Skin Editor** panel to close it.

Everything is now ready for us to test the Closed Captions we have added to the project.

10. Use the Preview icon to test the entire **Project** one more time.
11. When the project opens in the **Preview** pane, click on the **CC** button situated at the right-hand side of the Playbar to turn the Closed Captions on.
12. When the preview reaches slide 3, you should see the associated Closed Captions.

There are a few more things that we can do to fine-tune the look of the Text Captions. It will be done in the *Finishing Touches* section of the next chapter.

Closed Captioning a video file

The last thing that we will do in this chapter is to add Closed Captions to the video file we imported on slide 2. Note that you can add Closed Captions to a video file only if it has been imported as a **Multi-Slide Synchronized Video**. Perform the following steps to add Closed Captions to a video:

1. Use the **Filmstrip** to return to slide 2. It is the slide where we imported the video file back in *Chapter 4, Working with Animations and Interactive Objects.*
2. Click on the video to make it the active object. The **Properties** panel is updated.
3. In the **Video** accordion, click on the **Edit Video Timing** button. The **Edit Video Timing** dialog opens.

The **Edit Video Timing** dialog can be used to trim the imported video file. In the previous versions of Captivate, we had to use an external application named the *Adobe Captivate FMR editor* for this purpose. In this exercise, we do *not* want to *edit* the video file. We only want to add Closed Captions to it.

4. Click on the **Closed Captioning** tab situated at the top left corner of the **Edit Video Timing** dialog.
5. Click on the **+** icon to add a new Closed Caption. Type `Hi, I'm Damien. I'll be your guide during this demonstration.`
6. Click on the **+** icon a second time to add a second Closed Caption. Type `To get started, click on the Continue button at the bottom of your slide.`

Notice that two yellow vertical bars appear in the upper area of the **Edit Video Timing** dialog. Watch out! It is possible that these two bars share the same location, giving the false impression that there is only one vertical bar.

7. Move these vertical bars to synchronize the Closed Captions with the video file. This is the exact same procedure as for the slide audio Closed Captions.
8. Click on the Play button in the top left corner of the **Edit Video Timing** box to test the synchronization between the video and the Closed Captions. It will probably be necessary to adjust the position of the vertical bars and to retest the video a few times before you find the right settings.
9. When done, click on **OK** to validate the changes and close the **Edit Video Timing** dialog.
10. Click on the Preview icon and choose to preview the entire **Project**.
11. When the **Preview** pane appears, click on the **CC** icon of the Playbar to turn the Closed Captions on. Confirm that Closed Captions have been added to the video file of slide 2.

Extra credit

Closed captions can be added to the audio files generated by the Text-to-Speech feature using the exact same procedure as for the audio file recoded or imported in Captivate. In this extra credit section, you will add closed Captions to the Driving in Belgium application. As a reminder, these are the basic steps to follow:

- Use the **Filmstrip** to go to a slide that has an associated audio clip. They can be identified easily, thanks to the loudspeaker icon that appears next to the slide's thumbnail.

- In the **Slide Notes** panel, convert every note to Closed Captions using the **Audio CC** checkbox.
- Click on the **Closed Captioning** button to open the **Slide Audio** dialog.
- Move the vertical yellow marks to synchronize the Closed Captions with the audio clip.
- Use the **Play** button to test the good syncing between the audio and the Closed Captions.
- Repeat the procedure on every slide having an associated audio.
- To test the Closed Captions, don't forget to add the **CC** button on the Playbar using the **Skin Editor**.

This exercise concludes our overview of the Closed Captioning system of Captivate. Here is a quick summary of what we have learned:

- Closed Captions are associated either with a slide-level audio clip or with a Multi-Slide synchronized Video.
- The text of Closed Captions associated with a slide-level audio clip is found in the **Slide Notes** Panel.
- The text of Closed Captions associated with a video file is found in the **Closed Captioning** tab of the **Edit Video Timing** dialog box.
- In the resulting movie, the Closed Captions are turned off by default. It is the student who has to turn them on.
- Use the **Skin Editor** to add the **CC** button to the Playbar. The **CC** button is used by the student to turn the Closed Captions on or off.

Summary

In this chapter, we have imported *sound effects* on objects, *voice-over narration* on slides and *background music* on the entire project.

To produce these audio files, Captivate offers the ability to *record* our own clips, but we can also *import* audio clips produced in an external application or *convert* text typed in the **Slide Notes** panel to speech using one of the *Speech Agents* provided by Captivate or already present on the system.

Wherever they are coming from, these audio files make our eLearning content much more interesting, more interactive, and fun to use.

When adding voice-over narration, it is a good idea to add Closed Captions as well. The Closed Captions will greatly enhance the usability and accessibility of the Captivate movie. The same **Slide Notes** used for *Text-to-Speech* can also be used to generate the Closed Captions.

With the addition of audio files in our projects, we slowly reach the end of the post-production phase. Our projects are now completely different from the original rushes we had in our suitcase when entering the post-production studio.

In the next chapter, we will make our projects ready for the final publication by adding some finishing touches. We will ensure that the spelling is right, we will fine-tune the Playbar, add a Table of Contents, and many other things. When the project will be ready, we will then move on to the final phase of the process and make our movies available to the outside world by publishing them in various formats.

Meet the Community

Lieve Weymeis

Bio

Lieve Weymeis is a civil engineer and professional musician. After eight years of research in shell construction stability (several publications), she started her career as a college lecturer in the Construction and Real Estate departments, teaching several technical courses and **Information and Communications Technology** (**ICT**). She is known as a specialist in building site project management, blended learning, and eLearning.

As head of the Construction Department for 10 years, Weymeis introduced new pedagogical methodologies and the use of a Learning Management System. Presently she is researching blended learning, eLearning, and social media. She also develops eLearning courses and offers training in Adobe Photoshop®, InDesign®, Adobe Captivate®, and eLearning Suite software.

As a beta tester for Adobe Captivate, she was invited in 2009 to be a member of its Advisory Board. In 2010, she agreed to serve as a moderator for Adobe Captivate online Help. She is an active member of the Adobe Captivate Community on user forums, Twitter, and LinkedIn. She also writes a popular blog about eLearning Suite.

Contact info

Blog: `http://lilybiri.posterous.com/`

Twitter: `@Lilybiri`

My personal note

Lieve holds a special place in my heart because she and I are both from Belgium! Her blog on Captivate is one of the best around! During the writing of this book, Lieve celebrated her 100,000th visitor on her blog, and I feel that this milestone is totally deserved. Her involvement in the Captivate community is second to none. During your researches on the Internet, you'll see her name associated with an impressive collection of blog posts, forum replies, tutorials and articles. If you are on Twitter, Lieve is definitely someone you want to follow.

To finish this (long) personal note, I would like to take advantage of the fact that these lines will be printed out in a book to officially acknowledge my deepest thanks and my admiration for her work in the Captivate community.

6
Final Changes and Publishing

With the sound recorded, synchronized, and Closed Captioned, our work in the post-production studio is almost over. There are just a couple of things left to be done before the movie can be published.

Most of these *Final Changes* are options and features that we will set for the entire movie. It includes checking the spelling, entering the project metadata, choosing how the project starts and ends, and so on. The most important of these Final Changes is probably the *Skin Editor*. It will allow us to customize the Playbar and create a Table of Contents of the project among other things.

We will then focus on the third and last step of the Captivate production process: publishing the movie. Publishing the movie is the process by which we make our Captivate projects available to the outside world. Most of the time, we'll publish our movies in the Adobe Flash format or in the HTML5 format so that any student can enjoy the content of our online course across devices. However, Captivate can also publish the movie in many other formats. In this chapter we will:

- Check the spelling of the entire project
- Set the Start and End preferences of the movie
- Enter the project metadata to enhance the accessibility of the project
- Export the properties of a project and import them back in another project
- Customize the project Skin
- Add a Table of Contents
- Publish the project in various formats

At the end of this chapter, we will be ready to leave the post-production studio and push our eLearning content online!

Preparing our work

In this chapter, we will mainly work with the Encoder Demonstration file. Perform the following steps to get all files ready:

1. Open Captivate.
2. Open the `Chapter06/encoderDemo_800.cptx` file.

One of the exercises will make use of the Encoder Simulation.

3. Open the `Chapter06/encoderSim_800.cptx`.

At the end of this chapter, we will need to use our Video Demo project.

4. Open the `Chapter06/encoderVideo_800.cpvc`.
5. When all three files are open, ensure that the **Classic** workspace is the one in use.
6. Reset the **Classic** workspace by using the **Window | Workspace | Reset 'Classic'** menu item.

Captivate is now ready for the *Final Changes*!

Final Changes

With the completion of *Chapter 5, Working with Audio*, we can consider that the slides of our Encoder Demonstration project are all final. There are, however, a few more things to do before the movie can be published. In this section, we will discuss these *Final Changes* one by one.

Checking the spelling

Checking the spelling is probably one of the most fundamental *Final Changes*. After all, we are supposed to be teachers, and teachers know how to write with no mistakes! The Spell Checker of Captivate works like any other Spell Checker found in many other text authoring applications.

In Captivate 6, the Spell Checker has the ability to check the text typed in various locations throughout the project. This includes the text typed in the *Text Captions*, in the *Slide Notes*, in the *Text Animations*, in the *Buttons*, and in the *Table of Contents*.

Before we use the Spell Checker, we will take a quick look at its options using the following steps:

1. Open the **Preferences** of Captivate by using the **Edit | Preferences** (Windows) or the **Adobe Captivate | Preferences** (Mac) menu item.
2. On the left-hand side of the **Preferences** dialog, click on the **General Settings** category.
3. Click on the **Spelling Preferences** button to open the **Spelling Options** dialog, as shown in the following screenshot:

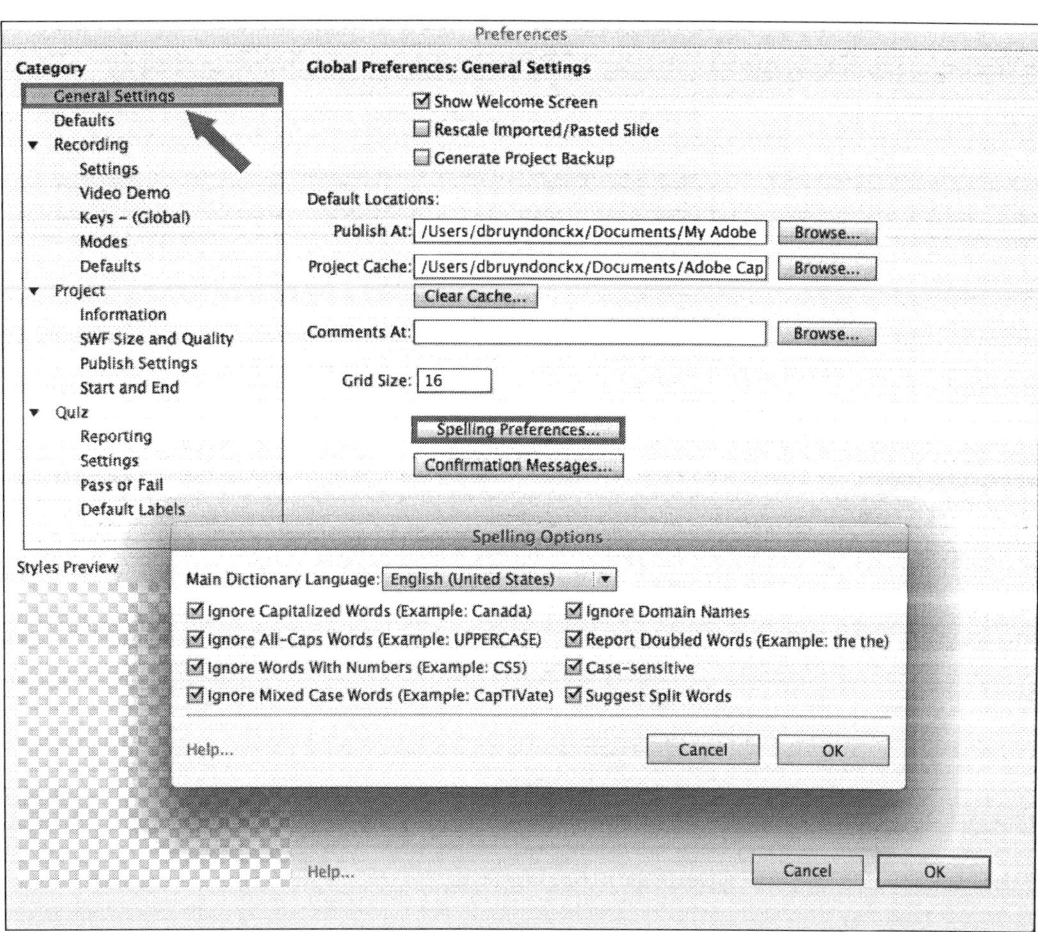

The main option of this box is the **Main Dictionary Language**. Notice that by default, the checkboxes of the **Spelling Options** dialog box are all selected.

4. Open the **Main Dictionary Language** drop-down list and take some time to inspect the available languages. Is yours in the list?
5. For this exercise, make sure to choose **English (United States)** as the **Main Dictionary Language**.
6. Take some time to inspect the other options of the dialog box. They should be pretty much self-explanatory. Make sure they are all selected before moving on.
7. Click on the **OK** button to close the **Spelling Options** dialog, then on **OK** again to validate the changes and close the **Preferences** dialog.

Now that we have a better idea of the available Spell Checker options, we will use the feature to check the spelling throughout the entire movie.

8. Use the **Project | Check Spelling** menu item (or the *F7* shortcut key) to launch the Spell Checker.

The first spelling error that the spell checker should pick-up is the **flv** file extension.

9. Click on the **Ignore All** button to ignore this error throughout the entire project.

One spelling error has been (intentionally) left over in the project on slide 3 where the word **bundel** is mistyped.

10. Take some time to inspect the **Check Spelling** dialog. It contains more or less the same options as any other Spell Checker found in virtually every text authoring applications.
11. Click on the **Options** button at the end of the **Check Spelling** dialog.

The same **Spelling Options** dialog as the one we accessed through the **Preferences** opens.

12. Leave all the **Spelling Options** at their current settings and click on **OK** to close the **Spelling Options** dialog.
13. At the bottom left corner of the **Check Spelling** dialog, click on the **Help** link.

Such a **Help** links can be found at the bottom left corner of many dialog boxes throughout Captivate. It opens the default browser and displays the Captivate Help page that specifically explains the options of the current dialog box. The **Help** link is an easy and fast way to access specific help content.

14. If you feel you need some additional explanations on the Spell Checker feature, take some time to review the currently open help page. When done, close your browser and return to Captivate.
15. In **the Check Spelling** dialog, make sure **bundle** is selected to replace **bundel** and click on **Change**.
16. Do the necessary changes if there are some more spelling errors to correct.

When done, an information box informs you that the check is complete and that a certain number of corrections have been made.

17. Click on the **OK** button to discard the information box.
18. Make sure you save the file before moving on.

With the spell check complete, the final phase of the post-production process is now underway. Checking the spelling in Captivate is as easy as checking the spelling in any other text-authoring application, but remember that it is an essential part of any professional eLearning project.

The following is a quick summary of what we have learned:

- Captivate contains a Spell Checker that works the same way as any other Spell Checker found in virtually every text-authoring application.
- The Spell Checker of Captivate has the ability to check the spelling of *all the text typed throughout the application*. It includes the text typed in the Text Captions, in the Slide Notes, in the Text Animations, on the Buttons, and in the Table of Contents.
- The **Spelling Options** can be accessed through the **Preferences** dialog or directly from the **Check Spelling** dialog.
- The **Help** link found at the bottom left corner of many dialog boxes opens the default browser and displays the help page specifically dedicated to that dialog box. It is a quick and easy way to access specific help content.
- Checking the spelling is an essential part of any professional eLearning project.

Start and End preferences

The second *Final Change* we will focus on will let us decide how the movie starts and how the movie ends. This is important to fine-tune the student's experience and to optimize the performances of the project when viewed over the Internet.

In the following exercise, we will explore the available Start and End preferences using the following steps:

1. If needed, return to the `Chapter06/encoderDemo_800.cptx` file.
2. Use the **Edit** | **Preferences** (Windows) or the **Adobe Captivate** | **Preferences** (Mac) menu item to open the **Preferences** dialog.
3. On the left-hand side of the **Preferences** dialog, select the **Start and End** category situated in the **Project** section.

Remember that the categories pertaining to the **Project** section of the **Preferences** dialog are specific to the current project only. Your screen should now display the dialog as shown in the following screenshot:

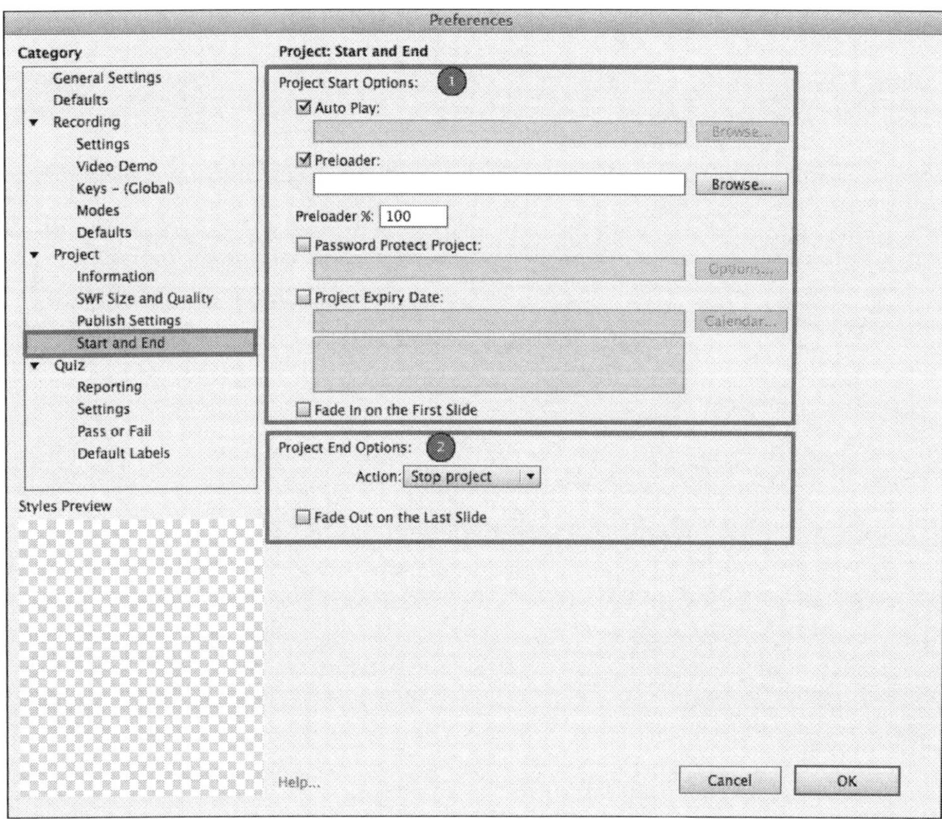

The **Start and End** preference page is divided into two sections. At the top of the page are the **Project Start Options** (1), as shown in the previous screenshot, and at the end of the page, are the **Project End Options** (2).

The following options are available under the **Project Start** section:

- **Auto Play** – If this option is selected, the project will start playing as soon as it finishes loading. If it is not selected, the student will have to click on the *Play* button to view the movie. In such situation, you can use the **Browse** button to choose an image that will be displayed until the student clicks on the *Play* button (Such an image is often called a *poster image*).
- **Preloader** – A Preloader is an Image or a Flash Animation (`.swf`) that is displayed while the movie is loading. If the Preloader box is selected and no Preloader file is supplied, Captivate uses its default Preloader, but we can also create our own custom Preloader or choose one in the *Gallery*.
- **Preloader %** – This is, to me, the most important option of this page. It represents the percentage of the file that has to be downloaded before the movie starts to play. If set to 50 percent, it means that the movie will start playing when 50 percent of the entire file is downloaded. The remaining 50 percent will be loaded while the beginning of the movie is being played. Use this option when the project is large and contains lots of audio or video. The student will have to wait less time before the movie starts to play.

Here is an interesting blog post from the Iconlogic's blog. Kevin Siegel details how to use the *Preloader* and the *Preloader %* options to broadcast your corporate brand, available at `http://iconlogic.blogs.com/weblog/2010/10/adobe-captivate-5-preload-your-corporate-brand.html`.

- **Password Protect Project** – This option is self-explanatory. Share the password only with those individuals that should be granted access to the project. Use this option if the project contains confidential information or if you want to share a beta-release of the project with a limited team of reviewers.
- **Project Expiry Date** – Use this option to set an expiration date for the project. The project will not be accessible if a student wants to access it after the expiration date.
- **Fade In on First Slide** – This option is turned on by default.

The following options are available under the **Project End** section:

- **Action** – The Action drop-down list is used to select an action that will be fired when the project is complete. By default, the **Stop project** action is performed.
- **Fade Out on Last Slide** – This option is turned on by default.

Now that we have a better understanding of the available options, we will fine-tune the **Start and End** preferences of our Encoder Demonstration.

4. Set the **Preloader** % option to `50 %`.

This particular movie contains a lot of sound and sound takes a lot of time to download. With the Preloader % option set to 50, the time spent by the student waiting for the movie to download is divided by 2.

5. Leave the remaining options at their default and click on **OK**.
6. Don't forget to save the file when done.

This concludes our overview of the **Start and End** preferences. Let's make a quick list of what we have learned:

- In the **Preferences** dialog, the options pages pertaining to the **Project** section are specific to the current project only.
- In the **Start and End** category, Captivate exposes lots of options and features that let us decide how the project starts and what happens when it has finished playing.
- These options can enhance the user experience, enforce some basic security, and optimize the loading time of the movie.

Project metadata and accessibility

A **metadata** is *data about data*. In the Captivate files that we are creating, the main data is the slides and all the objects and features that make up the project. The metadata of our projects are information such as the slide count, the author of the project, the description of the project, the resolution, and so on. All this information is *data about the data* or to use the proper word, *metadata*.

Some of these metadata (such as the slide count, the resolution, the length, and so on) are automatically generated by Captivate while other metadata has to be manually entered.

Metadata is essential if we want to create *accessible* projects. An **accessible** project is a project that can be accessed by people with disabilities. There are many things that we can do in a Captivate project to make it *accessible*. One of those things is to take the time to enter the metadata. These metadata will be used by the assistive devices of those with disabilities (devices such as Braille readers, screen readers, Text-to-Speech utilities) in order to let these special students enjoy the eLearning content we create in the best possible conditions.

Section 508

Many countries around the world have adopted some kind of accessibility standards, rules, and even laws. Most of the time, these standards are based on the **Web Accessibility Initiative** (**WAI** - see `www.w3.org/WAI`), a document developed by the **World Wide Web Consortium** (**W3C**). In the US legislation, these standards are implemented as an amendment of the US Rehabilitation Act of 1973. This amendment is commonly known as Section 508. When a project is *508 compliant*, it simply means that it complies with the accessibility requirements of this legal document.

In the following exercise, we will take the first step toward making our projects accessible by using the **Project Info** feature to enter the metadata of the project using the following steps:

1. If needed, return to the `Chapter06/encoderDemo_800.cptx` file.
2. Use the **Edit** | **Preferences** (Windows) or the **Adobe Captivate** | **Preferences** (Mac) menu item to open the **Preferences** dialog.
3. On the left-hand side of the **Preferences** dialog, click on the **Information** category situated in the **Project** section.

The upper section of the **Project Information** Preferences is used to manually enter the missing metadata, while the bottom section displays the automatically generated metadata. These are the (estimated) display time, the resolution, the slide count, and the number of hidden slides.

4. Type `My Fictional Training Company-MFTC` in the **Company** field.
5. Type `2012-MFTC` in the Copyright field.
6. Enter `Adobe Media Encoder-Demonstration` in the **Project Name** field.
7. Type `This project shows the students how to use the Adobe Media Encoder to convert a QuickTime movie, into Flash Video` in the **Description** field.

8. Fill the remaining fields (**Author**, **E-mail**, and **Website**) with your own name, e-mail address, and website URL. Note that none of these fields are mandatory. If you do not have a website, just leave the field blank.
9. Click on the **OK** button when done to close the **Preferences** dialog.

Back in the main Captivate interface, the **Project Info** panel gives you easy access to some of these metadata.

10. Click on the **Project Info** tab situated next to the **Properties** and the **Library** tabs in the upper-right edge of the workspace.
11. The **Project Info** panel opens and displays the automatically generated metadata.

The **Project Info** panel only *displays* some of the metadata. It *cannot* be used to *create* new metadata or to *modify* existing metadata.

By entering the project metadata, we have taken the first important step toward making our project 508 compliant. This is a very good point, but there is a lot more that can be done throughout the Captivate application to further enhance the accessibility of the project. There are some great blog posts on this subject as well as some very interesting pages in the official Captivate documentation:

- The accessibility page from the official Captivate documentation available at `http://help.adobe.com/en_US/captivate/cp/using/WSc1b83f70210cd1011d7107e311c7efcf707-8000.html`
- The Captivate Accessibility overview page on the Adobe website available at `http://www.adobe.com/accessibility/products/captivate/overview.html`
- Some useful tips and tricks regarding project info in Captivate 5 on the IconLogic blog by Kevin Siegel available at `http://iconlogic.blogs.com/weblog/2011/01/adobe-captivate-5-dont-quote-me.html`

This concludes this little discussion on project accessibility and metadata. Here is a quick summary of what we have learned:

- A metadata is data about data.
- Metadata is essential to make our project *accessible*.
- An accessible project is a project that can be accessed in good conditions by people with disabilities. These particular students use some specific input and output devices (such as Braille readers, Text-to-Speech utilities, and so on) that work much better if we take the time to enter some extra metadata in our projects.

- The accessibility guidelines and standards are commonly known as **Section 508** in reference of an amendment of the US Rehabilitation Act of 1973.
- Captivate automatically generates some of the metadata, while other metadata has to be entered manually.
- Use the **Project: Information** preferences to manually enter the project metadata.

Other project preferences

There are some more project preferences available in Captivate. Most of the time, the default settings for these particular options work just fine, so we won't modify any of these options in our Encoder Demonstration Project.

In the following exercises, we will simply take a look at these options and briefly discuss some of them:

1. If needed, return to the `Chapter06/encoderDemo_800.cptx` file.
2. Use the **Edit | Preferences** (Windows) or the **Adobe Captivate | Preferences** (Mac) menu item to open the **Preferences** dialog.
3. Open the **SWF Size and Quality** category situated in the Project section.

This particular **Preferences** page provides some options that let us control how the Captivate project will be converted into a Flash file during the upcoming publication process. Most of the time, we don't have to tamper with these settings as the default works just fine. We will just briefly discuss some of the available options:

- The **Advanced Project Compression** option: When selected, Captivate takes into account the differences between two consecutive slides instead of entirely publishing both slides. The goal is to generate the smallest possible Flash file. When this option is selected, the publication process may take a bit longer.
- The **Compress SWF File** option: Asks Captivate to compress the generated SWF file at the end of the publication process. This option helps reduce the SWF file size. Note that such a compressed Flash file requires Flash Player 9 or higher versions to play well.

The remaining options of this particular page are for the most part self-explanatory. If you want more information about any one of them, don't hesitate to click on the **Help** link at the bottom-left corner of the **Preferences** dialog.

4. Click on the **Publish Settings** category situated in the **Project** section of the left column of the **Preferences** dialog.

The **Publish Settings** category is the only page of the **Project** section that we haven't visited yet. It displays some additional options about how the project will be converted to Flash. Again, the default options work just fine for the vast majority of the project. We will just briefly discuss some of these options:

- **Frames Per Seconds** – Use this option if you want to embed your Captivate project in another Flash project that has a frame rate different than 30 frames per second. Otherwise, leave this option to its default value of **30** fps.
- **Publish Adobe Acrobat Connect metadata** – This option adds some metadata to the project, thus producing a slightly larger SWF file. This metadata is designed to facilitate the integration of the Captivate project in the *Acrobat Connect Pro* LMS from Adobe. If you do not have access to an *Acrobat Connect* server, this option is useless.

See this great blog post by Michael (known as the Captivate Guru) about how the Adobe Connect metadata affects the size of the resulting file, available at `http://www.cpguru.com/2008/12/30/reducing-the-file-size-of-your-captivate-projects/`.

- **Enable Accessibility**: This option also adds extra-information to the Captivate project, but it makes the project 508 compliant. **If this option is not selected, the accessibility options set throughout the project are useless**.
- **Externalize resources**: By default, Captivate produces a single SWF file containing the whole project. Consequently, this file can be very large and hard to download for the students. Externalizing resources tells Captivate to generate many smaller SWF files that reference each other. This option may help us optimize the download time of a large project, but makes it more difficult to push the Captivate project online once published. Note that some assets (like the inserted video files) are always externalized.

The other options of the **Preferences** page should be self-explanatory. Don't hesitate to click on the **Help** link if you need more information.

5. Click on the **Cancel** button to close the **Preferences** dialog and discard the eventual changes you've made along the way.

This concludes our tour of the project preferences. We will now try to apply the same preferences to another project.

Exporting the project preferences

Remember that the options pertaining to the **Project** section of the **Preferences** dialog are specific to the current project only.

If we want to apply the very same set of **Preferences** to another project, we have to export the **Preferences** of the current project and reimport them in the target project. In the following exercise, we will export the **Preferences** of the Encoder *Demonstration* and apply them to the Encoder *Simulation*:

1. If needed, return to the `Chapter06/encoderDemo_800.cptx` file.
2. Use the **File | Export | Preferences** menu item to export the preferences of the demonstration.
3. Save the preferences file as `Chapter06/encoderDemo_800_Preferences.cpr`. It should be the default name proposed by Captivate.
4. Click on **OK** to discard the information box telling you that the export is successful.

Note that the file extension of such a preference file is `.cpr`.

Now that we have exported the preferences of the *Demonstration* project, we will switch to the *Simulation* and import the demonstration preferences. At the end of this process, both projects will share the exact same project preferences.

5. Switch to the `Chapter06/encoderSim_800.cptx` file.
6. Use the **File | Import | Preferences** menu item to import a preference file in the project.
7. Browse to the `Chapter06/encoderDemo_800_Preferences.cpr` file and click on **Open**.

After a short while, an information box should appear on the screen telling you that the preferences were successfully imported.

8. Click on **OK** to discard the information box.
9. Use the **Edit | Preferences** (Windows) or the **Adobe Captivate | Preferences** (Mac) menu item to open the **Preferences** dialog.
10. Open the **Information** category situated in the **Project** section of the **Preferences** dialog.

The same metadata we entered in the Encoder *Demonstration* should have been applied to the *Simulation*.

11. Change the **Project Name** to `Adobe Media Encoder - Simulation`.
12. Change the project **Description** to `This project guides the student in using the Adobe Media Encoder to convert a QuickTime movie into Flash Video`.
13. Leave the other metadata to their current value and click on **OK** to validate the changes and close the **Preferences** dialog.
14. Use the **File | Save All** menu item to save both the Encoder *Demonstration* and the Encoder *Simulation* in one action.

The following is a quick summary of what we have learned about the remaining project preferences:

- Most of the time, the default settings of the **SWF Size and Quality** and the **Publish Settings** pages of the **Preferences** dialog work just fine.
- These settings may help us better control the size of the resulting Flash file and optimize the download time of the project. On the other hand, they can be quite technical and require some knowledge about Flash to be used with full efficiency.
- It is possible to export the preferences of one project and import them back into another project.

Working with the Skin Editor

The **Skin** of a project is a collection of elements that are, for the most part, displayed *around* the slides. It means that the elements of the Skin are *not* part of the actual eLearning content. They are used to interact with the Captivate movie and to enhance the overall user experience. A Skin is made of three main elements:

- The **Playback Controls** – Is the most visible element of the Skin. It contains the necessary buttons and switches that allow the student to control the movie during the playback. It also contains a progress bar that tracks the student's progression in the Captivate movie.
- The **Borders** – The Skin Editor lets us create borders around our movies. We can turn each of the four borders on and/or off and choose their width, color, and texture.
- The **Table of Contents** – The last element of a Skin is the Table of Contents. By default, it is turned off, but it is very easy to turn it on and generate a Table of Contents for the project.

Captivate is shipped with lots of predefined Skins that we can apply *as-is* to our projects for rapid development. We can also customize the existing Skins and save our changes as new Skins.

In this section, we will discuss each of the three Skin elements one by one. While doing so, we will slowly create a unique Skin that we will save and apply to all our projects. We will also uncover some more features of Captivate along the way.

Customizing the Playback Controls

The first and most visible element of the Skin is the Playbar. By default, the Playbar appears at the bottom of the movie, and contains the necessary buttons and switches to let the student control his/her progression in the Captivate movie.

In the following exercise, we will explore the available options of the Playbar and create a customized Playbar for our projects:

1. Return to the `Chapter06/encoderDemo_800.cptx` file.
2. Use the **Project | Skin Editor** menu item to open the **Skin Editor** floating pane, as shown in the following screenshot:

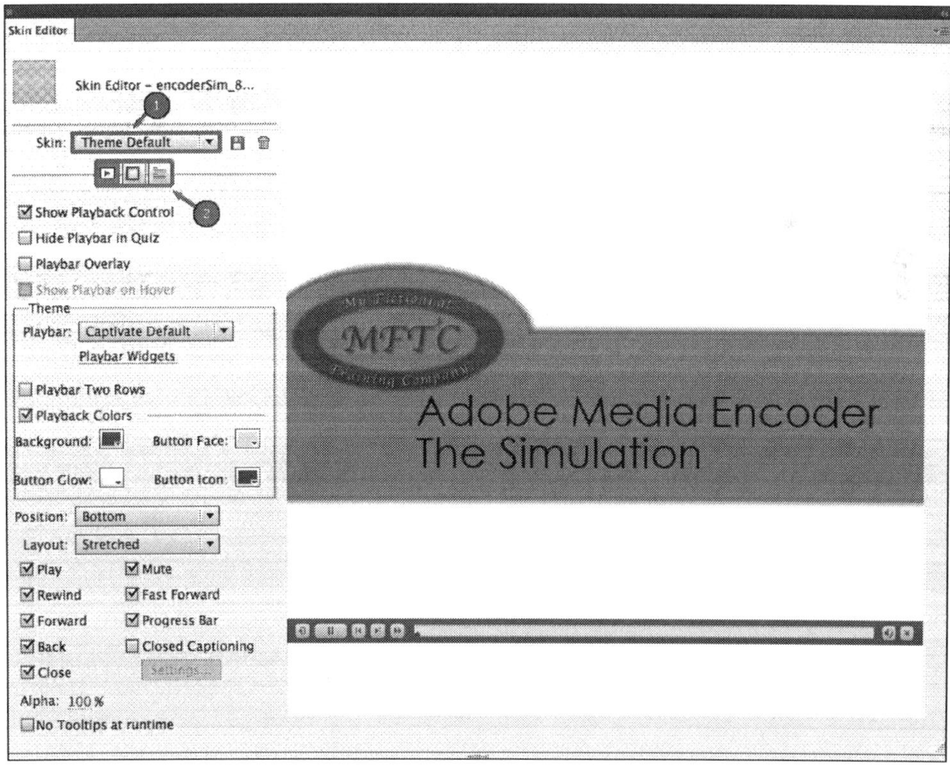

The **Skin Editor** is divided in two main areas. On the left-hand side, there are the Switches, Boxes, and Buttons that will let us customize the various elements of the Skin. On the right-hand side, there is a live preview of the first slide of the movie. This area of the **Skin Editor** is updated as we turn the options of the left area on and off.

In the upper-left area of the Skin Editor, notice two important controls. The **Skin** drop-down list (1), as shown in the previous screenshot is used to choose and apply one of the predefined Skins of Captivate to the project. Right below it, there are three icons (2). Each of them represents one of the main Skin elements: the **Playback Controls**, the **Borders**, and the **Table of Contents**.

3. Open the **Skin** drop-down list and choose any Skin you want.
4. The chosen Skin is applied to the movie and the preview area of the **Skin Editor** is updated.
5. Open the **Skin** drop-down list again and apply the **Captivate Default** Skin to the project.

The **Captivate Default** Skin is the one that will be used as the starting point of our own customized Skin.

6. *Deselect* the **Show Playback Control** checkbox.

When the preview updates, notice that the Playback Controls are not displayed anymore and that a gray bottom border appears where the Playback Controls used to be. This is very interesting and deserves further investigation.

By default, when a Playbar is applied, a **bottom border is also automatically applied to the movie**. This bottom border has **the same width as the Playbar**. The idea is to put the Playbar on top of the bottom border so that the Playback Controls do not overlap with the movie. This is a very good thing and, most of the time, it works just fine. That being said, this system **increases the overall height of the project**. If you remember the discussion we had in *Chapter 2, Capturing the Slides* about the resolution of the movie, this can be quite a problem in some situations.

We will now set the Skin, so that the Playback Controls are displayed without adding a single pixel to the height of the movie.

7. Click on the **Borders** icon. It is the second of the three icons situated just below the **Skin** drop-down list.
8. Deselect the **Show Border** checkbox.
9. Return to the previous screen by clicking on the **Playback Controls** icon situated right below the **Skin** drop-down list.

10. Select the **Show Playback Controls** checkbox to turn the Playbar back on.
11. Right below Show Playback Controls, select the **Playbar Overlay** checkbox. This is the option that allows the Playbar to overlap with the slide.
12. At the bottom of the **Playback Controls** page, set the **Alpha** of the Playbar to `30`.

By modifying the **Alpha** value of the Playbar, we create a semi-transparent Playbar so that the bottom part of the slide *can show through* the Playbar. This is how we can accommodate a Playbar **without increasing the overall height of the movie**.

13. Close the **Skin Editor** floating pane.
14. Use the Preview icon to preview the **Next 5 slides**. This will let us test the new Playbar configuration in the **Preview** pane.
15. When the preview is over, close the **Preview** pane.

In our example, we want the Playbar to be situated *inside* the border, so we will cancel our latest changes by reapplying the **Captivate Default** Skin.

16. Use the **Project | Skin Editor** menu to reopen the floating **Skin Editor** pane.
17. Open the **Skin** drop-down list. Notice that the Skin currently in use is the **Captivate Default (Modified)** Skin.
18. Apply *any* Skin of the list to the project.
19. Once the chosen Skin is applied, open the **Skin** drop-down list again.
20. Choose the **Captivate Default** Skin.

The original **Captivate Default** Skin is reapplied to the project. Basically, what we just did is *resetting* the **Captivate Default** Skin.

21. Deselect the **Rewind**, **Forward**, **Back**, **Close**, and **Fast Forward** checkboxes.
22. Make sure the **Play**, **Mute**, **Progress Bar**, and **Closed Captioning** checkboxes are selected.

After this operation, the Playbar contains three buttons in addition to the progress bar.

23. Click on the **Settings** button situated right below the **Closed Captioning** checkbox.
24. In the **CC Project Settings** dialog, choose the **Century Gothic** font **Family**, change the font **Size** to `14` and the number of **Lines** to `2`.
25. Click on the **OK** button to close the **CC Project Settings** dialog.
26. Take some time to explore the remaining options of the Playbar. Make sure you do not change any of them before moving on to the next step.

With the completion of this exercise, we can consider the Playbar as final! We will now experience our new Playbar in the **Preview** pane.

27. Close the floating **Skin Editor** pane.
28. Click on the Preview icon and choose to preview the entire **Project**.

When the movie starts to play, take a look at the Playbar. It contains three buttons and the progress bar as specified in the **Skin Editor** during the previous exercise.

29. Click on the **CC** button at the right edge of the Playbar to turn the *Closed Captions* on.

Notice that the Closed Captions appear in a semi-transparent rectangle that overlaps with the bottom area of the slide.

30. Close the **Preview** pane.

In the next section, we will explore the Borders. Borders are the second element of a Captivate Skin.

Working with Borders

The Borders are the second main element of a Captivate Skin. As we experienced in the previous section, adding a Playbar automatically adds a corresponding border, so that the Playbar does not overlap with the slide elements.

In the following exercise, we will experiment with the various Border properties:

1. Still in the `encoderDemo_800.cptx` file, use the **Project** | **Skin Editor** to return to the **Skin Editor** floating pane.
2. Click on the **Borders** icon situated right below the **Skin** drop-down list.

In the Borders page of the **Skin Editor**, notice that the Borders are currently enabled and that the Bottom border is turned on, as shown in the following screenshot:

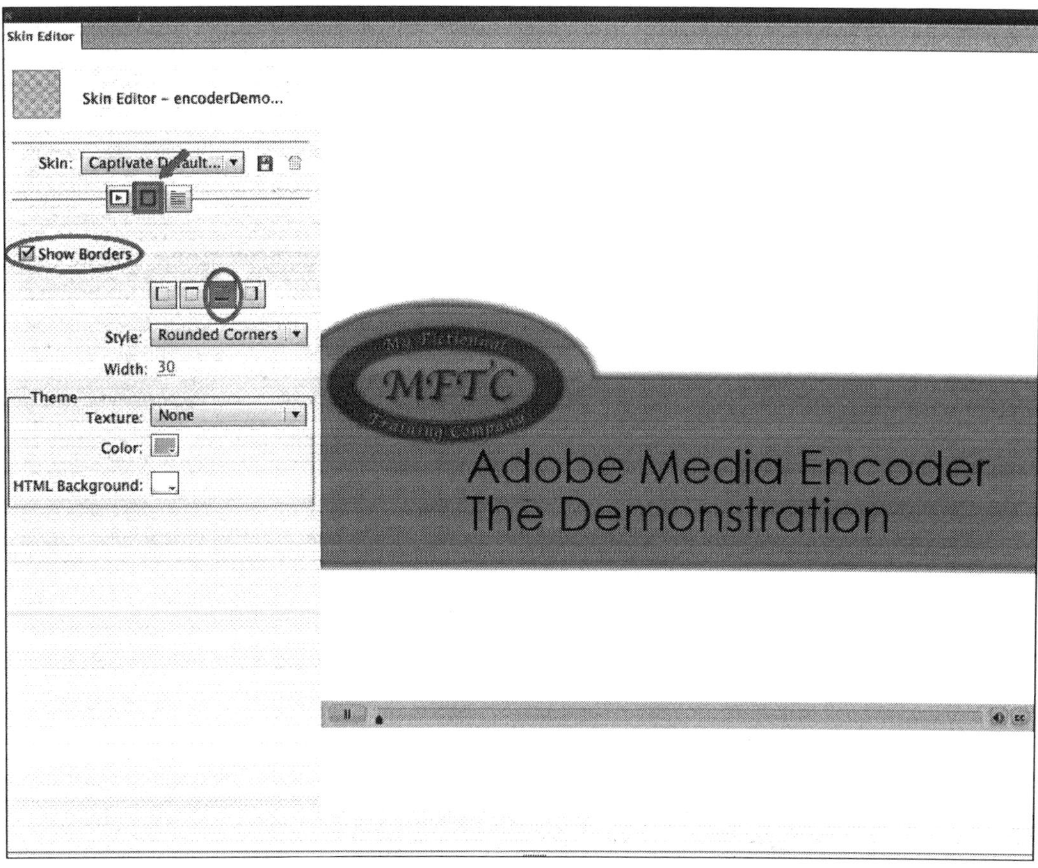

We will turn all four borders *on* and explore the available formatting options.

3. Click on the **Left** border, **Right** border, and **Top** border icons to turn them on.
4. In the **Style** drop-down list, choose the **Square Edge** style.
5. Click on the **Color** chooser. When the color palette opens, click on the **Color Picker**. It is the eyedropper icon situated in the top-right corner of the color chooser.
6. With the **color picker** enabled, take a close look at your mouse pointer. It should display an eyedropper icon. With this pointer active, click anywhere on the brown background, where the **Adobe Media Encoder - The Demonstration** Text Animation is located.

The *Color Picker* tool takes the color of the pixel we click on and applies it to the border. This tool is an incredibly fast and easy way to make two different elements share the very same color.

7. Open the **Texture** drop-down list and choose any texture you want.
8. Change the **Width** of the borders to `80`.

The previous steps illustrate all the available options for the borders. We will now arrange these options to fit the particular needs of our Encoder Demonstration.

Let's start with the most obvious change to be made: turning off this awful texture! (I do *not* like textures! They make the project look like my grandmother's kitchen!)

9. Open the **Texture** drop-down list again, and choose **None** at the very top of the list to turn the **Texture** off. With the **Texture** turned off, the brown border reappears.
10. Turn off the **Top**, **Left**, and **Right** borders. Leave only the Bottom border on.
11. Reduce the **Width** of the border to `30` pixels.
12. Close the floating **Skin Editor** pane and save the file.

Moving the Closed Captions outside of the slide

One of the problems that we have not solved yet is the Closed Captions overlapping with the slide. In this section, we will use the Rescale Project feature to add 50 pixels to the height of the movie. These extra pixels will be used to display our Closed Captions. Perform the following steps to move the Closed Captions outside the slide:

1. Still in the `Chapter06/encoderDemo_800.cptx` file, use the **Modify | Rescale Project** menu item to open the **Rescale Project** dialog.
2. In the upper area of the dialog, deselect the **Maintain Aspect Ratio** checkbox.

Remember that we only want to increase the Height of the project, not its Width.

3. Increase the **Height** of the project by 50 pixels. The new **Height** of the project should be **650** pixels.

Because the new Height is larger than the original Height, the bottom-left section of the **Rescale Project** dialog lights up. It contains the options specific to a higher project size.

4. Select the **Keep project the same size and position the objects** option.
5. Open the **Position Project** drop-down list and choose the **Top Center** option
6. Make sure the **Rescale Project** dialog looks like the following screenshot:

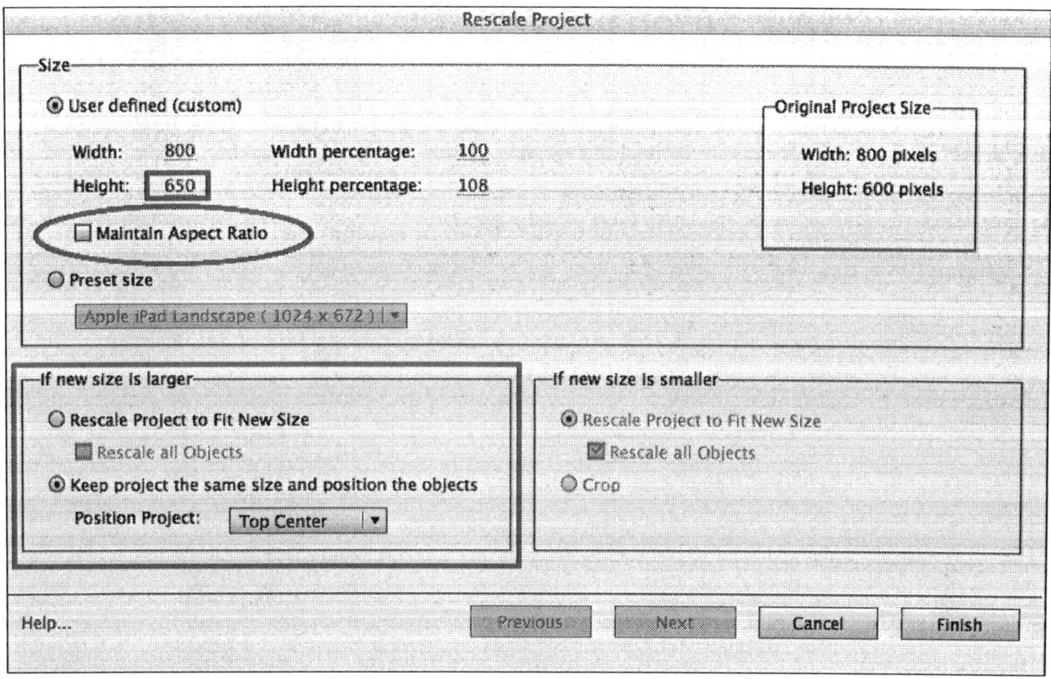

These settings will add 50 pixels to the height of the project without modifying the size of the actual slide. By selecting **Top Center** in the **Position Project** drop-down list, the extra 50 pixels will be inserted at the bottom of the project between the slide and the Playback Controls.

7. Click on the **Finish** button and discard the warning message to apply the changes.
8. Save the file when done.

Remember that rescaling a project is an action that *cannot* be undone, hence the warning message.

9. Use the Preview icon to test the entire **Project**.
10. In the **Preview** pane, click on the **CC** button of the Playbar to turn the Text Captions on.

They should now appear between the Playback Controls and the slide.

With the completion of the above exercises, the first two elements of the Skin (the Playback Controls and the Borders) are now in place. In the next section, we will focus on the third and last element of the Skin: the Table of Contents.

Adding a Table of Contents

The Table of Contents is the third and last element of the Skin. By default, the Table of Contents is turned off.

In the following exercise, we will turn on Table of Contents and explore the available options:

1. Still in the `encoderDemo_800.cptx` file, use the **Project | Table of Contents** to open the floating **Skin Editor** pane on the **Table of Contents** page.
2. Click on the **Show TOC** checkbox to turn the Table of Contents on.

By default, the Table of Contents appears on the left-hand side of the project and contains every single slide. At this moment, the slides are named **Slide 1**, **Slide 2**, and so on.

In the following section of this exercise, we will explore two ways to change the name of the slides in the Table of Contents.

The first way is to change the name of the slide directly in the **Skin Editor**.

3. Right below the **Show TOC** checkbox, double-click on the **Slide 1** title.
4. Change the name of the slide to **Introduction** and press the *Enter* key.

After a short while, the preview area displays an updated Table of Contents.

The second way of changing the slide name involves closing the **Skin Editor** and using the **Properties** panel of each slide to specify a slide *Label*.

5. Close the floating **Skin Editor** panel.
6. Use the **Filmstrip** to select slide 2. Make sure the **Properties** panel shows the properties of the *Slide* and not the properties of any of the slide element.
7. At the top of the **Properties** panel, type `Video Slide` in the **Label** field.
8. Press *Enter* to validate the change.

When it is done, take another look at the **Filmstrip**. The slide *Label* should be displayed below the corresponding thumbnail.

9. Use the same technique to enter a label for other slides of the project:
    - Slide 4 - Change the Label to `Beginning of the Demonstration`
    - Slide 22 - Change the label to `Ending slide`
    - The label of slide 3 should already be set
    - Leave the Label field of the other slides empty

10. Use the **Project | Table of Content** menu item to reopen the floating **Skin Editor** pane on the **Table of Contents** page.
11. Click on the **Reset TOC** icon situated below the list of TOC entries, as shown in the following screenshot:

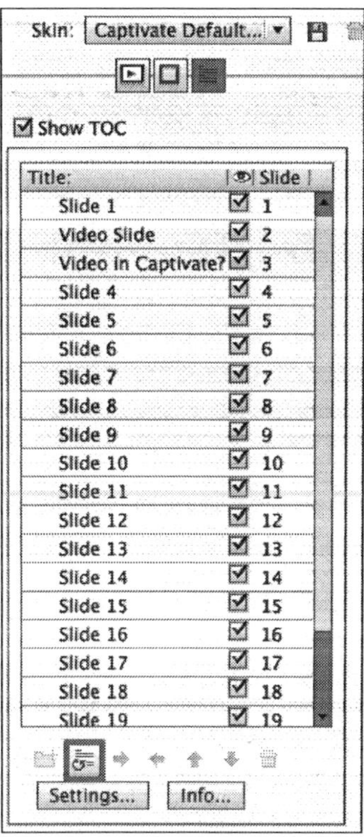

When clicking on this icon, Captivate inspects the slides of the project and re-generates the entries of the Table of Contents. Notice that the slide label, if any, is used as the **Title** of the TOC entry.

Also, notice that there is *no label for slide 1*. This tells us that **manually changing the name of the slide in the TOC editor does NOT add a corresponding label to the slide**.

About the slide labels

In the current exercise, we are using the slide labels to generate the entries of the Table of Contents, but adding labels to slides serves many other purposes as well. First of all, it makes our project easier to use and maintain. But the main benefit of the slide label is probably the enhanced accessibility it provides. The slide label is yet another metadata element used by the assistive devices of those with disabilities and is mandatory to make our eLearning projects 508 compliant.

We will now reenter a name for slide 1 and hide the unnecessary slides from the Table of Contents.

12. In the **Skin Editor**, double-click on the **Slide 1** title in the list of TOC entries. Retype `Introduction` and press the *Enter* key.
13. Uncheck the visibility checkbox for slides 5 to 21.

In the preview area of the **Skin Editor**, notice that the corresponding slides disappear from the Table of Contents. At this point there should be only five slides mentioned in the Table of Contents.

Finally, we will fine-tune the look and feel of the Table of Contents.

14. Click on the **Info...** button situated at the bottom of the **Skin Editor**, below the list of TOC entries. The **TOC Information** dialog opens.
15. In the **TOC Information** dialog, click on the **Project Information** button.

This last action *copies* the available project metadata to the corresponding fields of the **TOC Information** box.

16 Type `Encoder Demonstration` in the **Title** field of the **TOC Information** dialog.
17. At the bottom of the **TOC Information** dialog, change the Font to **Century Gothic**.
18. Click on the **OK** button to validate your choices and close the **TOC Information** dialog.

At this point, the Table of Contents is almost ready. The only remaining problem is the extra space required by the Table of Contents. To address this issue, we will ask Captivate to position the Table of Contents on top of the slide and to provide a little icon to toggle its visibility.

19. Click on the **Settings** button situated at the bottom of the **Skin Editor**, below the list of TOC entries and next to the **Info** button we used earlier in step 12.
20. At the top of the **TOC Settings** dialog, change the **Style** to **Overlay**. This is what will position the TOC on top of the slides.
21. In the **Color** section, click on the **Background** color and use the eyedropper tool to apply the same brownish color we used earlier as the background color of the Table of Contents.
22. Change the **Alpha** value to `65` %. This will create a semi-transparent Table of Contents.
23. Take some time to explore the other available options. When done, click on **OK** to validate your choices and close the **TOC Settings** dialog.
24. Close the floating **Skin Editor** pane and save the file.

The last thing to do is to test the newly added Table of Contents in the **Preview** pane.

25. Click on the Preview icon to preview the entire **Project**.

When the **Preview** pane opens, notice the small double arrow in the top-left corner of the slide.

26. Click on that small double arrow to reveal the Table of Contents.
27. Click on the same icon to turn the Table of Contents back off.

At the right edge of the Playbar, we have another solution to toggle the Table of Contents on and off.

28. Click on the **TOC** icon situated at the right edge of the Playbar to reveal the Table of Contents.
29. In the Table of Contents, notice that the already visited slides are identified by a checkmark.
30. In the Table of Contents, click on the **Beginning of the Demonstration** title. The demonstration directly jumps to the corresponding slide.

This illustrates how the Table of Contents can be used to navigate in the project.

31. Click on the **TOC** icon of the Playbar to hide the Table of Contents.
32. Close the **Preview** pane and save the file.

With the addition of the Table of Contents, we can consider that our Skin is final. It looks so great (no kidding!) that we want to apply it to the other projects that we are working on.

Applying the same Skin to another project

To create the Skin of the Encoder Demonstration, we used the **Captivate Default** Skin and we customized it. The final Skin is very different from the original **Captivate Default** Skin we used as a base. It is so different that we can consider it as an entire new Skin.

In the following exercise, we will save the new Skin and apply it to the *Simulation* project using the following steps:

1. Still in the `encoderDemo_800.cptx` file, use the **Project | Skin Editor** menu to reopen the floating **Skin Editor** pane.

The **Skin** drop-down indicates that the **Captivate Default (Modified)** Skin is currently in use.

2. Click on the **Save As** icon situated right next to the **Skin** drop-down list.
3. In the **Save As** box that pops up, name the new Skin `MFTC-Skin` and click on **OK** to close the box.
4. The **Skin** drop-down should now indicate that the new **MFTC-Skin** is in use.
5. Close the floating **Skin Editor** pane.

Now that the new Skin is saved, we will switch to the Simulation and apply the new Skin to that project a well.

6. Switch to (or open) the `Chapter06/encoderSim_800.cptx` file.
7. When in the Simulation project, use the **Project | Skin Editor** menu to open the **Skin Editor**. Notice that the **Captivate Default** Skin is currently applied to the project.
8. Open the **Skin** drop-down list.
9. Apply the new **MFTC-Skin** to the Simulation project.

When the **MFTC-Skin** is applied to the Simulation project, notice that only the *Playbar* and the *Border* parts of the Skin have been enabled. The Table of Contents is *not* present. That being said, the *settings* of the TOC have been carried over in the Simulation project, so if we decide to create a TOC for the Simulation, it will have the exact same look and features as the TOC of the Demonstration project.

Extra credit

In this extra credit section, you will generate a Table of Contents for the Simulation project. These are the general steps to follow:

- Add labels to the slides you wish to add to the TOC
- Open the **Skin Editor** and select the **Show TOC** checkbox
- Hide the slides you do not want to see in the TOC
- Click on the **Info** button and import the **Project Information** in the **TOC Information**
- Fine-tune the settings of the Table of Contents as needed
- Close the **Skin Editor** and test the entire project in the **Preview** Pane

With the completion of this exercise, we have reached an important milestone in the development of our Captivate projects: **the post-production phase of the workflow is complete**!

Here is a quick summary of what we have learned about the **Skin Editor** and the Table of Contents:

- A Skin is a collection of three elements: a **Playbar**, **Borders**, and a **Table of Contents**.
- By default, adding a Playbar to the project automatically adds a corresponding border. The idea is to place the Playbar on top of the border to avoid overlapping between the Playbar and the project.
- The **Skin Editor** allows us to customize the Playbar in many ways.
- We can also turn the Borders on and off and change their *width*, their *color*, and more.
- By default, the Table of Contents is turned off.
- It is possible to add *Labels* to the slides. These labels make it easier for us to work with the slides. They also further enhance the accessibility of the project, and are used as the default TOC entry titles.
- The **Skin Editor** provides many options to fine-tune the Table of Contents.
- Captivate ships with many predefined Skins for rapid development.
- When we modify one of the predefined Skins, we actually create a new Skin that can be saved and reapplied to another movie.

In the next part of this chapter, we will focus on the third and last main step of the workflow: making the project available to the outside world by publishing it in various formats.

Publishing

So far, we have been working in a `.cptx` file, which is the default native file type of Captivate. The `.cptx` file format is great when creating and designing our projects, but it has two major disadvantages:

- It can become very large. Consequently, it is difficult for us to upload the file on a website and for the student to download and view it.
- Opening a `.cptx` file requires Captivate to be installed on the computer system.

Publishing a Captivate movie is converting (the proper word is *Compiling*) the `.cptx` file to a format that can be easily downloaded and viewed by our students.

The primary format to publish our projects is the `.swf` format. `swf` (pronounced `swif`) stands for **ShockWave Flash**. It is the file format used by the free Adobe Flash player plugin installed in more than 98 percent of the computers connected to the Internet. It has two advantages as compared to the `.cptx` file:

- A `.swf` file is usually much lighter than its `.cptx` counterpart, making it much easier to upload and download across the Internet.
- Any browser equipped with the free Adobe Flash plugin is able to open and play the `.swf` file. This makes it incredibly easy to deploy our Captivate courses.

That being said, the `.swf` format has some major disadvantages:

- It requires the Adobe Flash Player plugin to be installed. If, for whatever reason, the plugin is not available, the `.swf` file cannot be played back.
- There is no more Flash Player plugin available for mobile devices. Consequently, a `.swf` file cannot be played back on a Smartphone or on a Tablet.

That's why other publishing formats are available in Captivate. In Captivate 6, the most effective alternative to the `.swf` format is to publish the project in HTML5. When published to HTML5, the project can be played back in any **modern** browser *without the need for an extra plugin*. HTML5-enabled projects can also be played back on mobile devices *including the iPhone, iPad, and iPod touch!*

HTML5 also has its caveats. At the time of this writing, (June 2012) HTML5 is still under development. Consequently, some features of Captivate are not yet supported in HTML5.

In this section, we will explore and discuss the various publishing options at our disposal in captivate.

Publishing to Flash

In the history of Captivate, publishing to Flash has always been the primary publishing option. Even though HTML5 publishing is a game changer, publishing to Flash still is an important capability of Captivate. Remember that this publishing format is currently the only one that supports every single feature, animation, and object of Captivate.

In the following exercise, we will publish our movie in Flash format using the default options:

1. Return to the `Chapter06/encoderDemo_800.cptx` file.
2. Click on the **Publish** icon situated right next to the Preview icon. Alternatively, you can also use the **File** | **Publish** menu.

The **Publish** dialog box opens, as shown in the following screenshot:

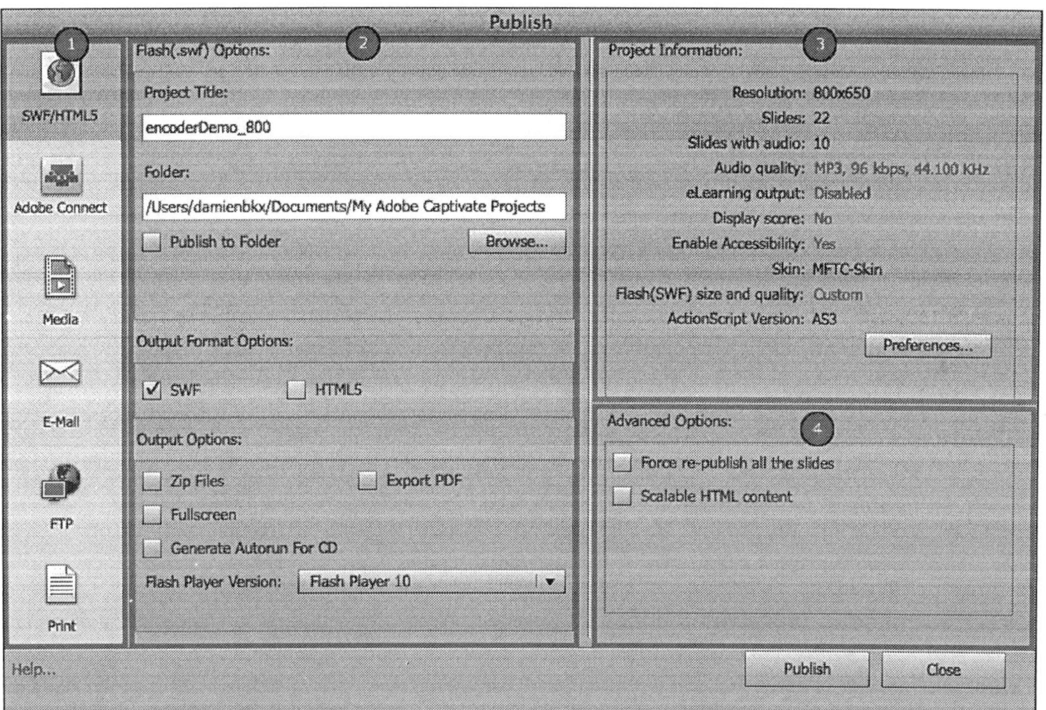

The **Publish** dialog box is divided into four main areas:

- The **Publish Format** area (1) – This is where we choose the format in which we want to publish our movies. Basically, we can choose between three options: SWF/HTML5, Media, and Print. The other options (E-mail, FTP, and so on) are actually suboptions of the SWF/HTML5, Media, and Print formats.
- The **Output Format Options** area (2) – The content of this area depends on the format chosen in the Publish Format (1) area.
- The **Project Information** area (3) – This area is a summary of the main project preferences and metadata. Clicking on the links of this area will bring us back to the various project preferences boxes we visited earlier in this chapter.
- The **Advanced Options** area (4) – This area provides some additional advanced publishing options.

We will now move on to the actual publication of the project in Flash Format.

3. In the *Publish Format* area, make sure the chosen format is **SWF/HTML5**.
4. In the **Flash(.swf) Options** area, change the **Project Title** to `encoderDemo_800_flash`.
5. Click on the **Browse** button situated just below the **Folder** field and choose to publish your movie in the `Chapter06/Publish` folder of your exercises folder.
6. Make sure the **Publish to Folder** checkbox is **selected**.
7. Take a quick look at the remaining options, but leave them all at their current settings.
8. Click on the **Publish** button at the bottom-right corner of the **Publish** dialog box.

When Captivate has finished publishing the movie, an information box appears on the screen asking if you want to view the output.

9. Click on **No** to discard the information box and return to Captivate.

We will now use the Finder (Mac) or the Windows Explorer (Windows) to take a look at the files Captivate has generated.

10. Use the Finder (Mac) or the Windows Explorer (Window) to browse to the `Chapter06/Publish` folder of your exercises.

Because we selected the **Publish to Folder** checkbox in the **Publish** dialog, Captivate has *automatically* created the `encoderDemo_800_flash` subfolder in the `Chapter06/Publish` folder.

11. Open the `encoderDemo_800_flash` subfolder to inspect its content.

There should be five files stored in this location:

- `encoderDemo_800_flash.swf` – This is the main Flash file containing the compiled version of the `.cptx` project
- `encoderDemo_800_flash.html` – This file is an HTML page used to embed the Flash file
- `standard.js` – is a JavaScript file used to make the Flash player work well within the HTML page
- `demo_en.flv` – is the video file used on slide 2 of the movie
- `captivate.css` – provides the necessary style rules to ensure the proper formatting of the HTML page

If we want to embed the compiled captivate movie in an existing HTML page, only the `.swf` file (plus, in this case, the `.flv` video) is needed. The HTML editor (such as Adobe Dreamweaver) will recreate the necessary HTML, JavaScript, and CSS files.

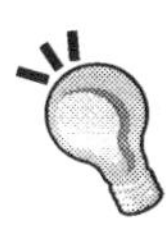

Captivate and Dreamweaver

Adobe Dreamweaver CS6 is the HTML editor of the Creative Suite and the industry leading solution for authoring professional web pages. Inserting a Captivate file in a Dreamweaver page is dead easy! First, move or copy the main Flash file (`.swf`) as well as the needed support files (in our case the `.flv` video file), if any, somewhere in the root folder of the Dreamweaver site. When done, use the Files panel of Dreamweaver to *drag-and-drop* the main `swf` file on the HTML page. *That's it!*

We will now test the movie in a web browser. This is an important test as it recreates the conditions in which our students will experience our movie once in production.

12. Double-click on the `encoderDemo_800_flash.html` file to open it in a web browser.
13. Enjoy the final version of the demonstration that we have created together!

Now that we have experienced the workflow of publishing our project to Flash with the default options, we will add some changes into the mix and create a scalable version of our project.

Scalable HTML content

Back in *Chapter 2, Capturing the Slides*, we had a discussion about choosing the right size for our project. One of the solutions was to use the new **Scalable HTML content** option of Captivate 6. Thanks to this new option, our eLearning content will be automatically resized to fit the screen on which it is viewed. Let's experiment with this option hands-on, using the following steps:

1. If needed, return to the `Chapter06/encoderDemo_800.cptx` file.
2. Click on the **Publish** icon situated right next to the Preview icon. Alternatively, you can also use the **File | Publish** menu.
3. In the *Publish Format* area, make sure the chosen format is **Flash(.swf) Options** area.
4. In the **Flash(.swf) Options** area, change the **Project Title** to `encoderDemo_800_flashScalable`.
5. Click on the **Browse** button situated just below the **Folder** field and ensure that the publish folder still is the `Chapter06/Publish` folder of your exercises.
6. Make sure the **Publish to Folder** checkbox is **selected**.
7. In the **Advanced Options** section (lower-right corner of the Publish dialog), select the **Scalable HTML content** checkbox.
8. Leave the remaining options at their current value and click on the **Publish** button at the bottom-right corner of the **Publish** dialog box.

A message informs you that object reflection is not supported in scalable content. We used object reflection on slide 3 to enhance the AMELogo image.

9. Click on **Yes** to discard the message and start the publishing process.

When Captivate has finished publishing the movie, an information box appears on the screen asking if you want to view the output.

10. Click on **Yes** to discard the information box and open the published movie in the default web browser.

During the playback, use your mouse to resize your browser window and notice how our movie is also resized in order to fit the browser window. Also notice that the reflection effect we used on the AMELogo image has been discarded.

Publishing to HTML5

Publishing to HTML5 is the killer new feature of Captivate 6.

One of the main goals of HTML5 is to provide a *plugin free paradigm*. It means that the interactivity and strong visual experience brought to the Internet by the plugins should now be supported *natively* by the browsers and their underlying technologies (mainly HTML, CSS, and JavaScript) *without* the need for an extra third-party plugin.

Because a plugin is no longer necessary to deliver rich interactive content, **any modern browser should be capable of rendering our interactive eLearning courses**. And that includes the browsers installed on mobile devices, such as Tablets and Smartphones.

This is an enormous change, not only for the industry, but also for us, the Captivate users and eLearning developers. Thanks to HTML5, our students will be able to enjoy our eLearning content across all their devices. The door is open for the next revolution of our industry: the **mLearning** (for Mobile Learning) revolution.

> **Blog posts**
>
> To get a better idea of what's at stake with HTML5 in eLearning and mLearning, I recommend these two blog posts, available at `http://blogs.adobe.com/captivate/2011/11/the-how-why-of-ipads-html5-mobile-devices-in-elearning-training-education.html` by Allen Partridge on the official Adobe Captivate blog and `http://rjacquez.com/the-m-in-mlearning-means-more/` by RJ Jacquez.

Using the HTML5 Tracker

At the time of this writing (June 2012), HTML5 is still under development. Some parts of the HTML5 specification are already final and well implemented in the browsers while other parts of the specification are still under discussion. Consequently, some features of Captivate that are supported in Flash are not yet supported in HTML5.

In the following exercise, we will use the HTML5 tracker to better understand what features of our Encoder Demonstration are supported in HTML5:

1. If needed, return to the `encoderDemo_800.cptx` file.
2. Use the **Window | HTML5 Tracker** to open the **HTML5 Tracker** floating panel.

The **HTML5 Tracker** informs us that some features that we used in this project are not (yet) supported in HTML5, as shown in the following screenshot:

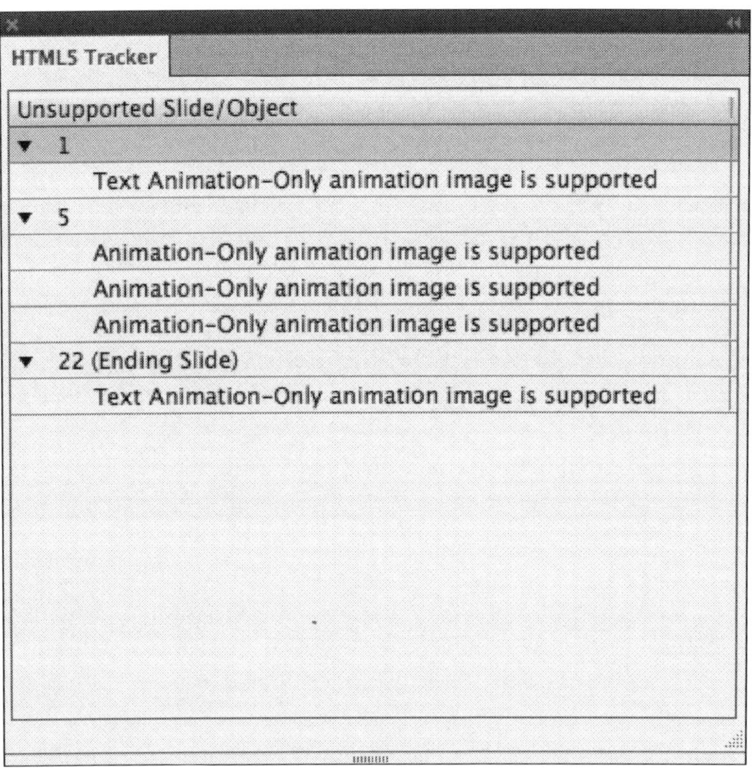

On slide 1 and slide 22, the Text Animations are not supported in HTML5. Same thing for the three orange arrow animations we inserted on slide 5.

3. Close the **HTML5 Tracker** panel.

A comprehensive list of all the objects and features that are not yet supported in the HTML5 output is available in the official Captivate Help at `http://help.adobe.com/en_US/captivate/cp/using/WS16484b78be4e1542-74219321367c91074e-8000.html`. Make sure you read that page before publishing your projects in HTML5.

In the next exercise, we will publish a second version of our Encoder Demonstration using the new HTML5 publishing option.

Publishing the project in HTML5

The process of publishing the project to HTML5 is very similar to the process of publishing the project to Flash. Perform the following steps to publish the project in HTML5:

1. If needed, return to the `encoderDemo_800.cptx` file.
2. Click on the **Publish** icon or use the **File | Publish** menu item to open the **Publish** dialog box.
3. In the left-most column of the **Publish** dialog, make sure you are using the **SWF/HTML5** option.
4. Change the **Project Title** to `encoderDemo_800_HTML5`.
5. Click on the **Browse** button and choose the `Chapter06/publish` folder of the exercises as the publish location.
6. Make sure the **Publish to Folder** checkbox is selected.
7. In the Output Format Option section, select the **HTML5** checkbox. Once done, uncheck the **SWF** checkbox.

This is the single most important setting of the entire procedure. Note that you can select both the SWF *and* the HTML5 options.

8. In the **Advanced Options** area of the **Publish** dialog, deselect the **Scalable HTML content** checkbox.
9. Leave the other options at their current settings and click on the **Publish** button.

Captivate informs us that some features used in this project are not supported in HTML5. This is something we already anticipated in the previous section of the book while looking at the **HTML5 Tracker** panel.

10. Click on **Yes** to discard the message and start the publication to HTML5.

The process of publishing to HTML5 is much longer than the publication to Flash. One of the reasons is that Captivate needs to open the Adobe Media Encoder to convert the `.flv` video used in slide 2 and the Full Motion Recording of slide 13 to the `.mp4` format.

When the publish process is complete, a second message appears asking if you want to view the output.

11. Click on **No** to discard the message and return to the standard Captivate interface.

We will now use the Windows Explorer (Windows) or the Finder (Mac) to take a closer look at the generated files.

12. Use the Windows Explorer (Windows) or the Finder (Mac) to go to the `Chapter06/publish/encoderDemo_800_HTML5` folder of the exercises.

You should find a bunch of files and folders in the `publish/encoderDemo_800_HTML5` folder, as follows:

- `index.html` – is the main HTML file. This is the file to load in the web browser to play the course.
- The `/ar` folder – contains all the needed sound clips in `.mp3` format.
- The `/dr` folder – contains all the needed images. Notice that the mouse pointers, the slide backgrounds, as well as all the Text Captions are exported as `.png` images.
- The `/vr` folder – contains the needed video files in `.mp4` format.
- The `/assets` folders – contains the needed CSS and JavaScript files.

We will now test this version of the project in a web browser.

> **Supported browsers and OS for HTML5**
>
> On the desktop, the HTML5 version of our eLearning project requires *Internet Explorer 9* or later versions, *Safari 5.1* or later versions or *Google Chrome 17* or later versions. For mobile devices, HTML5 is supported on iPads with iOS 5 or later versions. Make sure you use one of the browsers mentioned for the testing phase of this exercise.

13. Open the `index.html` file in one of the supported browsers.

When testing the HTML5 version of the project in a web browser, notice that the unsupported Text Animations of slide 1 and 22 have been replaced by a standard Text Caption with a Fade In effect.

- On slide 3, the effect we added on the AMELogo image is *not* reproduced in the HTML5 output. Surprisingly, *this was not mentioned in the HTML5 tracker panel*.

- On slide 5, the unsupported orange arrows Animations have been replaced by static images.
- On slide 16, the zooming animation is supported, but Text Captions that should be invisible are showing in the Zoom Destination area.

Apart from the few problems mentioned in the previous list, Captivate 6 does a pretty good job in converting our demonstration to HTML5.

That being said, HTML5 publishing is still an emerging technology. The room for improvement is enormous. In the coming years more parts of the HTML5 specification will be finalized and new techniques, tools, and framework will emerge. We will then be able to better implement HTML5 across devices, both in Captivate and throughout the entire Internet.

Publishing to PDF

Another publishing option available in Captivate is to publish our project as an Adobe PDF document. This process is very close to the Flash publishing process we covered previously. When converting to PDF, Captivate first converts the project to Flash and then embeds the resulting `.swf` file in a PDF document. To read the Flash file embedded in the PDF document, the free Adobe Acrobat Reader simply contains a copy of the Flash player.

Publishing the Captivate project to PDF is a great way to make the eLearning course available offline. The students can, for example, download the PDF file from a website and take the course in a train or in an airplane where no Internet connection is available. On the other hand, as the Captivate movie can be viewed offline, any Captivate feature that requires an Internet connection (such as reporting the scores to an **LMS (Learning Management System)**) will *not* work!

In the following exercise, we will publish the Encoder Demonstration to PDF:

1. Return to the `Chapter06/encoderDemo_800.cptx` file.
2. Click on the **Publish** icon situated right next to the **Preview** icon. Alternatively, you can use the **File | Publish** menu item.
3. In the *Publish Format* area, make sure the chosen format is **SWF/HTML5**. If needed, deselect the HTML 5 checkbox and make sure the .SWF checkbox is the only one selected.
4. In the **Flash(.swf) Options** area, change the **Project Title** to `encoderDemo_800_pdf`.
5. Make sure the publish **Folder** still is the `Chapter06/Publish` folder of the exercises.

6. Make sure the **Publish to Folder** checkbox is still **selected**.
7. At the end of the *Output Format Options* area, select the **Export PDF** checkbox.
8. Click on the **Publish** button situated in the lower-right corner of the **Publish** dialog.

When the publishing process is complete, a message tells you that **Acrobat 9 or higher is required to read the generated PDF file**.

9. Click on **OK** to acknowledge the message. A second information box opens.
10. Click on **No** to discard the second message and close the **Publish** dialog.
11. Use the Finder (Mac) or the Windows Explorer (Windows) to browse to the `Chapter06/publish/encoderDemo_800_pdf` folder.

There should be six additional files in the `Chapter06/publish/encoderDemo_800_pdf` folder. Actually, publishing to PDF is an extra option of the standard publishing to Flash feature.

12. Delete all but the PDF file from the `Chapter06/publish/encoderDemo_800_pdf` folder.
13. Double-click on the `encoderDemo_800_pdf.pdf` file to open it in Adobe Acrobat.
14. Notice that the file plays normally in Adobe Acrobat. This proves that all the necessary files and assets have been correctly embedded into the PDF file.

In the next section, we will explore the third publishing option of Captivate: publishing as a standalone application.

Publishing as a standalone application

When publishing as a standalone application, Captivate generates an `.exe` file for playback on Windows or an `.app` file for playback on Macintosh. The `.exe` (Windows) or `.app` (Mac) file contains the compiled `.swf` file plus the Flash player.

The advantages and disadvantages of a standalone application are similar to those of a PDF file. That is, the file can be viewed offline in a train, in an airplane, or elsewhere, but the features requiring an Internet connection will *not* work.

In the following exercise, we will publish the Captivate file as a standalone application using the following steps:

1. If needed, return to the `Chapter06/encoderDemo_800.cptx` file.
2. Click on the **Publish** icon situated right next to the **Preview** icon. Alternatively, you can use the **File | Publish** menu item.

3. Click on the **Media** icon situated on the left-most column of the **Publish** dialog box. The middle area is updated.
4. Open the **Select Type** drop-down list. If you are on a Windows PC, choose **Windows Executable (*.exe)** and if you are using a Mac, choose **MAC Executable (*.app)**.
5. If needed, change the **Project Title** to `encoderDemo_800`.
6. In the **Folder** field, make sure that the `Chapter06/Publish` folder still is the chosen value.

Take some time to inspect the other options of the **Publish** dialog. One of them allows us to choose a custom icon for the generated `.exe` (Win) or `.app` (Mac) file.

7. Leave the other options at their current value and click on the **Publish** button.

When the publish process is complete, an information box will ask you if you want to see the generated output.

8. Click on **No** to clear the information message and to close the **Publish** dialog.

Now that the standalone application has been generated, we will use the Finder (Mac) or the Windows Explorer (Win) to take a look at the `Chapter06/Publish` folder.

9. Use the Finder (Mac) or the Windows Explorer (Windows) to browse to the `Chapter06/Publish` folder of the exercises.
10. Double-click on the `encoderDemo_800.exe` (Win) or on the `encoderDemo_800.app` (Mac) to open the generated application.

Our Captivate movie opens as a standalone application in its own window. Notice that no browser is necessary to play the movie.

This publish format is particularly useful when we want to burn the movie on a CD-ROM. When generating a Windows executable (`.exe`), Captivate can even generate an `autorun.ini` file so that the movie automatically plays when the CD-ROM is inserted in the computer.

Publishing as a video file

When publishing a project as a video file, Captivate 6 generates an `.mp4` video file and proposes various video presets for the conversion. Actually, Captivate first generates a `.swf` file and then converts it to a video file.

After the video conversion, the video file will play on any media player that is capable to play the `.mp4` format. It is an ideal solution if we want to upload our movie on YouTube or if we want to make it available to non-Flash devices. On the other hand, the generated video file proposes a *linear* experience to the learner. That is, no more interaction and no more branching is possible. The student experiences the video from the beginning to the end in a linear fashion, as it is the case while watching a motion picture in a movie theatre or on TV. Consequently, converting a Captivate project to a video file is well suited for a Demonstration, but does not work well in case of a Simulation.

In the following exercise, we will convert our Encoder demonstration into an `.mp4` video using the following steps:

1. If needed, return to the `Chapter06/encoderDemo_800.cptx` file.
2. Click on the **Publish** icon situated right next to the **Preview** icon. Alternatively, you can also use the **File | Publish** menu.
3. If needed, click on the **Media** icon situated on the left-most column of the **Publish** dialog box.
4. Open the **Select Type** drop-down list and choose **MP4 video (*.mp4)**.
5. If needed, change the project title to `encoderDemo_800`.
6. Open the **Select Preset** drop-down list. Take some time to inspect the available options and choose **YouTube Widescreen HD**.
7. Make sure the **Folder** field still points to the `Chapter06/Publish` folder.
8. Click on the **Publish** button at the bottom-right corner of the **Publish** dialog.

Publishing to a video file can be quite a lengthy process, so be patient! First, you will see that Captivate converts the project to a `.swf` file. When that first conversion is over, Captivate opens a second box named **Adobe Captivate Video Publisher** and converts the `.swf` file to video. At the end of the whole process, the **Adobe Captivate Video Publisher** proposes to publish the generated video to YouTube or to open it.

9. Close the **Adobe Captivate Video Publisher** window.
10. As usual, use the Finder (Mac) or the Windows Explorer (Windows) to take a look at the `Chapter06/Publish` folder.
11. Double-click on the `encoderDemo_800.mp4` file. The video opens in the appropriate media player.

The generated video file can be uploaded to YouTube, DailyMotion, or any other video hosting service. You can also host the video on your own internal video-streaming server (such as a Flash Media server) if you have one available.

Publishing to YouTube

Captivate 6 includes a workflow that allows you to publish your Captivate movie to a video file and upload it on your YouTube account without even leaving Captivate.

In the following exercise, we will convert our Captivate file to a video and upload it to YouTube.

This exercise requires a YouTube account and the creation of a new channel on your account. If you do not have a YouTube account, you can create one for free or read through the steps of the exercise.

Perform the following steps to upload the video on YouTube:

1. Return to the `Chapter06/encoderDemo_800.cptx` file.
2. Click on the YouTube icon situated in the main toolbar.

When clicking on the YouTube icon, Captivate generates the slides as if we were publishing the movie in Flash format. When that first conversion is completed, Captivate opens the **Adobe Captivate Video Publisher** and converts the `.swf` file to `.mp4`. So far the process is exactly the same as the one we used in the previous section. At the end of the process, however, Captivate opens another window.

3. Enter your **Username** and **Password** to log on to your YouTube Account.
4. Once logged in, enter the relevant project information.
    - Enter the **Title** of the movie. This is the only required field.
    - Enter a **Description**. By default, the description entered in the Project Info preferences pane (if any) is used.
    - Enter a list of comma-separated **Tags**. These tags will help YouTube reference your video so that other YouTube users can find it easily.
    - Choose the best **Category** for your video.
    - Choose the level of **Privacy** (private or public).
5. Select the **I have read the terms & conditions** checkbox and click on the **Upload** button.

Captivate uploads the video to YouTube. When the process is complete, the Adobe Captivate Video Publisher shows the direct link of our video on YouTube.

6. Click on the **Close** button to close the **Adobe Captivate Video Publisher**.

As you can see, Captivate makes it easy to publish a project to YouTube!

YouTube best practices for Adobe Captivate 5.5 and higher version

Here is an interesting blog post by R.J. Jacquez, a former Adobe Evangelist and a well-know blogger in the eLearning community. RJ describes the upload to YouTube feature and gives some very interesting tips and tricks to convert a Captivate project to a YouTube video, available at `http://rjacquez.com/best-practices-for-publishing-to-youtube-in-the-new-adobe-captivate-5-5/`.

Publishing a Video Demo project

Due to its very nature, a Video Demo project can only be published as an `.mp4` video file. Of course, this video file can be uploaded to YouTube using the very same Publish to YouTube feature than the one we used in the previous section.

In the following exercise, we will return to our `encoderVideo.cpvc` file and explore the available publishing options:

1. Return to the `Chapter06/encoderVideo.cpvc` file.
2. Make sure the file opens in Edit mode.
3. If you are *not* in Edit mode, click on the **Edit** button at the lower-right corner of the screen. (If the **Edit** button is not displayed on the screen, it simply means that you already are in Edit mode).

When the file is open in *Edit* mode, take a look at the main toolbar at the top of the interface. Notice the same YouTube icon as the one we used when in a standard Captivate project. For this exercise, we won't use that YouTube icon, but the standard **Publish** icon instead.

4. Click on the **Publish** icon or use the **File** | **Publish** menu item.

The **Publish Video Demo** dialog opens. Unlike the **Publish** dialog that we used in a standard Captivate demonstration, the **Publish Video Demo** dialog does not let us publish our project in a wide variety of formats.

5. In the **Publish Video Demo** dialog, make sure the **Name** of the project is `encoderVideo`.
6. Click on the **...** button and choose the `Chapter06/publish` folder as the destination of the published video file.

7. Open the **Preset** drop-down. Take some time to inspect the available presets. When done, choose the **Video - Apple iPad** preset.
8. Make sure the **Publish Video Demo** dialog looks like the following screenshot and click on the **Publish** button:

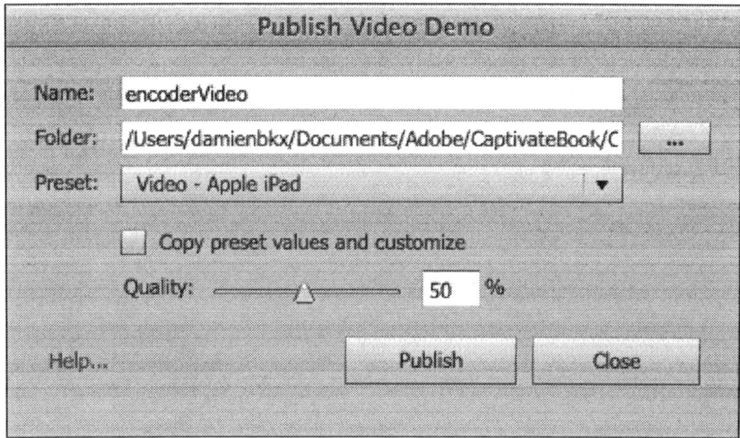

Publishing a Video Demo project can be quite a lengthy process, so be patient! When the process is complete, a message asks you what to do next. Notice that one of the options enables you to upload your newly created video to YouTube directly.

9. Click on the **Close** button to discard the message.
10. Use Windows Explorer (Windows) or the Finder (Mac) to go to the `Chapter06/publish` folder.
11. Double-click on the `encoderDemo.mp4` file to open the video in the default video player of the system.

Publishing a Video Demo project is nothing more than publishing a standard project to video. Remember that a Video Demo project can only be published as a video file. No other publishing options are available for a Video Demo.

Publishing to Word

The last important publishing option to cover is the publication of the Captivate movie as a Microsoft Word document. There are four formats available: *Handout, Lesson, Step by Step guide*, and *storyboard*.

This publication option requires both Captivate and Microsoft Word to be installed on the same system. If you do not have Microsoft Word installed on your computer, just read through the steps of this exercise.

In the following exercise, we will publish our Captivate movie as a Microsoft Word file using the *Handout* template:

1. Return to the `Chapter06/encoderDemo_800.cptx` file.
2. Click on the **Publish** icon situated right next to the **Preview** icon. Alternatively, you can also use the **File | Publish** menu.
3. Click on the **Print** icon situated at the end of the left-most column of the **Publish** dialog box.
4. Change the **Project Title** to `encoderDemo_800_handout`.
5. Make sure the **Folder** field still points to the `Chapter06/Publish` folder of the exercises.
6. In the **Export Range** section, make sure that **All** is selected. We could publish a smaller selection of slides if needed.

That's it for the usual options. Before clicking on the **Publish** button, we have a few more options available in the right-most column of the **Publish** dialog.

7. In the right-most area of the **Publish** dialog, open the **Type** drop-down list. Inspect the available options and choose the **Handouts** type.
8. In the **Handout Layout Options** section, leave the **Use table in the output** option selected.
9. Open the **Slides Per Page** drop-down and choose to have **2** slides on each Word page.
10. Select the **Caption Text**, the **Slide Notes**, and the **Include mouse Path** checkboxes.
11. Take some time to inspect the remaining options, but leave them all at their current value.
12. When ready, click on the **Publish** button.

Captivate generates the Word document according to the options set in the **Publish** dialog. When done, an information box appears asking if you want to view the generated file.

13. Click on **No** to discard the information box and close the **Publish** dialog.

14. Use the Finder (Mac) or the Windows Explorer (Windows) to browse to the `Chapter06/Publish` folder.
15. Double-click on the newly created `encoderDemo_800_handout.doc` file.

The file opens in Microsoft Word. Take some time to inspect the generated Word document. Can you find the effect of each of the boxes we selected in the **Publish** dialog?

Extra credit

In this extra credit section, you will test the remaining Microsoft Word publish options by generating a *Lesson*, a *Step by Step guide*, and a *storyboard*. These are the general steps to follow:

- Open the **Publish** dialog box.
- In the left-most column, ensure that the **Print** option is selected.
- Give the project a meaningful **Project Title**.
- In the right-most area of the **Publish** dialog, change the **Type** to **Lesson**, **Step by Step**, or **storyboard**.
- Experiment with the other options. Each **Type** has a specific set of options available, which are, for the most part, self-explanatory.
- When ready, click on the **Publish** button.
- Use the Finder (Mac) or the Windows Explorer (Windows) to browse to the `Chapter06/Publish` folder and test your files.

Other publishing options

When we open the **Publish** dialog box, there are three options in the left-most column that we did not cover in the previous sections. We will now briefly describe these remaining options:

- **Adobe Acrobat Connect Pro** – Adobe Connect pro is a server product from Adobe. One of the services offered by this enterprise solution is an LMS that integrates nicely with Captivate. If an Acrobat Adobe Connect pro server is available in your network, you can use this publishing option to convert the Captivate file to Flash (`.swf`) and upload the resulting file to the Acrobat Adobe Connect pro server.
- **E-Mail** – This option converts the Captivate file to Flash or as a standalone application and attaches the resulting file in an e-mail message. The message can be further customized in your e-mail client software.

- **FTP** – This option converts the Captivate file to Flash or as a standalone application and uploads the resulting file(s) to an FTP server.

These three options are nothing special. They just combine one of the main publishing options covered earlier with some kind of extra file transport action in order to facilitate a usual workflow.

This last exercise concludes our overview of the publishing options of Captivate. So let's make a quick summary of what we have learned:

- Publishing is the third and last step of the Captivate workflow. The idea is to make our eLearning content available to the outside world.
- Captivate proposes four main publishing formats: publishing to *Flash* or *HTML5*, publishing as a *standalone application*, publishing as a *video* file, and publishing as a *Microsoft Word* document.
- When publishing in a Flash format, Captivate generates a `.swf` file that can be played back by the free Adobe Flash Player plugin.
- The generated `.swf` file can be embedded in a PDF document for offline viewing. This option requires Adobe Acrobat, or Adobe Reader 9, or later versions.
- Publishing in HTML5 is a new capability of Captivate 6. A project published in HTML5 can be played back on virtually any mobile device, including iOS devices such as the iPhone and the iPad.
- Not every feature of Captivate is supported in HTML5. Use the **HTML5 Tracker** to find out what slides/objects of your project is not supported.
- When publishing as a standalone application, Captivate produces either an `.exe` file for playback on Windows or an `.app` file for playback on a Mac.
- Captivate 6 can produce `.mp4` video that can be optimized for YouTube and for playback on a mobile device.
- When publishing as a video or as a standalone application, the published project can no longer connect to the Internet. Consequently, some features that require an Internet connection (such as communicating with an LMS) will not work.
- When the project is published as a video file, it can only be experienced as a linear video that plays from the beginning to the end. Consequently, interactivity and branching are not supported.
- A Video Demo project can only be published as a `.mp4` video file.

Extra credit

In this extra credit section, you will open the Encoder Simulation and publish it in various formats.

These are the general steps to follow:

- Open the `encoderSim_800.cptx` file.
- Open the **Publish** dialog and publish the movie in Adobe Flash format.
- Reopen the **Publish** dialog and ask Captivate to generate a HTML5 output of our project. Don't forget to use the **Window** | **HTML5** Tracker panel prior to publishing in HTML5 in order to find out whether all the features used in the project are supported in HTML5.
- Return to the **Publish** dialog to create a Mac or a Windows executable depending on the OS you work on.
- Don't forget to test each and every generated file as soon as the publication process is finished.

Summary

At the end of this chapter, we can proudly turn off the lights and leave the post-production studio. We have gone through the three major steps of the production process, uncovering lots of Captivate features, tools, and objects along the way!

In this particular chapter, we first focused on some final changes we can apply to our movie before the publishing phase. We have checked the spelling, decided how the movie should start and end, added metadata to the project, and created a unique Skin among other things. A Captivate Skin is a collection of three elements: the Playback Controls, the Borders, and the Table of Contents.

When all these Final Changes had been taken care of, the movie was finally ready for publication.

In the second part of this chapter, we concentrated on the **Publish** dialog box where we covered the main publishing features of Captivate. Publishing is the process by which the movie is made available to the outside world.

Publishing to Flash is the main publishing option of Captivate. The Flash format supports every single feature of Captivate. HTML5 publishing is a new capability of Captivate 6. Even though it still needs to improve, HTML5 publishing opens the door of mLearning, which is the next revolution of our industry. Other publishing formats of Captivate include publishing as a standalone application, publishing as an `.mp4` video file, and publishing as a Microsoft Word document. The `.mp4` video files produced by Captivate can easily be uploaded on YouTube without even leaving the application.

With our project published in such a wide variety of formats, **the first part of this book is over!** In the next few chapters, we will concentrate on the most advanced features of Captivate.

The next chapter will focus on the *quizzes*. By adding Question Slides and Question Pools to the project, we will be able to produce complex quizzes in order to assess our student's knowledge. We will then configure our Captivate movie to report the result of the Quiz to a **Learning Management System** (**LMS**) using either the **Sharable Content Object Reference Model** (**SCORM**) or the **Aviation Industry Computer-based Training Committee** (**AICC**) standard. If you do not have access to an LMS, we will discuss an alternate method to help you track and assess your student's performances.

We still have lots of interesting discussions ahead, so stay tuned and let's meet in Chapter 7!

Meet the Community

Jim Leichliter

Bio

Jim Leichliter of CaptivateDev.com is a Software Developer with 13 years of experience and has a love for eLearning. Not only does he build Captivate Widgets, but he also helps clients integrate Captivate with third-party systems to create mashups, interactive games, and reporting solutions.

Contact details

Blog: `http://CaptivateDev.com`

Twitter: `@CaptivatePro`

E-mail: `Jim@CaptivateDev.com`

My personal note

Jim's website is another one of these resources that I cannot do without. His well-maintained blog helped me out in many situations I had to face with Captivate, but the real treasure proposed by Jim is his collection of free and commercial Captivate Widgets.

7
Working with Quizzes

Assessing the student's knowledge has always been one of the primary concerns of anyone involved in some kind of teaching activity. When it comes to eLearning, addressing the assessment issue is both a pedagogical and a technical challenge.

On the pedagogical side, one of the factors that characterize the eLearning experience is the fact that the learner sits alone in front of his/her computer. No one is around to assist the students. We, the teachers, have to leave lighthouses along the learner's path in order to make sure that the lonely learner does not get lost and confused. Constant assessment might help us keep our students on track. By giving them many opportunities to test and validate their new knowledge, our students can immediately identify the areas of the course that deserve more attention and can build any new knowledge on solid grounds.

On the technical side, Captivate contains a powerful quizzing engine that lets us insert different kinds of Question Slides in our movies. At the end of the Quiz, Captivate is able to send a detailed report to an LMS. An LMS is a **Learning Management System**. It is a server that is able to host eLearning content and to track the learner's progression into the online courses it hosts.

In this chapter, we will:

- Insert various kinds of Question Slides in our Captivate movies.
- Create a Question Pool and insert Random Question Slides in the project.
- Create a Pretest.
- Explore and set the Quiz Preferences.
- Provide feedback to the user by using the branching capabilities of the Question Slides and of the Quiz.
- Set up the reporting to an LMS server.

- Discuss the SCORM and AICC standards used to communicate the Quiz results to an LMS server.
- Publish an eLearning-enabled project.
- Use the alternative Quiz reporting features of Captivate in case no LMS is available.

Preparing our work

For the exercises of this chapter, we will use our Driving in Belgium application. Perform the following steps to prepare Captivate:

1. Open Captivate and ensure that the **Classic** workspace is currently applied.
2. Use the **Window | Workspace | Reset 'Classic'** to reapply the original default workspace.
3. Open the `Chapter07/drivingInBe.cptx` file.

At the end of the chapter, we will need to work with the Encoder Demonstration project.

4. Also, open the `Chapter07/encoderDemo_800.cptx` file.

Introducing the Quiz

During the first part of this chapter, we will insert a Quiz at the end of the Driving in Belgium project. When taking a Quiz such as the one we are about to create, it is very important to introduce the Quiz to the students and to precisely tell them what is going to happen. We will now copy-paste two slides from another project into the Driving in Belgium project. These two slides will be used to introduce the Quiz to the students and give precise directions about how the Quiz is supposed to take place using the following steps:

1. Make sure you are in the `Chapter07/drivingInBe.cptx` file.
2. Use the **Filmstrip** to go to slide 14.

Slide 14 is the last slide of the actual course. We want our Quiz to be inserted in between slide 14 and the final slide of the project where we thank our students for taking this online course.

3. Open the `Chapter07/dib_quizIntro.cptx` file.
4. In the **Filmstrip**, select both slides of the `dib_quizIntro.cptx` file.

5. Hit the *Ctrl* + *C* (Windows) or the *cmd* + *C* (Mac) shortcut to place both slides in the clipboard.
6. Return to slide 14 of the `drivingInBe.cptx` file.
7. Use the *Ctrl* + *V* (Windows) or the *cmd* + *V* (Mac) shortcut to paste the slides.

Remember that new slides are always inserted *after* the active slide. In our case, the two slides that we are pasting are included as slides 15 and 16 of the `drivingInBe.cptx` project.

8. Use the **Filmstrip** to return to slide 14.
9. Use the Preview icon to preview the **Next 5 slides**.

This gives you a chance to experience the new slides in a manner that is close to what our students will experience while taking the test.

10. When the preview is finished, close the **Preview** pane. Then, close the `dib_quizIntro.cptx` project.

At the end of this procedure, there should be 17 slides in the project.

Creating Question Slides

In Captivate, a Question Slide is a very special kind of slide. When inserting the first Question slide in a project, we automatically create a Quiz. There are many options that we can set either for each specific Question Slide or for the entire Quiz.

Captivate supports eight types of Question Slides. In this section, we will explore each of these question types one by one.

To get started, let's insert a first Question Slide in our project using the following steps:

1. Return to the `Chapter07/drinvingInBe.cptx` file.
2. Use the **Filmstrip** to go to slide 16.
3. Use the **Insert | Question Slide** menu item. The **Insert Questions** dialog box opens.

The **Insert Questions** dialog box provides a list of all the types of Question Slides available in Captivate. For this first example, we will add only one **Multiple Choice** question to the project.

4. In the **Insert Questions** dialog, select the **Multiple Choice** checkbox.
5. Open the **Graded** drop-down list associated with the **Multiple Choice** checkbox.

The drop-down list provides three options: **Graded**, **Survey**, and **Pretest**:

- A **Graded** question has right and wrong answers. For example, *Is Belgium a Multilingual country?* (True/False) is a question that has a right and a wrong answer, so it is a *Graded* question (by the way, the answer is *True!*).
- A **Survey** question is used to get the student's feedback. A Survey question has no wrong answer as it is used to gather the learner's opinion about something. For example, *Would you recommend this eLearning course to your friends?* (Yes/No) is a *Survey* question. There are no right or wrong answers to that question.
- A **Pretest** question is a question that is *not part of the quiz* and whose answer *is not reported* to the server. A Pretest is used to assess the student's knowledge *before* he/she takes the course. It is possible to add branching based on the outcome of a Pretest. For example, the student that passes the Pretest can skip the course if he/she wants to, but the student that fails the Pretest has to take the course to gain the required knowledge. Pretest is a new feature of Captivate 6.

In our case, we will add a single Graded Multiple Choice question.

6. Select **Graded** in the drop-down list.
7. Make sure that the **Insert Questions** dialog is set to add a single **Graded Multiple Choice** Question Slide to the project, as shown in the following screenshot:

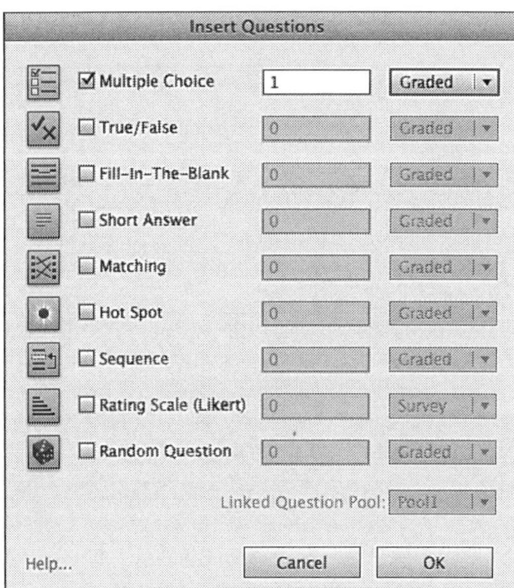

8. Click on the **OK** button to generate the Question Slide and to close the **Insert Questions** dialog.

Take a look at the **Filmstrip**. It now contains **19 slides**. It means that the operation we have just completed has added *two slides* to the project.

- As expected, the Multiple Choice Question Slide has been inserted *after* the slide that was selected. In our case, the Multiple Choice Question is slide 17.
- Because the new slide is the first Question Slide of the project, Captivate has also generated the **Quiz Result** Slide as slide 18.

The Quiz Result Slide contains a lot of automatically generated elements.

9. Use the **Filmstrip** to go to slide 18.
10. Inspect the various elements that have been automatically added to this slide.

Most of these elements are self-explanatory and need no further explanation. The only element that probably requires an explanation is the **Review Area**. This area is used to display a feedback message to the student at the end of the Quiz. The content of that message depends of the outcome of the Quiz.

The Quiz Result Slide is generated by default when a new Quiz is created (or in other words, when the first Question Slide is added to the project). It is possible to turn this slide off if we want to.

11. Use the **Quiz | Quiz Preferences** menu item to open the Quiz Preferences dialog.
12. On the left-hand side of the **Preferences** dialog, click on the **Settings** category of the **Quiz** section.

Watch out! There is another **Settings** category in the **Recording** section. Make sure you use the one in the **Quiz** section, as shown in the following screenshot:

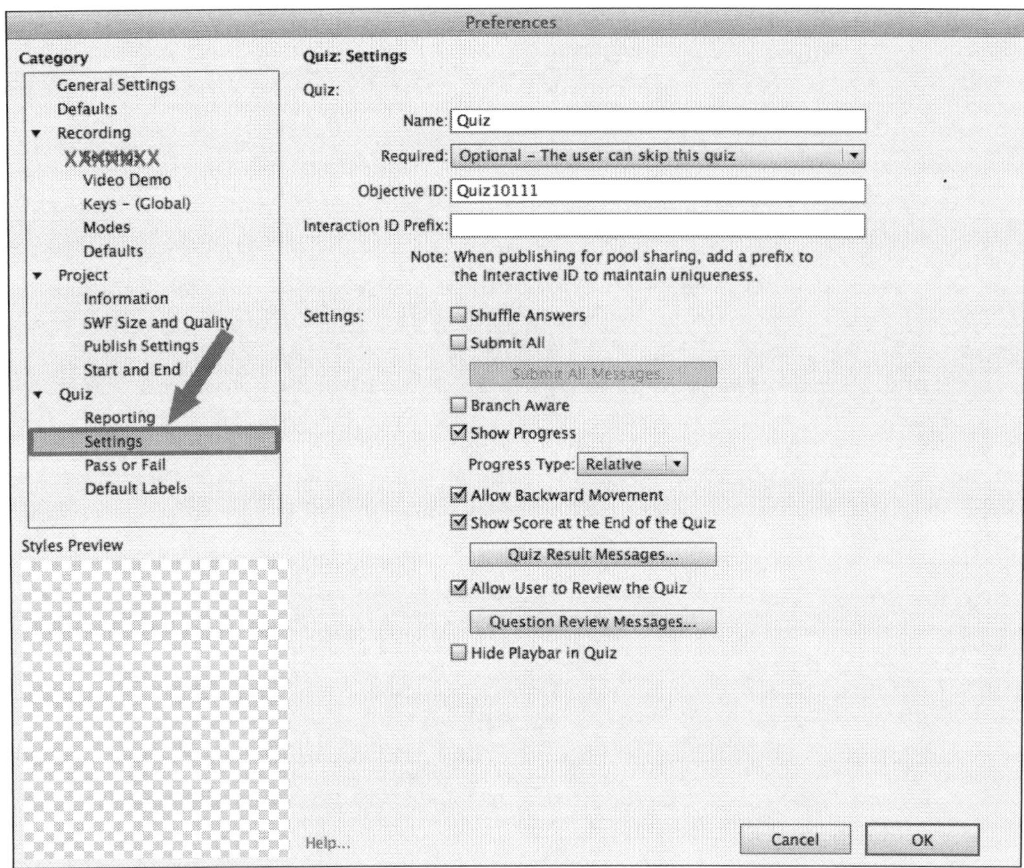

13. Deselect the **Show score at the End of the Quiz** checkbox.

With this option deselected, the **Quiz Result** Slide is turned off.

14. Click on the **OK** button to apply the changes and close the **Preferences** dialog.

When the operation is complete, take another look at the **Filmstrip**. Notice that slide 18 is grayed out and that an eye icon appears under the slide 18 thumbnail. It simply means that the slide is hidden. In other words, it is still in the project, but it won't be displayed to the student!

15. On the **Filmstrip**, click on the eye icon associated with slide 18.

This action turns the visibility of slide 18 back on. It also reselects the **Show Score at the End of Quiz** checkbox of the Quiz Preferences.

16. Use the **Quiz | Quiz Preferences** menu item to return to the **Preferences** dialog.
17. On the left-hand side of the **Preferences** dialog, click on the **Settings** category of the **Quiz** section.

Notice that the **Show Score at the End of Quiz** checkbox is *selected*. It means that turning the visibility of the Quiz Result Slide back on in the **Filmstrip** automatically reselects this checkbox!

18. Click on **Cancel** to close the **Preferences** dialog.

In the next section, we will study each and every question type one by one. The first question type we will focus on is the Multiple Choice question.

The Multiple Choice question

The basic principle of a Multiple Choice question is to ask a question and provide multiple possible answers. The student has to choose the correct answer from the list of available answers. In Captivate, we can go a step further and set multiple correct answers for the same question. In such a case, we have access to some advanced scoring options to determine what happens when a student's answer is partially correct.

In the following exercise, we will fine-tune the Multiple Choice question we added in the previous section using the following steps:

1. Return to the `Chapter07/drivingInBe.cptx` file.
2. Use the **Filmstrip** to go to slide 17.

Slide 17 is our first Question Slide. As you can see, lots of objects have been automatically generated on this slide.

Watch out! It is possible that some objects sit on top of other objects. For example, move the orange *Incomplete Caption* to reveal the *Success Caption*!

The purpose of most of the generated objects should be obvious, but some of them require more explanation.

- The **Review Area** is related to the **Review Quiz** button situated on the Quiz Result Slide. If the user clicks on that button at the end of the Quiz, he/she will be allowed to review the Quiz. In such a case, the Review Area is used to display an appropriate feedback message to the student.
- The student uses the four buttons at the bottom of the slide (**Clear**, **Back**, **Skip**, and **Submit**) to interact with the Quiz. It is possible to control the visibility of each of those buttons either for the entire Quiz or for each specific Question Slide.
- The **Progress Indicator** in the lower-left corner of the slide can also be customized in the Quiz Preferences.
- During the Quiz, the *feedback messages* situated on the right-hand side of the slide are all hidden by default. They are automatically revealed depending on the student's answer to the question.

Every single element of the Question Slide can be customized. If needed, we can even insert extra objects on the Question Slides (such as Images, Animations, or additional Text Captions) using the same techniques as for a standard slide.

Text Captions are used to display the question and the list of possible answers.

3. Double-click on the Text Caption that reads **Type the question here** to select it in Edit mode. When done, *triple-click* the same object to select its content.
4. Type `What are the three official languages of Belgium?` When done, hit the *Esc* key.
5. Resize the Text Caption so that the entire question sits on a single line of text.
6. If needed, move the Caption so that it does not overlap with any other slide element.
7. Double-click on the first possible answer to select it in Edit mode, then triple-click the very same object to select its entire content. Type `French` in the first possible answer.
8. Use the same technique to write `English` in the second possible answer.

To make this question more interesting, we need to add some more possible answers to the list.

9. Open the **Quiz Properties** panel situated at the right edge of the interface, next to the **Properties** and **Library** panels.

10. In the **General** accordion of the **Quiz Properties** panel, change the number of **Answers** to `5`. Captivate generates three more answers on the Question Slide.
11. Type `German`, `Dutch`, and `Spanish` in the newly generated answers.

At this moment, the Question Slide only accepts one of the answers from the list as the correct answer, but Belgium is a complicated country with three official languages! Fortunately, Captivate has an option that allows the multiple choice question to accept more than one correct answer.

12. In the **General** accordion of the **Quiz Properties** panel, select the **Multiple Answers** checkbox.

On the Question slide, this action changes the radio buttons associated with each of the possible answers to checkboxes. We will now tell Captivate what the right answers are.

13. On the Question Slide, select the three correct answers (**French**, **German**, and **Dutch**).

At this moment, the question is either entirely right (if the user selects all three correct answers) or entirely wrong (in every other case). A new feature of Captivate 6 allows us to define **Partial Scoring**. This advanced option is currently available on Multiple Choice questions only.

14. In the **General** accordion of the **Quiz Properties** panel, select the **Partial Score** checkbox.

Notice that by selecting the **Partial Score** checkbox, the **Points** and **Penalty** options of the **General** accordion are grayed out. When Partial Scoring is turned on, **each possible answer of the Multiple Choice question is assigned a specific score**.

15. Select the first possible answer of the Question Slide (**French**) and return to the **Properties** panel.
16. Open the **Advanced Answer Option** accordion and confirm that this specific answer is worth **5 Points**.
17. Select the second possible answer (**English**) and confirm it is worth **0 Points**.
18. Repeat the same procedure with the remaining possible answers. The **Dutch** and **German** answers should grant **5 Points** to the student, while the **Spanish** answer is worth **0 Points**.

Now that Captivate is able to tell the right from the wrong answers apart, we will finish off with this first Question Slide by fine-tuning some additional options.

19. In the **General** accordion of the **Quiz Properties** panel, select the **Shuffle Answers** checkbox.

The **Shuffle Answers** checkbox asks Captivate to display the possible answers in a random order each time a student takes the Quiz.

20. In the **Options** accordion of the **Quiz Properties** panel, deselect the **Incomplete** caption. This removes the orange feedback message from the Question Slide.
21. Also deselect the **Next** checkbox to remove the **Skip** button from the slide.
22. Take some time to inspect the remaining options of the **Quiz Properties** panel, but do not change any of them at this time.

Pay particular attention to the following:

- You can still change the question **Type** (**Graded** or **Survey**) in the **General** accordion.
- You can set a **Time Limit** to answer that particular question.
- You can set an **On Success** action and a **Last Attempt** action to implement *branching* on the Question Slides.

The last thing we will do on this first Question Slide is to take care of the two feedback messages.

23. Change the text of the green feedback message to `Great answer! Click anywhere to continue.`
24. Change the text of the red feedback message to `Sorry, your answer is not correct! The Official languages of Belgium are French, Dutch, and German. Belgian road signs might be in one or more of these languages. Click anywhere to continue.`
25. Move and resize these two feedback messages as you see fit. Remember that these two messages are not supposed to be displayed at the same time, so it is not a problem if they overlap.

This concludes our exploration of the Multiple Choice question type. As you can see, there is a big bunch of options available to help us precisely fine-tune our assessments.

The Short Answer question

The second question type we will focus on is the **Short Answer** question.

On Slide 5, we ask the learner if he/she uses *kilometers per hour* or *miles per hour* to measure speed. If the student clicks on *miles per hour*, a short course on how to convert m/h to km/h is taught on slide 7 and 8. The Short Answer Question Slide will be added as slide 9 to *immediately* test the student on this new knowledge.

This is the constant assessment technique at work! Notice that only the students taking the *miles per hour* branch will have to answer that question. Perform the following steps to add the Short Answer Question Slide:

1. Use the **Filmstrip** to go to slide 8 of the `Chapter07/drivingInBe.cptx` file.
2. Use the **Insert | Question Slide** menu item to open the **Insert Questions** dialog box.
3. Select the **Short Answer** checkbox. Make sure you add a single **Graded Short Answer** question.
4. Click on the **OK** button. Captivate inserts the new Question Slide as slide 9 and closes the **Insert Questions** dialog.
5. Change the title of the question to `Convert km/h to m/h.`
6. Change the question to `How much m/h makes 120 km/h?`
7. Move and resize these two Text Captions as you see fit.

We will now change the properties of the answer field and tell Captivate what is the correct answer to this question.

8. Select the **Answer** field. The **Properties** panel is updated and shows the properties of the **Answer**.
9. Type the following entries in the **Correct Entries** box (Click on the **+** icon to add an entry) `80`, `80mph`, `80 mph`, and `80 m/h`.
10. Make sure that the **Case-Sensitive** checkbox is *not* selected.

Remember that we want to test if the student can convert m/h to km/h. The proper spelling or the proper use of capital letters is not of concern here. That's why we have to accept many different correct entries.

This situation illustrates the difficulty to correctly set up a *Short Answer* question. We have to ask the proper question, so that the correct answer is obvious enough for a computer to correct it, but it has to be flexible enough to allow the students to type the same answer in different versions.

11. With the **Answer** object selected, enter the following properties in the **Transform** accordion:
    - **W**= `115`, **H** = `28`
    - **X** = `120`, **Y** = `90`
12. Select the **Submit** button and move it next to the answer field (**X**= `320`, **Y** = `222`).

We will now add an image to the Question Slide to make it more attractive and fine-tune the question properties.

13. Open the **Library** panel. Locate the `c43_speedLimit120.png` file in the **images** section.
14. Drag-and-drop the image from the **Library** to the slide.
15. With the image selected, use the **Transform** accordion of the **Properties** panel to enter the following value:
    - **W** = `120`, **H** = `120`
    - **X** = `55`, **Y** = `175`
16. Open the **Quiz Properties** panel.
17. In the **General** accordion, change the **Points** to `5` and the **Penalty** to `1`.

The **Penalty** will *remove* one point from the student's score if he/she gives the wrong answer to the question. This option is yet another new feature of Captivate 6.

18. In the **Options** accordion:
    - Deselect the **Incomplete** Caption. The orange feedback message disappears from the screen and the Success Caption is revealed.
    - Deselect the **Clear**, **Back**, and **Next** buttons. The corresponding objects are removed from the slide.
19. Leave all the other options of the **Quiz Properties** panel at their current settings.

Last but not least, we will enter the proper text in the correct and wrong feedback messages.

20. Change the text of the green message to `Great answer! 120 km/h (80 mph) is the speed limit on Belgian motorways. Click anywhere to continue.`
21. Change the text of the red message to `Sorry! 120 km/h makes approximately 80 MPH. Watch out, as 120 km/h is the speed limit on Belgian highways! Click anywhere to continue.`
22. Resize and position these two messages where you see fit. Remember that these two objects *are not supposed to be displayed at the same time*, so it is not a problem if they overlap.

That's it for the Short Answer question. Make sure your slide looks more or less like the following screenshot and save the file before moving on:

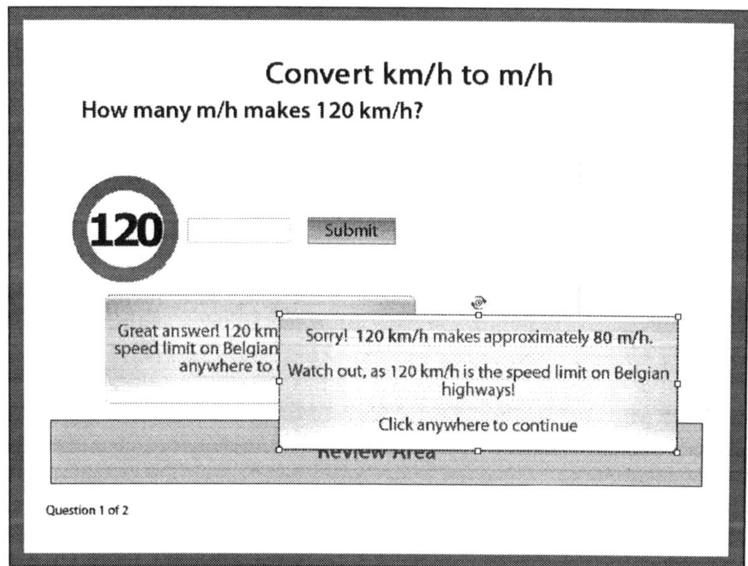

Adding the remaining Question Slides

To speed you up and let you focus on the Question Slides specifics, the remaining Question Slides of this project have already been created for you. They are stored in the `Chapter7/additionalQuestions.cptx` file. In the following exercise, we will simply copy-paste the questions of the `additionalQuestions.cptx` file into the `drivingInBe.cptx` file:

1. Open the `Chapter07/additionalQuestions.cptx` file.
2. Use the **Filmstrip** of the `additionalQuestions.cptx` file to select the first slide of this project.
3. Leave the *Shift* key down and select slide 6 in the **Filmstrip**.

This action selects from slide 1 to slide 6. In other words, you have selected all but the last slide of the `additionalQuestions.cptx` file. Notice that the last slide of this project is the automatic Quiz Result Slide of the Quiz.

4. Use the *Ctrl* + *C* (Windows) or the *cmd* + *C* (Mac) shortcut to *copy* the selected slides to the clipboard.
5. Return to slide 18 of the `drivingInBe.cptx` file.
6. Use the *Ctrl* + *V* (Windows) or the *cmd* + *V* (Mac) shortcut to paste the slides.

Six Question Slides are added to the project *after* slide 18. At the end of this exercise, there should be 26 slides in the `drivingInBe.cptx` file.

7. Save the `drivingInBe.cptx` file.
8. Close the `additionalQuestions.cptx` file.

The stage is set for us to explore the remaining question types available in Captivate.

The Matching Question

The next question type is the Matching Question. The basic idea is to provide two columns of elements. The student has to match an element of the first column with one or more element(s) of the second column. Perform the following steps to customize this Question Slide:

1. Still in the `Chapter07/drivingInBe.cptx` file, use the **Filmstrip** to go to slide 19.

Slide 19 is one of the slides that we copy-pasted from the `additionalQuestions.cptx` file.

2. Change the items of the first column to: `Motorways`, `National Roads`, and `Cities and Towns`.
3. Change the Items of the second column to: `50km/h`, `unlimited`, and `90 km/h`.

To make the question more interesting (and the answer more difficult to find), we will provide a different number of items in both columns.

4. Open the **Quiz Properties** panel.
5. In the **General** accordion of the **Quiz Properties** panel, increase the number of items of **Column 2** to `5`.
6. Select the **Shuffle Column 1** checkbox.

The **Shuffle Column 1** checkbox instructs Captivate to display the options of the first column in a random order each time a student takes the Quiz.

We will now change the text of the two extra items of Column 2 and show Captivate the correct answer to this question.

7. Type `120 km/h` and `30 km/h` in the two extra items of Column 2.
8. Click on the **Motorways** item of the first column to select it. Use the drop-down list at the left of the text to match it with the **120 km/h** item of column 2.

9. Use the same technique to:
   - Match **National Road** with **90 km/h**
   - Match **Cities and Towns** with **50 km/h**
10. Return to the **Quiz Properties** panel.
11. In the **General** accordion of the **Quiz Properties** panel, change the **Points** to `15`.

Note that many items of the first column can match the same item of the second column. This ability can be used to create very interesting and complex matching questions.

Before moving on to the next question type, feel free to move and resize the objects of this slide to your taste. Remember that when it comes to aligning and resizing objects, some great tools are available on the Align toolbar.

The True/False question

The third question type we will discuss is the True/False question. A True/False question is a Multiple Choice question with only two possible answers. By default, these two answers are *True* and *False* but we can change these defaults to anything we like (such as Yes/No, Man/Woman, and so on) as long as no more than two different answers are needed. Perform the following steps to fine-tune the True/False question type:

1. Still in the `drivingInBe.cptx` file, use the **Filmstrip** to go to Slide 20.

Slide 20 is a True/False question that we imported from the `additionalQuestions.cptx` file. Notice that the typing of the question has already been taken care of. Notice also that the two answers (**True** and **False**) do not integrate nicely with the question. Our first task will be to adjust the possible answers so the question makes sense.

2. Change the text of the **True** answer to `On the Right Side`. Resize the object accordingly.
3. Change the text of the **False** answer to `On the Left Side` and resize the object accordingly.

This illustrates that the possible answers of a True/False question can actually be something else than *True* and *False*. The important point here is to ask a question that has **no more than two possible answers**, whatever these answers are.

4. Make sure that **On the Right Side** is selected as the correct answer.
5. In the **General** accordion of the **Quiz Properties** panel, change the **Points** to `5`.

As you can see, the True/False question is actually a variant of the Multiple Choice question. It is a Multiple Choice limited to two choices! Don't forget to save the file before moving on to the next Question Slide.

The Fill-In-The-Blank question

The next question type is the Fill-In-The-Blank question. The idea is to take out one or more words from a given sentence. The student has to *fill in the blank(s)* either by typing the missing words or by choosing them from a drop-down list. Perform the following steps to use the Fill-in-The-Blank question type:

1. Use the **Filmstrip** to go to slide 21 of the `Chapter07/drivingInBe.cptx` file.

Slide 21 is yet another question imported from the `additionalQuestions.cptx` file.

Notice the **On Belgian motorways, the speed limit is 120 km/h** sentence that has been typed for you. This sentence is the one from which some words will be taken out. In our case, we will delete the word **Motorways** and replace it by a drop-down list of possible answers the students will have to choose from.

2. Select the word **Motorways**.
3. In the **General** tab of the **Quiz Properties** panel, click on the **Mark Blank** button.

Notice that a dashed line now underlines the selected word. This is how Captivate marks the words that are taken out of the original sentence. We will now tell Captivate that we want to replace this word by a drop-down list.

4. Double-click on the underlined word until a box pops up on the screen.
5. In the bottom-left corner of the box, change **User Input** to **Dropdown List** (1).
6. Click on the **+** icon (2) three times to add three more entries in the list. There should be four possible answers in the list.
7. The four propositions are *motorways, national roads, cities and towns,* and *railroad.*
8. Show Captivate the right answer by selecting the **Motorways** option in the list. (Notice that we can mark multiple propositions as correct).
9. Select the **Shuffle Answers** checkbox.

The Shuffle Answers checkbox asks Captivate to display the options of the drop-down list in a random order each time a student takes the quiz.

Make sure your list looks like the following screenshot before moving on:

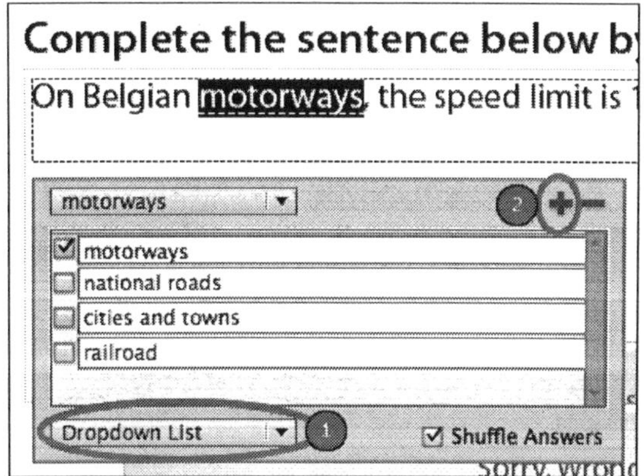

That's it for the Fill-In-The-Blank question. Of course, it is possible to mark more than one blank in the same sentence. In this case, Captivate will give the points of the question only if the whole sentence is correct. The question is either completely right or completely wrong!

The Hotspot question

The Hotspot question was a new feature of Captivate 3. The idea is to display an image on the slide and let the student choose the right spot(s) on this image. In our example, we will display road signs and ask the student to choose which sign corresponds to a given situation using the following steps:

1. Return to the `Chapter07/drivingInBe.cptx` file. Use the **Filmstrip** to go to slide 22.

Slide 22 has also been imported from the `additionalQuestions.cptx` file. Notice that an image containing various Belgian road signs have been added to the slide and that a single *Hotspot* is present on the slide. The student will be asked to click on the road sign(s) that gives the right of the way.

In this example, *two* of the road signs of the image are used to give the right of the way. Our next task will be to add one more Hotspot to the slide and to position the Hotspots above the right answers.

2. In the **General** accordion of the **Quiz Properties** panel, change the number of **Answers** to `2`.

This action generates a second Hotspot on the Question Slide.

3. Position the first Hotspot on top of the image of the first road sign and the second hotspot on top of the last road sign. Feel free to resize the Hotspots as needed.
4. Select one of the two Hotspots. In the **Fill & Stroke** accordion of the **Properties** panel, change the Stroke **Width** to `0` to turn off the border of the selected Hotspot.
5. At the top of the **Properties** panel, click on the **Save Changes to Existing Style** icon.

This action turns off the border of the remaining Hotspot. The goal is to create Hotspots that are invisible to the students.

6. Open the **Quiz Properties** panel and take a closer look at the available properties for a Hotspot question.

Make sure your Hotspot Question Slide looks similar to the following screenshot:

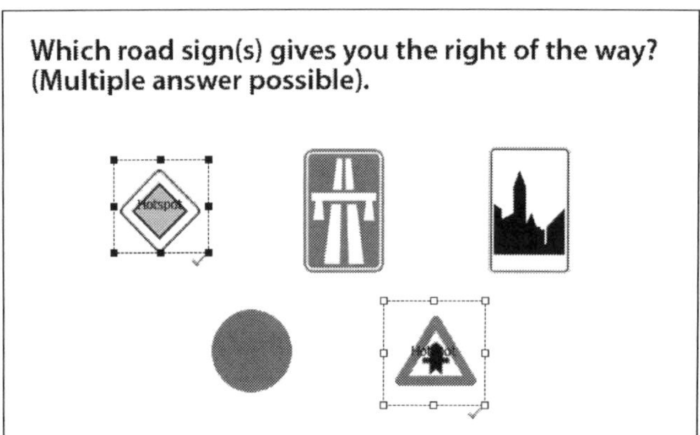

That's it for the Hotspot question! As you can see, there is nothing really difficult about this question type, just another great assessment tool in our teacher's toolset.

The Sequence question

The Sequence question was also a new feature of Captivate 3. The idea is to provide the student with a set of actions that have to be arranged in the correct order. Perform the following steps to use the Sequence question type:

1. Still on the `Chapter07/drivingInBe.cptx` file, use the **Filmstrip** to go to slide 23.

2. In the **General** accordion of the **Quiz Properties** panel, change the number of **Answers** to `5`.

This action generates three extra steps in addition to the two actions that were already present on the slide. We will now change the text of these five steps.

3. Change the text of the five steps to: `Get a nice parking slot - Turn off the engine. - Get out of the car. - Make sure the doors are locked. - Visit Belgium!`

Sizing the steps of the Sequence

For some strange reason, it is not possible to change the height of an individual step after the text has been typed in. If needed, make sure to enlarge these Text Captions *before* typing the actual items of the sequence.

In this case, there is no need to show Captivate the right answer. Captivate will simply display these steps in a random order each time a student takes the Quiz. The right answer is the order in which we typed the actions on the slide.

4. In the **General** accordion of the **Quiz Properties** panel, make sure the **Points** option is set to **10**. Also, add a **Penalty** of **2** points.

These options instruct Captivate to add 10 points to the score of the student in case the answer is right and to remove 2 points from the score when the answer is wrong. Remember that the **Penalty** option is one of the new features of Captivate 6.

This concludes our overview of the Sequence question type. There is one last question type to go through before we can test our Quiz in the Preview pane.

Creating surveys with Likert questions

This one is a bit special. It is the only question type that **cannot be graded**. The Likert question is used to gather feedback and opinions, so there are **no right or wrong answers** for this type of questions. The idea is to display statements on the screen and have the students specify their level of agreement to these statements using a rating scale.

In the following exercise, we will configure a Likert question using the following steps:

1. Go to slide 24 of the `Chapter07/drivingInBe.cptx` file.
2. In the **General** accordion of the **Quiz Properties** panel, change the number of **Answers** to `3`.
3. Open the **Rating Scale** drop-down list to reduce the scale to `3` items.

These actions create two extra statements and their corresponding objects on the slide. The **Rating Scale** option has left only three *levels of agreement* for each statement. This option is for the entire slide. It is not possible to set this option separately for each statement.

4. Change the text of the three statements to: `I learned interesting things in this online course` - `eLearning is a great learning solution` and `I would recommend this course to a friend.`
5. Change the label of the three columns to `Disagree`, `Neutral`, and `Agree`.
6. Feel free to move and resize the objects of this slide as you see fit.

This question is a *survey* question, so there are no right or wrong answers. Consequently, there are no green and no red feedback messages available.

We will provide some feedback to the student anyway by importing a regular slide in the middle of the Quiz, right after the survey question.

7. Open the `Chapter07/surveyFeedback.cptx` file.

This file contains a single slide that we will use as the feedback message of our survey in the `drivingInBe.cptx` file.

8. Copy-paste the single slide of the `surveyFeedback.cptx` file as slide 25 of the `drivingInBe.cptx` file.

This extra slide is situated after the Likert question, but before the Quiz Result Slide. This illustrates the possibility to add a regular slide in the middle of a Quiz.

> This extra slide also features another use of the new **Insert** | **Characters** feature. On this slide, transparent Text Captions have been carefully positioned right above the images of the actors. To give the illusion of text being written on the images, we have used two different **cursive fonts**, we have applied a **Rotation** to both Text Captions, and we have applied the **same timing** to the Text Caption and to the image it relates to.

9. Take some time to inspect the objects of this slide, their timing on the **Timeline** and, their properties in the **Properties** panel.

In this exercise, we have created a Likert survey question and we have added an extra slide in the middle of the Quiz to provide some feedback to the student.

Previewing the Quiz

Now that we have one example of every question type in the project, it is time to experience that Quiz hand-on! As we did not change any of the Quiz Preferences yet, we will live the default Quiz experience and have a better understanding of the available options. Perform the following steps to preview the Quiz:

1. Use the Preview icon to preview the entire **Project**.
2. View the entire project as if it was the first time and take the Quiz as a normal student would.
3. When you reach the **Quiz Results** Slide, click on the **Review Quiz** button.

The **Review Quiz** button takes you back to the first slide of the Quiz. Notice that the first slide of the Quiz is the Fill-In-The-Blank question where the student must convert m/h to km/h. The problem is that some students will *not* view this Question Slide, which leads to their test result being inaccurate. Use the Forward button of the Playbar to go through each Question Slide one by one. It is in Quiz Review mode that the **Review Area** makes more sense.

The Review Area is the big gray rectangle that we saw on the Question Slides. It is used to display a feedback message to the student where appropriate.

When you are back on the Quiz Results Slide, take some time to inspect the information it contains. Pay particular attention to the message in blue written at the end of the slide (**Sorry you failed** or **Congratulations, you passed**). It is a general feedback message that depends on the outcome of the Quiz as a whole. Obviously, we have to set a *passing score* in order to let Captivate know when to display one or the other message.

4. Click on the **Continue** button to move on to the last slide of the movie.
5. When done, close the **Preview** pane to return to Captivate.

Remember that we did not change any of the Quiz Preferences yet. In the upcoming *Quiz Preferences* section, we will review the options that will allow us to customize the Quiz. But before that, let's take a deeper look at the Pretest feature of Captivate 6.

Creating a Pretest

So far, we have created *Graded* and *Survey* questions in our Quiz. In this section, we will explore the *Pretest* questions. Basically, the Pretest questions look exactly like the Survey or the Graded questions. What makes them special is the following:

- Pretest questions are *not part of the Quiz*. Their result is *not* accounted for when generating the Quiz Result Slide.
- Pretest Questions are not part of the interaction report that is sent to an LMS (more on reporting to an LMS in the *Reporting scores to an LMS* section mentioned later in this chapter).

Pretest is a new feature of Captivate 6.

In the following exercise, we will insert a Pretest in the `encoderDemo_800.cptx` file using the following steps:

1. Open or switch to the `Chapter07/encoderDemo_800.cptx` file.
2. Use the **Filmstrip** to go to slide 2.

Creating a Pretest question is a process that is very similar to creating a standard Graded or Survey question, so the Pretest has already been created for you in the `chapter07/pretest.cptx` file.

3. Open the `chapter07/pretest.cptx` file.
4. Use the **Filmstrip** to select slides 1, 2, 3, and 4 of the `pretest.cptx` file.
5. *Copy* the selected slides and return to the `encoderDemo_800.cptx` file.
6. In the **Filmstrip** of the `encoderDemo_800.cptx` file, right-click on slide 2 and *Paste* the slides.

The four slides of the Pretest are inserted *after* slide 2. Slide 3 is a standard slide used to introduce the Pretest to the student. Slides 4, 5, and 6 are three Question Slides that form the actual Pretest. Slide 7 is the automatically generated Quiz Result Slide.

In order to better understand the Pretest feature, we will now test this project in the **Preview** pane to experience it hands-on.

7. Use the Preview icon to preview the entire **Project**.

While in the **Preview** pane, there are some *major* changes to notice. First of all, our Playbar is gone! When a Pretest is inserted into a project, Captivate 6 **automatically disables the Playback Controls** to prevent the student from skipping the Pretest.

After taking the entire Quiz, the Quiz Result Slide is displayed. **Regardless of the answers you provided during the Pretest, your score will always be 0 and the Total Question count will also always be 0**. Remember that the Pretest questions are *not* part of the actual Quiz!

8. Close the **Preview** pane when the preview is finished.
9. In the **Filmstrip**, right-click on the Quiz Result Slide (slide 7) and click on **Hide Slide** in the contextual menu.

Because the Pretest is not part of the Quiz, the Quiz Result Slide of this project is useless and can be safely turned off!

In *Chapter 11, Variables, Advanced Actions, and Widgets*, we will see how we can add branching depending on the outcome of the Pretest and how we can create a Pretest - only Quiz Result slide.

At the end of this set of exercises, we have inserted one question of each type in one of our project and a Pretest in another project. It is time to make a quick summary of what we have learned about quizzes and Question Slides:

- There are *eight types of Question Slides* available in Captivate.
- Each question can either be a **Graded**, a **Survey**, or a **Pretest** question. The only exception to this is the *Likert* question that can only be a *Survey* question.
- A Graded question *has right and wrong answers*. A Survey question is used to gather feedback and opinions from the students. It *does not have right or wrong answers*. A Pretest question *is not pat of the Quiz* and is used to assess the student's knowledge *before* he/she takes the online course.
- Use the **Insert** | **Question Slide** menu item to insert Question Slides to the project.
- When inserting the first Question Slide, Captivate *automatically* generates a **Quiz Results Slide**. This slide can be turned off in the Quiz Preferences.
- The **Quiz Properties** panel is used to set up the options specific to each type of Question Slides.
- Each graded question can be worth a different amount of **Points** when the student answers the question correctly. If the answer is not correct, it is possible to remove some points from the student's score by applying a **Penalty**.
- **Partial scoring** is available for Multiple Choice questions only.
- When a Pretest is inserted into a project, Captivate *automatically turns off the Playback Controls* of that project to prevent the students from skipping the Quiz.

In the next section, we will explore the available Quiz Preferences.

The Quiz Preferences

Now that we have a better idea on how a Quiz works by default, we will return to the Quiz Preferences dialog to take a deeper look at the available options using the following steps:

1. If needed, return to the `drivingInBe.cptx` file.
2. Use the **Quiz | Quiz Preferences** menu item to open the Preferences dialog.

By default, the Quiz Preferences dialog opens on the **Reporting** section. We will discuss the reporting options later in this chapter.

3. On the left-hand side of the **Preferences** dialog, click on the **Settings** category of the **Quiz** section, as shown in the following screenshot:

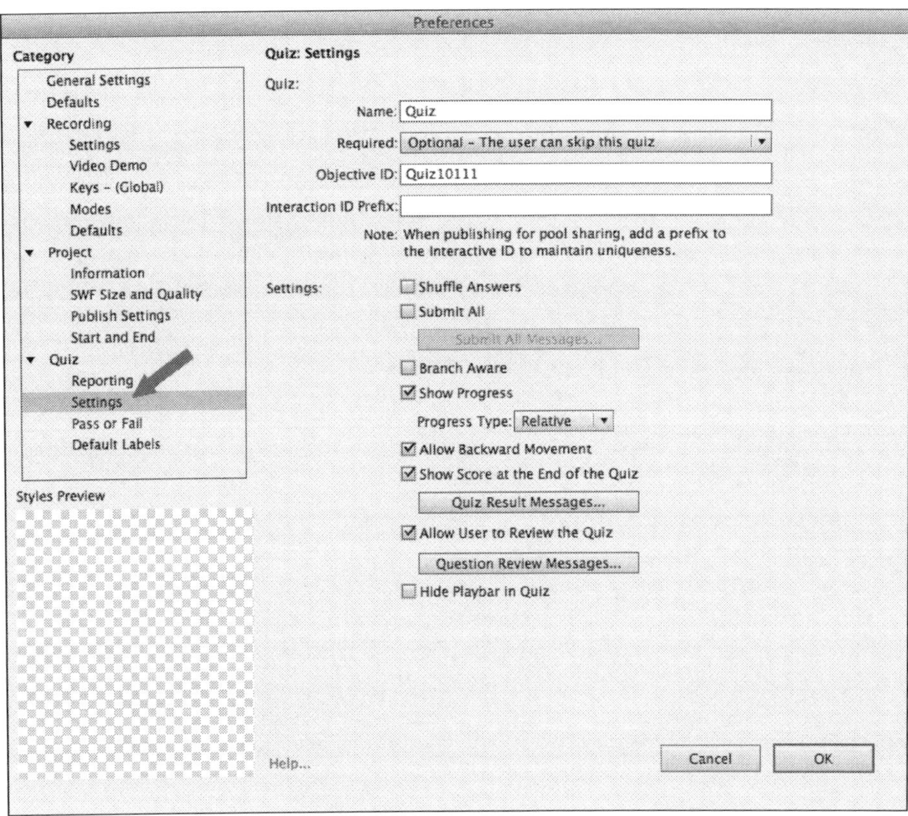

Take some time to review the options of this page. Most of them should be self-explanatory.

4. Deselect the **Show Progress** checkbox. This removes the progress indicator situated at the bottom-left corner of the Question Slides.

Remember that the Short Answer question of slide 9 will only be asked to the students that respond *miles per hour* to the question asked on slide 5. In other words, the Question count and the progress indicator of this particular project might be different for every student. For the progress indicator, no problem, we just decided to turn it off! But for the Question Slide count and for the score that shows on the Quiz Result Slide, we have a problem!

5. Select the **Branch Aware** checkbox to instruct Captivate to calculate the Question slide count and the student's score based on the questions that are *actually* asked to each specific student.

As it is the case with the Pretest, **Captivate disables the Playback Controls** when a **Branch Aware** Quiz is present in the project.

> **A customized progress indicator**
>
> Lieve Weymeis found a way to create a customized progress indicator using Advanced Actions and Variables, available at `http://lilybiri.posterous.com/customized-progress-indicator`. Advanced Actions and Variables will be covered in *Chapter 11, Variables, Advanced Actions, and Widgets.*

6. Deselect the **Allow Backward Movement** checkbox.
7. Click on **Yes** to remove the (now unneeded) **Back** buttons from the Question Slides.
8. Click on the **Quiz Results Messages** button. The **Quiz Results Messages** dialog opens.

The **Quiz Results Messages** dialog lets us customize the set of information that appears in the Quiz Results Slide, at the very end of the Quiz.

9. Deselect the **Correct Questions** and the **Total Questions** checkboxes.
10. Also, deselect the **Quiz Attempts** checkbox.
11. If needed, customize the **Pass Message** and the **Fail Message**.

12. Click on the **OK** button to validate your changes and close the box.
13. Click on the **Question Review Messages** button. The **Question Review Messages** dialog opens.

This box is where we can customize the messages that are displayed in the Review Area when the student reviews the Quiz. In our case, we won't allow the students to review the Quiz at all, so we will close this box without making any changes.

14. Click on the **Cancel** button to close the box.
15. Deselect the **Allow User to Review the Quiz** checkbox.

This action removes the **Review Quiz** button from the **Quiz Results** Slide and the **Review Area** from the Question Slides.

16. Click on the **OK** button to validate the changes and close the **Preferences** dialog.
17. Use the **Filmstrip** to go to slide 26.

Slide 26 is the Quiz Results Slide. Notice that it contains less information than before and that the **Review Quiz** button has been removed. This configuration matches the checkboxes configuration we applied on the Quiz Preferences dialog.

Setting the passing score of a Quiz

When the student reaches the Quiz Results Slide, Captivate displays a message that depends of the outcome of the Quiz. To display this message, Captivate must be informed of what the passing score of the Quiz is. If the student reaches that passing score, Captivate displays the *Passing Message*; otherwise, the *Failed Message* is displayed.

In this section, we will set the passing score of the Quiz and add some branching.

First of all, we will import two more slides in the project and place them *after* the Quiz. One will congratulate the student who passes the Quiz, and the other one will ask the students who failed to take the test again later using the following steps:

1. Open the `Chapter07/quizFeedback.cptx` file.
2. Use the **Filmstrip** to select both the slides of this file and copy them.
3. Return to slide 26 of the `drivingInBe.cptx` file and paste the slides.

After this procedure, the `drivingInBe.cptx` file should contain 29 slides, as shown in the following screenshot:

The stage is set! We will now return to the Quiz Preferences dialog to set the passing score of the Quiz and arrange branching.

4. Make sure you are *not* on slide 27 or 28 of the `drivingInBe.cptx` file.
5. Use the **Quiz | Quiz Preferences** menu item to return to the Quiz Preferences dialog.
6. Click on the **Pass or Fail** category situated in the **Quiz** section of the **Preferences** dialog.

The main Pass/Fail option is situated at the top of the dialog box. Notice that there are two ways to set the passing score for a Quiz: as a **percentage** or as a certain amount of **points** to reach. Notice also that the total points is the sum of the points set for all the Question Slides of our Quiz (excluding the point of the Pretest slides, if any).

7. In the **Pass/Fail Options** section, set the passing score to `50` %.

We will now decide what action has to be taken when the student passes or fails the test.

8. In the **If Passing Grade** section, set the **Action** to **Jump to Slide**. Then, select **Quiz Passed Feedback** from the **Slide** drop-down list.
9. In the **If Failing Grade** section, allow the user one attempt and set the **Action** to **Jump to Slide**. Then, select **Quiz Failed Feedback** from the **Slide** drop-down list.

Setting the Pass and Fail options and adding some branching on the Quiz is *that* easy! Before moving on to the next step, we will take a quick look at the **Default Labels** preferences pane.

10. Click on the **Default Labels** category situated on the left-hand side of the **Preferences** dialog.

The **Default Labels** preferences are used to change the default text and the default formatting of the various elements of a Question Slide. It is best to change these options *before* the first Question Slide is added to the project! In our case, it is too late! But don't worry; we will take care of the formatting of our Quiz in the next chapter.

11. Click on the **OK** button to validate the changes and close the **Preferences** dialog.

There is one more little thing to do in order to complete the branching system of the Quiz.

12. Use the **Filmstrip** to go to slide 27.
13. If needed, open the **Properties** panel and make sure it displays the properties of the entire slide.
14. Set the **on Exit** action to **Jump to Slide** and choose **slide 29** in the **Slide** drop-down list.
15. Use the Preview icon to test the entire **Project**. When done, close the **Preview** pane and save the file.

Apart from the formatting, our Quiz is now up and running. We will, however, add some spice to the mix by creating a Question Pool, but before that, let's make a quick summary of what we have just learned:

- By default, each Question Slide contains four buttons and a Review Area.
- By default, Captivate generates a **Quiz Results** Slides and displays it at the end of the Quiz.

- By default, the Quiz Results Slide contains the **Review Quiz** button that allows the student to return to each Question Slide and have a feedback on his/her work.
- We can allow the students to go backward in the Quiz, but a submitted answer cannot be changed for another answer.
- The Quiz Preferences dialog contains many options that let us fine-tune the student's experience. Some of these options are used to turn the objects of the Question Slides on or off.
- We can use the Quiz Preferences dialog to set the **passing score** of the Quiz and to add **branching** that depends on the general outcome of the Quiz.

Creating Question Pools

A **Question Pool** is a repository of Question Slides. The idea is to let Captivate randomly choose questions in the pool in order to create a unique Quiz for each student. We can have as many Question Pools as needed in a single Captivate project and each pool can contain an unlimited number of Question Slides.

Creating a Question Pool

In our case, we will create a single Question Pool, add four Question Slides to it, and ask Captivate to randomly choose one question from the pool and insert it into the Quiz.

The first action of this process is to create the Question Pool using the following steps:

1. Make sure you are still in the `Chapter07/drivingInBe.cptx` file.
2. Use the **Quiz | Question Pool Manager** menu item to open the **Question Pool Manager**.

The Question Pool Manager is divided into two main areas:

- On the upper-left side of the box, there is a list of all the Question Pools of the project. Just above the list of pools, the + and the - icons (1) are used to add or remove Question Pools.

- The right-hand side of the box shows the list of the Question Slides associated with the pool selected on the right-hand side. The **+** and the **-** icons (2) are used to add new Question Slides into the selected pool or to remove existing Question Slides from the selected pool, as shown in the following screenshot:

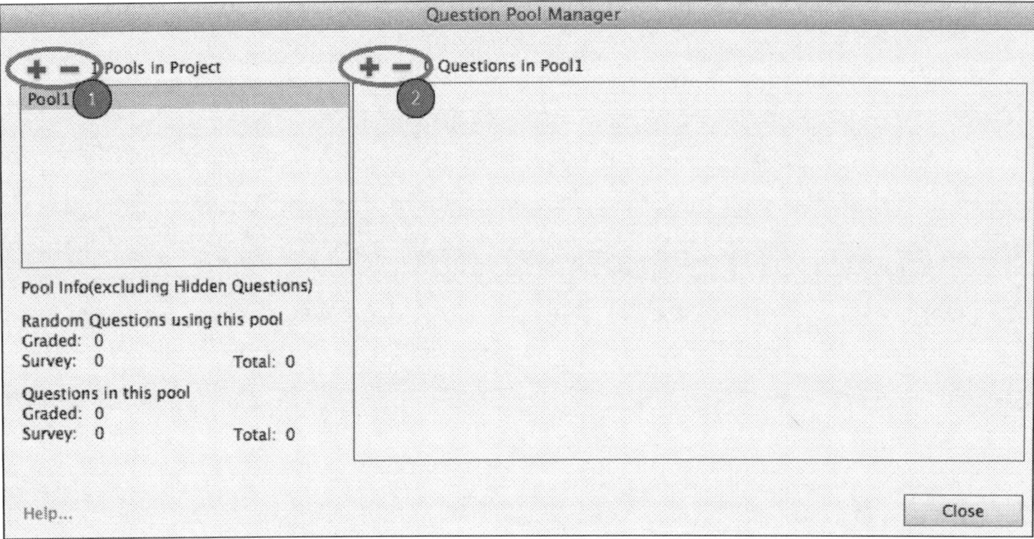

Notice that a first Question Pool named **Pool1** has been automatically created by Captivate when we opened the Question Pool Manager. We will now rename this Question Pool and add questions to it.

3. On the left-hand side of the **Question Pool Manager**, double-click on the **Pool1** entry of the list of pools.
4. Name the Pool `drivingInBelgiumPool1` and press the *Enter* key.
5. Click on the **Close** button to close the **Question Pool Manager**.

Now that we have a Question Pool available, we will add questions to it.

Inserting questions in a Question Pool

We could have used the **Question Pool Manager** to create new Question Slides and add them into the pool, but we will use another technique. Instead of creating new Question Slides to fill the new Question Pool, we will move some of the existing Question Slides of our Quiz into the new pool using the following steps:

1. Use the **Filmstrip** to go to slide 19. Hold the *Shift* key down and click on slide 22.

This operation selects four slides from slide 19 to slide 22.

2. In the **Filmstrip**, right-click one of the selected slide.
3. In the contextual menu, choose **Move Question to | drivingInBelgiumPool1**.

This operation removes the selected slides from the **Filmstrip** and moves them into the Question Pool.

4. Open the **Question Pool** panel that appears right next to the **Timeline** panel at the bottom of the screen. (If the **Question Pool** panel is not present on the screen, use the **Window | Question Pool** menu item to turn it on).

Four of our Question Slides should be displayed in the **Question Pool** panel indicating that they have been moved into the **DrivingInBelgiumPool1** correctly. Another way to access the same information is by using the Question Pool Manager.

5. Use the **Quiz | Question Pool Manager** to open the **Question Pool Manager** dialog.
6. Make sure that our Question Pool is selected on the left-hand side of the dialog, and take a look at the right-hand side.

When the **drivingInBelgiumPool1** is selected, the right-hand side of the **Question Pool Manager** dialog shows that four Question Slides are part of the pool.

7. Click on the **Close** button to close the **Question Pool Manager**.

Now that we have moved our Question Slides into the Question Pool, it is time to insert some random slides into the project.

Share Question Pools with other projects

You may have noticed the **Quiz | Import Question Pools** menu item. Using this feature, we can easily import a Question Pool from another project into this project.

Inserting Random Question Slides in the main project

Remember that the idea of a Question Pool is to have a repository of questions available in order to generate random quizzes. In this section, we will use our new Question Pool to insert a Random Question in our project using the following steps:

1. Use the **Filmstrip** to go to slide 18 of the `drivingInBe.cptx` file.

Slide 18 is the Multiple Choice question we created earlier in the *Creating Question Slides* section. It is the first question of the Quiz.

2. Use the **Quiz | Random Question Slide** menu item to insert a Random Question into the main project.

Captivate inserts the Random Question *after* slide 18. It means that the Quiz starts for each student with the same Multiple Choice question of slide 18. The second question of the Quiz will be randomly chosen by Captivate at runtime among the four questions of the pool. Finally, the third-graded question of the Quiz is the sequence question of slide 20 followed by the short survey of slide 21.

3. Use the **Filmstrip** to go to slide 19.
4. Open the **Quiz Properties** panel situated at the right-hand side of the screen.

The **Quiz Properties** panel of a Random Question holds only a fraction of the options that we used to see in the **Quiz Properties** panel of a regular Question Slide. Two of the available options are the **Points** and the **Penalty** properties.

5. Open the **Question Pool** panel situated right next to the **Timeline** at the bottom of the screen.
6. Select any Question Slide in the **DrivingInBelgiumPool1** Question Pool.
7. When the selected question appears in the main area of the Captivate interface, take a look at the **Quiz Properties** panel.

Notice that, here again, the **Quiz Properties** panel holds fewer options than the **Quiz Properties** panel of a regular Question Slide. Two of the missing options are the **Points** and the **Penalty** properties.

When combining the options of the **Quiz Properties** panel of the Random Question Slide in the main project with the options of the **Quiz Properties** panel of a Question Slide within a Question Pool, we obtain more or less the **Quiz Properties** panel of a regular Question Slide.

8. Return to slide 18 of the main **Filmstrip**. In the **General** accordion of the **Quiz Properties** panel, make sure that the **Points** property is set to **10** and that the **Penalty** property is set to **1**.

Now that we have inserted a Random Question in the project, we will test our movie and experience our random Quiz.

9. Use the Preview icon to test the entire **Project** in the **Preview** pane.

When you reach the Quiz, pay close attention to the Question Slides that are displayed. Try to answer the questions correctly, so that the **Quiz Passed Feedback** slide is displayed when the Quiz is over.

10. When you are done, close the **Preview** pane.
11. Use the **Preview** icon to test the entire project a second time.

When you reach the Quiz, notice that *you are not answering the exact same questions as for the first test*. Give wrong answers so that you fail the Quiz.

12. Make sure that the **Quiz Fail Feedback** slide is displayed at the end of the Quiz.

Our random Quiz is now up and running. It is time to make a quick summary of what we have learned:

- A **Question Pool** is a repository of Question Slides from which Captivate randomly picks questions in order to create random quizzes *on the fly*.
- A Captivate project can include as many Question Pools as needed. A Question Pool can contain as many Question Slides as needed.
- The **Quiz | Import Question Pool** menu item can be used to import a Question Pool of another project in the current project.
- Use the **Quiz | Question Pool Manager** menu item to create new Question Pools and to add Question Slides in the available pools.
- If the project already contains Question Slides, they can be moved in a Question Pool at any time.
- A Quiz can be a mix of regular questions and of Random Questions from many different Question Pools.
- The **Quiz Properties** panel of a Random Question contains only a fraction of the options available for a regular question. The remaining options are associated with the Question slide in the Question Pool.

Great! We now have a pretty good idea of what a Captivate Quiz is and of the myriad of options available. Now we want to be able to track the performance of the students that take our Quiz. This is where the LMS enters the stage.

Reporting scores to an LMS

LMS stands for Learning Management System. The Help files of Captivate give the following definition for an LMS:

> *You can use a learning management system (LMS) to distribute a computer-based tutorial created using Adobe Captivate over the Internet. A learning management system is used to provide, track, and manage web-based training.*

An LMS offers many services to both the teachers and the students involved in some kind of eLearning activity:

- An LMS is a website that is able to host our online courses.
- An LMS maintains a list of teachers and students. Thanks to this listing, an LMS can be used to enroll students in online courses and to define one or more teacher(s) for each course.
- An LMS is able to enforce the pedagogical decisions of the teacher. For example, the LMS can be set to give access to the next part of the course only if the current activity has been completed. Some LMSs can also enforce branching by automatically providing an additional activity for those students who have failed a Quiz, and so on.
- An LMS is able to communicate with our Captivate-powered eLearning content. This gives us access to many pieces of information such as the number of students that have taken the course, the time it took to complete an activity, the result of our quizzes and even a detailed report of every interaction performed by each student while taking the course.
- And much much more....

There are many LMSs available out there and there are a myriad of companies, schools, and universities that have deployed an LMS to deliver, track, and manage their web-based trainings. Some LMSs are commercially licensed and can be quite expensive, but there are also open-source LMS platforms that can be downloaded for free and easily deployed on a web server.

Moodle

Moodle is the name of the most popular and powerful open source LMS solution. Personally, I have used Moodle for many of the eLearning projects I have been working on and it never let me down! Even though it is very powerful, Moodle is not the easiest solution to learn and use. Packt Publishing has published an impressive array of titles on Moodle, providing the necessary documentation to get you started. More information on Moodle is available at `http://www.moodle.org`. More information about Packt books on Moodle is available at `http://www.packtpub.com/books/moodle`.

For a list of the most popular LMSs, see the following webpage on Wikipedia `http://en.wikipedia.org/wiki/List_of_learning_management_systems`.

SCORM and AICC

Each LMS has its pros and cons, and each contains a unique set of features. However each LMS must be able to host eLearning content created by a myriad of different authoring tools (Adobe Captivate being only one of the eLearning authoring tools available).

So the challenge is to have courses created by a myriad of different tools communicate with a myriad of different brands of LMS! This challenge is being addressed by two internationally accepted standards: SCORM and AICC. When choosing an LMS for your organization, make sure that the chosen solution is either SCORM or AICC-compliant; otherwise, you'll have a hard time making your courses communicate with the LMS. Captivate is both SCORM *and* AICC-compliant, so the courses created with Captivate can be integrated in virtually every LMS available on the market.

- **SCORM** stands for **Sharable Content Object Reference Model**. SCORM is maintained by the **Advanced Distributed Learning** (**ADL** - `http://www.adlnet.org/`) project of the US Department of Defense. SCORM is a *reference model*. It means that it aggregates standards created by other organizations. The goal is to build a single standard based on the work done by other organizations active in the eLearning field. See the Wikipedia page on SCORM at `http://en.wikipedia.org/wiki/SCORM`.
- **AICC** stands for **Aviation Industry Computer-based Training Committee**. The idea was to provide a unique training and testing environment for the aviation industry in order to ensure the same training and testing standard for all the airline companies in the world. For more info, see the AICC page on Wikipedia at `http://en.wikipedia.org/wiki/Aviation_Industry_Computer-Based_Training_Committee` or the official AICC website at `http://www.aicc.org/`.

Now that we have a better idea of what an LMS is and of the standards in use, we will enable reporting in our Captivate project.

Enabling reporting in Captivate

To have Captivate produce an LMS-ready content, we have to set options at different locations throughout the project:

- At *interaction level*, we have to decide which interaction has to be reported to the LMS. To be properly reported to the server, we have to assign a unique **Interaction ID** to each interaction we want to report. In Captivate, an interaction can be a **Question Slide** (except *Pretest* question), a **Click Box**, a **Text Entry Box**, or a **Button**.
- At *project level*, we have to decide which standard (such as SCORM, AICC, and so on) the project will use to send the data to the LMS and which data is to be included in the report. This is done in the Quiz Preferences dialog.

In the next exercise, we will make our Quiz ready to be integrated in a SCORM-compliant LMS. We will first inspect the options available at interaction level, before moving on to the project level reporting options.

At interaction level

In Captivate, an interaction is something that requires an action from the student. All three interactive objects of Captivate (Click Box, Text Entry Box, and Button) as well as all types of Question Slides fall under the *interaction* umbrella.

We already know that each of these interactions is able to stop the Playhead and wait for the student to interact with the project. We also know that the interactions implement the *branching* concept.

What we are about to discover is that each of these interactions can be reported to an LMS. To do so, we must assign each interaction with a unique **Interaction ID**. This Interaction ID is what makes data tracking by the LMS possible. Perform the following steps to assign each interaction with a unique interaction ID:

1. Use the **Filmstrip** to go to slide 9 of the `drivingInBelgium.cptx` file.
2. In the **Reporting** accordion of the **Quiz Properties** panel, deselect the **Report Answer** checkbox.

This particular Question Slide is not actually part of the Quiz, so we do not want this interaction to be part of the report that Captivate sends to the LMS. By deselecting the **Report Answer** checkbox, we made this Question Slide invisible to the LMS (but not to the Quiz Result Slide of the Captivate project as discussed in *The Quiz Preferences* section).

3. Use the **Filmstrip** to select slide 18 of the project.

Slide 18 should be the Multiple Choice question and the first Question Slide of the actual Quiz.

4. In the **Reporting** accordion of the **Quiz Properties** panel, make sure the **Report Answer** checkbox is *selected*.
5. Type `MC_Languages` in the **Interaction ID** field.
6. Use the same technique to define an **Interaction ID** for the other questions of the Quiz:
    - Use **SEQ_Parking** as the **Interaction ID** for the Sequence question of slide 20
    - Use **Survey_DrivingInBe** for the Likert question of slide 21
7. Return to the **Question Pool** panel situated next to the **Timeline** at the bottom of the screen.
8. Use the same technique to assign an **Interaction ID** to the Questions of the Question Pool:
    - Use **MATCH_SpeedLimit** for the Matching question
    - Use **TF_sideOfRoad** for the True/False question
    - Use **FIB_MotorwaysSpeedLimit** for the Fill-In-The-Blank question
    - Use **HS_RightOfWay** for the Hotspot question
9. Save the file when done.

Let's take another look at these *Interaction IDs*. Before the underscore is the type of interaction (MC for Multiple Choice, TF for True False, and so on) and after the underscore is the topic of the question. This is how I come up with meaningful unique names for the Interaction IDs. Feel free to use any other conventions in your projects.

Also notice that there are no spaces and no special characters in the Interaction ID. Captivate enforces these restrictions by turning every space and every special character typed in the Interaction ID field to an underscore.

10. Return to slide 19 of the **Filmstrip**.

Slide 19 is the Random Question Slide of our Quiz.

11. In the **Reporting** accordion of the **Quiz Properties** panel, make sure the **Report Answer** checkbox is selected.

Even though we assigned an Interaction ID to each Question Slide of the Question Pool, the Report Answer checkbox is located in the Quiz Properties panel of a Random Question in the main Filmstrip. So if the same Question Pool is used in many different projects, the developer of each project can decide whether to report the answers or not. If the answer is to be reported, the Interaction ID specified in the Question Pool is used in the reported data sent to the LMS.

12. Save the file when done.

Reporting Click Boxes and Text Entry Boxes

Before we move on to the next topic, we will take a quick look at the Encoder Simulation to find out how Click Boxes, Text Entry Boxes, and Buttons can be included in a Quiz and reported to an LMS using the following steps:

1. Open the `Chapter07/encoderSim_800.cptx` file. Use the **Filmstrip** to go to slide 2.
2. Select the **Continue** button at the lower-right corner of the slide.

With the button selected, take a look at the **Properties** panel and note that it contains a **Reporting** accordion. Open the **Reporting** accordion and take a look at the available options.

3. Use the **Filmstrip** to go to slide 4. Select the Click Box and take a look at the **Reporting** accordion of the **Properties** panel.
4. Use the **Filmstrip** to go to slide 13. Select the Text Entry Box and take a look at the **Reporting** accordion of the **Properties** panel.

Each of these three interactive objects can be added to the Quiz by selecting the **Include in Quiz** checkbox. Once included in the Quiz, these objects have the very same reporting capabilities as a regular Question Slide.

When selecting the **Include In Quiz** checkbox, but not the **Report Answer** checkbox, we include an interactive object in the Quiz without reporting the interaction to the LMS. We can use that feature to create *Training Simulations*. In a Training Simulation, the Click Boxes and Text Entry Boxes should be included in the Quiz for the students to have a feedback on the Quiz Results page, but the reporting should be turned off.

5. Close the `encoderSim_800.cptx` file without saving the eventual changes.

In this exercise, we have assigned a unique Interaction ID to the interactions that we want to report to the LMS. We have also turned off the reporting on the interactions that we do not need to track. In the next section, we will explore the project level reporting options.

At project level

When every interaction that we want to report has a unique Interaction ID, it is time to focus on the project level reporting options. This is where we will choose the standard (SCORM or AICC) that we want to use and configure the data that we want to report to the LMS.

In the following exercise, we will enable reporting to a SCORM-compliant LMS such as Moodle using the following steps:

1. If needed, return to the `Chapter07/DrivingInBe.cptx` file.
2. Use the **Quiz | Quiz Preferences** menu item to open the Quiz Preferences dialog. On the left-hand side of the **Preferences** dialog, make sure that you are on the **Reporting** category.
3. At the top of the page, select the **Enable reporting for this project** (1) checkbox.

When I teach a Captivate class, I often refer to this checkbox as being the *main circuit breaker* of the reporting system.

4. Open the drop-down list (2), as shown in the following screenshot:

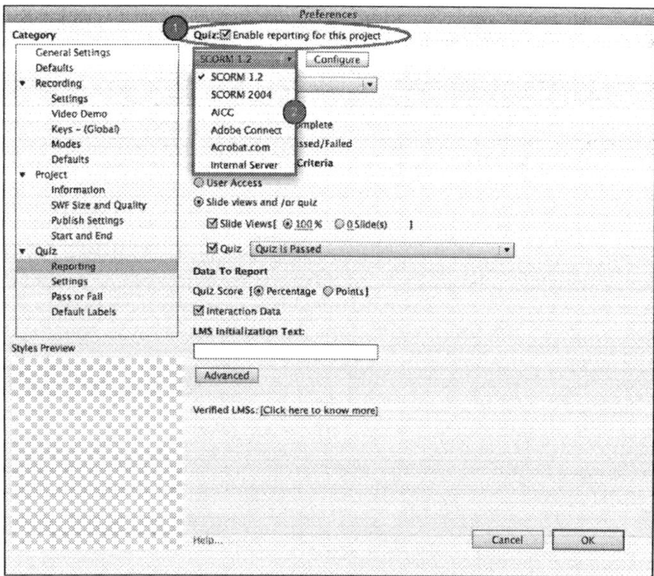

We now have to choose which type of LMS we want to use among the six options offered by Captivate. These options are:

- **SCORM 1.2** - Use this option for the Captivate project to use the SCORM 1.2 standard to communicate with the LMS.
- **SCORM 2004** - Use this option for the Captivate project to use the newer SCORM 2004 standard to communicate with the LMS.
- **AICC** - Use this option for the Captivate project to use the AICC standard to communicate with the LMS.
- **Adobe Connect** - This option is used to send the reporting data to an Adobe Connect server.
- **Acrobat.com** - Is the name of a cloud-based service from Adobe. It can be used as an alternate reporting method if no LMS is available in your organization.
- **Internal Server** - Use this option to have Captivate send the data to a server inside your organization. Of course, you should develop a server side script (in PHP or any other language) that will receive and process the data. To help you out, there are two sample files in the `/Templates/Publish` folder of your Captivate installation. These two files are called `internalserverread.php` and `internalServerReporting.php`.

At the time of this writing, the SCORM 2 specification is under development. No doubt that SCORM 2 compliance will be one of the new features of a future Captivate release.

5. Choose each of these options in the drop-down list one by one and notice how the **Preferences** dialog updates to show the options relevant to the chosen reporting method only.

In our case, we want to send the data to a Moodle LMS. The `http://docs.moodle.org/22/en/SCORM_FAQ` page of the official Moodle website tells us that Moodle is compatible with the SCORM 1.2 standard, and that the SCORM 2004 standard is only partially supported.

6. Choose the **SCORM 1.2** option in the drop-down list.

We will now choose how Captivate will report the status of the course. If there is a Quiz in the project, you probably want the status to be *Pass* or *Fail*. If the project does not contain a Quiz and you just want to track the completion status of the project, choose *Complete/Incomplete*.

7. In the **Status Representation** section, choose the **Incomplete | Passed/Failed** option.

We will now instruct Captivate that we want to consider this piece of eLearning content as *complete* when the student has passed the Quiz.

8. In the **Success/Completion criteria** section, choose the **Slide views and/or quiz** option.
9. Deselect the **Slide Views** checkbox, but leave the **Quiz is Passed** checkbox on.

Finally, we will decide what data we want to report to the LMS. Basically, we can choose to report only the final score of the student or to report the final score plus some details about each interaction. In our case, we want to report the score of the student as a percentage and we want to have access to the Interaction Data as well.

10. In the **Data To Report** section, choose to report the **Quiz Score** as a **percentage**.
11. Make sure the **Interactions Data** checkbox is *selected*.

As we have chosen the SCORM standard, there is one extra step to go through before we can publish our LMS-ready captivate project. This extra step is the creation of the SCORM manifest file.

Enabling reporting in a Quiz-less project

The reporting options are not limited to the projects containing a Quiz. Reporting can be used to track the completion status of a project only. Some LMS are able to reveal the next activity of a course when and only when they receive the *Complete* status report from the current activity.

Creating a SCORM manifest

A SCORM manifest is an `.xml` file named `imsmanifest.xml`. This manifest file is a very important piece of the SCORM package because it describes the course and the course structure to the SCORM-compliant LMS. Without this file, the LMS is unable to integrate the Captivate movie in a course and gather the tracking data sent by the project.

If this sounds too technical for you, don't worry! Captivate can generate that manifest file for you using the very simple procedure that follows.

1. Still in the **Reporting** category of the **Preferences** dialog, click on the **Configure** button situated at the top of the box.

The first section of the **Manifest** dialog is the **Course** section (1). The **Course** section is used to enter the metadata of the project. These metadata will be used by the LMS to display the course information to the student and to enhance the integration of the project into the LMS.

2. In the **Course** section of the **Manifest** dialog, enter the following information:
   - Identifier - `DrivingInBe101`
   - Title - `Driving in Belgium`
   - Description - Enter any meaningful description here!
3. Leave the other options at their current settings, as shown in the following screenshot:

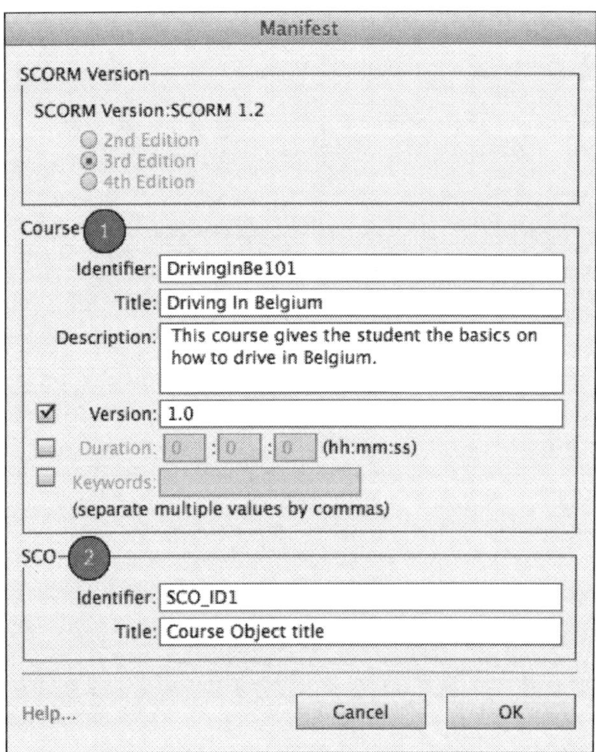

The second part of the Manifest dialog is called SCO (2), as shown in the previous screenshot. **SCO** stands for **Shareable Content Object**. This concept is at the heart of the SCORM standard.

In the SCORM specification, a course can be composed of many activities. Each of these activities has a unique SCO identifier. Using a SCORM Packager application (such as the *Multi SCO Packager* or *Reload*), it is possible to integrate a Captivate Project in a larger SCORM-compliant course containing lots of other content made by lots of other applications. That is why it is important to specify the SCO identity of our Captivate project. By default, Captivate generates a default SCO that is based on the name of the project. We can keep that default name or change it to something more specific.

The Multi SCO Packager

If you obtained Captivate as part of the eLearning suite, you have access to a very interesting little tool named the **Multi SCO Packager**. This small application is able to merge multiple projects, each having its own SCO identifier, in a single course package that can be uploaded all at once to the LMS. These projects can be Captivate projects, HTML pages made with Dreamweaver and the Course Builder extension, Flash projects, or SCORM-enabled PDF files. There is an interesting training video available on this application. It can be found on the following page:

`http://blogs.adobe.com/captivate/2011/10/training-using-multi-sco-packager-to-create-a-single-course-out-of-scos-from-captivate-flash-and-dreamweaver.html.`

4. Type `DrivingInBe101` in the SCO **Identifier** and `Driving in Belgium` in the SCO **Title**.
5. Click **OK** to validate the changes and close the dialog box.
6. Also click on the **OK** button of the **Preferences** dialog.

The project can now be published as an LMS-ready package. This is what we will cover in the next section.

The exact settings of the Reporting and Manifest dialogs depends on the LMS that you use. See this page from the *infosemantic* website for more information:

`http://www.infosemantics.com.au/adobe-captivate-learning-management-system-lms-guide.`

Publishing an eLearning-enabled project

As a Captivate user, publishing an eLearning-enabled project is not very different from publishing a normal project. Behind the scenes, however, Captivate generates a whole bunch of files to enable SCORM or AICC reporting. Use the following steps to publish a LMS-ready package:

1. Still in the `Chapter07/drivingInBe.cptx` file, click on the **Publish** icon to open the **Publish** dialog.
2. In the left-most column of the **Publish** dialog, choose to publish the movie in **SWF/HTML5** format (1).
3. Change the **Folder** to the `Chapter07/Publish` folder (2) of the exercise files.
4. In the **Output Format Options** section, make sure the **SWF** option is the only one selected (3).
5. In the **Output Options** section of the **Publish** dialog, select the **Zip Files** option (4).

When the **Zip Files** checkbox is selected, Captivate publishes the movie and creates a `.zip` archive containing all the generated files. Using this technique, we simply have to upload that single `.zip` file to the LMS to publish the entire SCORM package. A SCORM-compliant LMS is supposed to be able to unzip the package and to properly manage the files it contains.

6. Take a quick look at the **Project Information** section situated on the right-hand side of the **Publish** dialog. Confirm that **SCORM 1.2** is selected as the **eLearning output** option (5), as shown in the following screenshot:

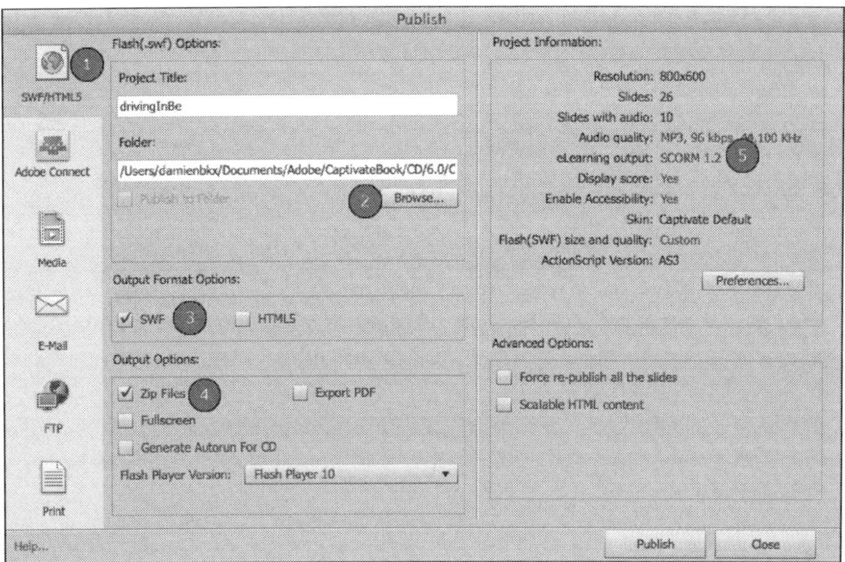

7. Click on the **Publish** button.

Take some time to read the important message that Captivate displays. Remember that we used the new **Penalty** option of Captivate 6 on some of the Question slides of our Quiz. Well bad news! This advanced scoring option is only supported in SCORM 2004.

8. Click on **Yes** to keep on going with the publication process anyway.

Captivate will simply ignore the **Penalty** option when publishing the movie.

9. Acknowledge the **Publish Complete** message by clicking on the **OK** button.

We will now leave Captivate and take a look at the generated `.zip` file.

10. Use the *Finder* (Mac) or *Windows Explorer* (Windows) to navigate to the `Chapter07/Publish` folder of the exercises files.

We should find the `drivinInBe.zip` file in this folder.

11. Unzip the file to take a closer look at its content.

And this is where the magic takes place! In the unzipped version of the file, we should find the same files as when we published a regular non-SCORM project (that is, the `.swf` file, a corresponding `.html` file, the `standard.js` JavaScript file, and the `captivate.css` file). But because we decided to produce a SCORM-compliant package, Captivate has generated lots of extra files. These extra files are used to enable communication between the LMS and the Captivate project.

The most important of these extra files is the `imsmanifest.xml`. This file is the manifest file and it must be stored at the root of the SCORM package. If you have an XML editor available, feel free to open this file and take a look at its content (but make sure you do not modify it!). The manifest file describes the course structure to the LMS using a SCORM-compliant XML format, as shown in the following screenshot:

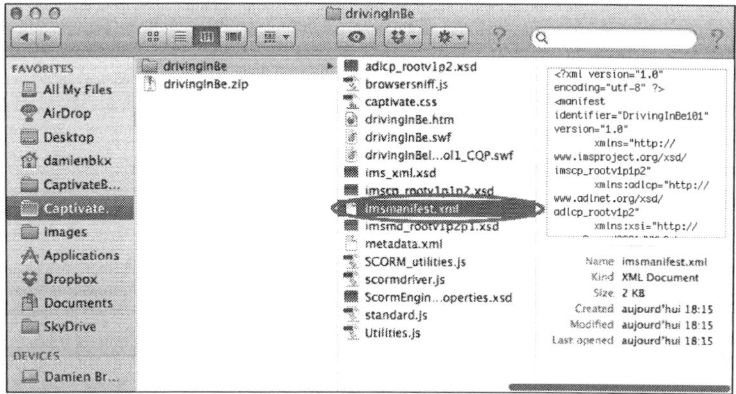

The actual extra files that Captivate generates depend on the standard being used (SCORM or AICC) and of the chosen version of SCORM.

Integrating the SCORM package in the LMS

Now that we have a SCORM package available, the last step of the process is to integrate it in an LMS. The exact methodology depends on the LMS in use, but all SCORM-compliant LMSs are supposed to accept the ZIP file generated by Captivate, to unzip it and to find their way around the files it contains, provided that a SCORM-compliant manifest can be found at the root level of the zip package.

Test your SCORM packages for free

If you do not have a SCORM-compliant LMS available, you can still test the SCORM features of your Captivate project by setting up a free account to SCORM Cloud at `https://cloud.scorm.com/sc/guest/SignInForm`. SCORM Cloud is a web-based LMS. Their free service can be used as a great testing platform, but if you want to use SCORM Cloud to host your real online courses, you'll have to upgrade to a paid subscription plan. See this great blog post about creating an LMS-ready file in Captivate and uploading it to SCORM cloud at `http://blogs.adobe.com/captivate/2011/11/demystifying-captivate%E2%80%93lms-integration.html`.

The following screenshot shows the `drivingInBe.zip` file ready to be uploaded to the Moodle LMS:

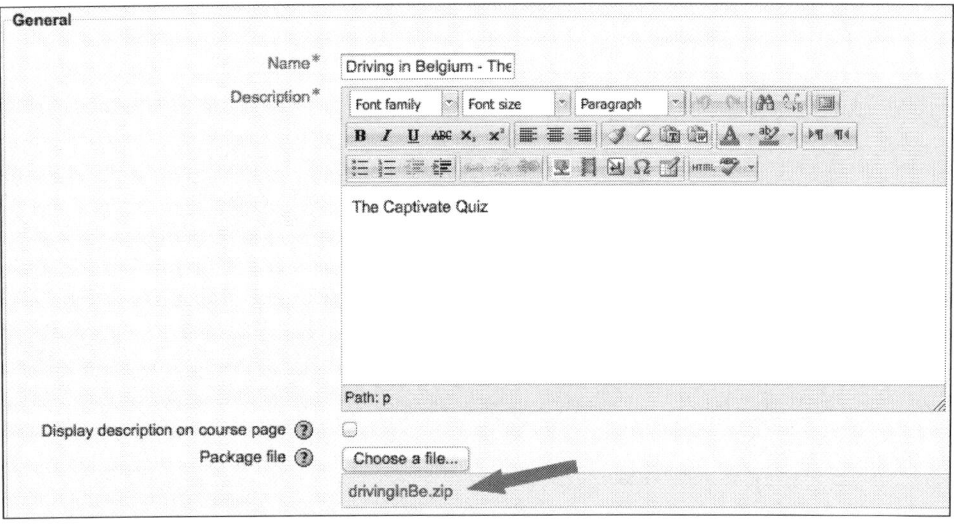

When the Captivate project is integrated in the LMS, the students are able to see the course and take the test online! Remember that when setting up the reporting options, we decided to report every single interaction to the server. We also assigned a unique Interaction ID to each interaction that we wanted to report.

The following screenshot shows the report as displayed by Moodle. The actual look and feel depends on your LMS. Note that most LMSs let us export this data in **CSV** (**Comma Separated Values**) format so that it can be further analyzed in a spreadsheet application such as Microsoft Excel or Apple Numbers:

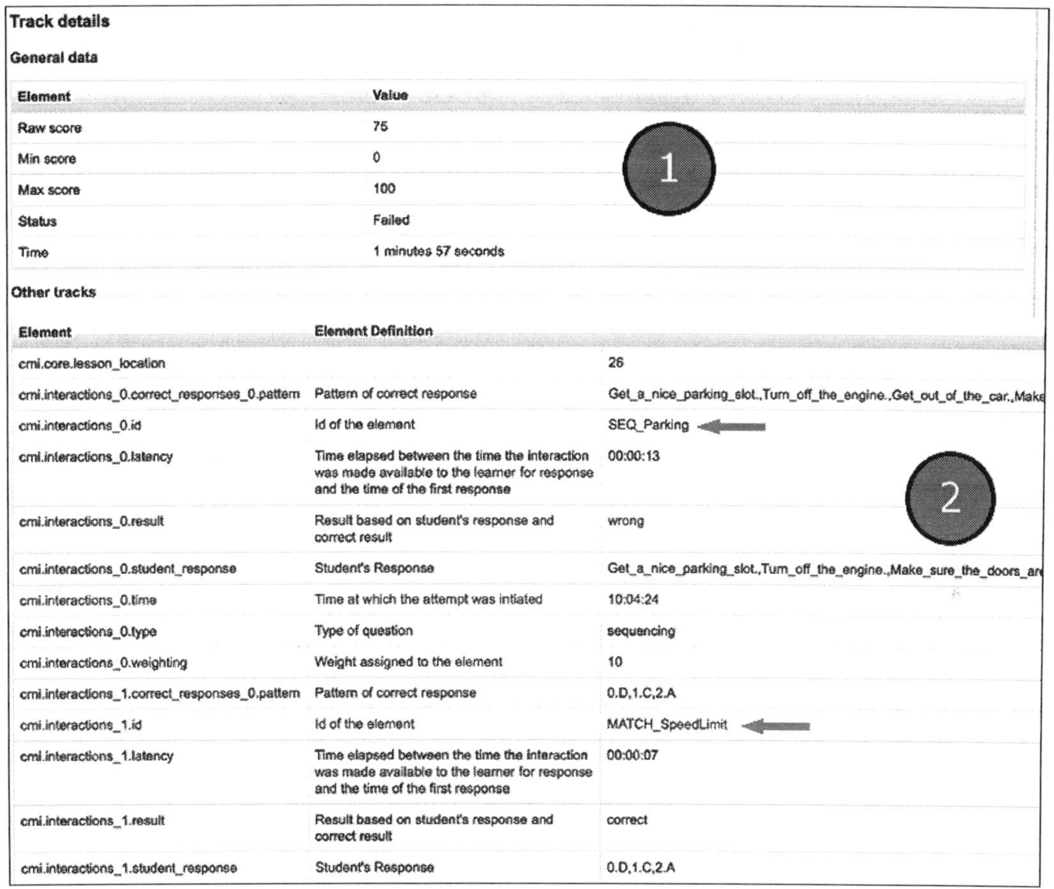

Track details

General data

Element	Value
Raw score	75
Min score	0
Max score	100
Status	Failed
Time	1 minutes 57 seconds

Other tracks

Element	Element Definition	
cmi.core.lesson_location		26
cmi.interactions_0.correct_responses_0.pattern	Pattern of correct response	Get_a_nice_parking_slot.,Turn_off_the_engine.,Get_out_of_the_car.,Make
cmi.interactions_0.id	Id of the element	SEQ_Parking
cmi.interactions_0.latency	Time elapsed between the time the interaction was made available to the learner for response and the time of the first response	00:00:13
cmi.interactions_0.result	Result based on student's response and correct result	wrong
cmi.interactions_0.student_response	Student's Response	Get_a_nice_parking_slot.,Turn_off_the_engine.,Make_sure_the_doors_ar
cmi.interactions_0.time	Time at which the attempt was intiated	10:04:24
cmi.interactions_0.type	Type of question	sequencing
cmi.interactions_0.weighting	Weight assigned to the element	10
cmi.interactions_1.correct_responses_0.pattern	Pattern of correct response	0.D,1.C,2.A
cmi.interactions_1.id	Id of the element	MATCH_SpeedLimit
cmi.interactions_1.latency	Time elapsed between the time the interaction was made available to the learner for response and the time of the first response	00:00:07
cmi.interactions_1.result	Result based on student's response and correct result	correct
cmi.interactions_1.student_response	Student's Response	0.D,1.C,2.A

The upper part (1) of the previous screenshot shows the general information reported by SCORM such as the student's score, the status, and the time it took to take the Quiz.

The bottom part of the screenshot (2) shows the detailed interaction report. Notice how the Interaction IDs we created in Captivate are used in this report (shown as arrows in the previous screenshot).

We now have a better idea of how Captivate reports the scores to an LMS. Keep in mind though that Captivate can only *send* the data to the server. It is up to the LMS application to implement a system that is able to retrieve, archive, process, and display the reported data. Consult the documentation of your LMS for details about how it implements SCORM.

Before moving on to the next step, let's make a quick summary of what we have learned:

- Captivate is able to send data about the completion status of the project and the Quiz results to a **Learning Management System** (LMS).
- An LMS is a system that is able to host, deliver, and manage our online courses. An LMS is also able to track the student's progression in the online courses.
- To enable communication between a piece of eLearning content and an LMS, the industry has developed two widely accepted standards: **AICC** and **SCORM**. Captivate supports both standards, which means that a Captivate-powered course can be integrated in *virtually any LMS*.
- Negative scoring (such as the **Penalty** option of Captivate 6) is only supported in SCORM 2004.
- Captivate is able to report both the completion status of the project (Complete/Incomplete or Passed/Failed) and detailed information about each interaction.
- In Captivate, an interaction is anything that requires an action from the user. It can be a Question Slide, a Click Box, a Text Entry Box, or a Button.
- In order to enable reporting of every interaction, it is necessary to assign a unique Interaction ID to each interaction that needs to be reported.
- When choosing the SCORM standard for reporting, it is necessary to generate a manifest file. The manifest file is called `imsmanifest.xml` and is used to describe the structure of the SCORM package to the LMS.
- When publishing an eLearning-enabled project, select the **Zip Files** checkbox in the **Publish** dialog. A SCORM-compliant LMS is supposed to be able to unzip the file and correctly manage the files it contains. This makes it easy for us to deploy our projects in an LMS.
- When publishing an eLearning-enabled content, Captivate generates a lot of extra files to enable SCORM or AICC support.

- The exact method of integrating the course in the LMS depends on the LMS in use. It is necessary to consult the documentation of your LMS before publishing your Captivate files.

Using Acrobat.com as an alternate reporting method

If you do not have access to an LMS, Captivate provides an alternate reporting method. This alternate method uses the *Acrobat.com* cloud service to replace the LMS used in the traditional reporting workflow.

Acrobat.com is a set of cloud-based services from Adobe. One of the greatest things about Acobat.com is the free 2 GB storage space that can be used to share large files with other people (and more specifically with our students). But Acrobat.com is not only about file storage and sharing. It is a whole array of free and paying cloud-based services, including the ability to convert files to PDF online, form design, and much more.

The exercises of this section require that you, as well as each of your students, have an Acrobat.com account. A free Acrobat.com account is one of the goodies brought to you by your Adobe ID, so if you already have an Adobe ID, you're all set for this section. If you do not have an Adobe ID, it is easy to create one for free on the `www.adobe.com` website or on the `www.acrobat.com` website. If you do not want to sign up for a free Acrobat.com account, you will not be able to perform the exercises of this section. Just read through the steps to have an idea of the workflow.

In the next exercises, we will use Acrobat.com as an alternate reporting method. Make sure you have an Adobe ID before starting this procedure.

Configuring the Captivate project for Acrobat.com reporting

First of all, we will configure our Captivate project for Acrobat.com reporting using the following steps:

1. Use the **Filmstrip** to go to slide 23 of the `Chapter07/drivingInBe.cptx` file.

Slide 23 should be the automatically generated **Quiz Results** Slide. Note that this slide contains a single button labeled **Continue**.

2. Use the **Quiz | Quiz Preferences** menu item to open the **Reporting** category of the **Preferences** dialog.
3. Open the **SCORM 1.2** drop-down list and choose **Acrobat.com** instead.
4. Click on the **Configure** button situated next to the drop-down list.
5. In the top-most area of the **Configure Acrobat.com Settings** dialog, enter your Adobe ID credentials.
6. In the lower area of the **Alternate Reporting** dialog, enter the following information:
    - Company/Institute: `MFTC`
    - Department: `Training`
    - Course: `Driving In Belgium`

Note that all these fields are mandatory, as shown in the following screenshot:

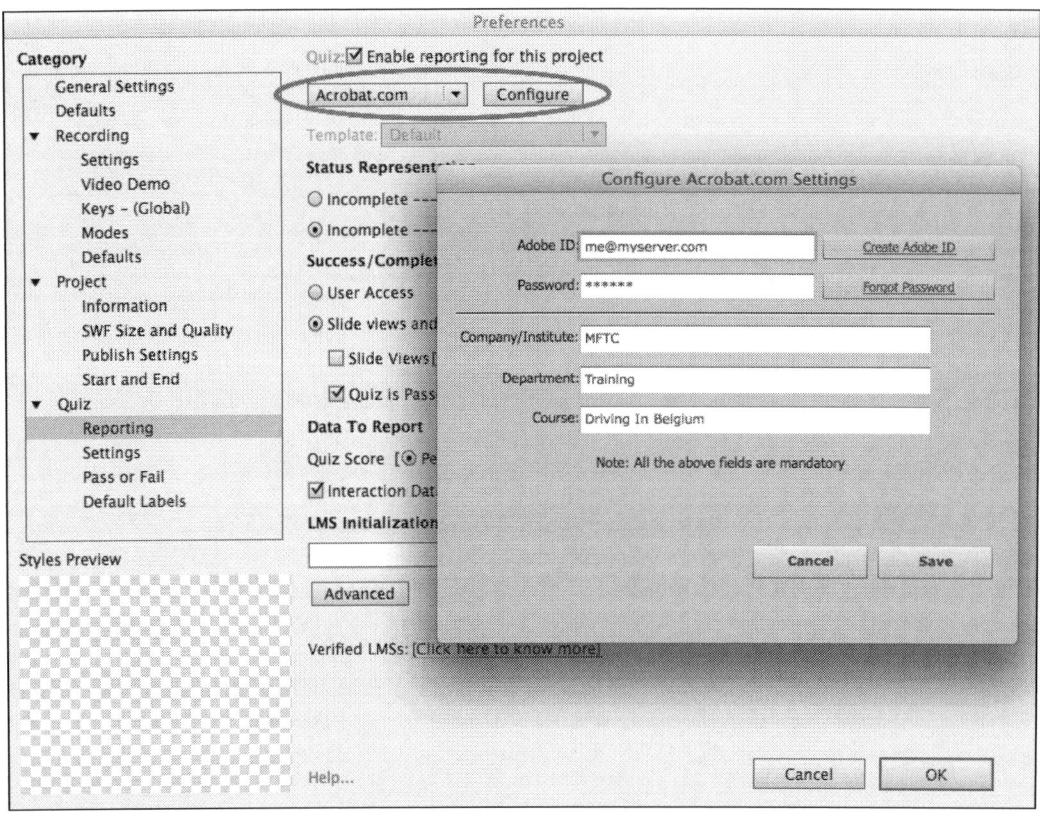

7. Click on the **Save** button. Captivate logs in to the Acrobat.com service and retrieves the necessary information.
8. Click on **OK** to close the **Preferences** dialog.

Notice that the Quiz Results Slide (slide 24) now contains a second button labeled **Post Results**. When the student clicks on this button, the Quiz results are uploaded to the Acrobat.com service.

Uploading the files to Acrobat.com

Now that our project is properly configured, we will take advantage of the File Sharing service provided by Acrobat.com to upload our project and share it with our students using the following steps:

1. Use the **File | Collaborate | Share files on Acrobat.com** menu item to open the corresponding dialog box.
2. Enter your Adobe ID credentials in the box and click on the **Sign In** button. Captivate connects to the Acrobat.com service and moves on to the second step of the Wizard.
3. Select the **PDF** checkbox to have Captivate convert our project into a PDF file and send it to Acrobat.com.
4. Click on the **Next** button to go to the next step of the Wizard.
5. In the **To** field, enter the e-mail addresses of the students you want to share your project with.

Optionally, we can type a nice introduction message for our students. Also note that your own e-mail address is automatically added in the **CC** field.

6. Click on the **Send** button to convert the project to PDF, send the file to Acorbat.com, and send the e-mail messages to the selected students.

This operation can be quite lengthy depending on the size of the project and the speed of your Internet connection.

Add students to the course

Thanks to your address being added automatically in the CC field, a copy of the project is sent to yourself. You can then allow more students to access the course by sending them the link to the file. Note that each student needs an Adobe ID to download the course from Acrobat.com and to report the results of the Quiz.

Taking the Quiz

Once the students have access to the download link, they can log in to Acrobat.com using their own Adobe ID and download the PDF File. In the following exercise, you will pretend to be a student in order to download and experience the online course as a real student would using the following steps:

1. By now, you should have received an invitation e-mail from Acrobat.com with a link to our shared PDF file. Click on the link to open the Acrobat.com website.
2. Once on the Acrobat.com website, sign in with your Adobe ID credentials and click on the **Sign in** button. You will be automatically redirected to the shared file.
3. Click on the **Download** button situated at the top-left corner of the Acrobat.com screen to download the file to your computer.
4. Open the downloaded file with Adobe Acrobat or Adobe Reader and take the course as a normal student would.
5. Once you reach the Quiz Results page, click on the **Post Result** button.
6. Follow the onscreen instructions to sign in to Acrobat.com and upload your Quiz result to the cloud.
7. When the movie is finished, close the Adobe Acrobat or Adobe Reader application.

Note that each student must have a valid Adobe ID to access the download and to publish the Quiz results to the server.

When viewing such a PDF file, it is important to use the official Adobe Acrobat or Adobe Reader application. Third-party PDF readers (such as Foxit Reader) might not implement all the required features to make the Acrobat.com integration work as advertised.

Using the Adobe Captivate Quiz Result Analyzer

For the last step of the process, we will return into the role of the teacher and examine how we can retrieve the Quiz Results from the server and what are our options to analyze the data.

To achieve these goals, we will use an external application that is part of the Captivate bundle. This application is called the **Adobe Captivate Quiz Result Analyzer**.

The Quiz Result Analyzer is an *Adobe AIR* application. It means that it will work the exact same way on every platform, but it also means that the AIR runtime must be installed on your computer to run the Adobe Captivate Quiz Result Analyzer.

[More information on Adobe AIR can be found at the following URL: `http://www.adobe.com/products/air.edu.html`.]

The Adobe Captivate Quiz Result Analyzer installer can be downloaded for free on the Adobe website at the following address: `www.adobe.com/go/cp5_quizanalyzer`.

Once you have downloaded the `AdobeCaptivateQuizresultAnalyser.air` file double-click on it and follow the onscreen instructions to install the application.

The following exercise begins when the installation of the Quiz Result Analyzer is complete:

1. Open the Adobe Captivate Quiz Result Analyzer application.
2. At the top of the screen, select **Acrobat.com** in the **Source** (1) drop-down and click on the **Sign in** button.
3. Enter your Adobe ID credentials and sign in to Acrobat.com. Once you have signed in, your name and a **Sign out** button appear at the top-left corner of the interface (2).
4. Choose **MFTC** in the **Organization** drop-down, **Training** in the **Department** drop-down, and **Driving in Belgium** in the **Course** drop-down (3). When done, click on the **Generate Report** button.

We could have uploaded more than a single Captivate project in the same course. Each of these projects is then considered a lesson inside a single course. In our case, the Driving In Belgium course is made of a single lesson.

5. Double-click on the **drivingInBeAcrobat** lesson to drill down through the data and have a list of all the students who have taken the Quiz.

At this time, only one student (yourself) has taken the Quiz. (4), as shown in the following screenshot:

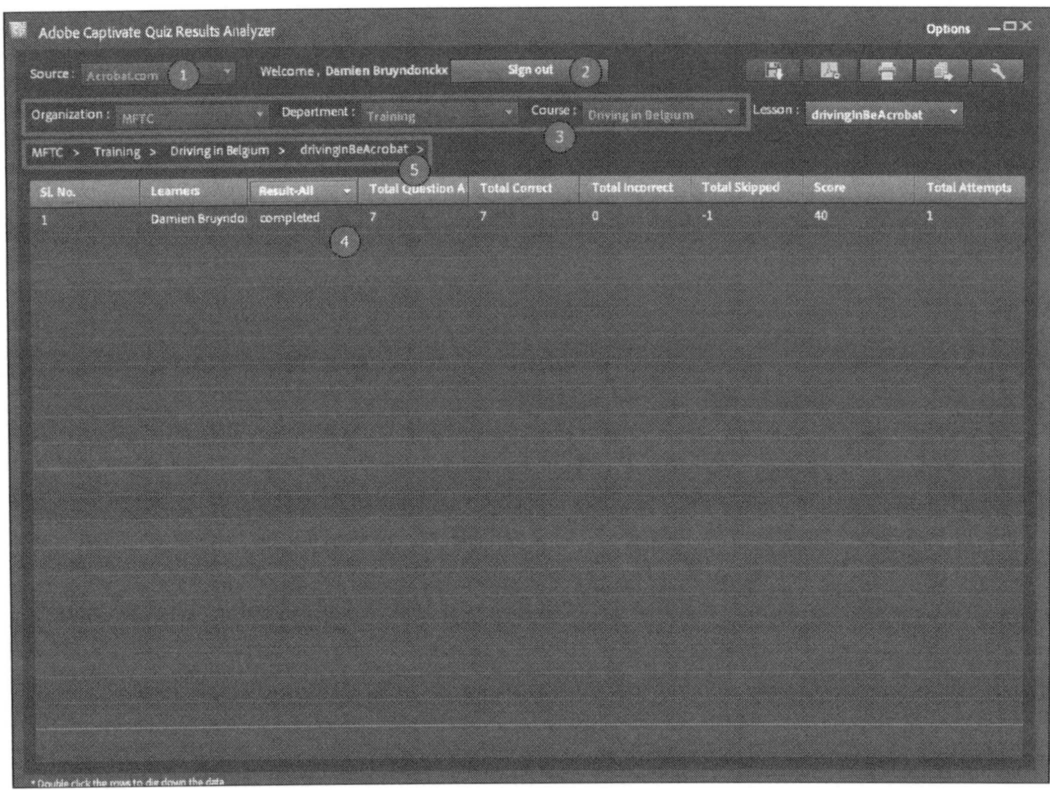

It is possible to go even deeper in the data and see the details of each interaction within the Captivate project.

6. Double-click on your name to have a detailed report on your performances in the Quiz.

Take your time to browse through the available data. Notice how the Interaction ID we typed earlier in Captivate is used to generate this report. Right above the report, use the breadcrumb (5), as shown in the previous screenshot to go back up the data tree and display the report of another user, of another lesson, or of another course.

7. At the top-left corner of the application, click on the **Export to CSV** icon to export the current report to CSV, as shown in the following screenshot:

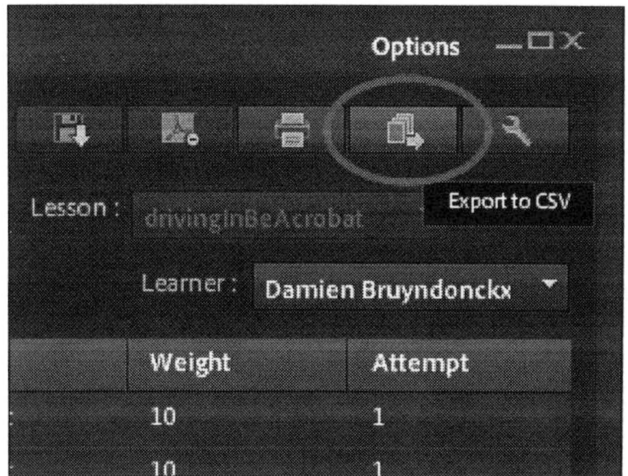

The exported CSV file can be opened with any spreadsheet application (such as Microsoft Excel or Apple Numbers) in order to be further analyzed.

This exercise concludes our exploration of the alternate reporting method using Acrobat.com as the LMS. Before moving on to the next chapter, let's make a quick summary of what we have learned:

- If no LMS is available, you can use Acrobat.com as an alternative reporting method.
- This solution requires the teacher (you) and every student to have a valid Adobe ID.
- Acrobat.com is a set of online services provided by Adobe. These services include a free 2 GB storage space to share large files with colleagues, customers, or students.
- To use Acrobat.com as the LMS, follow the basic four-step workflow:
    - Configure the Acrobat.com reporting in the Quiz Preferences
    - Upload your file to Acrobat.com
    - Let the students take the Quiz
    - Use the Quiz Result Analyzer to visualize, analyze, and export the Quiz results
- The Quiz Result Analyzer is a free AIR application that is shipped with Captivate or that can be downloaded from the Adobe Website.

To finish off with this topic, I would like to share this video from the Adobe TV website. This video explains how to use Acrobat.com as an alternate reporting method and has been created using Adobe Captivate, available at:

`http://tv.adobe.com/watch/publish-and-track-results/reporting-without-having-to-use-lms/`.

Summary

With the addition of Question Slides and quizzes, our project is not a simple demonstration or simulation anymore. It is a full-featured eLearning package that is able to integrate nicely in virtually every LMS on the market. On the pedagogical side, we have discovered the eLearning answer to the assessment issue, which is one of the primary concerns of any teacher. On the technical side, we have discovered the SCORM and AICC standards that make communication between our eLearning content and an LMS possible.

In this chapter, we have discussed each of the eight question types of Captivate. We then created a Question Pool before exploring the Quiz Preferences and the myriad of options available to customize our quizzes. In the second part of this chapter, we discussed how the Quiz results and the interactions can be reported to an LMS. Finally, we discovered how Acrobat.com can be used as an alternative reporting method if no LMS is available.

In the next chapter, we will add Master Slides, Templates, and Themes to the mix. These features will help us achieve a consistent look and feel among the slides of a project as well as across projects.

Captivate still has some interesting features waiting to be uncovered. Let's meet in the next chapter to pursue our exploration.

Meet the Community

Rick Zanotti

Bio

Rick Zanotti is the president and founder of the RELATE Corporation, and the host of the eLearning Chat online TV shows.

With over 35 years of experience in IT and Learning, Rick is an Entrepreneur, Instructional Designer, Multimedia Author, Voice-over Talent, Video Producer, Podcaster, and Management Consultant.

Prior to RELATE, Rick was a Vice-president of Information System, Director of IT, Systems Analyst, and senior Project Leader for companies like LFP, Marsh & McLennan, Day Runner, and Citibank NA.

Rick is also an internationally known martial artist and author. He has taught the police, the military personnel, and many students in several countries.

Rick studied Engineering and Business Administration with a minor in Information Systems.

Rick and Leslie have been married for over 26 years and have one married daughter and two dogs. Rick, born in Buenos Aires, Argentina, is also fully bilingual in Spanish.

Rick Zanotti has been involved with Adobe Captivate since it was originally called FlashCam, then RoboDemo, and now what you see today. He is a member of the Adobe Captivate Advisory board and has helped influence many features and bug fixes working with Adobe engineer.

Contact details

Website: `www.relate.com`

Twitter: `@rickzanotti`

Facebook: `rickzanotti`

Google+: `rickzanotti`

Shows: **video netcasts**

eLearnChat: `http://vimeo.com/channels/elearnchat`

SchreckTeck: `http://vimeo.com/channels/schreckteck`

RELATE: `http://www.youtube.com/user/relatecasts`

My personal note

When I discovered Rick's eLearn chat show, I immediately became a big fan! I enjoy watching Rick chat with some of the greatest and most influential individuals of the eLearning industry. It helps me grab the big picture of where our industry is going to and helps me identify the key players of the community.

Don't hesitate to bookmark the eLearn chat channel on Vimeo. You won't regret it!

8
Templates, Master Slides, and Themes

In this chapter, we will concentrate on the cosmetic part of the project. Our primary goal will be to reach a high level of consistency in the look and feel of our eLearning content. Remember that our students are alone in front of their computer with no one around to guide them. In the previous chapter, we briefly discussed how consistency in the learning strategy can be used as a lighthouse along the student's path to knowledge. In this chapter, we will discover that a consistent look and feel is yet another one of these lighthouses that we can leave behind for the students.

Captivate proposes four features to help us achieve this high level of consistency. The first feature is the *Styles* and the *Object Style Manager*. This feature has been already discussed in *Chapters 3, Working with Standard Objects* and *Chapter 4, Working with Animations and Interactive Objects*, and will be used again in this chapter. The other three features are the **Master Slides**, the **Templates**, and the **Themes**. These will be introduced in this chapter.

In addition to addressing the consistency issue, the proper use of Master Slides, Templates, Styles, and Themes will dramatically speed up the development of our eLearning content.

In this chapter, we shall:

- Experiment with the predefined Themes of Captivate.
- Create a new Theme from scratch.
- Create a full set of Master Slides.
- Add Placeholder Objects on the Master Slides.
- Apply these Master Slides to the slides of the project.
- Fine-tune the look and feel of the objects using the Styles.

- Save the Styles in our Theme.
- Create a brand new Template.
- Add Placeholder Slides to the Template.
- Create a new Captivate project from a Template.

Preparing our work

At the beginning of this chapter, we will work on a brand new blank project. Later on, we will use our Driving in Belgium application. Perform the default steps to make Captivate ready:

1. Open Captivate and ensure that the **Classic** workspace is currently applied.
2. Use the **Window** | **Workspace** | **Reset 'Classic'** to reapply the original default workspace.
3. Open the `Chapter08/drivingInBe.cptx` file.

That's it! We're all set for the Master Slide, Themes, and Template adventure!

Experimenting with Themes

Captivate 6 introduces this new feature called **Themes**. Captivate ships with a few ready-to-use Themes right out of the box. In order to have a better idea of what a Theme is, let's start with some simple experiments using those predefined Themes:

1. Once in Captivate, use the **File** | **New Project** | **Blank Project** menu item to create a new blank project. You can also use the **Blank Project** link on the right-hand side of the Welcome screen, if the Welcome screen is visible.
2. In the **New Blank Project** dialog, use the **Select** drop-down menu to choose a size of **800 x 600** for the project. When done, click on the **OK** button.

Captivate creates a new blank project of the chosen size. A single slide is automatically added to the **Filmstrip** (1) This slide already contains a bunch of elements. Notice the **Themes Panel** (2) that spans across the entire width of the stage, as shown in the following screenshot:

If the Themes panel is not automatically displayed on the screen, use the **Themes | Show/Hide Themes Panel** menu item to turn it on.

Currently, our new blank project is using the default *White* Theme.

The Elements of a Theme

A Captivate Theme is a collection of graphical elements and assets. In the next few pages, we will try to discover what Themes are made of by manipulating different Themes and exploring the way they affect the slides and objects of the project.

The Master Slides

To better understand what Themes are, our first stop is the **Master Slide** panel using the following steps:

1. Open the **Master Slide** panel. By default it is situated at the bottom of the screen, next to the **Timeline**.

If the **Master Slide** panel is not displayed, use the **Window | Master Slide** menu item to turn it on.

The *White* Theme contains an entire set of predefined **Master Slides**. Each of these Master Slides proposes a predefined layout that we can apply *as is* to any slides of the project. To ensure visual consistency across the Master Slides of the Theme, the first Master Slide of the panel is known as the Main Master Slide (1).

The Main Master Slide contains the visual elements that are common to most (if not every) slides of the project, as shown in the following screenshot:

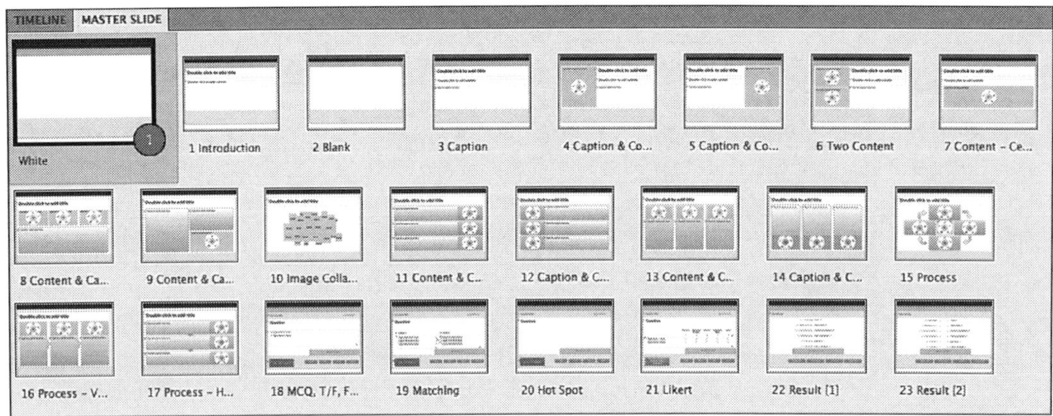

In Captivate 6, it is possible to create new slides based on one of the Master Slides of the Theme.

2. Select the first slide of the project in the main **Filmstrip**.
3. Use the **Insert** | **New Slide from** | **Caption** menu item.

Captivate creates a new slide based on the *Caption* Master Slide of the Theme. The new slide already contains a bunch of Text Captions. Actually, the elements contained in the slides are not *real* Text Captions *yet*. These elements are **Text Caption Placeholders**. They are used to predefine the location, the size and, other formatting options of a future Text Caption.

4. Double-click on the **Double click to add title** Placeholder.
5. Type some text into the Text Caption and hit the *Esc* key.

Now that some text has been typed into the object, it is not a Placeholder anymore, but an actual Text Caption. The size, position, font family, font size, color, and so on. of this Text Caption are inherited from the Placeholder, while the content of the Text Caption has just been typed in.

6. Use the **Insert** | **New Slide from** | **Two Content** menu item.

Captivate inserts yet another slide in the project, but this time, it is based on the *Two Content* Master Slide of the Theme. This slide also contains some placeholders. On the right-hand side of the slide, three Text Caption Placeholders are displayed. On the left-hand side of this slide, there are two **Content Placeholders**.

7. Pass your mouse over the icons of the Content Placeholders. Notice that each icon corresponds to a Captivate object.
8. Click on the **Image** icon of the Content Placeholder shown by the red arrow in the following screenshot:

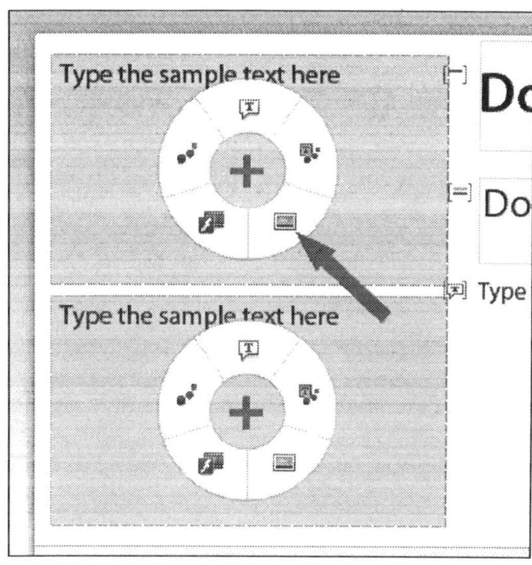

When you click on this icon, Captivate immediately opens the **Select Image from Library** dialog. From this dialog, we can choose the image to insert in the Placeholder.

9. Click on **Cancel** to close the dialog without inserting any image.
10. Do the same experiment with the other icons of the Placeholder.

Each of these icons act as a *shortcut* that inserts different kind of content in the Placeholder. This illustrates the basic idea of the Themes and the Placeholders. The Themes and the Placeholders provide ready to use layouts containing shortcut icons to the various objects of Captivate. As such, Themes and Placeholders are both tremendous time savers. They enable us to *rapidly* develop our pieces of eLearning content.

11. Use the **Insert | Question Slide** menu item to open the **Insert Questions** dialog.
12. Set the dialog so it inserts **1 Graded Multiple Choice** question, **1 Graded Short Answer** question, and **1 Graded Matching** question. When done, click on **OK** to close the dialog and insert the Question Slides.

Captivate inserts *four* new slides in the project. The three Question Slides we asked for plus the automatic Quiz Result Slide.

13. Use the **Filmstrip** to select slide 6. It should be the Matching Question we just inserted.
14. Open the **Properties** panel and make sure it displays the properties of the **Slide**.

In the **General** accordion of the **Properties** panel, notice that Captivate has *automatically* applied the **Matching** Master Slide to this question, as shown in the following screenshot:

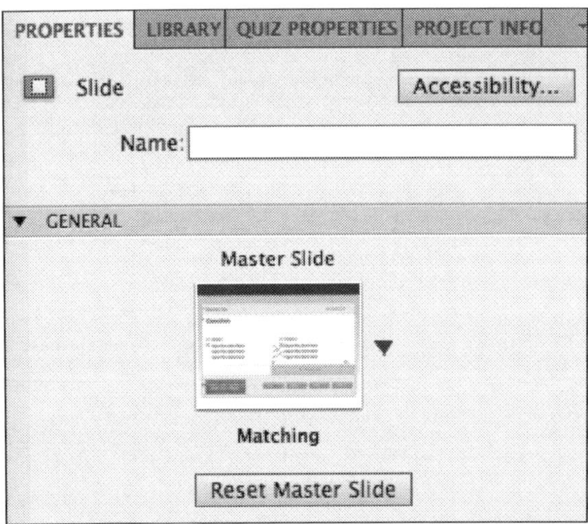

This is where the true magic of the Themes is revealed. When a new slide is inserted into the project, Captivate will always try to determine the best Master Slide to apply. In this case, Captivate has decided that the Matching Master Slide was the one to use, which is exactly what we need. Again, this is *rapid* eLearning at work!

15. Use the **Filmstrip** to browse the other two Question Slides as well as the automatic Quiz Result Slide. Use the **Properties** panel to see what Master Slide has been *automatically* applied by Captivate.

The Styles

In this section, we will apply another Theme to the project and see how this change affects the slides and the objects using the following steps:

1. If needed, use the **Themes | Show/Hide Themes Panel** menu item to turn the Themes panel on.

2. Click on the **Timeworn** Theme to apply it to the project.
3. Read the warning message and click on **Yes** to continue.

The new Theme is applied to the slides of the project.

4. Use the **Filmstrip** to go through the slides of the project one by one.

While doing so, notice how the new Theme affects the look and feel of your project. The most obvious change probably is the new background image, but a Theme is far more than that. Take a close look at the Text Captions for instance. You will see that their formatting has been affected by the new Theme as well.

This illustrates that, in addition to Master Slides, a Theme contains **Object Styles**. So by applying another Theme on a project, we also update the styles of the objects.

The Skin

The third component of a Theme is the **Skin**. Remember that a Skin is a collection of three elements: the Playback Controls, the Borders, and the Table of Contents. Let's make an experiment using the Skin Editor to apply a Theme to the Project:

1. Use the **Project** | **Skin Editor** menu item to open the floating **Skin Editor** panel.

In the Playback Controls page of the Skin Editor, notice that the currently applied Skin is the **Theme Default** (1). The color of the *Playback Controls* element of this Theme is defined in the **Theme** section (2) of the **Skin Editor**, as shown in the following screenshot:

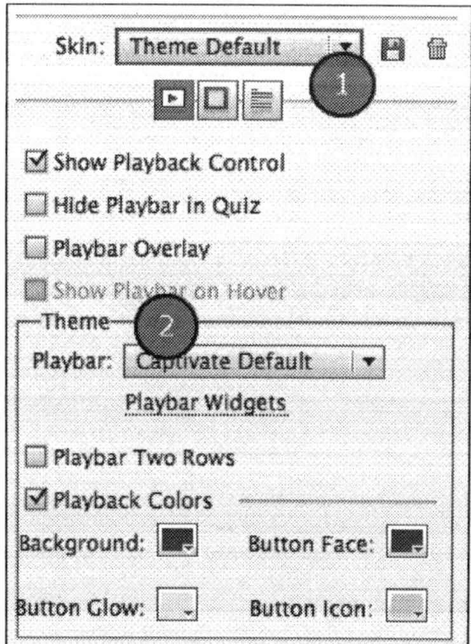

2. Close the floating **Skin Editor** panel without making any change.
3. Use the **Project | Table of Contents** menu item to reopen the floating **Skin Editor** panel, but on the **Table of Contents** page.
4. Select the **Show TOC** icon.

Take some time to inspect the look and feel of the Table of Contents in the Preview area of the **Skin Editor** panel and note how it uses the same general look and feel and the same color scheme as the rest of the Theme.

5. Close the floating **Skin Editor** panel when ready.

We will now apply yet another Theme to the project and return to the Skin Editor to take a look at the changes.

6. If needed, use the **Themes | Show/Hide Themes Panel** menu item to turn the Themes panel on.
7. Apply the **Clean Blue** Theme to the project.
8. When the new Theme is applied, use the **Project | Skin Editor** menu item to reopen the floating **Skin Editor** panel.

Take some time to inspect the look and feel of the Playback Controls and of the Table of Contents in the Preview area of the **Skin Editor** panel. Notice that the Clean Blue Theme we just applied to the project has completely changed the look and feel of these elements.

9. When done, close the floating **Skin Editor** panel.
10. Also close the file without saving it.

We now have a much better understanding of what a Theme is. In the next section, we will create our own Theme and apply it to the Driving in Belgium project, but, for the moment, let's make a quick summary of what we have learned:

- A **Theme** is made of a collection of graphical assets and styles. It is used to quickly define the look and feel of an entire project.
- Captivate ships with a bunch of predefined Themes. These are available in the Themes panel that is displayed across the width of the stage. Use the **Themes | Show/Hide Themes panel** menu item to turn the Themes panel on or off.
- A Theme is composed of three basic elements: a collection of **Master Slides**, the **Styles** to apply to the objects of the project, and the **Skin** of the project.
- When we insert a new slide in the project, Captivate tries to determine the best Master Slide to apply to the new slide.

Creating a Theme

In this section, we will return to the `drivingInBe.cptx` file and create a new Theme. To do it, we will first apply one of the predefined Themes of Captivate 6 to the project. We will then fine-tune all three components of this Theme one by one starting by the **Master Slides**, then the **Styles**, then the **Skin**. Perform the following steps to create a new Theme:

1. If needed, return to the `Chapter08/drivinInBe.cptx` file.
2. Use the **Themes | Show/Hide Themes panel** to turn the Themes panel on.

We will use the **Blank** Theme as a starting point to create our own custom Captivate Theme.

3. Apply the **Blank** Theme to the project.

By applying the **Blank** Theme to the project, we modify the overall look and feel as well as some of the styles of our project.

4. Use the **Themes | Save Theme As** menu item to create a new Theme based on the **Blank** Theme.
5. Save the new Theme as `Chapter08/MFTC-Theme.cptm`.
6. Acknowledge the successful creation of the new Theme by clicking on the **OK** button.

Note the file extension used for Themes is `.cptm`.

With our new Theme saved, we can safely move on to the next step and customize the Master Slides of the Theme.

Customizing the Master Slides of the Theme

The idea behind the Master Slides is quite simple. The goal is to create a set of slides in which we place backgrounds and other objects that are common to many slides in the project (such as logos, headers, footers, and so on). Once the Master Slides are created, we can apply them to the standard slides of our project in order to have them share the elements defined in the Master Slide.

If you are a PowerPoint or a Keynote user, this process probably sounds very familiar. Use the following step to open the Master Slide panel (if needed):

1. If needed, open the **Master Slide** panel. By default, the **Master Slide** panel is situated at the bottom of the screen, next to the **Timeline**.

The Blank Theme that we applied to the project already contains nine Master Slides (1) in addition to the Main Master Slide (2), as shown in the following screenshot:

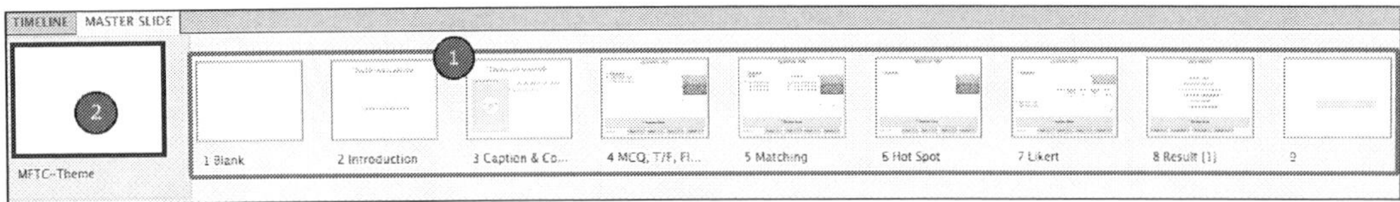

First, we will customize the Main Master Slide.

Customizing the Main Master Slide

The Main Master Slide is the first one in the Master Slide panel. The Main Master Slide contains the graphical elements shared by most (if not all) slides of the project. Note that by default, the name of the Theme (here **MFTC-Theme**) appears below the Main Master Slide thumbnail, as shown in the previous screenshot. Perform the following steps to customize the background of the Main Master Slide:

1. In the **Master Slide** panel, click on the Main Master Slide to make it the active object.
2. If needed, open the **Properties** panel. Make sure it shows the properties of the Main Master Slide.
3. Use the **Insert** | **Image** menu item to insert the `images/mftcContentTemplate.jpg` image on the Master Slide.
4. Right-click on the image we just imported. In the contextual menu that opens, click on the **Merge with the background** menu item.
5. Take some time to read the information message that appears on the screen. Click on the **Yes** button to acknowledge the message and merge the image with the background, as shown in the following screenshot:

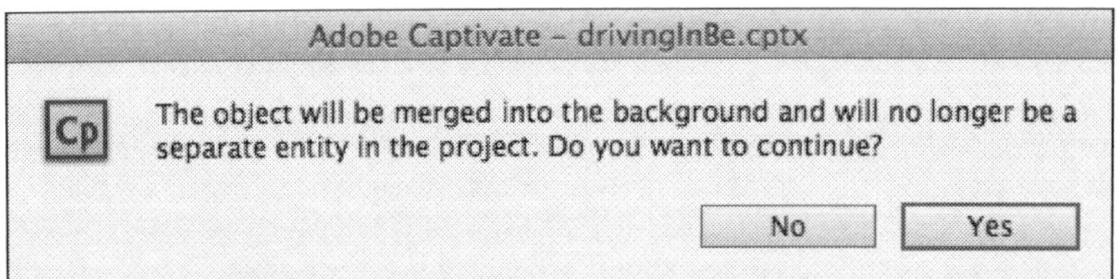

By merging a picture into the background, the picture becomes the slide itself. Consequently, it cannot be manipulated as an object anymore and it disappears from the **Timeline**.

Take a look at the **Master Slide** panel and notice that the new background of the Main Master Slide is used by all the other Master Slides of the project.

Adding a Master Slide to the Theme

We will now add a new Master Slide to the project. We will call it the *Title* Master Slide and use another image as its background by performing the following steps:

1. With the Main Master Slide selected in the **Master Slide** panel, use the **Insert | Content Master Slide** menu item to insert a new Master Slide in the project.

The new Master Slide is inserted as Master Slide number 2. Note that by default, it uses the background of the Main Master Slide, which is *not* what we want in this case.

2. Select the newly inserted Master Slide in the **Master Slide** panel.
3. At the very top of the **Properties** panel, enter `Title` in the **Name** field.

The new name appears below the Master Slide thumbnail in the **Master Slide** panel. The next step is to remove the default background image that is inherited from the Main Master Slide and to replace it with another background image.

4. At the top of the **Properties** panel, deselect the **Use Master Slide Background** checkbox.
5. Still in the **Properties** panel, click on the Folder icon situated below the **Background** field.
6. In the **Select Image from Library** dialog box, select the `mftcTitleTemplate.jpg` image situated in the **Backgrounds** section.
7. Click on **OK** to apply the new background and to close the **Select Image from Library** window.

The new **Title** Master Slide now uses another background image than the one used by the other Master Slides of the project, as shown in the following screenshot:

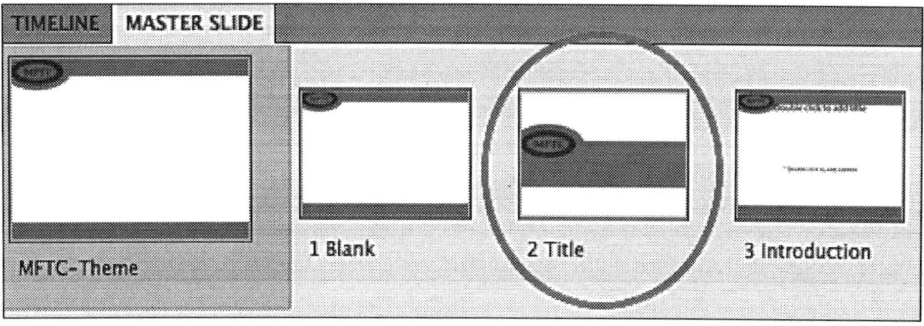

Adding Placeholders to the Master Slides

In our project, we have three *Title Slides*. The first one is the very **first slide** of the project. The second one is **slide 16**, which introduces the Quiz. The third one is **slide 26**, which is the last slide of the project. In addition to sharing the same background image, these three slides contain a Text Animation with similar properties. To speed up the development of the future eLearning projects that will be using this Theme, we will now add a Text Animation Placeholder on the **Title** Master Slide using the following steps:

1. In the **Master Slide** panel, select our new **Title** Master Slide.
2. Use the **Insert | Placeholder Object | Text Animation** menu item to add a Text Animation Placeholder on the Master Slide.
3. Move the Placeholder Object roughly to the center of the brown area in the middle of the slide.

When the Text Animation Placeholder is selected, notice the **Effect** drop-down list of the **General** accordion of the **Properties** panel. It is the very same **Effect** drop-down list as the one that is used when configuring an actual Text Animation.

4. In the **General** accordion, change the **Effect** to **Waltz**.

The other options of the Text Animation (such as the text content) depend on the actual Text Animation object that will be placed in this Placeholder at design time.

Applying the Master Slides to the slides of the project

In this section, we will use the Master Slides of our Theme to implement a consistent look and feel for all the slides of the project. We will start by applying the **Title** Master Slide to slides 1, 16, and 26 using the following steps:

1. Use the **Filmstrip** to go to slide 1 of the project.
2. Make sure that the **Properties** panel shows the properties of the **Slide** and not the properties of one of the objects of the slide.
3. In the **General** accordion of the **Properties** panel, use the **Master Slide** drop-down list to apply the **Title** Master Slide to this particular slide.

Notice that the **Name** we added earlier to the Master Slide now helps us locate it in the drop-down list!

4. Still in the **General** accordion of the **Properties** panel, select the **Use Master Slide Background** and the **Master Slide Objects On Top** checkboxes.

5. Repeat the same sequence of actions to apply the Title Master Slide to slides 16 and 26.

We will now apply the **Blank** Master Slide to the content slides of the project.

6. Use the **Filmstrip** to return to slide 2.
7. In the **General** accordion of the **Properties** panel, confirm that the **Blank** Master Slide is in use.
8. Also make sure that the **Use Master Slide Background** and the **Master Slide Objects On Top** checkboxes are both *selected*.
9. Repeat the same sequence of actions from slides 3 to 8 and from slides 10 to 15.

Finally, we will apply the proper Master Slide to the Question Slides of our project.

10. Return to the **Master Slide** panel situated at the bottom of the screen.

The **Master Slide** panel contains five Master Slides that are specially designed for the Question Slides and the Quiz Result Slide. The **MCQ, T/F, FIB, Sequence** Master Slide shall be applied to the *Multiple Choice* questions, the *True/False* questions, the *Fill-In-The-Blank* questions, and the *Sequence* questions. The **Matching, Hotspot,** and **Likert** Master Slides have been designed to be applied to the corresponding Question Slides. Finally, the **Result** Master Slide is to be used on the automatic Quiz Result Slide.

11. Use the **Filmstrip** to go to slide 18.
12. In the **General** accordion of the **Properties** panel, confirm that this slide uses the **MCQ, T/F, FIB, Sequence** Master Slide.
13. Repeat the same procedure with slides 20, 21, and 23. Slide 20 should use the same **MCQ, T/F, FIB, Sequence** Master Slide then slide 18. Slide 21 should use the **Likert** Master Slide and slide 23 should use the **Result** Master Slide.
14. Return to the **Question Pool** panel (if needed, use the **Window | Question Pool** menu item to turn the panel on).
15. Use the same procedure as above to ensure that all four Question Slides of the Question Pool use the Master Slide that corresponds to their question type.

When these checks are done, each slide of the project should share the same general look and feel with minimal effort on our side!

Modifying a Master Slide

The Master Slides already helped us *achieve* a high level of consistency within our project. Now they will help us *maintain* this consistency over time.

A Master Slide can be much more than a simple background. A Master Slide can contain many of the objects that are found on any regular slide (such as Text Captions, Highlight Boxes, and Image).

In the following exercise, we will add a Text Caption to the Main Master Slide and see how this change affects regular slides of the project using the following steps:

1. Return to the **Master Slide** panel situated at the bottom of the screen, next to the **Timeline** and the **Question Pool** panels.
2. Select the Main Master Slide.
3. Use the **Insert** | **Standard Objects** | **Text Caption** menu item to insert a new Text Caption on the Master Slide.

While the **Insert** | **Standard Objects** menu is open, notice that some of the objects are grayed out and thus, unavailable for insertion on a Master Slide. The unavailable objects are the three interactive objects, the Zoom Area, the Rollover Slidelet, and the Mouse. The other Standard Objects can be inserted on a Master Slide using the very same technique as for a regular slide.

4. Replace the text of the Text Caption by `Copyright MFTC - 2012`.
5. Place your mouse cursor in the Text Caption, right before the **C** of **Copyright**. In the **Format** accordion of the **Properties** panel, click on the **Insert Symbol** icon and insert the **Copyright** symbol followed by a space, as shown in the following screenshot:

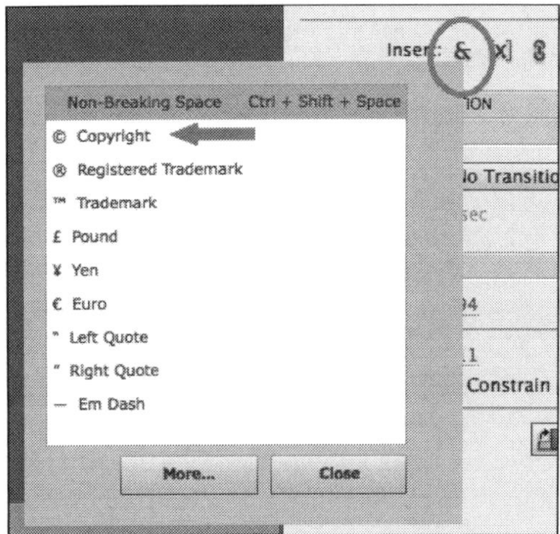

6. In the **Character** accordion of the **Properties** panel, change the font **Size** of the entire Text Caption to `12` points.
7. In the **Transform** accordion of the **Properties** panel, give the new Text Caption the following options:
   - Deselect the **Constrain proportions** checkbox
   - Change the size of the Text Caption to **W** = `150` and **H** = `30`
   - Change the position of the Text Caption to **X** = `10` and **Y** = `555`
8. In the **Transition** accordion, change the **Effect** to **No Transition** if needed.

By adding a nice copyright notice on the Main Master Slide, we have added a copyright notice on every single Master Slides and, consequently, on every standard slide of the project. Let's check it out!

9. Use the **Filmstrip** to return to the first slide of the project.

The copyright notice we inserted on the Main Master Slide is visible in the bottom-left corner of slide 1.

10. Browse the remaining slides of the project one by one. Pay close attention to the copyright notice!

Not bad! Our copyright notice integrates nicely with most of our slides. Only the slides that are using the Title Master Slide (slides 1, 16, and 26) must be adjusted. Also note that thanks to the Master Slide system, the copyright notice has the very same appearance, size, and position on every single slide that displays it. Did you say *Consistency*?

11. Return to the **Master Slide** panel and select the **Title** Master Slide.
12. In the **General** accordion of the **Properties** panel, *deselect* the **Show Main Master Slide Objects** checkbox.

This action removes the copyright notice from the Title Master Slide and, consequently, from all the slides of the project that are based on this Master Slide.

The Master Slide part of our new Theme is now finished. Before moving on to the next section, let's save the changes made to the Theme:

13. Use the **Themes | Save Theme** menu item to save the new Master Slide configuration into our custom `MFTC-Theme.cptm` file.

Now that the Theme is saved, let's make a quick summary of what we just learned:

- To create a new Theme, apply one of the predefined Themes to your project and use the **Themes | Save Theme As** menu item.
- A Theme is saved as a `.cptm` file.
- Use the Main Master Slide to quickly define the general look and feel of the project.
- By default, all the Master Slides of the project use the same background as the Main Master Slide. Deselect the **Use Master Slide Background** checkbox of a Master Slide so that it uses another background.
- It is possible to prevent the objects of the Main Master Slide to appear on the individual Master Slides by deselecting the **Show Main Master Slide Objects** checkbox.
- Use the **Insert | Content Master Slide** menu item to insert a new Master Slide in the project.
- The changes made on a Master Slide are reflected on the standard slides that are using that Master Slide.

In the next section, we will use the Styles and the Object Style Manager to fine-tune the look and feel of the objects we have inserted in the project. We will also save these styles into the Theme so they can be easily reused on subsequent projects.

Adding Styles to the Theme

Remember the good old Object Style Manager we discussed in *Chapter 3, Working with Standard Objects*? If not, don't worry, we will use it again in this section. Along the way, we will discover some new features of Captivate that will further help us rapidly implement a consistent design throughout the entire project.

Styling the Standard Objects

Let's start by giving the proper look and feel to the Standard Objects of the project using the following steps:

1. Use the **Filmstrip** to return to slide 2.

There should be two Text Captions on slide 2. The top-most Text Caption is supposed to be the title of the slide, but by applying the *Blank* Theme mentioned earlier in *Creating a Theme* section, the formatting of this Text Caption has been reset. We will now repair the formatting of this Text Caption so it looks like a title again!

2. Select the Text Caption that reads **Drive in Belgium the safe way**.
3. In the top-most area of the **Properties** panel, notice that this Text Caption currently uses the **[Default Caption Style]**.
4. In the **Character** accordion of the **Properties** panel, change the font **Family** of the selected Text Caption to **Century Gothic** and the font **Size** to `49` points.

Now that the Text Caption has recovered the proper look and feel, we will save its current formatting properties in a new style and apply that style to the other Text Caption of the same type throughout the entire project.

5. In the top-most area of the **Properties** panel, click on the **Create New Style** icon.
6. Change the name of the new style to `MFTC-Title` and click on the **OK** button.
7. In the top-most area of the **Properties** panel, click on the **Apply this style to** icon.
8. In the drop-down list, choose the **[Default Caption Style]**. This applies the new **MFTC-Title** style to every Text Captions of the project that are currently using the **[Default Caption Style]** style.
9. Use the **Filmstrip** to browse the slides of the project one by one.

Ensure that the remaining *Title Text Captions* of the project are now properly formatted.

Next, we will repair the formatting of the Smart Shapes of slides 4 and 14.

10. Use the **Filmstrip** to return to slide 4.
11. Click on the Rounded Rectangle Smart Shape that we use as a picture frame.

Remember that we used the new Group feature of Captivate 6 to group this Rounded Rectangle with the image. By clicking once on the Rounded Rectangle, **you actually select the entire group of objects**, not the Rounded Rectangle alone!

12. Click on the Rounded Rectangle a second time to select this object within the group.

Notice that **white** selection handles now surround the Rounded Rectangle and that **green** handles surround the entire group. The presence of these green handles is the visual clue telling us that the active selection is a single object within a group, as shown in the following screenshot:

With the Rounded rectangle selected, let's change its formatting options and save them in a style.

13. In the **Fill & Stroke** accordion of the **Properties** panel, change the **Fill** color of the Rounded Rectangle to the solid color `#AB8F1D`.
14. Make the object completely opaque by changing the Alpha value to `100`.
15. Change the **Stroke** color to `#4C421D`.
16. Finally, change the stroke **Width** to `3` pixels.

Make sure the Rounded Rectangle now looks like the one in following screenshot:

In order to quickly apply this new formatting to the other Smart Shapes of the project, we will now save current formatting properties of the Rounded Rectangle in a style and apply this style to the other Smart Shapes of the project.

17. With the Rounded rectangle still selected, click on the **Create New Style** icon of the **Properties** panel.
18. Name the new style `MFTC-SmartShape` and click on the **OK** button.
19. In the top-most area of the **Properties** panel, click on the **Apply this style to** icon.
20. In the drop-down list, choose the **[Default Smart Shape Style]**.
21. Use the **Filmstrip** to go to slide 14.

The three Smart Shapes of slide 14 should have the same general look and feel as the Rounded Rectangle of slide 4. But the Smart Shapes of slide 14 contain some text that needs to be properly formatted as well.

22. Select any of the three Smart Shapes of slide 14.
23. In the **Character** accordion of the **Properties** panel, change the font **Family** to **Century Gothic** and the font **Size** to `20` points.
24. In the **Format** accordion, change the alignment to **Align Left** and the **Left Margin** to `20` pixels.
25. In the top-most area of the **Properties** panel, click on the **Save changes to Existing Style** icon to update the style and the other two Smart Shapes of the slide.

Extra credit

There is one last standard object type to style in this project. It is the **Rollover Area** associated with the Rollover Objects of slides 14 and 15. In this extra credit section, you will select one of the Rollover Areas of slides 14 or 15, make it completely invisible, and save that formatting in a new style that you will name `MFTC-RolloverArea`. Then, you will apply the new style to the other Rollover Areas of the project.

Styling the Question Slides

In this section we will quickly style the Question Slides of our project. To do so, we will define formatting properties and apply styles **to the Placeholder Objects of the Master Slides** used by the Question Slides of the project. Perform the following steps to style the Question Slides:

1. Return to the **Master Slide** panel. If the panel is not open, use the **Window | Master Slide** menu item to turn it on.

2. Select the **MCQ, T/F, FIB, Sequence** Master Slide.
3. Select the **Question Title** Placeholder.

In the top-most part of the **Properties** panel, notice that the style currently applied to the Question Title is the **Default Question Title Style**.

4. In the **Character** accordion of the **Properties** panel, change the font **Family** to **Century Gothic**, change the font **Size** to `35`, and deselect the **Bold** icon.
5. In the top-most part of the **Properties** panel, click on the **Create New Style** icon.
6. Name the style `MFTC-questionTitle` and click on the **OK** button.
7. Click on the **Apply this style to** icon situated right below the **Style** drop-down.
8. In the box that opens, select the **[Default Question Title Style]** and click on **OK**.

This operation applies our new **MFTC-questionTitle** style to the Title Placeholders of the project. Don't hesitate to browse to the other Master Slides of the project to check it out! When done, make sure you return to the **MCQ, T/F, FIB, Sequence** Master Slide to continue with this exercise.

The next step is to take care of the **size** and the **positioning** of the Question Title.

9. Select the Title Placeholder of the **MCQ, T/F, FIB, Sequence** Master Slide.
10. Enter the following values in the **Transform** panel:
    - Deselect the **Constrain Proportions** checkbox
    - Position the Title Caption at **X** = `50` and **Y** = `100`
    - Resize the Title Caption to **W** = `700` and **H** = `40`

It is possible that the Question Title overlaps with other objects of the Master Slide.

11. In the top-right corner of the **Transform** accordion title bar, click on the small arrow icon. In the menu that opens, choose **Apply to all Items of this type**, as shown in the following screenshot:

Thanks to this feature, we apply the current values of the **Transform** accordion to all the other objects of the projects that are of the same type. In our case, the Question Title of every Question Slide now has the same size and the same position!

We will use the very same workflow for the *Question* Text Caption.

12. Still on the **MCQ, T/F, FIB, Sequence** Master Slide, select the Question Placeholder. (**Question Placeholder** should be written at the top of the **Properties** panel).
13. In the Character accordion, change the font **Family** to **Century Gothic** and the **Size** to `25` points.
14. Save the new formatting as a new style named `MFTC-question`.
15. Apply the new style to every object that currently uses the **[Default Question Text Style]**.
16. In the **Transform** accordion, enter the following values:
    - **X** = `50` and **Y** = `140`
    - **W** = `700` and **H** = `70` (Deselect the **Constraint Constrain Proportions** box)
17. Use the small icon at the top-right corner of the **Transform** accordion to apply these values to the other objects of the project that are of the same type.

Styling the Buttons

In this section, we will concentrate on the **Submit** and the **Clear** buttons of the Question Slides. Perform the following steps to style these buttons:

1. Return to the **MCQ, T/F, FIB, Sequence** Master Slide.
2. Select the **Submit** button of the Master Slide.
3. Make sure the **Properties** panel is displayed on the right-hand side of the screen.
4. In the **General** Accordion, change the **Button Type** to **Image Button**.
5. Click on the Folder icon situated right next to the **Button Type** drop-down. Choose the `images/buttons/mftcSubmit_up.png` image of the exercises files.

When browsing for the image file, notice that the `images/buttons` folder contains **three versions** of the Submit button, as shown in the following screenshot:

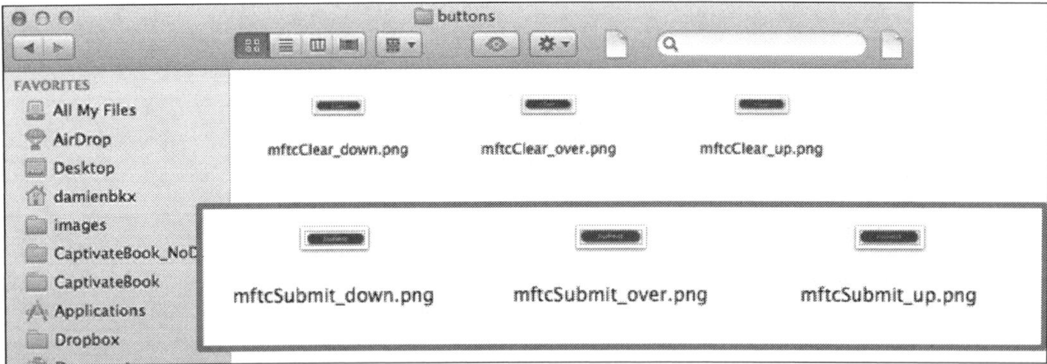

- One version ends with `_up` and is the normal state of the button
- Another version ends with `_over` and is used to change the appearance of the button when the student passes his/her mouse over the button
- The third version ends with `_down` and is used when the student has his/her mouse over the button and the mouse button down

Captivate is able to recognize these three states providing that all three images are stored in the same location and that the name of the file ends with *_up*, *_over*, and *_down*.

6. Use the **Properties** panel to create a new style after the current look and feel of the **Submit** button. Name this new style `MFTC-questionSubmit`.
7. Use the very same procedure to change the look and feel of the **Clear**, **Next**, and **Back** buttons. Use the images stored in the `images/buttons/` folder and create three new styles named `MFTC-questionClear`, `MFTC-questionNext`, and `MFTC-questionBack`.

The next step is to apply these new styles to the buttons of the other Master Slides of the theme. Because all the buttons of the Question Slides share the same [Default Quiz Button Style] regardless of the action they perform (Submit, Clear, or else), we cannot use the **Apply this style to** icon as we did for the Text Captions. Instead, we will have to manually apply our new styles to the buttons of the remaining Master Slides.

8. Go to the **Matching**, **Hotpsot**, and **Likert** Master Slides and manually assign our four new styles to the corresponding buttons.

Now that all the buttons of our Master Slides have the right *look*, we will use the **Transform** panel to assign a precise *position*.

9. Return to the **MCQ, T/F, FIB, Sequence** Master Slide select the **Submit** button.
10. Use the **Transform** accordion of the **Properties** panel to position the **Submit** at **X**= `645` and **Y**= `550`.
11. Select the **Clear** button and position it at **X** = `500` and **Y** = `550`.

The **Clear** button currently overlaps with the **Next** button.

12. Use the same technique to move the **Next** button to **X** = `355` and **Y** = `550`, and the **Back** button to **X** = `210` and **Y** = `550`.

We will now use the **Apply to all items of this type** feature to apply these values to the buttons of the other Question Slides as well.

13. Click on the **Submit** button to make it the active object.
14. Open the small icon at the top-right corner of the **Transform** panel and click on the **Apply to all items of this type** icon.
15. Repeat the same operation with the **Clear**, **Next**, and **Back** buttons.
16. Save the file and use the Preview icon to test the entire **Project**!

Cool! Thanks to the *Master Slides*, the *Styles*, and the *Apply to All* icon, we have been able to create an attractive look and feel and to **consistently** use it throughout our application.

The Styles part of our custom Theme is now finished! The last thing to do is to save these new styles into the Theme.

17. Use the **Themes | Save Theme** menu item to save these changes into our custom `MFTC-Theme.cptm` file.

Extra credit

In this extra credit section, you will use the same tools to arrange the objects of the remaining Master Slides. Feel free to lay them out as you see fit and to create new styles as needed. Here are some tips and tricks to help you do the job:

- Stay in the Master Slide panel and apply your formatting and positioning choices to the Placeholder Objects.
- Use the Styles whenever possible. They make it incredibly easy to apply the same formatting properties to lots of different objects.

- Use the small *Apply to all* icon at the top of the accordions of the **Properties** panel to quickly apply the same properties to many objects of the same type.
- Use the tools of the Align toolbar. Remember to use the **Window | Align** menu item to turn the Align toolbar on. By default, it appears in the top-left area of the workspace.
- Use the files of the `images/buttons` folder to define the look of the buttons of the **Result** Master Slide.

When you are done, don't hesitate to return to the main **Filmstrip** and to the **Question Pool** to take a look at the Slides and Question Slide of the project. You should see that they all share the same look and feel and that the objects present on these slides all have a consistent formatting.

By modifying the look and feel of the Master Slides and by applying styles to the Placeholder Objects, you modified the actual objects on the actual slides as well.

If a Master Slide is not properly applied to one of the standard slides of the **Filmstrip**, use the **Reset Master Slide** button of the **Properties** panel.

In the next section, we will concentrate on the Skin, which is the last component of a Theme, but before that, a quick little summary of the key points to remember:

- The styles and formatting changes applied to the Placeholder Objects of the Master Slides are reflected on the corresponding standard slides of the **Filmstrip**.
- Use the Apply To All icon at the top-right corner of the accordions to quickly apply the values defined in that accordion to the other objects of the same type/style throughout the entire project.
- An Image Button accepts three states. The `_up` state, the `_down` state, and the `_over` state. Use three different images to define each of these three states.

Adding a Skin to the Theme

In addition to the Master Slides and the Styles, a Theme can also contain a Skin. In this section, we will return to the **Skin Editor** and define the default Skin of our custom Theme using the following steps:

1. Still in the `drivingInBe.cptx` file, use the **Themes | Skin Editor** menu item to open the **Skin Editor** floating panel.

In *Chapter 6, Final Changes and Publishing,* we used the **Project | Skin Editor** menu item to open the **Skin Editor** floating panel. In Captivate 6, because the Skin is one of the components of a Theme, the **Themes** menu also provides an access to the **Skin Editor**.

Now that the **Skin Editor** is open, notice that the **Show Playback Control** checkbox as well as most of the other checkboxes of the **Skin Editor** are grayed out! This is due to the **Branch Aware** checkbox of the Quiz Properties that we have selected in the previous chapter. When a Pretest or a Branch Aware Quiz is present in the project, **the Playback Control and the Borders are disabled**.

The solution is to return to the Quiz Properties dialog in order to temporarily deselect the **Branch Aware** checkbox. Then we will return to the Skin Editor to setup the default Skin of the Theme before returning to the Quiz Properties to turn the **Branch Aware** checkbox back on.

2. Close the floating **Skin Editor** panel.
3. Use the **Quiz | Quiz Preferences** menu item to return to the Quiz Preferences dialog.
4. In the left-hand side of the **Preferences** dialog, click on the **Settings** category of the **Quiz** section.
5. Deselect the **Branch Aware** checkbox and click on the **OK** button.

Now that the **Branch Aware** checkbox is deselected, we should have access to the options of the **Skin Editor**.

6. Use the **Themes | Skin Editor** menu item to reopen the floating **Skin Editor** panel.
7. In the **Theme** section of the **Skin Editor**, make sure the **Playback Colors** checkbox is *selected*.
8. Change the colors of the Playback Control bar as you see fit, as shown in the following screenshot:

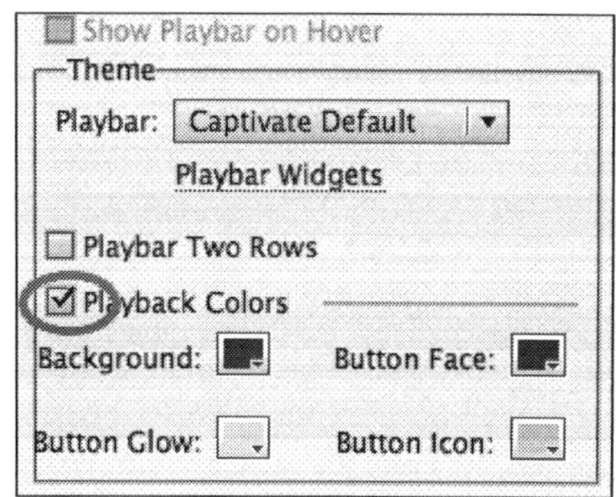

9. When done, go to the **Table of Contents** page of the **Skin Editor** and select the **Show TOC** checkbox.
10. Use the techniques covered in *Adding a Table of Contents* section from *Chapter 6, Final Changes and Publishing* to customize the Table of Contents as you see fit.

The design choices that you are making in the **Skin Editor** will ultimately be saved in our Theme and become the default settings of all the future projects based on that Theme.

11. Because we do not want this particular project to display a Table of Contents, deselect the **Show TOC** checkbox and close the floating **Skin Editor** panel.
12. When done, use the **Themes | Save Theme** menu item to save the changes made to the Theme.

Our custom Theme is now complete! It has a set of **Master Slides** providing ready-made slide layouts, it contains lots of **Object Styles** and it has a customized **Skin**. Before moving on to the next section, we will return one last time to the **Quiz Properties** dialog in order to turn the **Branch Aware** checkbox back on for this project.

13. Use the **Quiz | Quiz Preferences** menu item to return to the Quiz Preferences dialog. Open the **Settings** category of the **Quiz** section and select the **Branch Aware** checkbox. When done, click on the **OK** button.

In the next section, we will use our new Theme to create a Template, but before that, let's quickly summarize what we have learned in this section:

- The Skin is the third component of a Theme
- Captivate 6 automatically disables the Playback Controls and the Border components of the Skin if a Pretest or a Branch Aware Quiz is present in the project
- By saving a Skin into a Theme, we make it the default Skin of all the projects that will use this Theme

Working with Templates

The basic idea of a Template is to create a project that can be used as the starting point of another project. When creating a project from a Template, a **stencil copy** of the Template is created which serves as the starting point of the new project. In the new project, the teacher can edit, remove, and add objects with no restrictions.

A Template can contain the same slides and objects that a regular project contains. The preferences applied to the Template become the default Preferences of the projects that are based on the Template. A Theme can be applied to a Template. It then becomes the default Theme of the projects that are based on that Template.

In the next exercise, we will create a Template that will be used for all the demonstrations created by the developers of the MFTC company. The instructional and visual designers at MFTC decided that:

- The demonstrations should have a resolution of 800 x 600 pixels
- The demonstrations should use our custom MFTC-Theme
- Each demonstration should begin with a Title Slide containing a text animation that uses the *Waltz* effect
- The second slide of each demonstration is a slide explaining the objectives of the demonstration
- The actual screenshot-based demonstration begins on the third slide
- When the demonstration is finished, a summary slide should emphasize the key points of what has been learned
- After the summary, the last slide should contain a text animation similar to the one found on the first slide

Creating a Template

To help the company enforce these rules, we will create a Template that the eLearning developers will have to use to create their demonstrations. This Template will not only help in producing consistent content and design across projects, but will also speed up the development process of the eLearning courses by reusing common design, properties, and content. Perform the following steps to create a Template that will help developers create their demonstrations:

1. Save and close every open project.
2. On the right column of the Captivate Welcome screen, click on the **Create New | Project Template** link.
3. In the **New Project Template** box, select the **800 x 600** resolution and click on **OK**.

The first rule is already enforced! All the demonstrations that will be based on this Template will all use the same 800 x 600 resolution.

4. To apply another Theme to the project, use the **Themes | Apply a New Theme** menu item. Then, browse your hard disk and apply the `chapter08/final/MFTC-Theme.cptm` Theme to the project.

Second rule enforced! All future Demonstrations based on this Template will use our custom `MFTC-Theme.cptm`. Also notice that our new **MFTC-Theme** has been added to the Themes panel.

5. Make sure that the **Properties** panel shows the properties of the first slide of the project.
6. In the **General** accordion of the **Properties** panel, use the **Master Slide** drop-down menu to apply the **Title** Master Slide of the Theme to the selected slide.
7. At the top of the **Properties** panel, change the slide **Name** to `Intro Slide`.

Third rule enforced! The first slide of the Template contains a Text Animation Placeholder with the Waltz effect pre-selected!

8. Use the **Insert | New Slide from | Caption & Content - Left** to insert a new slide based on the **Caption & Content - Left Master Slide** of our Theme.
9. Use the **Properties** panel to change the **Name** of this slide to `Objectives of Demo`.

Fourth rule enforced! The second slide of the Template is ready to receive text and other content. The layout and styling of that content is already predefined in the Theme and in the Master Slides!

Adding Placeholder Slides

The third slide is where the actual screenshot-based demonstration should begin. When developing the Template, we do not know how long that demonstration will be and how many slides it will last. We only know that it should begin on slide 3. To enforce this rule, we will add a **Placeholder Slide** to the Template.

In Captivate, there can be two kinds of Placeholder Slides.

- A **Recording Slide Placeholder** is meant to be replaced by a screenshot-based recording using the techniques covered in *Chapter 2, Capturing the Slides*.
- A **Question Slide Placeholder** is meant to be replaced by a Question Slide. We can use it to enforce the presence of a Quiz in the project as well as to determine, right in the Template, the number of Question Slides the Quiz should contain.

In our case, a Recording Slide Placeholder is what we need. Perform the following steps to add a Recording Slide Placeholder:

1. If needed, use the **Filmstrip** to go to slide 2 of the Template.
2. Use the **Insert | Placeholder Slides | Recording Slide Placeholder** menu item to add a Recording Slide Placeholder at the end of the Template.

Fifth rule enforced! The Recording Placeholder Slide is added as slide 3 of the Template.

Notice that the options of the **Properties** panel are all grayed out when the slide is selected. Notice also that the icons of the vertical Object toolbar, as well as most of the options of the **Insert** menu are also grayed out.

We will now create the last two slides of the Template. Because they will be very similar to the first two slides, we will copy-paste and modify the first two slides of the project.

3. In the **Filmstrip**, select the first two slides of the project and hit the *Ctrl* + *C* (Windows) or *cmd* + *C* (Mac) shortcut to copy the slides.
4. Use the **Filmstrip** to go to the last slide of the Template (the Placeholder Slide) and hit the *Ctrl* + *V* (Windows) or *cmd* + *V* (Mac) shortcut to paste the slides at the end of the Template.
5. Use the **Filmstrip** to reorder the slides we have just pasted. The **Intro Slide** should be the last one.
6. When done, go to the fourth slide of the Template. In the **Properties** panel, change its **Name** to `Summary Slide`.
7. Move to the last slide of the Template and change its **Name** to `Ending Slide`.

Sixth and Seventh rules enforced! The last two slides of the Template are used to emphasize the key points learned during the demo and to add a nice animation when the project is finished.

For the sake of this example, we will consider this Template as finished. Keep in mind though that we could go much further in the development of a Captivate Template. For example, we could define the project properties and the LMS reporting methods right in the Template. These would become the default used by the future projects based on that Template.

8. Save the Template as `Chapter08/MFTC-Demo.cptl`.

Notice that the file extension used for a Captivate template is `.cptl` and not `.cptx` as for a regular project.

Creating a new Captivate project from a Template

In this section, we will play the role of an eLearning developer that has to use the Template we have just created to develop a new Captivate demonstration for the MFTC Company using the following steps:

1. Close every open file so that you can see the Captivate Welcome screen.
2. In the right column of the Captivate Welcome screen, click on the Create New **From Template** link, as shown in the following screenshot:

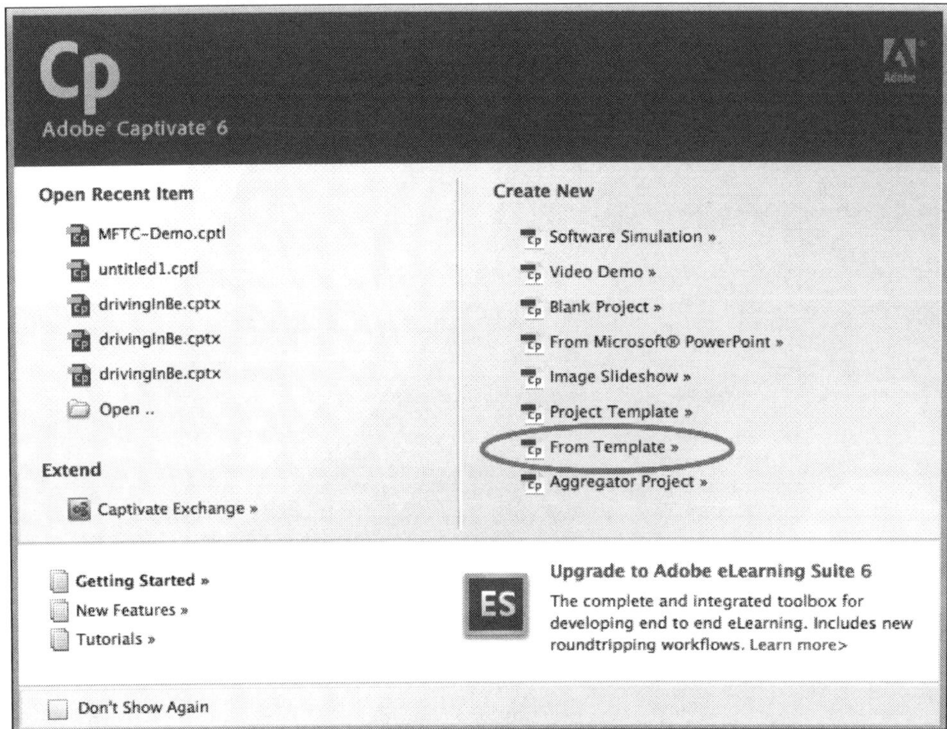

3. Navigate to the `Chapter08/MFTC-Demo.cptl` template file situated in the exercises folder and choose it as the base of a new project.

The new project that opens in Captivate is a *stencil copy* of the Template we created previously. Note that the new project has the `.cptx` file extension.

Before moving on, we will quickly perform a first test on this file.

4. Use the Preview icon to preview the entire **Project**.

When the project appears in the **Preview** pane, notice that the Placeholder Text Animation object of slide 1 does *not* appear in the final output. Also notice that the *Recording Slide Placeholder* is *not* part of the final output as well. Actually, the slide count (see the top-left corner of the **Preview** pane) is 4, and not 5.

As long as the Placeholder Objects and slides have not been replaced by actual objects and slides, they do not appear in the compiled version of the project.

5. Close the **Preview** pane to return to Captivate.
6. Use the **Filmstrip** to go to the first slide of the project.
7. Double-click on the **Text Animation** Placeholder to turn it into an actual Text Animation object.
8. Double-click on the Text Animation object to change its properties. Type `Welcome to the Demonstration`. Change the **Font** to **Century Gothic** and the **Size** to **45**. Click on **OK** to validate the change and generate the Text Animation object.
9. Move the Text Animation roughly to the center of the brown area of the slide.

Notice how fast it was to insert this Text Animation object on the first slide. Fast development is one of the big advantages of using Templates and Placeholder Objects.

In the **Properties** panel, notice that the default effect used by this object is the **Waltz** effect. This reflects what we decided on the Title Master Slide.

10. In the **Properties** panel, try to change the **Waltz** effect to any other effect of your choice.

No warning messages appear on the screen to tell us that this property is locked on the Template and cannot be changed. In other words, the developer *has the freedom to override the choices made on the Template*. Remember that the Template only sets the *default* properties of slides and objects, but *it does not force the developer* to use them on the final version of the project.

11. Use the **Filmstrip** to go to slide 3 of the project.

Slide 3 is the Recording Slide Placeholder. Remember that it did *not* show in the **Preview** pane while testing the project.

12. Double-click on the Recording Slide Placeholder.

Captivate switches to Recording Mode and displays the red recording area. All the options discussed in *Chapter 2, Capturing the Slides* are available in the Recording window, except for the size of the red recording area, which is locked by the Template at 800 x 600 pixels.

13. Click on the **Cancel** button to return to the standard Captivate interface.
14. Close the project without saving it.

This exercise concludes our overview of the Templates. Before moving on to the next chapter, let's make a quick summary of what we have learned about Templates.

- A Captivate Template is a *blueprint* used as a starting point for standard Captivate projects.
- A Template can contain the very same objects and slides as a standard project.
- The Theme applied to a Template serves as the default Theme for all future projects based on that Template.
- Placeholder Slides are used to mark the location of a screen recording or the location of Question Slides in the Template.
- A Template only sets the *default* properties and objects, but it does not strictly enforce them. In other words, a developer can override the choices made on a Template.
- A Template file has a `.cptl` file extension.

Summary

In this chapter, we have concentrated on the cosmetic part of our project. We discovered that, when properly implemented, the look and feel of the project plays a critical role in the success of the eLearning teaching strategy.

More specifically, it is the *consistency* of the look and feel that helps the students find their way around our eLearning content. Remember that, while taking our online courses, the students are alone in front of their computer, so it is important to create a consistent learning environment in which they feel comfortable enough to concentrate only on their learning.

By using the *Styles*, the *Master Slides*, the *Themes*, and the *Templates*, we have achieved a very high level of consistency in a record time and with minimal effort!

In the first part of this chapter, we have use the predefined Themes of Captivate to better understand what Themes are and how they work. We then moved on to the creation of our own customized Theme. Finally, we have created a Template and we used that Template to create a new project.

In the next chapter, we will discuss the close relationships between Captivate and other applications. As part of the Adobe line of products, Captivate integrates nicely with other Adobe Applications such as Photoshop and Flash. However, some interesting workflows have been developed between Captivate and a few third-party products as well. For example, we will create a new Captivate project by converting an existingPowerPoint presentation. We will also discuss how we can localize our eLearning content using a workflow that involves exporting content to Microsoft Word and importing it back into Captivate.

Meet the Community

In this Meet the Community section, I'll introduce you to two individuals from the same family. Together with two other members of the family, they own and manage Infosemantics, an Australian-based company specialized in eLearning development and Captivate widgets.

Rod Ward

Bio

Director of Infosemantics. Rod is a Technical Author, Information Designer, and eLearning Developer with over a decade of industry experience. Based in Perth since 1986, he has worked for companies large and small across Australia. Rod's specialties are the design and development of eLearning courses using sound instructional design principles and Adobe's suite of eLearning software tools.

Tristan Ward

Bio

Tristan is a Flash and ActionScript expert. He builds many of the Flash animations and interactivity add-ins included in Infosemantics' Captivate eLearning courses. Tristan is deservedly famous throughout the Adobe Captivate world for his Widget King blog, which contains many articles about creating AS3 Widgets using his WidgetFactory API, now the leading platform for creating AS3 Widgets for Captivate. He's also our go-to guy for video editing.

Contact details

Website: `http://www.infosemantics.com.au/`

Twitter: **Rod**: `@Infosemantics`/**Tristan**: `@WidgetFactory`

Tristan's blog: `http://www.infosemantics.com.au/widgetking/`

My personal note

When doing my researches for this book, the names of Rod Ward and Tristan Ward came out quite often. You definitely want to follow these two guys on Twitter! If you plan on developing your own Captivate Widgets, Tristan's blog is the ultimate online resource.

9
Using Captivate with Other Applications

In this chapter, we will explore how Captivate can be used with other applications. These applications include other Adobe products such as Adobe Flash Professional and Adobe Photoshop, and also third-party applications such as Microsoft Word and Microsoft PowerPoint.

There are many benefits in using Captivate with these external applications. If your company already has lots of training material made with PowerPoint, you'll be able to recycle this existing material and build on what already exists, rather than starting everything from the ground up again. By integrating Microsoft Word in the workflow, we can export the Text Captions and the Slide Notes to a Microsoft Word document and send it out to a translation service where the translators won't need any knowledge of Captivate to do their job. By exporting the Captivate project into Flash Professional, we'll be able to leverage the full power of the Flash Platform in our Captivate project.

In this chapter, we will:

- Create a new Captivate project from a PowerPoint presentation
- Add a PowerPoint slide in an existing Captivate project
- Explore the *round-trip editing* workflow between Captivate and PowerPoint
- Localize a Captivate project by exporting the Text Captions and Slide Notes to Microsoft Word, and reimporting them back into Captivate once translated
- Export the project to an XML file
- Import a Photoshop document into Captivate
- Export the Captivate project to Flash Professional

Preparing our work

To begin with this chapter, we won't need any of the files we worked on earlier, so the only thing to do is to reset the workspace of Captivate and get started. In order to do that, perform the following steps:

1. Open Captivate.
2. Ensure that the **Classic** workspace is applied.
3. Use the **Window | Workspace | Reset 'Classic'** menu item. This will re-apply the default **Classic** workspace to the Captivate interface.

Most of the exercises of this chapter require external applications to be installed on your system along with Captivate. If you do not have access to these applications, just read through the steps of the exercises to have a basic idea of the feature.

Captivate and PowerPoint

In this section, we will cover the tight integration that unites Microsoft PowerPoint and Adobe Captivate. This integration includes many features, such as creating a brand new Captivate project from a Microsoft PowerPoint presentation or including some slides of a presentation in an existing Captivate project.

Captivate shares these features with another software product from Adobe called **Adobe Presenter**. Adobe Presenter is a Microsoft PowerPoint plugin. In PowerPoint 2007 and later versions, Presenter installs an extra ribbon at the top of the PowerPoint interface. Presenter can be used to publish a PowerPoint presentation in Flash using a technique that is very similar to what is found in Captivate. Presenter also includes the ability to add narration and subtitles to a PowerPoint presentation and features the same quiz engine as the one used in Captivate. Presenter can be obtained as a standalone product or as part of the eLearning Suite and is only available on Windows. For more information on Presenter, visit `http://www.adobe.com/products/presenter.html`.

Converting an existing presentation to Captivate

We will start by converting an existing PowerPoint presentation into a new Captivate project.

Viewing the presentation in PowerPoint

If PowerPoint is available on your system, take some time to take a look at the presentation before inserting it into Captivate. To view the presentation, perform the following steps:

1. Open Microsoft PowerPoint.
2. When in PowerPoint, open the `Presentations/AdobeCaptivate.ppt` presentation situated in the exercises files.
3. Use the **Slide Show | View Slide Show** menu item to start the slideshow.

While viewing the presentation, focus your attention on the following:

- The presentation is made of 10 slides.
- There is a transition set up between all the slides of the presentation.
- On the first and last slide, the text is animated using an effect that has no equivalent in the **Effects** panel of Captivate.
- The presentation is mainly composed of text and images. Most of it is animated.
- Some of the effects used to animate the objects of PowerPoint have an equivalent in Captivate, but some do not.
- Sometimes, a mouse click is needed to go to the next step of the presentation, but sometimes not. Some slides of the presentation include Slide Notes.
- Slide 9 includes two links to the Adobe website.

Spelling errors and typos have been *intentionally* left over in the presentation. Please, refrain from correcting them. They will be used to demonstrate *round-tripping* between Captivate and PowerPoint in a short while.

4. Close PowerPoint without saving the changes made to the presentation.

We will now convert this presentation into a Captivate project and see how the PowerPoint features we pointed out are carried over (or not) into Captivate.

Creating a Captivate project from a PowerPoint application

In this section, we will convert the file we have just viewed in PowerPoint, into a Captivate project.

.ppt or .pptx?

When importing a `.pptx` file, it is required that PowerPoint is installed on the computer along with Captivate. When importing a `.ppt` file, PowerPoint is not needed. That's the reason why we chose to use `.ppt` files in this book instead of the newer `.pptx` file format. We do provide the `.pptx` files in the exercise download for you to experiment with the `.pptx` files if needed.

The following exercise starts on the Captivate Welcome screen:

1. On the right-hand column of the Captivate Welcome screen, click on the **From Microsoft PowerPoint** link.
2. Browse to the `presentations/AdobeCaptivate.ppt` file situated in the exercises folder and click on **Open**.

Captivate converts the PowerPoint slides into Captivate slides one by one. This operation can be quite lengthy, so be patient! When the conversion is finished, Captivate opens the **Convert PowerPoint Presentations** dialog box.

3. At the top of the dialog box, change the **Name** of the project to `AdobeCaptivateIntro`.
4. Open the **Preset Sizes** drop-down and change the resolution of the project to **800 x 600**.

Notice that Captivate lets you choose which PowerPoint slides to include in the project. Use the **Clear All** and **Select All** buttons to quickly select or deselect the entire set of slides. In our case, we want to import the whole presentation into Captivate, so make sure every PowerPoint slide is selected before moving on.

5. At the end of the dialog box, set the **Advance Slide** option to **On mouse click**.
6. Make sure the **Linked** checkbox is *selected*.

It is very important to get these last two options right! The **Advance Slide** option lets us decide how Captivate advances from one slide to the next one. By choosing **On mouse click**, we ask Captivate to generate a Click Box on top of every imported slide. This Click Box stops the Playhead and waits for the student to click on the slide.

When the student clicks on the slide, the Playhead is released and the movie continues to the next step.

The **Linked** checkbox is even more important. Captivate proposes two ways to insert a PowerPoint presentation in a project. They are as follows:

- When **Linked** is *not* selected: We create an **Embedded** presentation. It means that the PowerPoint presentation is entirely integrated into Captivate and does not maintain any kind of link with the original PowerPoint file.
- When the **Linked** checkbox *is* selected: It creates a **Linked** presentation. The PowerPoint presentation is also embedded into Captivate, but Captivate maintains a link between the project and the original PowerPoint presentation. This link can be used to update the Captivate file when a change is made to the PowerPoint presentation.

Make sure the **Convert PowerPoint Presentations** dialog looks like the following screenshot before moving on:

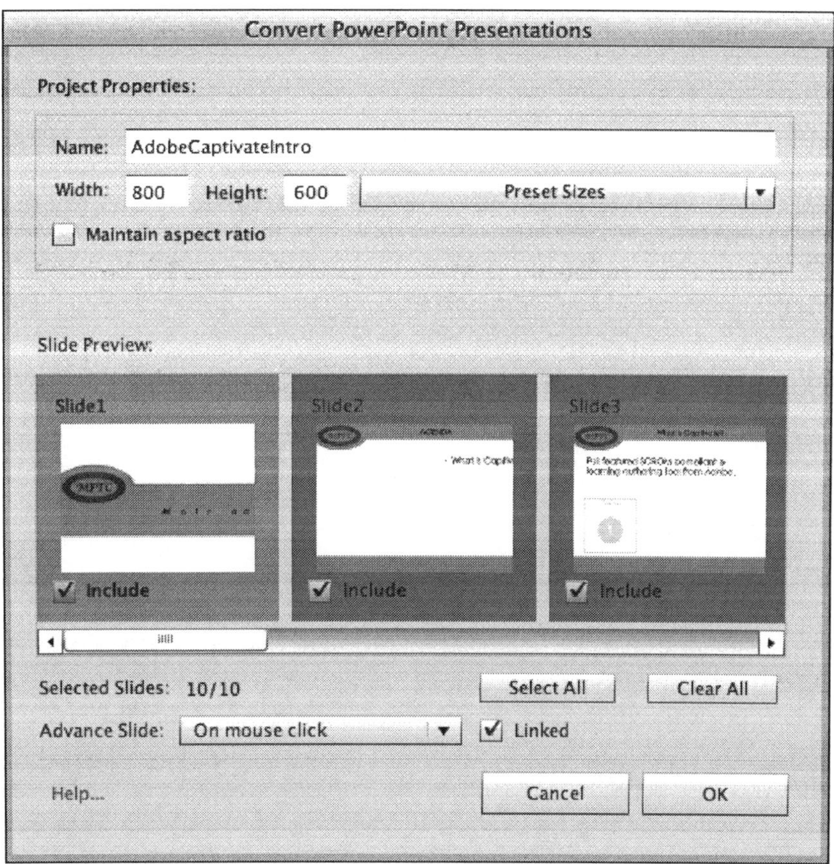

7. Click on the **OK** button.
8. Take some time to read the message that appears on the screen. Click on **Yes** to acknowledge the message and clear the message box.

Captivate creates a new project from the original PowerPoint presentation. This process can take some time, so be patient. When the importation is finished, a 10-slide project is loaded into the Captivate application. In the **Filmstrip**, notice that each slide has a **Name** that is derived from the slide title as entered in PowerPoint.

We will now test the movie to see how well (or how bad) Captivate handles the PowerPoint conversion process.

9. Save the file as `Chapter09/AdobeCaptivateIntro.cptx`.
10. Use the Preview icon to preview the entire **Project**.

Take the necessary time to test the entire project and notice that:

- Captivate does a pretty good job in converting a PowerPoint presentation into a Captivate movie
- Most animations are carried over from PowerPoint, even if a corresponding effect does not exist in Captivate
- The transitions are correctly imported and played back
- On slide 9, the links are functional

11. Close the **Preview** pane when done.

That's it for the final result as seen by the students. We will now take a closer look at the Captivate interface to discover other properties from the original presentation that are carried over in Captivate.

12. If needed, use the **Filmstrip** to return to the first slide of the project.
13. Use the **Window | Slide Notes** menu item to open the **Slide Notes** panel. Remember that, by default, this panel appears at the bottom of the screen, next to the **Timeline**.

The Slide Notes typed in PowerPoint have been imported in the **Slide Notes** panel of Captivate. Remember that these **Slide Notes** can be converted to *Speech* and to *Closed Captions*. The fact that Captivates imports this data from PowerPoint is a great productivity feature and a huge timesaver.

14. Use the **Filmstrip** to go to slide 2.
15. At the bottom of the screen, open the **Timeline** panel.

In PowerPoint, this slide holds quite a few pieces of text arranged in a bulleted list. We would expect the same slide in Captivate to contain a lot of Text Captions. Unfortunately, the PowerPoint to Captivate conversion process does not go *that* far. In Captivate, each PowerPoint slide is considered as a single animated object. The individual components of this animation do not show in the **Timeline** panel.

This can be a big problem if we want to modify a PowerPoint slide that was imported to Captivate. However, we selected the **Linked** checkbox when importing the slides, so Captivate knows where the original PowerPoint file is located. This will enable us to update the slides if needed.

Round Tripping between Captivate and PowerPoint

Round Tripping is the process by which we can invoke PowerPoint from Captivate, edit the presentation in PowerPoint, and return to Captivate. If you are working on Windows, this process can be done without even leaving Captivate, as PowerPoint can be displayed right within the Captivate interface. If you are working on a Mac, you'll be redirected to the actual PowerPoint application.

> The following exercise requires both PowerPoint and Captivate to be installed on your computer. On Windows, Office 2003 (SP3) or higher is required. On Mac, Office 2004 and up will do.

In the next exercise, we will experiment with the *Round-Tripping* workflow to modify a slide in PowerPoint and return to Captivate using the following steps:

1. In Captivate, use the **Filmstrip** to go to slide 4.
2. Right-click anywhere on the slide and choose **Edit With Microsoft PowerPoint | Edit Presentation**:

If you get a message saying the Captivate is unable to open the PowerPoint presentation because of a permission problem, return to PowerPoint to make sure the presentation is closed before starting this procedure in Captivate.

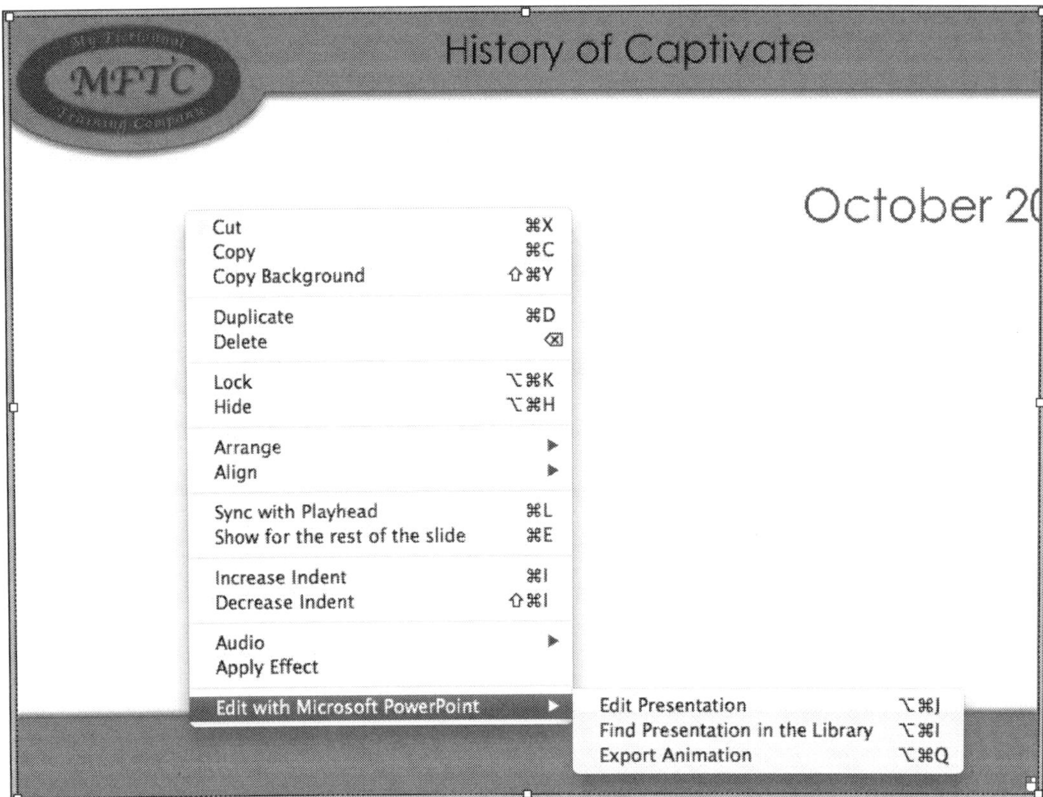

What follows depends on the operating system we are working on:

- On **Windows**: PowerPoint opens within the Captivate Interface, allowing us to edit the presentation using all the tools and features of PowerPoint *without even leaving Captivate*.
- On **Mac**: PowerPoint automatically opens in its own separate window and loads the presentation we want to edit.

Pay close attention to the remaining steps of this exercise, as the round-tripping experience is very different on Windows than from the one on Mac:

3. [MAC Only]: When PowerPoint is open, go to slide 4 of the PowerPoint presentation.
4. [Everyone]: On slide 4, change **October 204** to `October 2004`.
5. [MAC Only]:Use the **File** | **Save** menu item of PowerPoint to save the presentation.
6. [Mac Only]: Return to Captivate. A message asks if we want to import the updated presentation. Click on **Yes** and let Captivate make the necessary changes in the project.

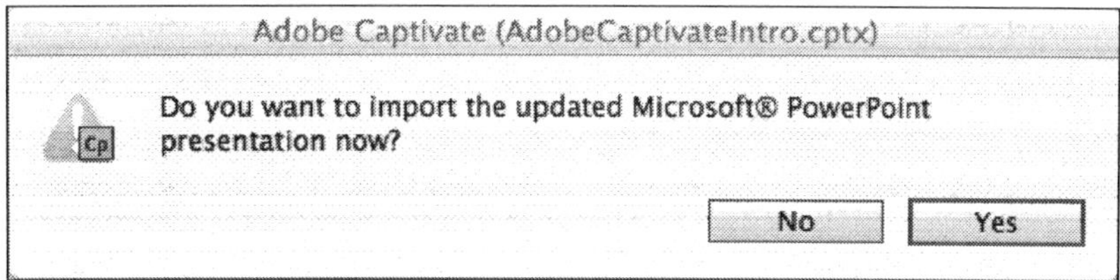

7. [MAC Only]: Close the PowerPoint application manually.
8. [Windows Only]: Click on the **Save** button situated in the upper-left corner of the interface. PowerPoint closes and the Captivate project is automatically updated.
9. [Everyone]: Save the Captivate file when done.
10. [Everyone]: Use the Preview icon to preview the entire **Project**.

When the preview reaches slide 4, pay close attention to the text in the main textbox. The modification done in PowerPoint should be reflected in the Captivate project.

The previous exercise describes a *round-trip editing* between Captivate and PowerPoint. The procedure begins in Captivate when the eLearning developer explicitly triggers this workflow.

Updating a linked PowerPoint presentation

In the next exercise, we will open PowerPoint and modify the presentation in the PowerPoint application. We will then return to Captivate and update the project accordingly. The steps are as follows:

1. Open the `presentations/AdobeCaptivate.ppt` in PowerPoint.
2. Go to slide 3 of the presentation and change **SCROM** to `SCORM` in the main textbox.

3. **Save** the presentation and **close** PowerPoint.
4. Return to Captivate and use the **Filmstrip** to go to slide 3 of the project.

This time, the change we made in PowerPoint is *not* reflected in Captivate. This is because we updated the presentation directly in PowerPoint. We did not start the procedure from Captivate, as it was the case in the previous exercise. However, we selected the **Linked** box when importing the presentation into Captivate. We will now use this link to have the changes made in PowerPoint reflected in our Captivate project.

5. Open the **Library** panel situated next to the **Properties** panel on the right-hand side of the screen.
6. In the **Presentations** section of the **Library**, locate the **AdobeCaptivate** presentation.

Notice the red dot in the **Status** column as shown in the following screenshot. It indicates that the linked PowerPoint presentation and the Captivate project are out of sync:

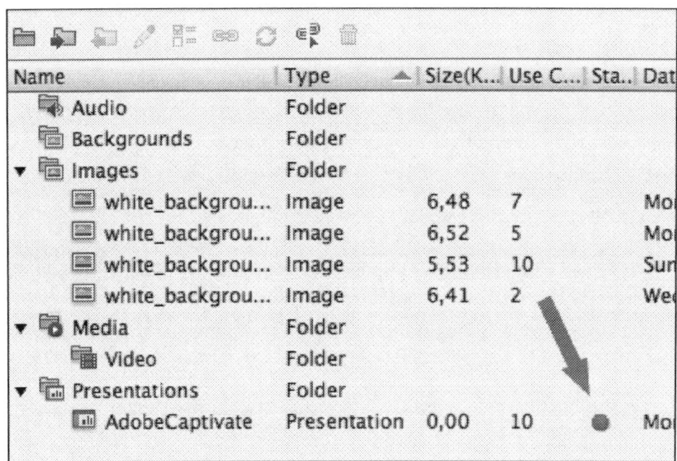

7. In the **Library** panel, right-click on the **AdobeCaptivate** presentation.
8. Click on the **Update** item of the contextual menu that opens. Confirm the operation by a click on the **Update** button of the **Update Library Items** dialog.

This refreshes the linked presentation and puts the Captivate project and the PowerPoint presentation back in sync. At the end of the process, the **Status** color should turn back to green.

9. Click on the **OK** button to acknowledge the successful completion of the update process.

Using the **Library** panel, there are a few more operations that can be done on a PowerPoint presentation.

10. Right-click on the **AdobeCaptivate** presentation again.
11. In the contextual menu, click on the **Change To "Embedded"** menu item.
12. Click on **OK** to clear the acknowledgement message.

After this operation, the link between the Captivate project and the PowerPoint presentation is broken. Any changes made to the external PowerPoint file will no longer be reflected in the Captivate project.

13. In the **Presentations** folder of the **Library**, right-click on the **AdobeCaptivate** presentation one last time.
14. In the contextual menu, click on the **Change To "Linked"** menu item.
15. Browse to the `/Chapter09` folder of the exercises files and save the file as `AdobeCaptivate_linked.ppt`.
16. Again, click on the **OK** button to clear the message.
17. Save the Captivate project when done.

This operation saves the embedded PowerPoint presentation as a new PowerPoint file and creates a link between this new file and the Captivate project. Notice that it is not possible to actually *recreate* the link to the *original* PowerPoint file. Instead, we create a *new* PowerPoint file, and link that new file to the Captivate project.

Inserting a PowerPoint slide in a Captivate project

In the previous section, we discussed how to convert an entire PowerPoint presentation into a *new* Captivate project. But sometimes, only a few PowerPoint slides must be inserted into an *existing* Captivate project.

In the next exercise, we will insert a single PowerPoint slide in the Encoder Demonstration project:

1. Open the `chapter09/endoderDemo_800.cptx` file situated in the exercises folder.

Extra credit

Before inserting a new PowerPoint slide into the project, you will apply the Theme we created in the previous chapter, to it. Remember to use the **Themes | Show/ Hide Themes Panel** menu item to turn the Theme panel on, if needed. If our **MFTC-Theme** is not listed in the Themes panel, you can use the **Themes | Apply a New Theme** menu item and look for the `MFTC-Theme.cptm` file on your hard disk. When done, don't forget to control the slides of the project one by one as some styles will have to be adjusted after the Theme is applied.

Importing a PowerPoint slide in an existing Captivate project

We will now add one more slide to the Encoder Demonstration:

1. Use the **Filmstrip** to go to slide 26 of the project.

Slide 26 should be the last slide of the screenshot-based demonstration and the second to last in the project.

2. Use the **Insert | PowerPoint Slide** menu item.
3. In the box that opens, make sure that **Slide 26** is selected.

The PowerPoint slide(s) will be inserted *after* the slide selected in this dialog box.

4. Click on the **OK** button and navigate to the `presentations/mediaEncoder.ppt` presentation situated in the exercises folder. Click on the **Open** button.
5. In the **Convert PowerPoint Presentations** dialog, open the **Advance Slide** drop-down and select the **Automatically** option.

This time, we do not want Captivate to generate an extra Click Box on top of the slide, as we did when converting a PowerPoint file earlier in this chapter. Instead, we will add a button at the lower-right corner of the slide, that will pause the Playhead and wait for the student to release it.

6. Leave the other options at their current value and click on the **OK** button.
7. Take some time to read the message and click on **Yes** to acknowledge and clear it.

The PowerPoint slide is inserted as slide 27 of the Encoder Demonstration project. We will now customize this slide and add a **Continue** button.

8. In the **Timeline**, extend the duration of the slide to **13** seconds.

9. Use the **Insert | Standard Objects | Button** or the corresponding icon in the vertical Object toolbar to insert a new button on the slide.
10. At the top of the **Properties** panel, use the **Style** drop-down menu to apply the **MFTC-ButtonContinue** style to our new button.

The **MFTC-ButtonContinue** style has been brought into this project as part of the **MFTC-Theme**.

11. In the **Action** accordion, make sure that the **On Success** action is set to **Go to the next slide**.
12. Move and resize the button so it fits nicely in the lower-right corner of the slide.
13. In the **Timeline** panel, move the button to the very end of the slide **Timeline**.
14. Use the Preview icon to test the entire **Project**.
15. Save the file when done.

In this exercise, we have inserted a PowerPoint slide in the middle of an *existing* Captivate project. This presentation has been inserted in the **Library** of the project and can be edited using the same *Round-Tripping* capabilities as discussed earlier in this chapter.

This exercise concludes our overview of the integration between PowerPoint and Adobe Captivate. Before moving on, it is time to emphasize the key points of what we have learned. They are as follows:

- It is possible to convert an entire PowerPoint presentation into a Captivate project.
- Captivate can import both, a `.ppt` and a `.pptx` file. A `.ppt` file can be imported in Captivate even if PowerPoint is not installed on the computer. When importing a `.pptx` file however, PowerPoint must be installed on the system along with Captivate.
- When converting PowerPoint to Captivate, most animation effects and transitions are carried over, even if they are not natively supported by Captivate.
- Each PowerPoint slide is imported as a single animation. In the **Timeline**, it is not possible to access each individual object of the original PowerPoint slide.
- An imported presentation *cannot* be updated in Captivate. To update a presentation, it is necessary to use PowerPoint.
- An imported PowerPoint presentation is either an **Embedded** presentation or a **Linked** presentation.

- An *Embedded* presentation is entirely integrated into the Captivate project.
- A *Linked* presentation is also integrated in the Captivate project, but it maintains a link with the original PowerPoint presentation. This link can be used to keep the PowerPoint presentation and the Captivate project in sync.
- **Round Tripping** is a concept that enables us to invoke PowerPoint from within Captivate, update the presentation in PowerPoint, and import the changes back into Captivate.
- The actual *Round-Tripping* experience depends on the operating system in use (Mac or Windows).
- It is possible to insert only a few PowerPoint slides in the middle of an existing Captivate project.

In the next section, we will use a workflow that involves Captivate and Microsoft Word to localize a Captivate project.

Importing PowerPoint versus animating native Captivate objects

In the early versions of Captivate, the **Effects** panel did not exist and so, it was very common to create slides in PowerPoint and insert them in Captivate. Since the introduction of the **Effects** panel, any native object of Captivate can be animated in ways that are very similar to what is found in PowerPoint. I think that the PowerPoint integration is a great tool to recycle existing content made in PowerPoint, or to involve non-Captivate developers in the production process, but new content should be developed entirely in Captivate whenever possible.

Localizing a Captivate project using Microsoft Word

In this section, we will create the French version of our Encoder Demonstration. To produce the French version of the project, there are three basic things to do. They are as follows:

- Re-record the screenshots of the demonstration using the French version of the Adobe Media Encoder application
- Translate the Text Captions and the Slide Notes
- Translate the other assets (such as the video file or additional imported images)

In the following exercise, we will concentrate on the second step of this process, which is, Translating the Text Captions and the Slide Notes:

1. Open the `Chapter09/encoderDemo_800_fr.cptx` file.
2. Use the **Filmstrip** to go to slide 4 of the project.

Notice that the background of slide 4 is a screenshot of the French version of the Adobe Media Encoder. The same is true for the other screenshot-based slides of the project. Notice also that, for the purpose of this exercise, the Pretest has been removed from the French project. Apart from these (not so) small details, this project is the very same project as the English one we did together.

To get the French screenshots in the English project, I followed these simple steps:

- I installed a French version of Captivate on my computer (actually in a virtual machine) and I used it to re-record the same screenshots as the ones we recorded in *Chapter 2, Capturing the Slides*.
- I opened our English project and used the **Save As** menu item to save it as `encoderDemo_800_fr.cptx`. At that point, both projects were exactly the same.
- I used the **File | Import | External Library** menu item to open the Library of the French project into the English project.
- I inserted the **Backgrounds** of the external **Library** to the corresponding English slides and used the **Merge With Background** feature to override the old English background with the new French background.

After this simple procedure, the file you just opened was ready for the second step of the process, that is, the translation of the Text Captions and the Slide Notes using Microsoft Word.

The following exercise requires Microsoft Word to be installed on the computer along with Captivate.

We will now export the Text Captions and the Slide Notes to Microsoft Word.

3. Make sure you are still in the `Chapter09/encoderDemo_800_fr.cptx` file.
4. Use the **File | Export | Project Captions and Closed Captions** menu item to export the Text Captions and the Slide Notes to a Word document.
5. Save the file as `Chapter09/encoderDemo_800_frCaptions.doc`.

When the export is complete, Captivate displays a message, asking if we want to see the generated Word document.

6. Click on the **Yes** button to open Microsoft Word and view the generated Word document:

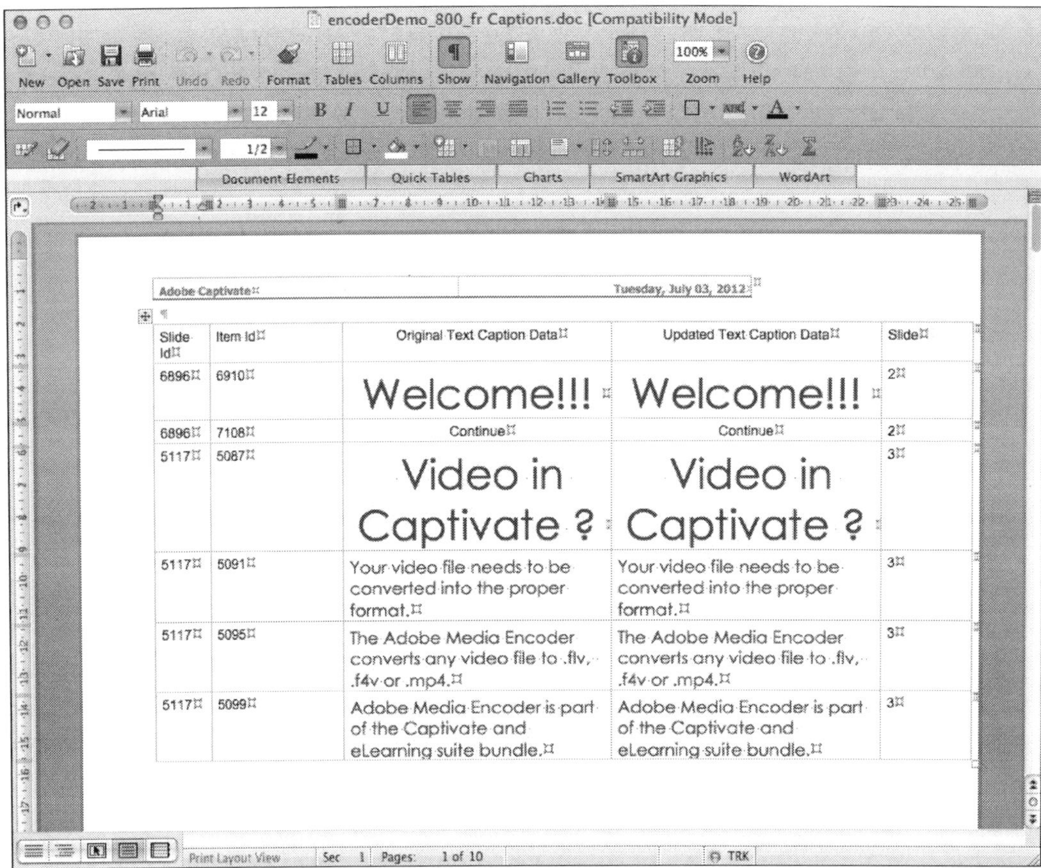

The generated Word document is a five-column table. The first two columns hold the **Slide ID** and **Item ID**. **Those two columns should not be tampered with**. When the translated text will be imported back into the project, these two pieces of information will be used by Captivate to uniquely identify the object into which the text needs to be imported.

The third column is the original text as written in the source language. The fourth column is where the translator will do his or her job. **The translated text should be entered in the fourth column of the table**.

Finally, the last column is the number of the slide on which the object is found.

7. Change the text in the fourth column of the Word document.

If you don't know French, don't worry. For the sake of this exercise, you can translate the first few captions in any language you want (or just update the text in any way!). When it is done, save and close the Word document.

We will now import the updated Text Captions and Slide Notes back into the Captivate project.

8. Return to Captivate in the `encoderDemo_800_fr.cptx` file.
9. Use the **File | Import | Project Captions and Closed Captions** menu item.
10. Import the `Chapter09/encoderDemo_800_frCaptions.doc` file.

Captivate imports the Word document, reads the data it contains, and updates the Text Captions and Slide Notes of the project. This process can be quite lengthy, so be patient. When the import process is complete, use the **Filmstrip** to browse through the slides of the project, and see the updated Text Captions and Slide Notes.

11. Don't forget to save the `encoderDemo_800_fr.cptx` file when done.

This simple workflow is only one step in the translation of an eLearning project into a foreign language. At this point of the exercise, the screenshots, the Text Captions, and the Slide Notes have been updated. However, the localization work is *not* over. The Text Animations (on slide 1 and slide 22) are not yet translated, the video file on slide 2 needs to be updated, and all the narration must be re-recorded in French and imported in the project.

These remaining actions are beyond the scope of this book, but all the techniques needed to complete them have been discussed in the previous chapters.

In the next section, we will discuss another feature that can help us localize a Captivate project.

Exporting the project to XML

In this section, we will export the project as an XML file. The exported file will include much more information than what was included in the Word document we exported in the previous section. According to the official Adobe Captivate blog, the exported XML file contains the following:

> *Text Captions, Text Animations, Rollover Captions, Default text and correct entries in Text Entry Box, Success/Failure/Hint Captions and button text for all interactive objects, Text Buttons, Slide Notes, Text and Rollover Captions in Rollover Slidelets, Quiz Buttons and Feedback captions, Project Info, Project Start and End options, text messages for password and Expiry Messages*

> See the original post at `http://blogs.adobe.com/captivate/2009/05/quick_editing_of_text_using_xm_1.html`.

Here are the steps to export our project to an XML file:

1. If needed, return to the `chapter09/encoderDemo_800.cptx` file.
2. Use the **File** | **Export** | **To XML** menu item.
3. Export the project as `chapter09/encoderDemo_800.xml` in the exercises folder.

When the export is finished, Captivate asks if we want to open the resulting XML file.

4. Click on **No** to close the message box and return to Captivate.

The resulting XML can be opened and updated with any XML editor. When the editing is done, the **File** | **Import** | **From XML** menu item can be used to import the updated data back into Captivate.

Importing a Photoshop file into Captivate

Photoshop is one of the oldest and most famous applications from Adobe. It is an amazing image-editing tool aimed at the professional designer. Lots of design companies around the world, use Photoshop as one of their primary tools to develop the look and feel of the projects they work on.

It is not uncommon to have a designer use Photoshop to create the look and feel of a Captivate-powered eLearning project, so the Captivate engineering team has come up with a specific feature that helps us import a Photoshop file in Captivate.

In Photoshop, each piece of the image is stored on a separate **layer**. At the bottom of the layer stack is the *background* layer. The other layers are arranged on top of the background in a way that is similar to what is found in the **Timeline** of Captivate.

The *Import from Photoshop* feature **is able to retain the layers and layer comps** of the original Photoshop file during the importation process. If you know Photoshop, you probably understand the huge benefit of such a feature.

The following screenshot is the Photoshop file, which we will import into our Captivate project along with its Layers panel as seen in Photoshop:

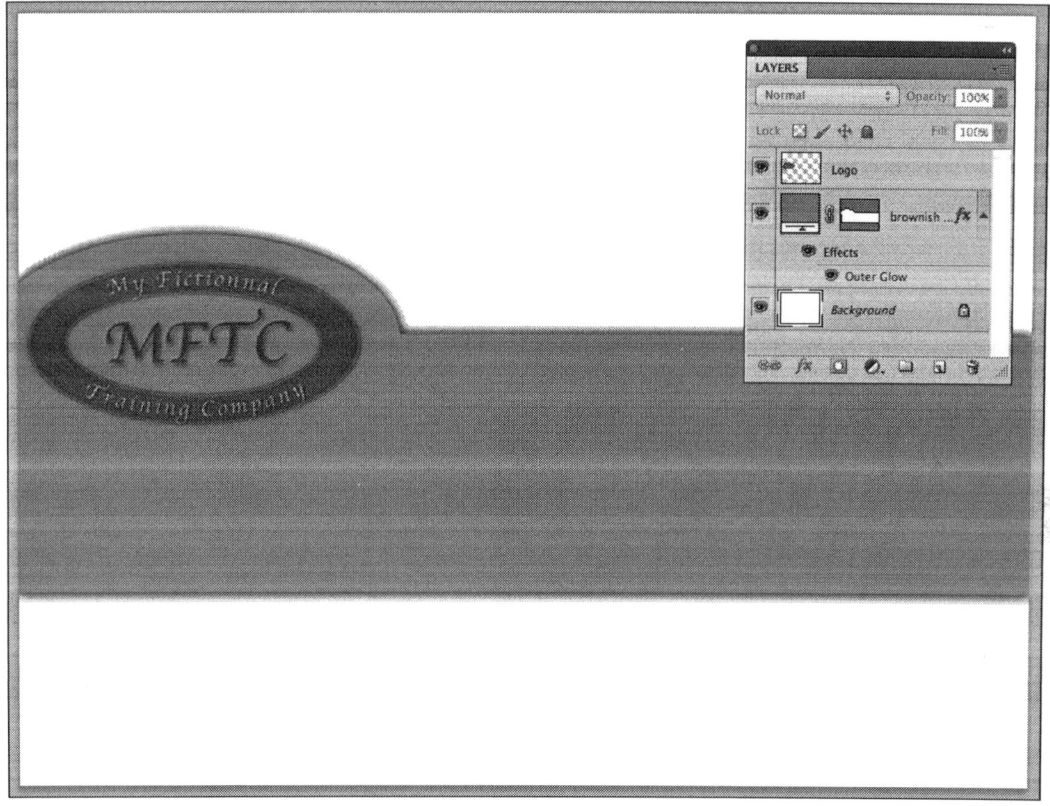

Notice that this image has three layers. They are as follows:

- At the bottom of the stack, the **Background** layer is a white rectangle that covers the whole image.
- Right above it, is the **Brownish Shape** layer. It is the brownish area at the center of the slide. Notice that an *Outer Glow* effect is applied to this layer.
- At the top of the stack, the **Logo** layer holds the MFTC logo.

We will now import this Photoshop document to create a new version of the introduction slide of our Driving In Belgium project.

For the sake of clarity, close every open project before starting the following exercise:

5. Open the `Chapter09/drivingInBe.cptx` file.
6. When the project is open, make sure you are on slide 1.
7. Use the **Insert | Blank Slide** menu item to insert a new slide in the project. This new slide is inserted as slide 2.

Notice that Captivate automatically applies the **Blank** Master Slide to the new slide. That's why the copyright notice is displayed on our new slide. Notice also that, the **Use Master Slide Background** checkbox of the **Properties** panel is *deselected* by default. That's why the new slide is blank and does not display the default project background.

8. In the **Properties** panel, open the **Master Slide** drop-down and apply the **Title** Master Slide on slide 2.
9. Select and delete the default Text Animation.

Slide 2 should now be completely blank! Now, let's start the actual Photoshop importation.

10. Still on slide 2, use the **File | Import | Photoshop File** menu item to start the procedure.
11. Import the `Images/mftcTitleTemplate.psd` Photoshop file situated in the exercises folder. (Notice that the file extension of a Photoshop file is `.psd`.)

Captivate opens the **Import "mftcTitleTemplate.psd"** dialog box:

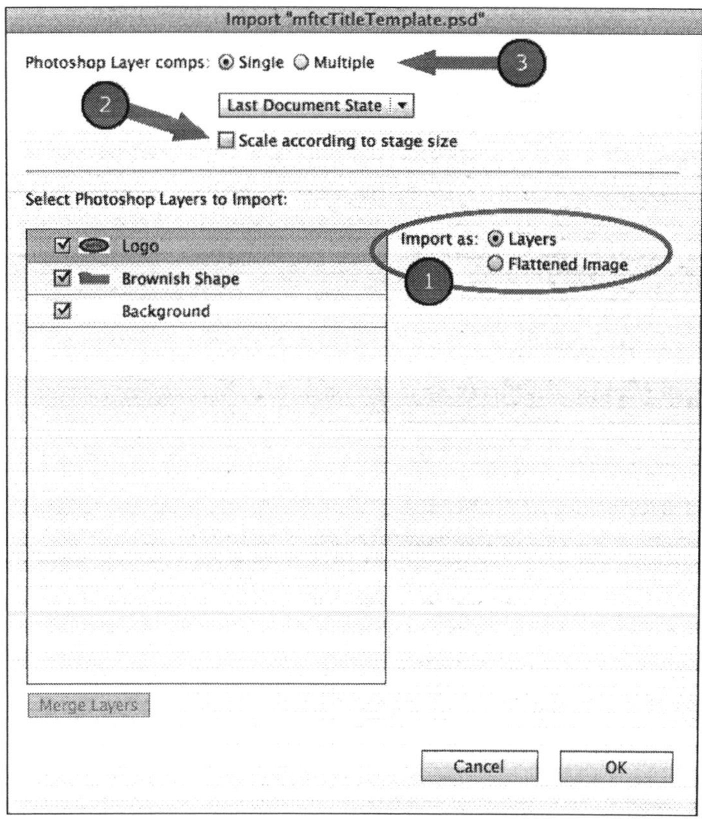

First of all, notice that we can import all the **Layers** of the original Photoshop file or import a **Flattened Image**(1). A **flattened image** is an image where all the layers have been combined into one single image.

Notice also the **Scale according to stage size** checkbox (2). If ticked, the Photoshop image will be automatically enlarged or reduced to fit the size of the Captivate project.

Photoshop users should notice the **Photoshop Layer comps** option at the top of the dialog (3).

12. Make sure that **Import as Layers** (1) is selected.
13. In the main area of the dialog, *deselect* the **Background** layer. We do not want that blank layer to be part of the imported data.
14. Click on the **OK** button to import the remaining two Photoshop layers in Captivate.
15. When the importation is complete, switch to the **Timeline** panel of slide 2.

This is where the import from Photoshop feature will show its awesomeness. *Two* images show up in the **Timeline** panel of Slide 2. This means that **a separate image has been created for each of the imported layers**. These two images can be arranged on the **Timeline** and animated using the **Effects** panel of Captivate.

16. Return to slide 1 and copy paste the Text Animation that it contains on slide 2.
17. When done, delete the first slide of the project.

The first slide of the project now contains three objects: two images from the imported Photoshop file and a Text Animation.

18. Arrange these three objects on the **Timeline** as you see fit. Don't hesitate to use the **Effects** panel as well. The goal is to come up with the greatest introduction slide ever!
19. When done, save and close every open file.

In the next section, we will export our Captivate project to Flash Professional, but before that, let's quickly summarize what we have learned in this section:

- Photoshop is a professional image-editing application developed by Adobe. Many designers around the world use Photoshop, and so, it is not uncommon that Photoshop is used to design the look and feel of a Captivate project.
- Photoshop uses a layer-based system to create complex compositions.
- Captivate contains a specific tool to import a Photoshop file into the project.
- We can import a *Flattened Image* into Captivate or *maintain the layers* found in the Photoshop file during the importation.
- If the Photoshop layers are maintained, each layer is imported *as a separate image* in Captivate. This allows us to arrange these images on the **Timeline** and apply different effects to the different parts of the imported image.

Exporting to Flash Professional

Adobe Flash Professional and Captivate have a lot in common. Both applications are used primarily to generate `.swf` files that can be played back by the free Flash Player plugin.

That being said, the Flash technology has a lot more to offer than what is actually used by Captivate to produce our eLearning content. On the other end, Adobe Flash Professional is the ultimate Flash authoring tool. By using Adobe Flash Professional, a Flash developer is able to leverage the full power of the Flash technology.

It is possible to export a Captivate project to Flash Professional where a Flash developer is able to tweak our Captivate projects in many ways that are not possible in Captivate.

In the following exercise, we will export our Captivate project to Flash Professional CS5.5 or CS6.

The following exercise requires Flash Professional to be installed on the computer along with Captivate. If you obtained Captivate as part of the eLearning suite, Flash Professional is included in your license and you're all set for this exercise.

The steps to export our Captivate project to Flash Professional CS5.5 or CS6 are as follows:

1. Open the `Chapter09/encoderDemo_800.cptx` Captivate file.
2. Depending on the version of Flash available on your system, use the **File** | **Export** | **To Flash CS6** or the **File** | **Export** | **To Flash CS5.5** menu item.

If Flash Professional is not installed on your system, these menu items should be grayed out.

3. In the **Export To Flash Options** dialog box, change the **Location** to the `Chapter09/FlashPro` folder of the exercise files.
4. Take some time to explore the remaining options of the dialog, but leave them all at their current setting.
5. Click on the **Export** button as shown in the following screenshot:

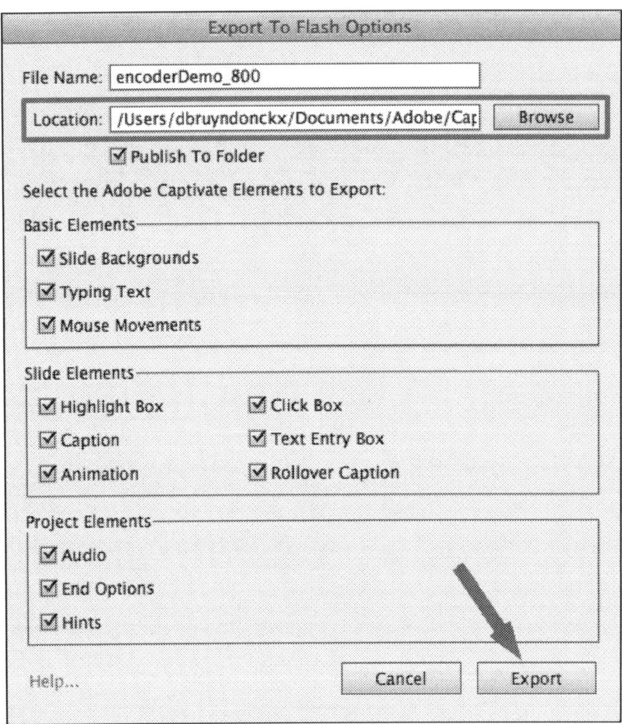

Captivate generates the slides and exports the project as a Flash file, with a `.fla` extension. When done, Flash CS6 (or CS5.5) opens, and our eLearning content loads into Flash Professional. When in Flash, we have access to the underlying code of our Captivate project, as shown in the following screenshot:

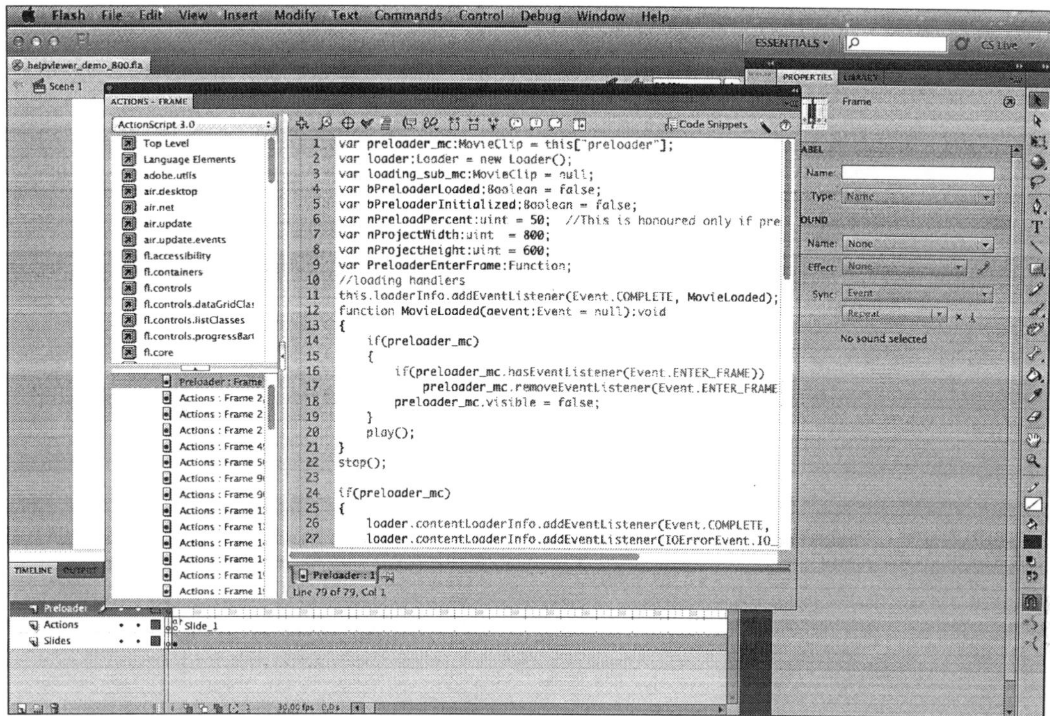

Learning how to leverage all that power in Flash Professional is beyond the scope of this book, but give the generated `.fla` file to a Flash developer and he or she will know what to do with it!

This discussion concludes our overview of the export to Flash feature. Let's quickly summarize what we have learned in this section:

- Adobe Flash Professional and Adobe Captivate are both used to generate Flash content.
- Captivate only uses a small part of the power of Flash.
- It is possible to export the Captivate project to Flash, to leverage the full power of the Flash technology.
- Exporting the Captivate project to Flash generates a `.fla` file that can be opened by the Adobe Flash Professional application. When the project is finished, it is necessary to compile it into a `.swf` file. The `.swf` file is the one that the Flash player is able to read.

Summary

In this chapter, we have explored some of the workflows that integrate Captivate with other applications. Some of these applications, such as Photoshop and Flash, are part of the Adobe product line, and others, such as Microsoft Word and Microsoft PowerPoint, are third-party applications.

By using the PowerPoint workflow, the eLearning developer is able to recycle existing content made in PowerPoint. When it comes to localization, we can export the Text Captions and the Slide Notes as a Microsoft Word document, send it to a translation service and import it back into Captivate. There is no need for the translators to know about Captivate to make this workflow work. When importing a Photoshop file into Captivate, we can decide to maintain the layers of the original Photoshop file, which gives us a great deal of flexibility, to further customize the imported images using the tools of Captivate. Exporting the project to Flash, gives us access to the full power of the Flash Technology.

When used correctly, these workflows are huge time savers that help us streamline the production process of our eLearning content.

Our projects are almost finished now. In the next chapter, we will explore how we can set up a review process. We will make our project available to a team of reviewers. Each of these reviewers will add their comments to the project and send them back to us using various techniques including e-mail and Acrobat.com. We will then import these comments into our Captivate project and address the reviewer's feedback.

Meet the Community

Kevin Siegel

Bio

Kevin Siegel is the founder and president of IconLogic, Inc. He has written more than 100 step-by-step computer training books on Adobe Captivate, AdobeRoboDemo, Adobe Dreamweaver, QuarkXPress, Adobe InDesign, Camtasia Studio, and more.

Kevin spent five years in the U.S. Coast Guard as an award-winning photojournalist and has more than two decades of experience as a print publisher, technical writer, instructional designer, and eLearning developer. He is a certified technical trainer, has been a classroom instructor for more than 20 years, and is a frequent speaker at trade shows and conventions. Kevin holds multiple certifications from companies such as Adobe and the CompTIA.

His company, **IconLogic** offers online training classes on Captivate that are attended by students from all over the world. The company also offers full development and one-on-one mentoring on Captivate and other eLearning development tools.

Contact details

Kevin's email: `ksiegel@iconlogic.com`

IconLogic's website: `www.iconlogic.com`

IconLogic's blog: `www.iconlogic.blogs.com`

My personal note

As an Adobe Captivate Certified Instructor, I have had a chance to teach lots of Captivate classes for various customers using Kevin's courseware. His courseware "Adobe Captivate 5: The Essentials" and "Adobe Captivate 5: Beyond the Essentials" have been parts of my instructor life for the last two years.

Besides his great courseware, Kevin maintains a great blog on Captivate and eLearning that you definitely want to bookmark.

10
Reviewing a Captivate Project

Despite our great level of professionalism and lots of testing throughout the development phase of the project, we have most probably left lots of mistakes, inconsistencies, and technical bugs behind. These errors must be removed from the project before the final publication. The problem is that we have been working so hard and so long on these projects that we are just not able to see those little details anymore.

By letting reviewers in the project, we bring in fresh eyes and open minds. Most of the time, their feedback is an invaluable asset that helps us take a step back and see what our projects are really capable of in the real world, outside the eLearning studio.

This is not only about going the extra mile. Such a review process is an essential part of any professional project.

In this chapter we will:

- Discuss the review process in general
- Initiate a review process by using our own internal server or Acrobat.com
- Install and use the Captivate Reviewer to generate comments
- Import the comments from various reviewers into Captivate
- Use the Captivate commenting tools to approve, reject, and respond to comments.

Preparing our work

In this chapter, we will mainly work with our Encoder Demonstration project. Perform the basic steps to ready Captivate:

1. Open Captivate.
2. Ensure that the **Classic** workspace is the one being used.
3. Use the **Window | Workspace | Reset 'Classic'** to reapply the default interface.
4. Open the `Chapter10/encoderDemo_800.cptx` file.

Captivate is now ready for the exercises of this chapter.

The Review process at a glance

There are two kinds of individuals and three important steps that make up a traditional review process.

Obviously, the two kinds of individuals are:

- The **Author(s)** of the project: That's us! We have created the project, and we are the ones that initiate and manage the reviewing workflow. We know the project by heart, and we have Captivate installed on our computers.
- The **Reviewer(s)**: These are the ones that will view and comment on our work. Some of them might know about Captivate, but some don't know anything about the technical part of our work (which is exactly what we need to have a fresh and open-minded feedback). Consequently, lots (if not all) of our reviewers do *not* have Captivate available on their systems.

Now, let's take a look at the reviewing workflow itself. What are the different steps of this process and what are the tools and strategies available in Captivate to leverage each of these steps.

In Captivate, the reviewing process can be summarized in three main steps:

- The **Distribution Step**: In the Distribution Step, we make our projects available to the reviewers. Basically, we have two options to distribute our projects to the reviewer: our own **internal server** (in other words, a location that can be accessed by every reviewer. It can be a shared network drive or using a third-party cloud-based service such as Dropbox or Skydrive.) or **Acrobat.com**. In both cases, an e-mail can be sent to the reviewers to invite them to the review. Note that a single review can include reviewers from Acrobat.com mixed with reviewers using an internal server.

- The **Reviewing Step**: In this step, each reviewer watches the movie and inserts comments in the project. As most of our reviewers do *not* have Captivate installed on their system, Adobe has created the **Adobe Captivate Reviewer** AIR application. The reviewers will use this special commenting application to create their comments. Note that it is *not* possible to create *new* comments from within Captivate, so the reviewers who have Captivate available still have to use the Adobe Captivate Reviewer application to create their comments.
- The **Collection Step**: The Collection Step takes place in Captivate. In this step, we import the comments sent by the reviewers into our project. The comments can be downloaded automatically from Acrobat.com or from our own internal server (or cloud based service), or inserted manually in the project from an XML file sent by a reviewer as an e-mail attachment. Once all the comments are inserted in Captivate, we can review and address them.

In the next few pages, we will discuss each of these three steps one by one, starting with the Distribution Step.

Distributing the project

In this step, we make the project available to our reviewers. To allow the reviewers to view and comment the project without using Captivate, we will actually *publish* the project, but using yet another publication format than the ones we have already discussed. Perform the following steps to distribute the project:

1. Use Windows Explorer (Win) or the Finder (Mac) to browse to the `Chapter10/encoderDemo_review` folder.
2. Notice that this folder contains a subfolder named `comments`. The comments made by the reviewers will be stored in that location.

Now that the stage is set, let's go back to Captivate and start the *Distribution Step* of our review process.

3. Return to Captivate. If needed, open the `Chapter10/encoderDemo_800.cptx` file.
4. When the file is open, use the **File | Collaborate | Send for Shared Review** menu item to open the **Send for Shared Review** dialog. Alternatively, you can also use the **Collaborate** icon of the main toolbar.
5. At the top of the dialog, make sure that the name of the project is `encoderDemo_800`. Make the necessary adjustments if needed.
6. Open the **How do you want to collect comments from your reviewers?** drop-down list and choose the **Automatically collect comments on my own internal server** option.

Note that the **Automatically collect comments on my own internal server** option is also the one to choose when you decide to use a third-party cloud-based service such as Dropbox or Microsoft Skydrive to make the project available to your reviewers.

Make sure that the **Send for Shared Review** dialog looks like the following screenshot before continuing:

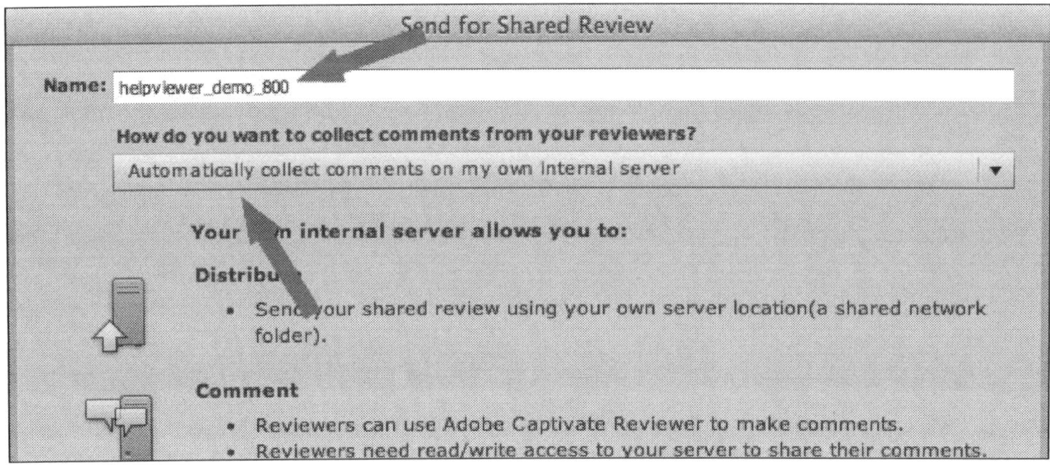

7. Click on the **Next** button to make the second step of the wizard appear on the screen.

The second step of the wizard is where we choose the location to publish our Captivate Review file and the associated comments. Usually, we want that folder to be any location that can be accessed by all reviewers (a shared folder on a network drive or a folder on the Cloud). In our case, we will use the `Chapter10/encoderDemo_review` folder and pretend it is a shared location.

8. Click on the **Browse** button.
9. Choose the `Chapter10/encoderDemo_review` folder as the `Publish` folder.
10. Choose the `Chapter10/encoderDemo_review/comments` folder as the `Comments` folder.

If we need to send an invitation e-mail to our reviewers, we can select the **SendMail** checkbox, but we will not do it for this exercise (The two sub-options of the **SendMail** checkbox will be discussed in the next section).

11. Make sure the **SendMail** checkbox is *not* selected and click on **Publish**.

Captivate generates the slides using a process similar to what we have seen when using the *Publish* dialog we covered in the *Publishing* section of *Chapter 6, Final Changes and Publishing*. When this process is finished, we can take a look at what really happened by using Windows Explorer (Win) or the Finder (Mac) to explore the generated file.

12. Use Windows Explorer (Win) or the Finder (Mac) to navigate to the `Chapter10/encoderDemo_review` folder.

This folder contains the `encoderDemo_800.crev` file. A `.crev` file is a special kind of `.swf` file used for commenting a Captivate project. The `.crev` file can only be opened by the *Adobe Captivate Reviewer* application.

In the **Send for Shared Review** dialog discussed previously, the two sub-options of the **SendMail** checkbox are used to attach the `.crev` file as well as the *Adobe Captivate Reviewer* AIR application to the generated e-mail.

Exploring the .crev file

The `.crev` file is actually a `.zip` file. If you want to explore the contents of the `.crev` package, change the `.crev` extension to `.zip` and use any archive utility to unzip the file. In the archive, you should find the usual `.swf` file plus an extra `.properties` file that can be opened with Text Edit (Mac) or Notepad (Win). Make sure you rename the `.zip` file with the original `.crev` extension before continuing the exercises of this chapter.

Our Captivate project is now published as a `.crev` file on a location where it can be accessed by our team of reviewers. We are ready for the second step of the reviewing workflow.

Commenting a Captivate project

In the second step of this workflow, we will pretend to be one of the reviewers. We will use the Adobe Captivate Reviewer application to add our comments to the project.

Installing the Adobe Captivate Reviewer application

The Adobe Captivate Reviewer is a free AIR application that is shipped with Captivate. Normally, it should have been installed with the rest of the Captivate 6 package. On the Mac, the `Adobe Captivate Reviewer.app` file can be found in the `/Applications/Adobe` folder. On Windows, it is situated in the `C:\program files\Adobe` folder. For the reviewers that do not have Captivate, the AIR installation package of this application can be downloaded from the Adobe website at `http://www.adobe.com/go/cp5_reviewerapp`. Also remember that the AIR runtime must be installed on the system in order to install and run an AIR application.

To install the AIR runtime, use the following URL: `http://get.adobe.com/air/`.

Make the reviewer application work on a Mac

Mac users have one more operation to do before they can use the Adobe Captivate Reviewer application. The exact procedure is described in the following referenced knowledge base article and it involves working with the command line in the Terminal application. The following procedure has been written for the Adobe Captivate Reviewer 2.0. If you have Version 2.5 or Version 6, make sure you make the necessary changes in the paths to the application file. The changes are available at `http://helpx.adobe.com/captivate/kb/cant-load-files-captivate-reviewer.html`.

The next exercise begins when the Adobe Captivate Reviewer application is installed and when the fix described in the above referenced knowledge base article has been applied (if working on a Mac).

Using the Captivate Reviewer to create new comments

With the Captivate Reviewer application installed and the `.crev` file available to the reviewers, all the required conditions are met for us to add our comments to the Captivate project. Perform the following steps to create new comments:

1. Open the Adobe Captivate Reviewer AIR application. (On Windows, run it as an administrator).
2. If it is the first time you are running the application, enter your name, e-mail address, and click on the **Login** button.
3. When the application is ready, click on the **Load Adobe Captivate Movie** button situated in the middle of the screen.
4. Browse to the `Chapter10/encoderDemo_review/encoderDemo_800.crev` file we published in *Distributing the project* section.

The movie loads in the Adobe Captivate Reviewer application. Notice the icons situated at the lower-left and at the lower-right corners of the application, as shown in the following screenshot:

- In the **lower-left corner** of the application are the Playback Controls (1). These icons are used to control the movie as it plays in the *Adobe Captivate Reviewer* application. The traditional *Play/Pause*, *Forward/Rewind*, and *Mute* buttons (plus a few others) can be found in this area.
- In the **lower-right corner** of the application are the icons used to manage the comments (2). The first icon, for instance, is used to create a new comment. Pass your mouse over the icons situated in that area to have a brief description of each available tool. Most of the time, the purpose of these icons is self-explanatory.

Now that we have a better idea of how the Adobe Captivate Reviewer works, let's play the movie and add some comments.

5. Click on the **Play** button to start playing the movie in the Captivate Reviewer.
6. When you feel that a comment is needed, click on the **Add Comment** (1) icon.

A comment is added at the current location of the Playhead and the movie is paused.

7. Type your comment in the box and click on the **Add** button (2).
8. The comment is added and the movie continues to play.

Notice the small dot that stays on the progress bar (3). It marks the exact location of the comments we just added in the movie, as shown in the following screenshot:

9. When you feel a second comment is needed, use the same procedure to add a second comment.

Add as many comments as needed to the movie, just like a real reviewer would do.

10. When done, click on the **Save Comments** icon situated in the lower-right corner of the application.

When you click on the **Save Comments** icon, an XML file with your comments is saved in the `Chapter09/encoderDemo_Review/comments` folder as specified in Captivate when we initiated the shared review. Remember that this folder is supposed to be in a location that can be easily accessed by every reviewer.

Exporting the comments

If the reviewer does not have access to the shared location, he/she shall receive the `.crev` file as an e-mail attachment. The reviewer opens the `.crev` file with the Captivate Reviewer Application installed on his/her system and adds comments to the project as described in the Using the Captivate Reviewer to create new comments section.

Because those reviewers do *not* have access to the shared folder where the comments are saved, they must *export* their comments rather than *save* them.

To export the comments, use the **Export Comments** icon of the Captivate Reviewer application. The **Export Comments** icon is highlighted in the following screenshot:

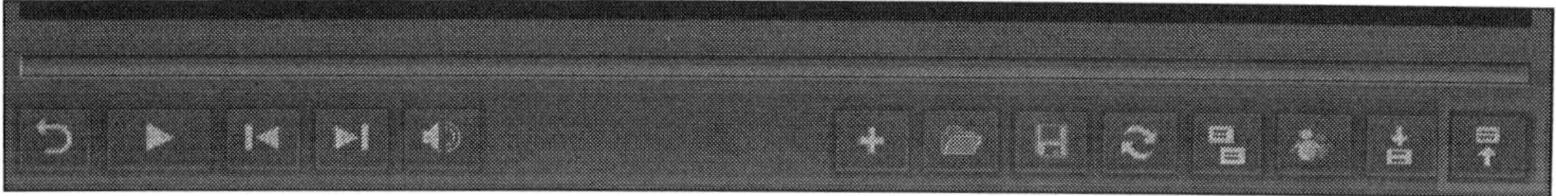

This procedure generates an XML file that needs to be sent back to the author of the project.

In the next section, we will return to Captivate and import those XML files in the project.

Collecting and addressing the comments

When the reviewers have sent their comments back to us (on a shared drive, using a cloud-based service, by e-mail, or using Acrobat.com), we can move on to the third and last step of the reviewing workflow. In this step, we have to import the comments into the main Captivate project and address the feedback of our reviewers:

1. Return to Captivate and open the `Chapter10/commentFiles/encoderDemo_800.cptx` file.
2. Use the **Window | Comments** menu item to open the **Comments** panel.

By default, the **Comments** panel appears at the bottom-right corner of the interface. At the very bottom of the **Comments** panel, a set of eight icons are used to manage the comments. Two of these icons can be used to import comments into the project. They are as follows:

- The **Import Comments** icon (1) is used to manually import the comments into Captivate. These comments are stored in XML files sent via e-mail by the reviewers with no access to the comment's storage location.

- The **Refresh icon** (2) is used to import the comments of the reviewers that have access to the shared folder where the comments are stored, as shown in the following screenshot:

We will now import the three XML files situated in the `Chapter10/commentFiles` folder of the exercises.

3. Click on the **Import Comments** icon situated at the bottom of the **Comments** panel.
4. Import the `Chapter10/commentFiles/bill@mftc.com.xml` file.
5. Repeat this operation with the other two XML files of the `Chapter10/commentFiles` folder.

After importing these three files, there should be ten comments from three different reviewers in the project.

Addressing the comments in Captivate

Take a look at the **Filmstrip** and note that there is an additional icon next to some of the slides. This icon is used to mark the slides with one or more associated comment(s). In the case of this project, Slide 2 is the first slide that has one (or more) comment(s) associated. Perform the following steps to address these comments:

1. Use the **Filmstrip** to go to Slide 2.
2. Take a look at the **Timeline** panel of Slide 2.

There should be two gray dots somewhere on the **Timeline**. They mark the exact position of the comments associated with slide 2.

3. Move your mouse over the first gray dot. A yellow message displays the comment. In the **Comments** panel, the corresponding comment is selected.
4. Click on the **Accept** button situated at the bottom of the **Comments** panel.
5. If needed add a message in the message box. When done, click on the **OK** button to validate your reply.
6. In the **Timeline** of slide 2, click on the second gray dot. This action selects the corresponding comment in the **Comments** panel.

This comment asks us to modify the look and feel of the **Continue** button.

7. Apply the **MFTC-ButtonContinue** style to the button and accept the comment.
8. In the **Comments** panel, click on the second comment to select it.

When clicking on the second comment of the **Comments** panel, Captivate automatically takes us to the slide 5 of the project where that comment is located. In the **Timeline** of slide 5, notice that there are *three comments* associated with that particular slide as indicated by the three dots present in the **Timeline**.

9. Move your mouse over the three dots of the **Timeline** to read the comments.

According to these comments, all our three reviewers have a hard time reading the question!

10. Open the **Properties** panel and make sure it shows the properties of the slide.
11. At the top of the **Properties** panel, click on the **Reset Master Slide** button.

This action reapplies the Master Slide. After this operation, the question and the answers do not overlap anymore, but some extra buttons are displayed at the bottom of the slide.

12. In the **Options** accordion of the **Quiz Properties** panel, deselect the **Back** and the **Next** checkboxes to remove the corresponding buttons from the slide.
13. Return to the **Comments** panel and accept the comments of slide 5.
14. Address the remaining comments of the project. You can either **Accept**, **Reject**, or **Reply** to a comment.

The ability to reply to the comments makes it possible to start real conversations with our reviewers around various aspects of the project being reviewed.

15. When done, click on the **Save Comments** icon to save your new comments and replies to the XML file on the shared network drive.

Earlier in the *Collecting and Addressing the comments* section, we discussed two ways of importing comments into the Captivate project. The method to use depends on whether the reviewers have access to the shared location where the comments are stored or not. The very same discussion is valid the other way around now that we have to make our new comments and replies available to our reviewers:

- The reviewers having access to the comments will use the **Refresh** button of their Adobe Captivate Reviewer application to import the new comments and participate in the discussion.

- For the other reviewers, we have to use the **Export Comments** icon to create a new `.xml` file that has to be sent by e-mail. Those reviewers will have to manually import this updated XML file into their Adobe Captivate Reviewer application to see the comments and participate in the discussion.

Using Acrobat.com in the Review process

Remember that Acrobat.com can be used as the storage location for the comments. This makes it much easier to distribute and refresh everyone's comments, but it requires that every individual involved in the review process has a free Acrobat.com account

For more information on using Acrobat.com in a review process, see this blog post from the official Adobe Captivate blog:
`http://blogs.adobe.com/captivate/2010/08/using-acrobat-com-for-adobe-captivate-project-reviews.html`.

Ending a review

When the eLearning developer decides that the review has come to an end, there is one last operation to do in Captivate using the following steps:

1. At the top of the **Comments** panel, click on the **End Review** icon.
2. Confirm that we want to end the review and delete all the comments.

This short exercise concludes our overview of the commenting workflow in Captivate. Before moving on to the last chapter, let's make a quick listing of what we have learned in this chapter:

- Captivate offers a reviewing workflow that allows us to gather the feedback of individuals not involved in the development of the project.
- Such feedback is of vital importance in order to come up with a truly professional and efficient piece of eLearning content.
- Basically, Captivate offers two options to manage the workflow: **Acrobat.com** or our own **internal server**. When choosing Acrobat.com, it is required that every reviewer has a free Acrobat.com account.
- The reviewing workflow of Captivate is composed of three main steps. In the **Distribute** Step, we initiate the workflow and make the project available to the reviewers. The **Comment** Step is where the reviewers add their comments to the project, and the **Collect** Step is where we gather everyone's comments and address them in Captivate.

- Third-party cloud-based services (such as Dropbox or Microsoft SkyDrive) can be used to make the project available to the reviewers and to store their comments.
- To add their comments to the project, the reviewers use the free Adobe Captivate Reviewer AIR application. Thanks to this application, it is not necessary to own Captivate in order to participate in a Captivate Review.
- The `.crev` file is a special kind of `.swf` file used for commenting. It is the preferred file type of the Captivate Reviewer AIR application.
- In Captivate, it is possible to **Approve**, **Reject**, and **Reply** to comments.

Summary

By letting external reviewers into the project, we have confronted our work to the outside world. Thanks to the feedback of our reviewers, we now have a much better idea of what our project is capable of in the wild.

For the success of such a review process, it is important to choose the reviewers correctly. Try to have the largest possible panel of profiles among your reviewers. Take some technical reviewers to chase the bugs. Also take some designers to have feedback on the look and feel and the ergonomics of your work. And don't forget to bring in the average guy that represents the intended target audience to have a feedback on how the course is perceived by the students.

In this chapter, we have explored the three basic steps of the review workflow (Distribute, Comment, and Collect) and we have been in the skin of both the project owner and the reviewer.

In the **Distribute** Step, we had two options to make our project available to the reviewers, our own server, or Acrobat.com.

In the **Comment** Step, we used the Adobe Captivate Reviewer. It is an AIR application, which means that it can run on virtually any desktop computer provided that the AIR runtime is installed on the system. Thanks to this small application, it is not required to own Captivate in order to view and add comments to a Captivate project. This allows virtually anyone to be part of a Captivate Review.

In the **Collect** Step, we first imported the comments into Captivate before going through the comments of our reviewers. We have accepted some comments and rejected some others. By replying to the comments, we could also start real discussions with our reviewers. Eventually, we decided that the review had to come to an end and we deleted all the comments associated with the project.

In the next chapter, we will discuss one of the most powerful and advanced features of Captivate. Thanks to the **Variables** and the **Advanced Actions**, we will be able to add an even higher degree of interactivity and customization to our projects. We will also discuss the **Widgets** and the brand new **Smart Interactions**. Widgets are external modules developed by the community (for the most part) that can be downloaded from the Internet. They are used to extend the capabilities of Captivate.

Captivate still has some gems waiting to be uncovered in the next and final chapter of this book. See you in the next chapter….

Meet the Community

Shivaswamy Viswanath

Bio

Having 14 years of experience in the Software Industry, Vish has worked in various capacities at Design Firms, Multimedia Firms, Product Development, and Training. Graduated with Bachelors in Science and diploma in Web and Multimedia Technologies, he has experience in User Experience Design, eLearning content authoring, Audio/Video Editing, Multimedia Authoring, Web Production, and Product Testing. Currently holding the Product Evangelist role at Adobe Systems, Vish engages the community with eLearning Products of Adobe.

Contact Details

Twitter: `@vish_adobe`

Blog: `http://blogs.adobe.com/captivate`

My personal note

Being an Adobe evangelist for Captivate and eLearning suite, Vish is in constant contact with the community. He is one of the main contributors to the official Adobe Captivate blog. He travels the world to meet with the community members and represent Adobe at various eLearning related events. As you'll progress into the Captivate world, Vish is one of those individuals that you'll likely encounter.

11
Variables, Advanced Actions, and Widgets

In this last chapter, we will take advantage of the Flash foundations of Captivate. The Flash technology includes a programming language called **ActionScript**. This language is one of the most powerful tools included in the Flash platform. It can be used to implement virtually anything that Flash is capable of (and that means a lot of things indeed!). When publishing our project to Flash, Captivate generates a lot of ActionScript code behind the scenes. It is the Flash Player that executes this ActionScript at runtime.

If we decide to publish our projects to HTML 5, Captivate generates a lot of JavaScript code behind the scenes. It is the browser that executes this JavaScript code at runtime.

Captivate exposes part of this technology to the eLearning developer. Now let's be honest, we won't *actually* be writing *real* ActionScript or JavaScript in Captivate (being an ActionScript or JavaScript developer is a full-time job that requires proper training and real programming skills), but we will be able to create some small scripts anyway, using buttons, drop-down lists, and dialog boxes. In Captivate, these small scripts are called **Advanced Actions**.

Thanks to these Advanced Actions, we will be able to dramatically enhance the eLearning experience of the students. We can for example:

- Dynamically generate text in Text Captions based on student input
- Show and hide objects in response to system or user actions
- Trigger a sequence of actions instead of a single action when a Click Box or a Button is clicked, and so on

Most of the time, these Advanced Actions need to store and read data in the memory of the computer, so we need a robust system to manage these pieces of data. This task is handled by the **Variables**. Basically, a variable is a named space in the memory of the computer in which we can store a piece of data. When referencing the name of a variable, we can access the data it holds and use this data in our Advanced Actions.

Those with advanced programming skills can also create **Widgets**. A Widget is a Flash file written in (real) ActionScript that can be inserted in a Captivate project. Widgets are created outside of Captivate using Flash Professional or Flash Builder. Thanks to the Widgets, we are able to add extra features to Captivate.

In this chapter, we will:

- Discuss and use the System Variables
- Store student input in a User-Defined Variable
- Use variables to generate text dynamically
- Create Standard and Conditional Advanced Actions
- Discuss, insert, and customize Widgets
- Discuss, insert, and customize a Smart Learning Interaction.

Preparing our work

In this chapter, we will return to the Driving In Belgium project.

1. Open Captivate.
2. Make sure that the **Classic** workspace is applied and use the **Windows | Workspace | Reset 'Classic'** menu item to re-apply the default interface.
3. Open the `Chapter11/drivingInBe.cptx` file situated in the exercises folder.

Great! Captivate is now ready to take us into the Variables adventure.

Variables

Every single programming language in the world makes use of *variables* to store and retrieve data to and from the memory of the computer. ActionScript and JavaScript are no exception! In Captivate, it is enough to know that a variable is a named space in the memory of the computer in which data can be read or written.

To make it short, a variable is made of two things:

- A **name**: This name must comply with strict naming rules and conventions. In ActionScript for instance, the name of a variable cannot contain any spaces or special characters (such as @ é, è, ç, à, #, ?, /, and so on). When writing a script, the programmer uses the name of the variable to access the data it holds.
- A **value**: The value is the piece of data that the variable contains. This value can change (vary) during the execution of the script or each time the script is executed, hence the name *Variable*.

For example, `st_firstName = "Damien"` defines a variable.

- `st_firstName` is the **name** of the variable
- `Damien` is the **value** of the variable

Next time the script is executed, we might have `st_firstName = "Bill"` or `st_firstName = "Linda"`, depending on the first name of the student who is taking the course.

In most programming languages, when a variable is created (the proper word is *Declared*), the programmer must specify the *type* of data that the variable will hold (data types include Text String, Integer, Date, Boolean, and so on), but Captivate has decided to keep things simple, so we won't have to worry about data types in our scripts.

System and User-Defined variables

In Captivate, we have two kinds of Variables available: the **System** Variables and the **User-Defined** Variable.

- The **System Variables** are *automatically created* by Captivate. We can use them in our scripts to retrieve information about the movie, the system, or to control various aspects of the movie.
- The **User-Defined Variables** are our own custom variables that we create for our own specific use.

Exploring the System Variables

Enough talking for now! Let's go back to Captivate and start our hands-on exploration of variables.

1. Return to the `Chapter11/drivingInBelgium.cptx` file in Captivate.

2. Use the **Project | Variables** menu item to open the **Variables** dialog box.
3. Open the **Type** drop-down list and choose **System** (1).

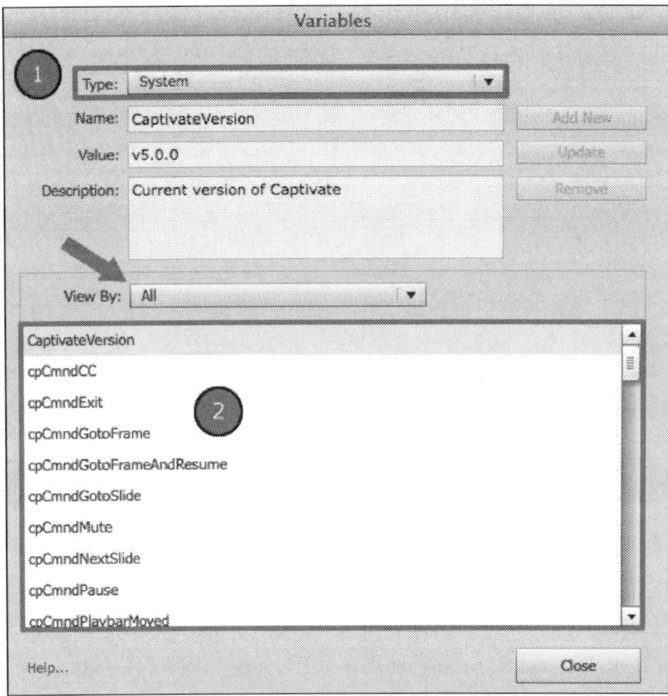

When selecting **System** in the **Type** drop-down, the list of all the available system variables appear in the main area (2) of the **Variables** dialog. Notice the **View By** drop-down (see the arrow in the preceding screenshot) that lets us filter the variables by their category.

4. Open the **View By** drop-down and take some time to examine the available options. When done, select the **Movie Information** category.

The variables *not* pertaining to the **Movie Information** category are filtered out of the **Variables** dialog.

5. Select the **CaptivateVersion** variable.

The upper area of the **Variables** dialog now displays the information of the **CaptivateVersion** variable. The **CaptivateVersion** variable gives us access to the current version number of Captivate.

6. Take some time to review the other **System** variables available.
7. When done, click on **Close** to close the **Variables** dialog.

Now that we have a better idea of the available system variables, we will use some of them to dynamically generate some Text Captions.

Generating text dynamically

We can include Variables in our Text Captions and in various other places where text is supported. To be more exact, we will use the names of the variables to specify what piece of data we want to print on the screen. At runtime, the Flash Player (or the browser) will replace the *name* of the variable with the current *value* of the variable.

In the next exercise, we will create a small note on the last slide of the project with the version of Captivate used to create the movie.

1. Return to the `Chapter11/drivinginBe.cptx` file and use the **Filmstrip** to go to the last slide of the project (Slide 26).
2. Insert a new Text Caption on the last slide. Type `This project is powered by Captivate` in the Text Caption.
3. Apply the Transparent Caption style to the Text Caption and move it to the bottom-left corner of the slide.
4. In the **Timeline**, make the Caption **Appear After 0 sec** and **Display for** the **Rest of** the **Slide**.

So far, so good! This is just about inserting and formatting a new Text Caption. Now, what we want to do is to insert a piece of *Dynamic Text* in the Text Caption, so that the version number of Captivate is automatically added at the end of the Text Caption.

5. Double-click on the new Text Caption and place your cursor at the end of the text, after the word **Captivate**.
6. Add a space in the Text Caption after the word **Captivate**.
7. In the **Format** accordion of the **Properties** panel, click on the **Insert Variable** icon.

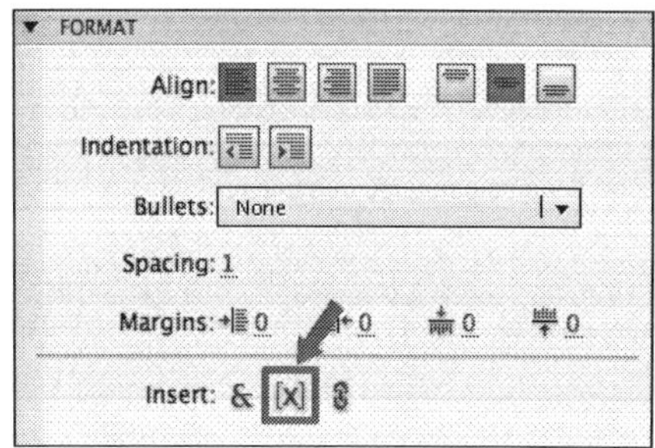

This action opens the **Insert Variable** dialog. We will use this dialog box to choose the variable whose value is to be added to the Text Caption.

8. In the **Insert Variable** dialog, change the **Type** from **User** to **System,** if necessary.
9. In the **View By** drop-down list, choose the **Movie Information** category.
10. Open the **Variables** drop-down and choose the **CaptivateVersion** variable from the list of available variables.
11. Click on **OK** to add the variable to the end of the Text Caption.

With this sequence of actions, we have added the **CaptivateVersion** system variable to the end of our new Text Caption.

Notice that the name of the variable is surrounded by two $ signs. The Text Caption now reads **This project is powered by Captivate $$CaptivateVersion$$**. At runtime, the **$$CaptivateVersion$$** part of the sentence will be replaced by the value of the *CaptivateVersion* variable.

We will now test our new Text Caption in the **Preview** pane.

12. Use the **Filmstrip** to return to slide 25.
13. Use the Preview icon to preview the movie **From This Slide**.
14. When the last slide appears in the **Preview** pane, pay close attention to the Text Caption we have added in the previous exercise.
15. Close the **Preview** pane when done and save the file.

Normally, the Text Caption should read: **This project is powered by Captivate 6.0.0!**

This first experience with variables teaches us what a **Dynamic Text** is: it is a piece of text that is generated *on the fly at runtime*.

Extra credit: generating a Quiz Result Slide for the Pretest

In this section, you will create a Quiz Result Slide for the Pretest that we added to the Encoder Demonstration project. To do it, you will use the **cpQuizInfoPretestScorePercentage** system variable. This brand new system variable of Captivate 6 gives us access to the result of the Pretest expressed as a percentage.

The general steps of this exercise are the following:

- Open the `Chapter11/encoderDemo_800.cptx` and `Chapter11/pretestFeedback.cptx` files
- Copy the two slides of the `pretestFeedback.cptx` file and paste them as slides 8 and 9 of the `encoderDemo_800.cptx` project
- On slides 8 and 9, replace the XXX part of the Text Captions by the **cpQuizInfoPretestScorePercentage** system variable
- Set the actions of the buttons of the two new slides to implement proper branching
- Test the entire movie several times to ensure that every Text Caption shows the right information and that every button takes the student to the right slide

Don't forget to save and close the files when done!

Using User-Defined variables

What is true with *System* variables is also true with *User-Defined* variables. In the next exercise, we will create a User-Defined variable to store the first name of the student that is taking the course. To capture the value of that variable, we will use a Text Entry Box and ask the student to type his/her first name in it.

Creating a User-Defined variable

First of all, let's create the variable:

1. Return to the `Chapter11/drivingInBe.cptx` file.
2. Use the **Project | Variables** menu item to open the **Variables** dialog box.
3. Make sure that **User** is selected in the **Type** drop-down.
4. Click on the **Add New** button to create a new variable.
5. Type `txt_studentFirstName` in the **Name** field.

This will be the name of our new variable. Remember that the name of a variable must comply with a strict set of rules and conventions:

- A variable name cannot contain any space
- A variable name cannot contain any special characters

In addition to these rules, some names are reserved by ActionScript and JavaScript and cannot be used as the names of our User-Defined variables.

See the Captivate Help at `http://help.adobe.com/en_US/captivate/cp/using/WSDF6E7000-1121-4808-B61B-CCAB6A554AD3.html` for a complete list of ActionScript-reserved names.

In this case, the name of the variable is `txt_studentFirstName`.

- I use the **txt_** prefix to specify that this variable will hold a piece of Text
- **studentFirstName** is the actual name of the variable

To make the name *human eye-friendly*, I used what the developers call the *Camel Case*. The idea is to use a capital letter each time a space should be needed. This way, ActionScript and JavaScript are happy (no spaces) and the human eye is happy as well!

6. Leave the **Value** field empty. A Text Entry Box will be used to capture the value of this variable.
7. Optionally, add a meaningful **Description** to the new variable.
8. Click on **Save** to create the variable and **Close** the **Variables** dialog.

Now that the variable exists, we will add a Text Entry Box to the second slide of the project. It will be used to capture the value of the variable.

Capturing values with Text Entry Boxes

First of all, let's insert the new Text Entry Box.

1. Use the **Filmstrip** to go to slide 2 of the `Chapter11/drivingInBe.cptx` file.
2. Use the **Insert | Standard Objects | Text Entry Box** menu item or the corresponding icon in the vertical Objects toolbar to create a new Text Entry Box.

As covered in *Chapter 4, Working with Animations and Interactive Objects*, Captivate inserts up to five objects that make up the Text Entry Box system (three feedback Captions, one Submit button, and the Text Entry Box itself). In the case of this particular Text Entry Box, we do not need all these objects so we will fine tune the properties of this Text Entry Box to disable the objects we do not need.

3. Make sure the Text Entry Box is the selected Object (The **Text Entry Box** mention appears at the top of the **Properties** panel).

4. In the **Options** accordion of the **Properties** panel, deselect the **Success**, **Failure**, and **Hint** checkboxes if needed. The corresponding captions disappear from the slide.

Now comes the option that will mark the change between a regular Text Entry Box and a Text Entry Box used to capture data.

5. In the **General** accordion of the **Properties** panel, make sure the **Validate User Input** checkbox is *not* selected.

There are no right and wrong answers for this particular Text Entry Box, so we do not need to validate what the user types in the object against a list of correct entries. Consequently, the Correct Entries Box associated with the object is not displayed. We will now associate this Text Entry Box with the `txt_studentFirstName` variable we created in the previous section.

6. In the **General** accordion of the **Properties** panel, open the **Variable** drop-down list.
7. Select the `txt_studentFirstName` variable from the list of available variables.

Our Text Entry Box is now associated with the `txt_studentFirstName` variable. It means that **whatever the student will type in the Text Entry Box will become the value of the** `txt_studentFirstName` **variable**.

8. In the **Action** accordion of the **Properties** panel, change the **On Success** action to **Go to the next slide**.
9. Move and resize the **Text Entry Box** and the associated **Submit** button so it fits nicely on the stage.
10. In the **Character** accordion of the **Properties** panel, adjust the formatting to your taste. The choices you make here apply to the text that the student will type in the box.
11. Move the Text Entry Box to the end of the **Timeline**.

Our Text Entry Box is now ready to capture the first name of the student and to associate that particular value with the `txt_studentFirstName` variable.

Using User-Defined variables to dynamically generate Text

The last step of this exercise is to use the `txt_studentFirstName` variable and its associated value to generate a piece of dynamic text.

1. Use the **Filmstrip** to go to slide 3 of the `Chapter11/drivingInBelgium.cptx` file.

2. Insert a new Text Caption to the slide.
3. Type **Welcome** followed by a space in the new Text Caption. Leave your cursor after the space.
4. In the **Format** accordion of the **Properties** panel, click on the **Insert Variable** icon.
5. In the **Insert Variable** dialog, choose to insert the `txt_studentFirstName` **User** variable.
6. Change the **Maximum length** to **30** characters to accommodate longer first names.
7. When the **Insert Variable** dialog looks similar to the following screenshot, click on the **OK** button:

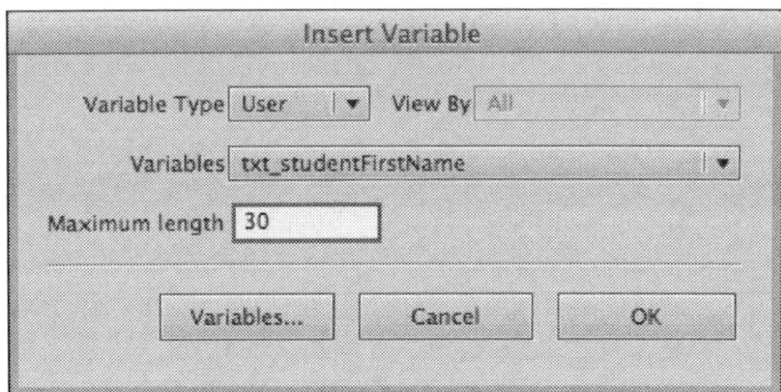

This action inserts the `txt_studentFirstName` variable in the new Text Caption and encloses it in double `$` signs. The full text of the Caption now is **Welcome $$ txt_studentFirstName$$**. Remember that at runtime, the **$$txt_studentFirstName$$** part of the sentence will be replaced by the first name of the student as typed in the Text Entry Box of the previous slide.

8. Adjust the *formatting*, the *position*, and the *timing* of the new Text Caption so it integrates nicely with the other elements of the slide.
9. When done, save the file and use the Preview icon to preview the whole **Project**. On the second slide, type your first name in the Text Entry Box and click on the **Submit** button. On slide 3, your name should be displayed in the Text Caption.
10. Close the **Preview** pane and save the file when done.

This exercise concludes our first exploration of system and user-defined variables. Before moving on to creating more variables and using them in advanced actions, let's make a quick summary of what we have learned so far.

- A **Variable** is a named space in the memory of the computer. When referencing the *name* of a variable, we access the *data* that the variable holds.
- There are two types of variables in Captivate. The **System** variables are automatically created by Captivate. The **User-Defined** variables are ours to create.
- It is possible to add variables in Text Captions. This creates **dynamic texts** in the project.
- A dynamic text is a text that is created *on the fly at runtime*. The Flash Player or the JavaScript engine of the browser simply retrieves the current value of a given variable to generate the content of a Text Caption.
- A Text Entry box can be associated to a User-Defined variable to capture the data of the variable. Once captured and stored in a variable, that piece of data can be used in any script or in any Text Caption.

Advanced Actions

An Advanced Action is a small script that is executed at runtime by the Flash Player or by the JavaScript engine of the web browser. These Advanced Actions can be used to manipulate the data contained in variables or to manipulate the objects of Captivate.

In Captivate, there are two families of Advanced Actions:

- The **Standard Actions** are simple procedures that are always executed the same way.
- The **Conditional Actions** are a bit more complex. They can evaluate if a given condition is *true* or *false* and act accordingly. Consequently, they do not always perform the same set of actions each time they are executed.

In the next exercise, we will create a couple of Standard Actions to get a sense of what they can achieve.

The Standard Action

The Standard Action is the simplest form of Advanced Actions that can be created in Captivate. A Standard Action is simply a list of instructions that the Flash Player or JavaScript will execute *one by one* and *in order* at runtime.

Automatically turning on Closed Captions with an Advanced Action

Our first example of Advanced Action will manipulate one of the many System Variables of Captivate to automatically turn on the Closed Captions when the movie starts.

First, let's find out the name of the variable to manipulate.

1. Still in the `drivingInBe.cptx` file, use the **Projects | Variables** menu item to open the **Variables** dialog.
2. Use the **Type** drop-down list to display the **System** Variables.
3. In the **View By** drop-down, choose the **Movie Control** category.
4. Select the first variable of the list named `cpCmndCC`.

The description says it all! This variable is a *Boolean* variable. It means that it can only have two values: 1 or 0. When the value of the variable is set to 1, the Closed Captions are turned on, but if it is set to 0, the Closed Captions do not appear. So basically, what we have to write is an Advanced Action that assigns the value 1 to the `cpCmndCC` System Variable and make Captivate execute that action when the movie starts.

5. **Close** the **Variables** dialog.
6. Use the **Project | Advanced Actions** menu item to open the **Advanced Actions** dialog.
7. In the top-left corner of the dialog, type `displayCC` in the **Action Name** field.

Note that the name of the action must comply with the same strict rules than the name of the variables (No spaces and no special characters).

8. In the **Actions** area of the dialog, double-click on the first line of the table.

This adds a first step to the Advanced Action. In the first column, a red dot indicates that the action is invalid in its current state. When this first instruction will be finished, the red dot should turn green. In the second column, there is a drop-down menu containing a list of possible actions we have to choose from.

9. Open the **Select Action...** drop-down and take some time to inspect the list of possible actions.
10. When done choose the **Assign** action in the list.
11. Open the **Select Variable** drop-down and take some time to inspect the available variables.

The **Select Variable** drop-down list proposes a list of variables whose value can be changed. (The `CaptivateVersion` variable for instance is *not* listed, because we *cannot* change the value of this variable. It is a *read only* variable).

12. At the very top of the list, select the `cpCmndCC` variable.
13. Open the second **Variable** drop-down list and choose **Literal**.
14. Type `1` in the field that appears and press *Enter*.

The whole sentence becomes `Assign cpCmndCC with 1`. In plain English, it translates to *Turn on Closed Captions*. Notice that the red dot in front of the action turns green. This is an indication that Captivate understands our action, which is a very good news!

15. Double-click on the second line of the table to add a second step into the action.
16. In the **Select Action...** drop-down, choose the **Continue** action.

The red dot at the beginning of the second line of the table turns green right away, because the `Continue` action does not require any kind of extra parameter to work.

Make sure the **Advanced Actions** dialog looks like the following screenshot before continuing with this exercise:

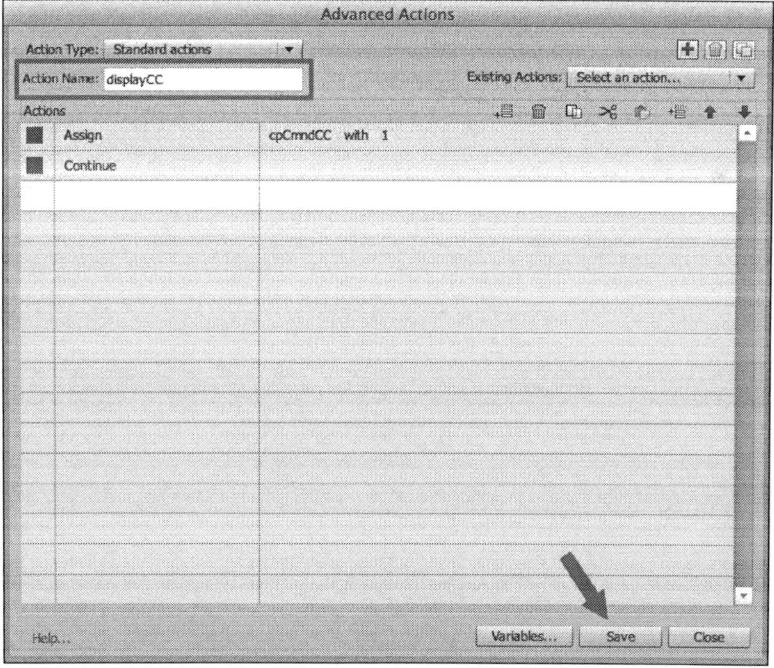

17. Click on the **Save** button at the bottom of the dialog to save the Advanced Action.
18. Acknowledge the successful saving of the Advanced Action and **Close** the **Advanced Action** dialog.

Our Advanced Action is now ready, but one last piece of the puzzle is still missing. We need to Tell Captivate *when* we want our action to be executed. In other words, we need to bind our action to the **event** that will *trigger* the action.

There are lots of possible events in Captivate, some of them are **system events** (such as the start of a movie, the beginning of a slide, and so on) and some of them are **student-driven events** (typically, a click on a button). In our case, we will ask Captivate to execute our action when the second slide of the movie is played.

19. Use the **Filmstrip** to go to slide number 2. Make sure that the **Properties** panel shows the properties of the slide.
20. In the **Action** accordion of the **Properties** panel, open the **On Enter** drop-down list.
21. Take some time to inspect the possible actions. When done, choose **Execute Advanced Action** in the list.
22. Make sure that our **displayCC** action appears in the **Script** drop-down.

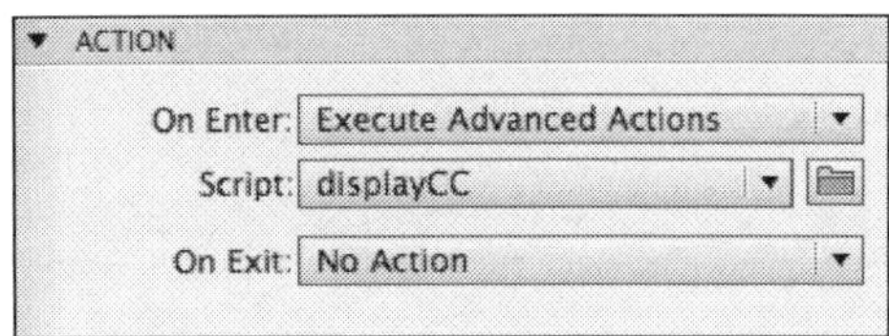

23. Save the file and use the Preview icon to preview the entire **Project**.

In the **Preview** pane, the Closed Captions should automatically be turned on when the playhead reaches slide 2.

This first example of an Advanced Action illustrates how an Advanced Action can be used to manipulate a system variable and how to bind an action to an event. By automatically turning on the Closed Captions, we enhance the overall experience of our beloved students.

Don't forget that other System Variables can be manipulated in the very same way allowing us to do things like muting or un-muting the sound, setting the audio volume, jumping to a slide, hiding the Playback controls, and more.

Extra credit

The last slide of the project with associated audio (and consequently with associated Closed Captions) is slide number 15, so it is safe to turn off the Closed Captions when the playhead exits slide 15. In this extra credit section, you will build a second Advanced Action that turns off the Closed Captions by assigning the value `0` to the `cpCmndCC` system variable. Captivate should execute this second Advanced Action when the student clicks on the **Continue** button of slide 15.

The main steps are as follows:

- Use the **Project | Advanced Actions** menu item to open the Advanced Actions dialog.
- Create a second Advanced Action named `hideCC` that assigns the value `0` to the `cpCmndCC` system variable and then, goes to the next slide. Don't forget to *save* the Advanced Action before closing the **Advanced Actions** dialog.
- On slide 15, in the **Properties** panel of the **Continue** button, bind the `hideCC` Advanced Action to the **On Success** event.
- Save the file and preview the entire **Project**. In the **Preview** pane, make sure that the Closed Captions are turned *on* at slide 2 and are turned *off* at the end of slide 15.

This second example illustrates how an Advanced Action can be bound to a student-driven event (the click on a button) instead of a System event.

Conditional Actions

The second kind of Advanced Actions available is the **Conditional Action**. A Conditional Action is a bit more complex than a Standard Action in that it is able to *evaluate if a condition is true or false* and act accordingly.

To illustrate this capability, we will add a new slide in the project after slide 12. On that new slide, we will display a feedback message to the student that is specific to the way they answered the two preceding questions.

Remember that we ask the students two questions in the first part of the movie (the measurement unit they use to measure speed and if they drive on the right or on the left side of the road). If we aggregate the answers of those two questions, we face three different situations.

Situation	Speed Units	Side of road	Score	Meaning
1	Km/h	Right	2	Ok to drive in Belgium
2	MPH	Left	0	Change all your habits to drive in Belgium
3	MPH Km/h	Right Left	1	Change some driving Habits to drive in Belgium

To keep track of the answers, we will assign a score to each of the possible answers. A score of 1 if the student does the same thing as in Belgium and a score of 0 if the student's habits are different from the Belgian ways of driving.

Our Conditional Action will display a feedback message that depends on the score of the student.

Creating the necessary variables

We will begin this exercise by creating yet another User-Defined Variable. We will use it to store the score of the student as he/she progresses into the project and answers questions.

1. Return to Captivate and use **the Project | Variables** menu item to return to the **Variables** dialog.
2. Click on the **Add New** button to create a new variable.
3. In the **Name** field, type `num_studentScore`.

`num_studentScore` will be the name of our new variable. The `num_` prefix states that this variable will hold a data of type of number.

4. In the **Value** field, give this variable an initial value of **0**.

The action of giving an initial value to a variable is called **initialization**. In the programmer's jargon, we would have said **Declare the** `num_studentScore` **variable and** ***initialize*** **it to 0**.

5. Optionally, type a description in the **Description** field.
6. Click on the **Save** button to save the new variable.

Make sure the **Variables** dialog looks like the following screenshot:

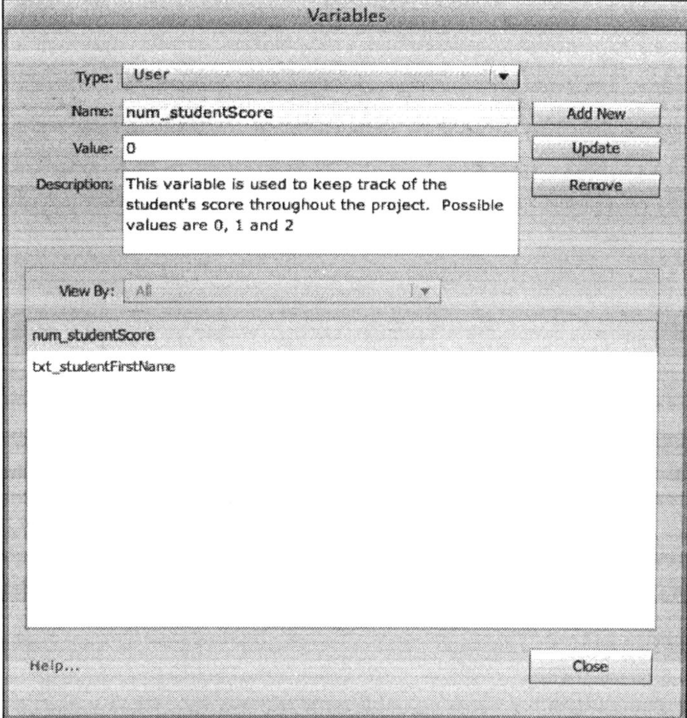

7. Click on the **Close** button to close the **Variables** dialog.
8. Don't forget to **Save** the file when done.

Now that we have created this variable, we are ready to track the score of the students throughout the entire project.

About naming variables

We already discussed the fact that the name of a variable must comply with strict naming rules (no space, no special characters, and so on). That being said, *any* name that complies with these rules is *not* right. When naming variables, it is important to stick to **conventions** in addition to complying with the rules, especially when working on a team. If no naming convention exists among the developers of a team, everyone will end up with his/her own naming rules and habits and it will be virtually impossible to keep track of the variables and to maintain the projects over time. In our case, we used the `txt_` and `num_` prefixes, then the name of the variable uses the Camel Case, but any other convention will do! The bottom line is: complying with the technical rules is *not* enough!

Assigning a score to each possible answers

At the beginning of the project, each student has a score of 0. Technically, we have translated this situation by *initializing* our `num_studentScore` variable to 0. Now the score of each student will evolve depending on the answers given in the project.

There are two places where the score of the student can evolve:

- **When entering slide 6**, the score has to increase by 1 point. Slide 6 is the feedback slide when the student chooses the *Km/h* answer to the first question.
- **When entering slide 11**, the score has to be incremented by 1 again. Slide 11 is the feedback slide when the student answers *On the right side* to the second question.

We will now create an Advanced Action that increments the `num_studentScore` variable by 1 point and have Captivate execute that action when entering slide 6 *and* when entering slide 11.

1. Use the **Project | Advanced Actions** menu item to open the **Advanced Actions** dialog.
2. At the top-left corner of the dialog, enter the name `incrementStudentScore` in the **Action Name** field.
3. In the main area of the **Variables** dialog, double-click on the first line of the table to add the first instruction to the Advanced Action.
4. Open the **Select Action...** drop-down and choose the **Expression** action from the list.
5. Open the **Select Variable...** drop-down and choose the `num_studentScore` variable from the list.
6. Open the next drop-down list and select the **Variable** option. Open the same drop-down list a second time and select the `num_studentScore` variable from the list.
7. Open the **Operator** drop-down and choose `+` from the list.
8. Open the last drop-down list and choose the **Literal** option. When done, type `1` in the field.
9. Click anywhere outside of the first line of the table to validate the expression. The red dot in front of the expression should turn green.

The entire expression now reads `num_studentScore = num_studentScore + 1`. In plain English, we add 1 to the current value of the `num_studentScore` variable, or in other words, we *increment* the `num_studentScore` variable by 1.

10. Double-click on the second line of the table to add a second instruction to this Advanced Action.
11. Open the **Select Action...** drop-down and choose the **Continue** action from the list.
12. Make sure your Advanced Action dialog looks like the following screenshot:

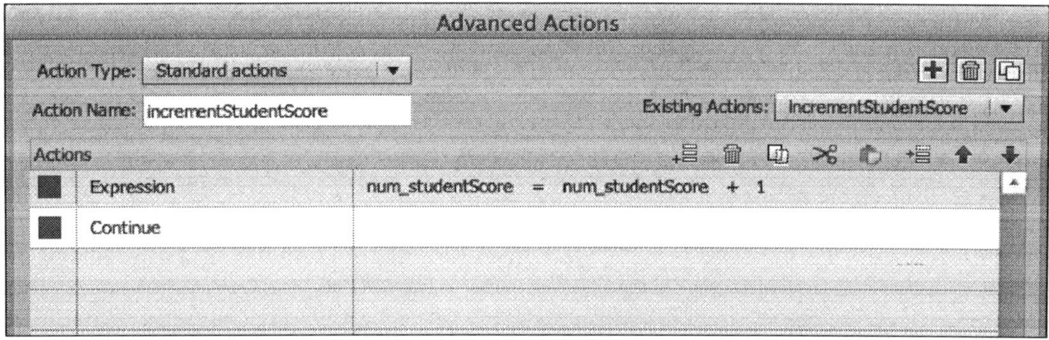

13. Click on the **Save** button to save the action and click on **Close** to close the Advanced Action dialog.

The next step is to bind this action to an event in the Captivate project.

14. Use the **Filmstrip** to go to slide 6 of the project.
15. Make sure that the **Properties** panel shows the properties of the **Slide**.
16. In the **Action** accordion, open the **On Enter** drop-down and select **Execute Advanced Actions** from the list.
17. Open the **Script** drop-down and select the `incrementStudentScore` script from the list.
18. Use the **Filmstrip** to go to slide 11 and repeat the same sequence of actions to bind the `incrementStudentScore` action to the **On Enter** event of slide 11.

Depending on the student's answers to the questions, our `num_studentScore` variable can now have three different values.

- If the student uses *Miles per Hours* and drives on the *left* side of the road, the `incrementStudentScore` action is never executed and the `num_studentScore` variable stays at its initial value of 0.
- If the students used *Kilometers per Hours* and drives on the *right* side of the road, the `incrementStudentScore` action is executed twice and the final value of the `num_studentScore` variable is 2.
- In the in-between situation, the `incrementStudentScore` action is executed only once and the final value of the `num_studentScore` variable is 1.

In the next step of the exercise, we will insert a new slide in the project and prepare three feedback messages to face the three situations described previously.

Giving names to objects

First of all, we will insert a new slide in the project and prepare three standard Text Captions on it.

1. Use the **Filmstrip** to go to slide 12 of the `drivingInBe.cptx` file.
2. Open the `Chapter11/DIB_feedback.cptx` file.
3. Copy the only slide of the `Chapter11/DIB_feedback.cptx` file and paste it as **slide 13** of the `drivingInBe.cptx` file.

The slide you just copied contains three Text Captions that are situated on top of each other in the center of the slide. In the **Timeline** panel, note that these three Text Captions are set to be displayed at the very same time and that they all last 6 seconds.

At runtime, only one of these Text Captions will be displayed to the student. The chosen Text Caption will depend on the student score as described in the preceding table. To make this possible, all three Text Captions will be initially hidden from the stage. An Advanced Action will then be used to check the score of the student and turn the visibility of the right Text Caption on.

In the next exercise, we will prepare this system by assigning a name to each Text Caption and by turning their visibility off.

4. Still on the new slide 13, use the **Timeline** to select the topmost Text Caption.

This first Text Caption will be used when the `num_studentScore` variable is 0.

5. Make sure the **Properties** panel shows the properties of the selected Text Caption.
6. At the top of the **Properties** panel, change the **Name** of the Text Caption to `TC_feedback0Points`.

This name will make it much easier for us to pinpoint this particular object while writing the Conditional Action. The second thing is to do is to instruct Captivate that this Text Caption will be hidden by default.

7. Still in the **Properties** panel of this Text Caption, deselect the **Visible in output** checkbox.

Notice that this action does *not* remove the object from the stage in Captivate. To hide the object from the stage in Captivate, it is necessary to turn off the associated eye icon in the **Timeline** panel.

8. In the **Timeline**, close the *Eye* icon associated with the **TC_feedback0Points** Text Caption.
9. Use the **Timeline** to select the middle Text Caption.
10. In the **Properties** panel, change the **Name** of that Text Caption to `TC_feedback1Point` and deselect the **Visible in output** checkbox.
11. In the **Timeline**, close the Eye icon associated with the **TC_feedback1Point** Text Caption.
12. Select the last Text Caption. Change its name to `TC_feedback2Points` and deselect its **Visible in Output** checkbox. Also hide it from the stage by closing the associated eye icon in the **Timeline** panel.

In this exercise, we have changed the names of three Text Captions. The names we give to the objects must comply with the same naming rules as the Variables (no spaces and no special characters). Remember that observing the technical requirements is *not* enough! It is much better if you also comply with some kind of naming convention. In this exercise, the `TC_` prefix stands for *Text Caption* the rest is the name of the object in camel case.

At the end of this exercise, your **Timeline** should look like the following screenshot:

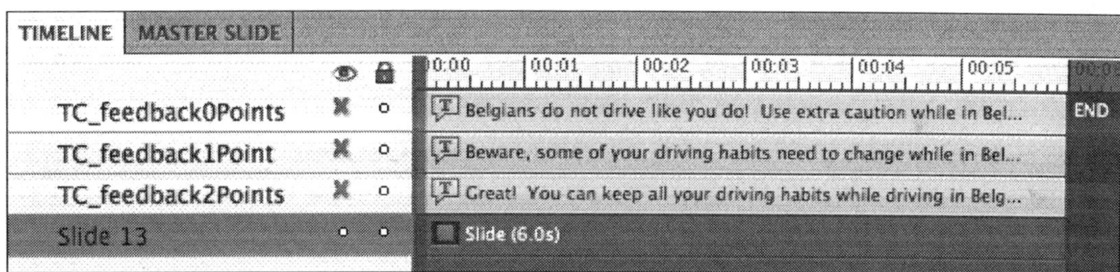

Let's make one last experiment before moving on to the next step.

13. Use the **Filmstrip** to return to slide 12.
14. Once on slide 12, use the Preview icon to preview the **Next 5 Slides**.
15. When the preview reaches slide 13, confirm that no Text Caption appears in the **Preview** pane.
16. When done, close the **Preview** pane and save the file.

The stage is set! The feedback messages are ready and we have a variable with three possible values to test against. The last piece of the puzzle is to create a Conditional Action that will evaluate the value of the `num_studentScore` variable and decide which of our three feedback messages must be revealed to the student.

Conditionally showing and hiding objects

In this section, we will create the conditional advanced action that will combine all the pieces of the puzzle together. When it will be done, we will bind this action to the **On Enter** event of slide 13.

1. Still in the `drivingInBe.cptx` file, use the **Project | Advanced Actions** menu item to open the **Advanced Actions** dialog.
2. In the top-left corner of the **Advanced Actions** dialog, open the **Action Type** drop-down and select **Conditional Actions** from the list.

The **Advanced Actions** dialog is updated and it shows the interface that we will use to create a *conditional* Advanced Action.

3. Still in the top-left corner of the dialog box, type `showScoreFeedback` in the **Action Name** field.

Remember that the name of an action cannot contain any spaces or special characters.

We will now dig into the *real* stuff and create our Conditional Advanced Action. We will start by coding the first-case scenario, when the `num_studentScore` variable has a value of 0.

4. At the top of the box, double-click on the blue **Untitled** button and change the text to **Score 0**.

This step is optional and has no technical influence on how this action will be executed. By adding a title to a branch of a Conditional Action, we make our job easier when debugging and maintaining this action in the future.

5. In the **If** part of the box, double-click on the first line of the table to add the first condition.
6. Open the **Variable** drop-down and select the **Variable** option from the list. Then, open the list again to select the `num_studentScore` variable.

7. Open the **Select comparison operator** drop-down and choose the **is equal to** option from the list of available operators.
8. Open the last drop-down and choose **Literal** from the list, then type `0` in the field.

The whole expression should now read `num_studentScore is equal to 0` and the red button at the beginning of the table row should turn green.

Notice the **AND** word at the end of the table row. It tells us that we can add more conditions and that the conditions will be united by an AND operator. In other words, **every individual condition should be true for the entire condition to be true**.

9. Open the **Perform actions if** drop-down and choose the **Any of the conditions true** option from the list.

Notice that the AND keyword switches to OR. In this case, **the entire condition is true if any of the individual condition is true**.

10. Open the **Perform actions if** drop-down and choose the **Custom** option from the list.

In this situation, it is up to the developer to choose between AND or OR at the end of every single condition. This allows us to create complex conditions. In our case, we only have a single condition, so the choice between AND and OR is not important.

11. Open the **Perform actions if** drop-down one last time and choose the **All conditions are true** option to return to the default situation.
12. In the **Actions** area of the dialog, double-click on the first row of the table to add a first action.
13. Open the **Select Action** drop-down and choose **Show** from the list of available actions.
14. Open the **Select Item** drop-down and choose the **TC_feedback0Point** item from the list.
15. Add a **Continue** action in the second row of the **Actions** area.

The red dots in front of these two actions should both be green. Notice how the name we added to the Text Caption in the previous section comes in handy now. Make sure the **Advanced Actions** dialog looks like the following screenshot before continuing:

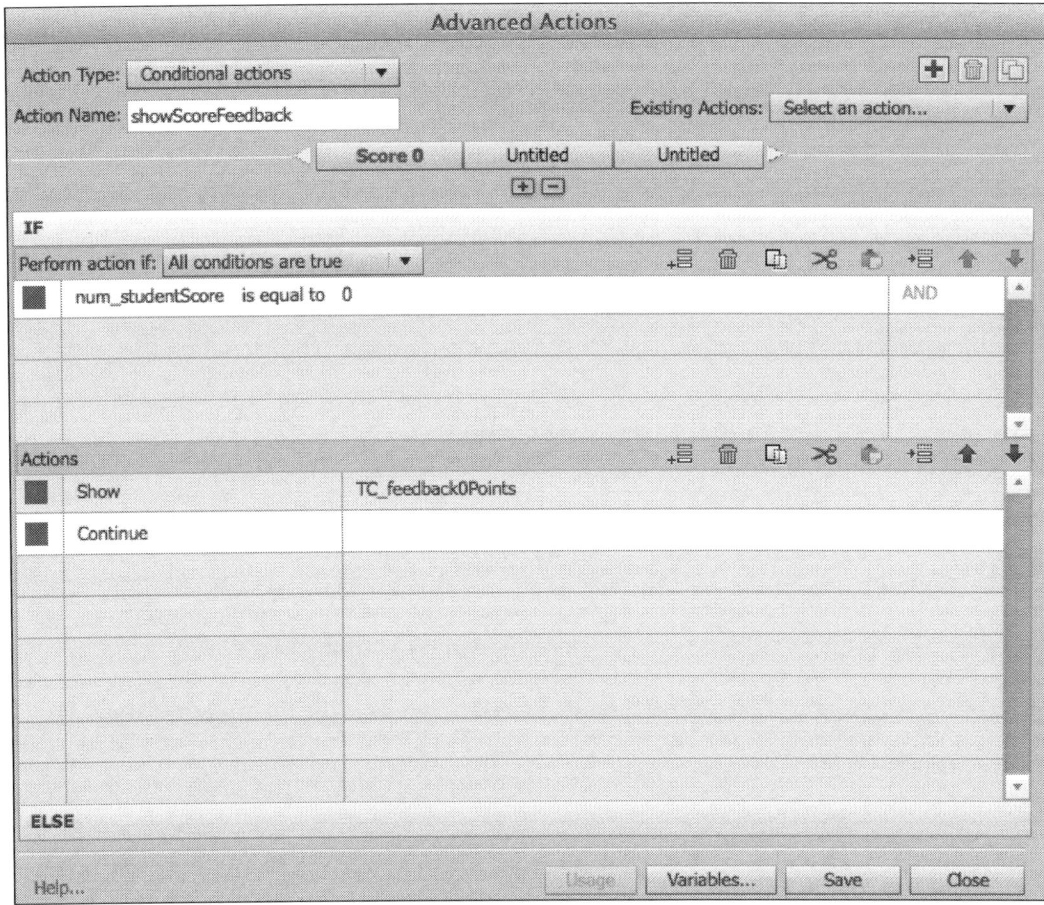

So far, we have coded the first of three possibilities only. We will now add a second decision to this Advanced Action to cope with the second situation.

16. At the top of the Conditional Action, double-click on the first **untitled** button. Rename this button **Score 1**.

This opens a second *If … Else* table in the Advanced Actions dialog. In Captivate, such a table is called a **decision**. By default, a Conditional Advanced Action contains three *decisions*, hence the three buttons at the top of the interface.

17. In the **IF** part of the second decision, double-click on the first line of the table to add a first condition.

18. Open the first drop-down and choose **Variable** from the list. Open the same drop-down again and choose the `num_studentScore` variable from the list of available variable.
19. In the second drop-down list, choose the **Is equal to** operator.
20. Open the last drop-down and choose **literal** from the list, then type `1` into the field that appears.

The condition should now read `num_studentScore is equal to 1` and the red dot in front of the condition should turn green. With the condition in place, we can move on to the bottom part of the dialog where we will set up the corresponding action.

21. Double-click on the first line of the **Actions** area.
22. Open the **Select action** drop-down and choose the **Show** action from the list.
23. Open the **Select Item** drop-down and choose the **TC_feedback1Point** item from the list. In the second row of the table, set the second action to **Continue**.

Our Conditional Action now accommodates two out of three situations. Before moving on to the next step, make sure that the Advanced Action dialog looks like the following screenshot. Notice at the top of the dialog box the two decisions that we renamed.

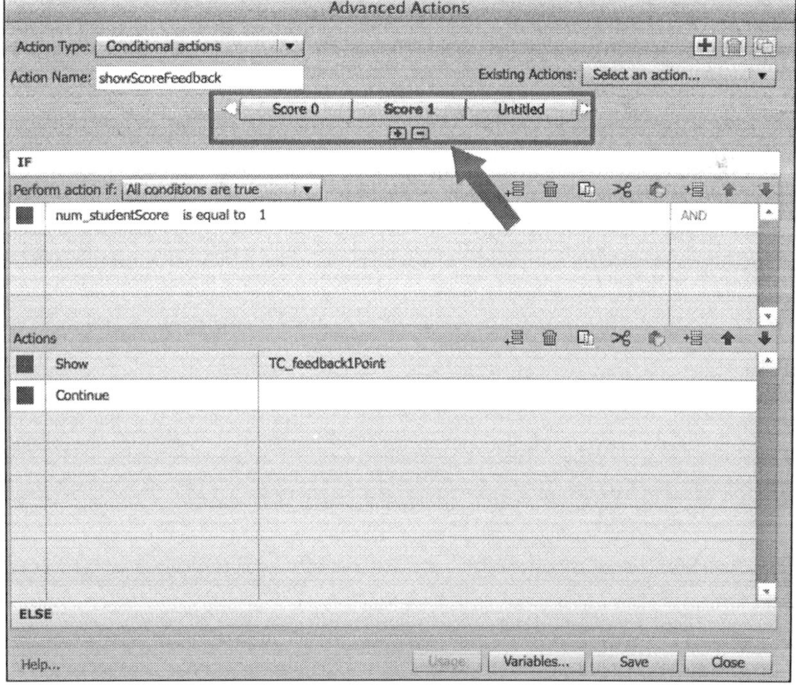

To code the last situation, we will simply add a third decision into the mix.

24. Double-click on the third (**untitled**) decision and rename it **Score 2**.
25. In the **IF** panel of the third decision, use the preceding techniques we discussed to code the condition so it reads `num_studentScore is equal to 2`.
26. In the **Action** panel, set the first action to `Show TC_feedback2Points` and the second action to `Continue`.
27. Make sure the **Advanced Actions** panel looks like the following screenshot. Notice the three decisions at the top of the dialog.

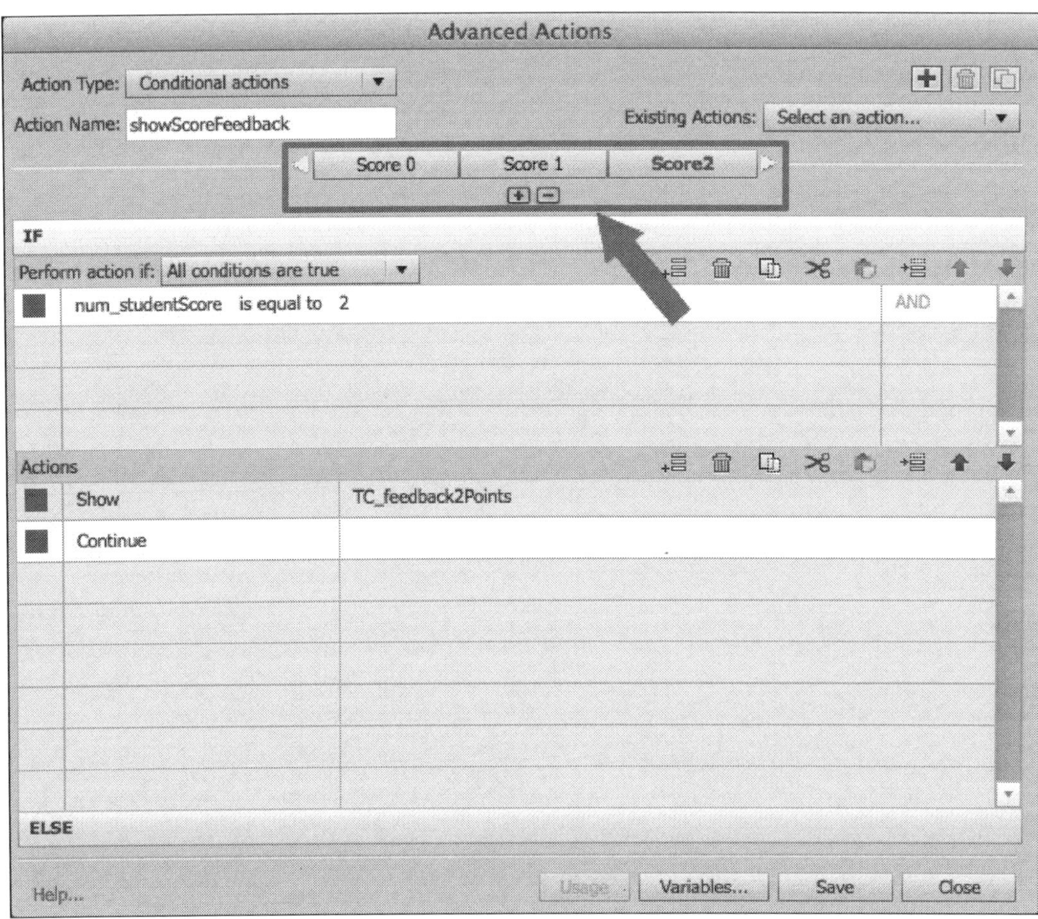

28. At the bottom of the **Advanced Actions** dialog, click on the **Save** button to save the changes made to the Action. Acknowledge the successful save of the script and click on the **Close** button to close the **Advanced Actions** dialog.

Finally, we will instruct Captivate that this action should run when entering slide 13.

29. Use the **Filmstrip** to go to slide 13.
30. In the **Properties** panel of slide 13, open the **On Enter** drop-down.
31. Choose **Execute Advanced Actions** from the drop-down list.
32. Choose the **showScoreFeedback** action in the **Script** drop-down.

We must also change the Action of the **Continue** button of slide 11.

33. Use the **Filmstrip** to go to slide 11 and select the **Continue** button.
34. In the **Action** accordion of the **Properties** panel, change the **Action** to **Jump to Slide**. Choose to jump to **slide 13** in the **Slide** drop-down.

For the testing phase, we will preview the entire project three times in order to test each of the three possible situations. Each time a test is run, we will answer differently to the question and see if the right feedback message shows up on slide 13.

35. Use the preview icon to preview the entire **project**. When the preview reaches slide 13, pay close attention to the message that is displayed.
36. Repeat this operation two more times. Make sure that you answer differently to the first two questions each time.

Normally, all three tests should run fine. The message displayed on slide 13 depends on the value of the `num_studentScore` variable which itself depends on the answers of the student.

Using a Conditional Action to implement Branching with the Pretest

In this section, we will return to the Encoder Demonstration project. Remember that this project begins with a Pretest.

1. If needed, open the `Chapter11/encoderDemo_800.cptx` project.

The Pretest is composed of three question slides. These question slides are slides 4, 5, and 6 of the project. Slide 7 is the automatically generated Quiz Result Slide. Remember that because the Pretest Question Slides are not actually part of the Quiz, the Quiz Result Slide displays a score of 0 regardless of the outcome of the Pretest. That's why we decided to hide slide 7 and to replace it with slides 8 and 9. Earlier in this chapter, we used a System Variable to display the student's score on these two slides.

In the next exercise, we will instruct Captivate to display slide 8 if the student has passed the Pretest and slide 9 if the student has failed the Pretest.

2. Use the **Filmstrip** to go to slide 6 of the project.

Slide 6 is the last question slide of the Pretest. Since slide 6 is a Question Slide, options are available in the **Quiz Properties** panel.

3. Open the **Quiz Properties** panel of slide 6. By default it is situated on the right side of the screen next to the **Properties** and **Library** panels.
4. In the **Action** accordion of the **Quiz Properties** panel, click on the **Edit Pretest Action** button.

This opens the **Advanced Actions** dialog box. A Conditional Advanced Action named **CPPretestAction** *automatically* loads into the dialog box.

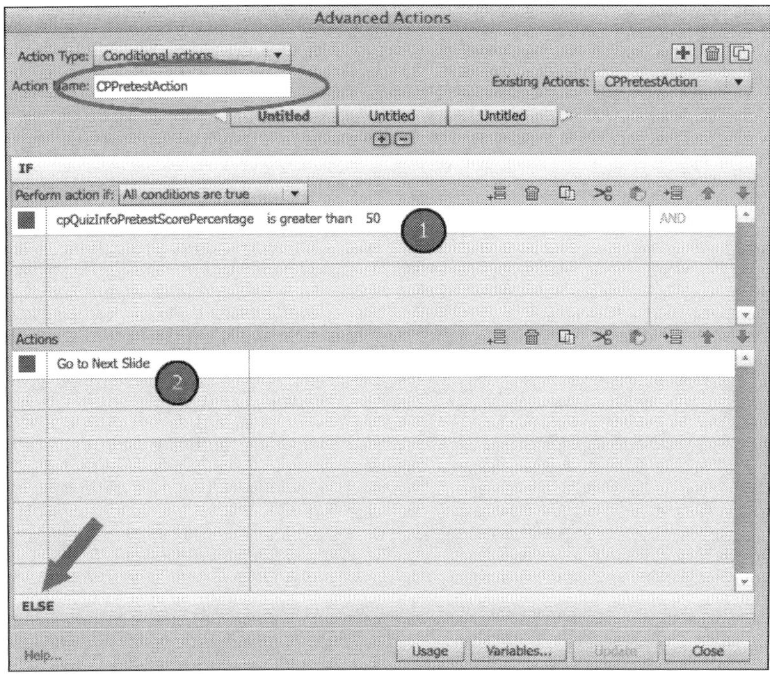

Captivate has automatically generated the **CPPretestAction** when we inserted the first Pretest Question Slide in the project. This action is automatically triggered at the end of the Pretest. Note that it uses the `cpQuizInfoPretestScorePercentage` system variable and compares it to 50 (1). By default, the action is set to **Go to Next Slide** (2).

5. Double-click on the **Go to Next Slide** action. Then, open the **Select Action** drop-down and choose the **Jump To Slide** action.
6. Open the **Select Slide** drop-down and choose to jump to slide **8 Pretest Success**.

The first part of the branching is finished! Captivate knows that it has to display slide 8 if the value of `cpQuizInfoPretestScorePercentage` is greater than or equal to 50, or, in other words, if the student has passed the Pretest. In every other situation, the student fails the Pretest and Captivate has to display slide 9 to the student.

7. At the bottom of the **Advanced Actions** dialog, click on **ELSE** (see the red arrow in the preceding screenshot).

Note that the default action of the **ELSE** clause also is the **Go to next slide** action. Obviously, we have to change it to *Jump to slide 9*.

8. Double-click on the **Go to Next Slide** action. Then, open the **Select Action** drop-down and choose the **Jump To Slide** action from the list.
9. Open the **Select Slide** drop-down and choose to jump to slide **9 Pretest Fail**.
10. Click on the **Update** button at the bottom of the **Advanced Actions** dialog to save the changes made to the **CPPretestAction** script.
11. Acknowledge the successful update of the script and close the **Advanced Actions** dialog.

Now that we have modified the `CPPretestAction`, Captivate knows what to do when the student passes or fails the Pretest. To make sure everything works as expected, some testing is needed.

12. Use the Preview icon to test the entire **Project**.

Make sure to test the project twice. For the first time, you should fail the Pretest and confirm that Captivate shows slide 9. For the second time, make sure you pass the Pretest, so Captivate displays slide 8 and gives you the opportunity to skip the Demonstration.

If everything works as expected, we have finished our exploration of Advanced Actions. Let's make a quick summary of what we have learned.

- There are two kinds of Advanced Actions in Captivate: the **Standard Actions** and the **Conditional Actions**.
- A Standard Action is a simple list of instructions executed *one by one* and *in order* at runtime. A Conditional Action checks if a condition is met before executing an action.
- When Creating a Conditional Action, we can create as many **decisions** as needed. Each decision is executed one by one by Captivate regardless of the outcome of any preceding decision.
- The Advanced Actions can be used to manipulate System or User-Defined Variables as well as to manipulate the objects of the project.
- It is possible to give a name to any objects added in Captivate. This makes it easier to manipulate these objects with Advanced Actions.
- It is necessary to bind an action to an **event** to instruct Captivate about *when* an action should be executed.
- There are two kinds of events in Captivate, the **System Events** and the **Student-Driven Events**.
- The System Events *are fired automatically* by the project. Example of system events are the beginning or the end of a slide, the start of the project, and so on.
- The Student-Driven Events are fired *by an action from the student*. The typical Student-Driven Event is a click on a button, but it can also be a click on a Click Box, the answer to a Question Slide, and so on.
- When we insert a Pretest in our project, Captivate automatically creates the `CPPretestAction` Conditional Advanced Action. This Advanced Action is automatically triggered at the end of the Pretest. We can use it to implement branching based on the outcome of the Pretest.

This concludes our discussion on Variables and Advanced Actions. It is one of the most advanced topics found in Captivate so don't worry if it is still a bit blurry for you. With time and experience, you'll be able to take full advantage of this powerful tool.

For more on Advanced Actions, make sure you subscribe to Lieve Weymeis' blog at `http://lilybiri.posterous.com/`. She is a world-class specialist of Advanced Actions and her blog is second to none when it comes to Variables, Advanced Actions, and other advanced tips and tricks on Captivate.

We will now move on to the next topic of this chapter and discuss the **Widgets**.

Widgets

According to the help files of Captivate:

> *Widgets are configurable SWF objects created in Flash. Widgets can help provide enhanced interactivity and rich content rapidly*

To make it short, a Widget is an external `.swf` file that adds an extra feature to the already rich set of tools provided by Captivate. These Widgets are created outside of Captivate in Adobe Flash Professional or in Adobe Flash Builder.

Creating Widgets

Creating Widgets is reserved to developers with knowledge of Flash and ActionScript, so it is beyond the scope of this book. If you have such knowledge, and want to start programming your own Captivate Widgets, make sure you subscribe to Tristan Ward's blog at `http://www.infosemantics.com.au/widgetking/`. You can also read the following tutorials to get you started: `http://blogs.adobe.com/captivate/2009/06/captivate_widgets_tutorial_cre.html` and `http://blogs.adobe.com/captivate/2010/10/flex-based-widgets.html`.

Some Widgets are shipped with Captivate, but the ultimate goal of Widgets is to let anyone create and share their homemade Widgets, so most Widgets can be downloaded from the Internet. Some can be downloaded for free while others are for sale.

Locating Widgets

By default, Captivate looks for the Widgets in the `[Captivate Install Path]/Gallery/Widgets` folder, but Widgets can be located anywhere on your hard disk.

1. Open Windows Explorer (Win) or the Finder (Mac) and browse to the `[Captivate Installation]/Gallery/Widgets`.

We already discussed the *Gallery* earlier in the book (see *Chapter 4, Working with Animations and Interactive Objects*, and *Chapter 5, Working with Audio*). As a reminder, the *Gallery* is a folder that contains various assets that we can use in our projects.

The `Widgets` folder of the `Gallery` contains a lot of `.swf` files and some `.wdgt` files. These are the two file extensions used to create Widgets. Each of the files present in the `Gallery/Widgets` folder is a *Widget* that we can insert in our Captivate Projects.

2. Return to Captivate and use the **Window | Widget** menu item to open the **Widgets** panel.

By default, the **Widgets** panel appears at the bottom-right corner of the screen, below the **Properties** panel.

3. Inspect the list of available Widgets and compare it with the files situated in the `Gallery/Widgets` folder.
4. At the very bottom of the **Widgets** panel, click on the very first icon named **Change Path**.

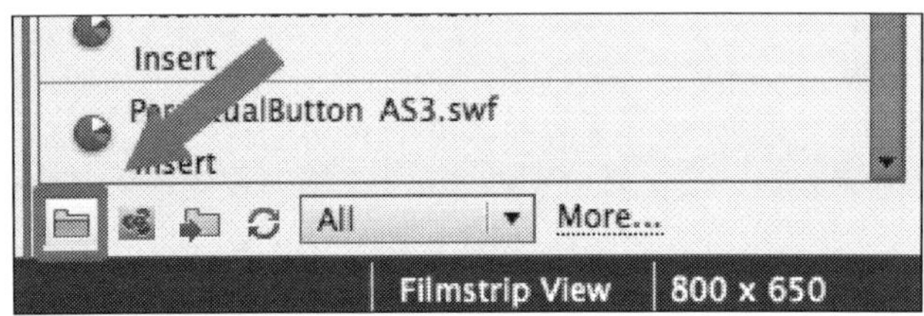

The window that opens when clicking on this icon lets us choose another folder on our hard disk from which Captivate retrieves the Widgets that appear in the **Widgets** panel. Thanks to this icon, we can store our Widgets anywhere on our computer.

5. Click on the **Cancel** button to close the dialog box without changing the path.

For the following exercises, we will use Widgets that are provided with Captivate, so make sure that the Path is set to `[Captivate Installation]/Gallery/Widgets`.

You may be wondering what is the difference between a *Widget* and a standard `.swf` *animation* as the ones we inserted in our project back in *Chapter 4, Working with Animations and Interactive Objects*. Both objects are external `.swf` files and both are situated in the `/gallery` folder of Captivate.

The answer is simple and is what makes Widgets truly awesome. Unlike the standard `.swf` animations of *Chapter 4, Working with Animations and Interactive Objects*, we can **customize** the widgets right within Captivate.

Modifying Widgets

For the ActionScript developers reading these pages, Adobe provides the source files of these Widgets in the `[Captivate Installation]/Gallery/Widgets/Source` folder. Feel free to inspect the code and to customize these widgets at will. If you come up with a nice Widget, don't forget to make it available to the community!

Understanding the three types of Widgets

Captivate proposes three types of Widgets: the **Static Widgets**, the **Interactive Widgets**, and the **Question Widgets**.

In this section, we will study each of these three Widget types one by one.

Static Widgets

Captivate proposes many objects that we can insert on the slides of our projects. We have studied most of these objects throughout this book, so they have no more secrets for us by now.

A **Static Widget** is **an extra object** that we can add to our slides. It has the same basic capabilities as any standard objects of Captivate. It is visible on the **Timeline** and can be synchronized with the rest of the objects of the slide.

In the next exercise, we will insert a *Static Widget* in the Driving in Belgium project.

1. Return to the `Chapter11/drivingInBe.cptx` file.
2. Use the **Filmstrip** to go to slide 26.

Remember that slide 25 is shown only to those students that pass the quiz. The Widget that we will add to this slide is called the *Certificate Widget*. It automatically generates a completion certificate that the student can print.

3. Return to the **Widgets** panel. Locate the **CertificateWidget.swf** in the panel and click on the corresponding **Insert** link.

The *Certificate Widget* is inserted on the slide and the **Widget Properties** dialog pops up in the center of the screen.

The **Widget Properties** dialog lets us customize the Widget being inserted in various ways. Its content depends on the Widget being inserted. It is up to each Widget developer to develop this dialog box and to provide options to customize the Widget. Sometimes, there are very few customizations available, and sometimes, like when using the Certificate Widget for instance, lots of options are available. Refer to the documentation of each Widget for explanation, support, and troubleshooting.

We will now use the **Widget Properties** dialog to customize the Certificate Widget that we are inserting.

4. Type **Driving In Belgium** in the **Course Name** field.
5. Click on the *Folder* icon situated next to the Logo field. Choose the `images/mftcLogo.png` file situated in the exercise files as the logo.
6. In the **Font Settings** section of the dialog, change the font **Family** to **Century Gothic**.
7. Leave the other options at their current setting. The **Widgets Properties** dialog should look like the following screenshot:

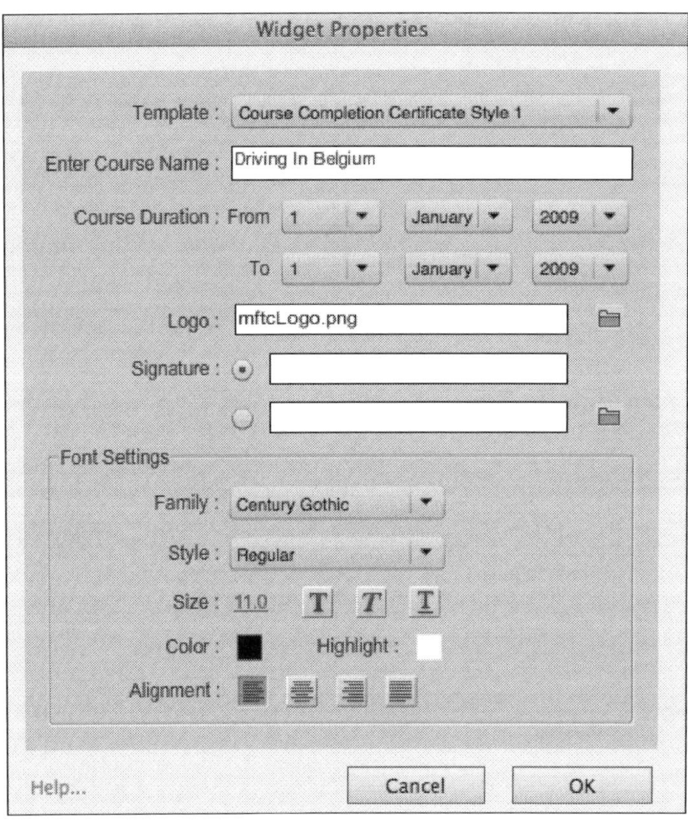

8. If everything is fine, click on **OK** to validate these settings and insert the Widget.
9. Move and resize the Widget so that it does not overlap the other objects of the slide.
10. Return to the **Properties** panel.

In the **Properties** panel of the Certificate Widget, notice that most of the accordions are the same as those used for the standard objects of Captivate. Also notice that the Widget appears in the **Timeline**, so we can arrange it in time using the same techniques as for the other objects of Captivate. Only the first accordion of the **Properties** panel is specific to the Widget.

11. Click on the **Widget Properties** button situated in the **Animation** accordion of the **Properties** panel.

The **Widget Properties** button brings us back to the **Widget Properties** dialog where we can further customize the Widget. Remember that the content of this box is different for each Widget.

12. Click on **Cancel** to close the **Widget Properties** dialog without doing any changes.
13. Save the file and use the Preview icon to test the entire **Project**.

Make sure you pass the test to see the slide containing the Certificate Widget.

Interactive Widgets

Captivate proposes three interactive objects: the *Click Box*, the *Text Entry Box*, and the *Button*. Remember that these three objects have the power to stop the playhead and wait for the student to interact with the movie.

An Interactive Widget is **an extra interactive object**. It has the same basic capabilities as the existing interactive objects of Captivate. That is, it can stop the playhead, interact with the student, and implement Branching.

In the next exercise, we will replace the **Let's go** button of slide 3 with the `NextButton AS3.wdgt` Widget:

1. Return to the `Chapter11/drivingInBe.cptx` file.
2. Use the **Filmstrip** to go to Slide 3.
3. Once on slide 3, select the **Let's Go** button and *delete* it.
4. Open the **Widgets** panel.

By default, it is displayed on the bottom right side of the screen below to the **Properties** and the **Library** panels.

Notice the drop-down list at the very bottom of the **Widgets** panel.

5. Open the drop down list at the bottom of the **Widgets** panel and choose the **Interactive** option.

This drop-down list acts as a filter to help us locate the Widgets more easily.

6. From the list of Interactive Widgets, locate the `NextButton AS3.wdgt` Widget and insert it on the slide.
7. The **Widget Properties** dialog box opens.

Notice that the **Widget Properties** dialog of this Widget is *not* the same as the one we used for the *Certificate Widget* we inserted in the previous section. Remember that each Widget has its own **Widget Properties** dialog.

This particular Widget does *not* offer any room for customization, so we will simply click on the **OK** button to insert the Widget on the slide.

8. Click on the **OK** button to insert the Widget on the slide.

The **Next** button is inserted into the slide. Notice that it comes with a *Success Caption*, a *Failure Caption*, and a *Hint Caption*. This tells us that this is an *Interactive* Widget. Its capabilities are similar to the other interactive objects of Captivate.

9. With the **Next** button selected, open the **Properties** panel.

Notice that the accordions of the **Properties** panel of this Widget are similar to those of the other interactive objects of Captivate.

We will now use these accordions to adjust the properties to our new **Next** button:

10. In the **Options** accordion, deselect the **Success**, **Failure**, and **Hint** captions.
11. In the **Action** accordion, set the **On Success** action to **Go to the next slide**.
12. Move the button to the lower-right area of the slide.
13. In the **Timing** accordion, make the Widget **Appear After 3 sec**onds, **Display For** the **rest of** the **slide**, and **Pause After 1 sec**.

These settings are reflected on the **Timeline**. When done, save the file and test the movie. Normally, The Interactive Widget should behave like any other interactive objects of Captivate.

Question Widgets

The Quiz engine of Captivate proposes quite a few question types that we can add in our projects. A Question Widget is **an extra question type** that we can include in our Quizzes. It has the same basic capabilities as any regular Question Slide of Captivate and its answers can be reported to an LMS using the same technique as the one used to report the answers of any other question types of Captivate.

1. Return to the `Chapter11/drivingInBe.cptx` file and open the **Widgets** panel.
2. At the bottom of the **Widgets** panel, open the drop-down list and choose **Question** from the list of available options.

By default, Captivate contains only one Question Widget named the `MCQ AS3.swf`. It is a *Multiple-Choice Question* Widget written in ActionScript 3. In the next exercise, we add one more question to the Quiz, using the `MCQ AS3.swf` widget.

3. Use the **Filmstrip** to go to slide 21 of the project. Slide 21 should be the sequence Question Slide of our quiz.
4. In the **Widget** panel Locate the `MCQ AS3.swf` Widget in the **Widgets** panel and click on the associated **Insert** link.

Captivate inserts a new Question Slide in the **Filmstrip**. This new Question Slide is a Widget Question. We will now change the various Text Captions associated with this new question and set up the multiple choices.

5. Change the content of the Text Caption that reads **Widget Question** to **Multiple Choice**.
6. Change the content of the Text Caption that reads **Type the question here** to **What best describes the Belgian way of driving?**

So far, so good! Nothing new for us! Just a bunch of Text Captions to adjust. We will now dig into the heart of this Question Widget and provide the multiple answers our students will have to choose from.

7. Double-click on the **Widget Question** rectangle situated in the middle of the slide.

This action opens the **Widget Properties** dialog. Remember that this dialog box is specific to each Widget. Note that two possible answers are already provided into the **Widget Properties** dialog.

8. Click once on the **Add** button add one possible answer on the list. You should now have a total of three possible answers in the **Widget Properties** dialog.

9. Type the following answers in each of the Answer fields:
    - `Belgian do not drive!`
    - `Belgian drive on the right side of the road.`
    - `Belgian use Miles per Hour to measure speed.`
10. To mark the correct answer, first deselect the currently selected answer, then, select the answer **B** checkbox.

Take some time to inspect the other available properties of this Widget, but leave them all at their current settings. Make sure that the **Widget Properties** box is similar to the following screenshot:

11. If everything looks fine, click on the **OK** button to validate the changes and close the box.
12. In the **Quiz Properties** panel, open the **Reporting** accordion.
13. Type `WMC_belgianWays` as the **Interaction ID**.

WMC stands for **W**idget **M**ultiple **C**hoice. Notice that the accordions of the **Quiz Properties** panel are the same as the accordions of any other Question Slide of Captivate.

14. In the **Options** accordion, deselect the **Incomplete** option. This action removes the orange feedback message from the slide.
15. Also deselect the **Next** option to remove the **Next** button from the slide.
16. Change the content of the two remaining feedback messages. Move and resize them as you see fit.
17. Use the Preview icon to test the entire movie.

Make sure the Widget Question works as expected. When done, close the **Preview** pane and save the file.

Where to find Widgets?

In addition to the Widgets provided by Captivate, many Widgets can be found on the Internet. Some are for free and some are for sale. In this section, I would like to introduce some reference sites where great Widgets can be found. This section is *not* intended to be a comprehensive list of *all* the greatest Captivate sites, but I feel like these are a good starting point to start your own research.

Adobe Captivate Exchange

The first reference is the Adobe website itself, and more specifically, a section of the site called **Adobe Exchange**. On Adobe Exchange, you'll find lots of plugins, widgets, scripts, extension, and so on for various Adobe products including Captivate. Adobe Captivate Exchange can be accessed right from within the Captivate interface.

1. Return to Captivate and open the **Widgets** panel.
2. At the end of the **Widgets** panel, click on the second icon to access **Adobe Captivate Exchange**.

This action opens your default web browser and takes you to the Adobe Captivate Exchange website where lots of great assets can be found including Widgets, sounds, images, and so on.

Blogs and websites

- **Cpguru**: Another great website for widgets is `www.cpguru.com`. Both free and commercial Widgets can be found on this site and you can even request Michael to develop a custom widget just for you. Michael also maintains a great Captivate blog on this website.
- **CaptivateDev**: `www.captivatedev.com` is maintained by Jim Leichliter. He provides lots of free and commercial Widgets for Captivate and also runs his own blog. You certainly want to bookmark this site while working with Captivate.
- **Infosemantic**: Infosemantic is an Australian company that specializes in developing Widgets for Captivate. Their Widgets can be found on their website at `http://www.infosemantics.com.au/`. The list of their free Captivate Widgets can be found at `http://www.infosemantics.com.au/adobe-captivate-widgets/download-free-trial-widgets`.

Working with the Smart Learning Interactions

Smart Learning interactions are a new feature of Captivate 6. A **Smart Learning Interaction** is a complex interactive object with lots of built-in behavior. Smart Learning interactions and Widgets have a lot in common. First, it is possible to download more interactions from the Internet. Second, Smart Learning Interactions can be customized in various ways.

As a new feature of Captivate 6, Smart Learning Interactions are entirely compatible with both Flash and HTML 5, which is not the case for most Widgets.

In the next exercise, we will add one slide to the Driving In Belgium project and add a Smart Interaction onto it.

1. If needed, return to the `Chapter11/drivingInBe.cptx` file.
2. Use the **Filmstrip** to go to the first slide of the project.
3. Use the **Insert | New Slide from | Blank** menu item to insert a new slide based on the Blank Master Slide of the Theme.

The new slide is inserted as slide 2 of the project.

4. Add a *Continue* button to the slide. Use the **MFTC-ButtonContinue** style and position it at the bottom-right corner of the slide. Make sure its action is **Go to the next slide**.

The stage is set! Our next task will be to add a Smart Learning Interaction on this new slide.

5. Use the **Insert | Interaction** menu item to open the **Select Interaction** dialog.

The **Select Interaction** dialog shows a list of all the Interactions available in Captivate 6. Notice the **Download More** link (see the red arrow in the following screenshot) that lets us download some more interactions from the Internet.

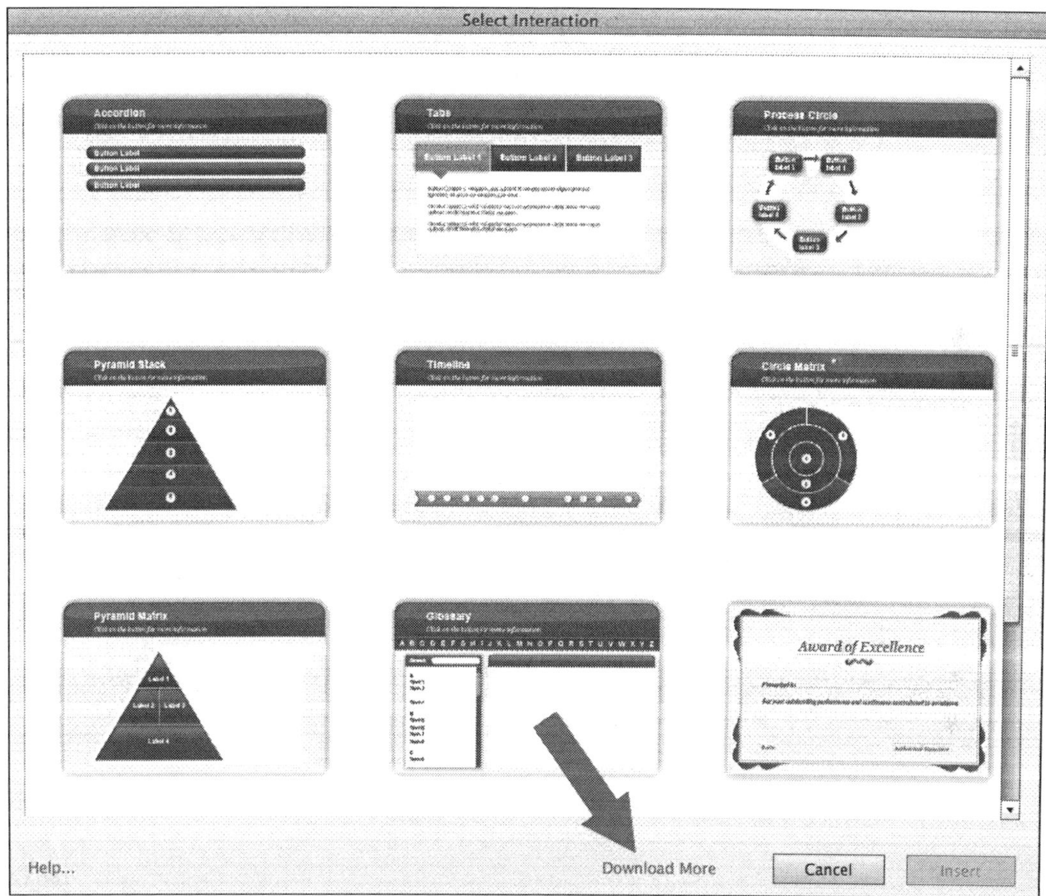

6. Take some time to inspect the available interactions. When done, select the **Accordion** interaction (the first one on the list) and click on **Insert** to insert it onto slide 2.

This action inserts the Accordion Smart Interaction onto slide 2 and opens the **Configure Interaction** dialog box. We will use it to customize both the content and the look and feel of our accordion.

7. Use the left column of the **Configure Interaction** dialog, to choose a Theme of your liking (In the example of the `Chapter11/final` folder, we choose Theme 7).
8. Click on the **Custom | Header** section of the left column of the **Configure Interaction** dialog.
9. At the top of the **Custom | Header** section, turn the Header **Off**.

That is for the look and feel of the interaction. We will now customize the content of the accordion.

10. In the main area of the **Configure Widget** dialog, *double-click* on the first button of the accordion and change its **Title** to `Description`.
11. Double-click on the Content area of the first accordion and type a short description of the project.

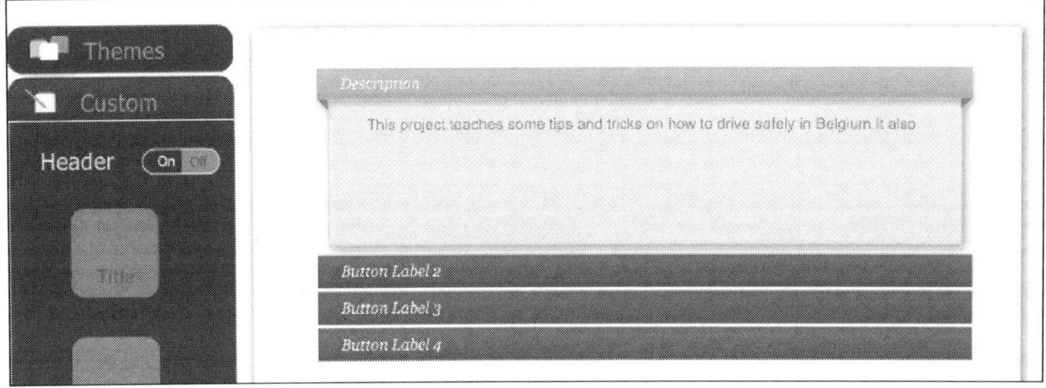

12. Change the **Button Label 2** title to `Target Audience` and the **Button Label 3** title to `Length of the project.`
13. Double-click on the **Button Label 4** and click on the *Minus* button to delete it from the accordion.

You should now have three panels left in the accordion as shown on the following screenshot:

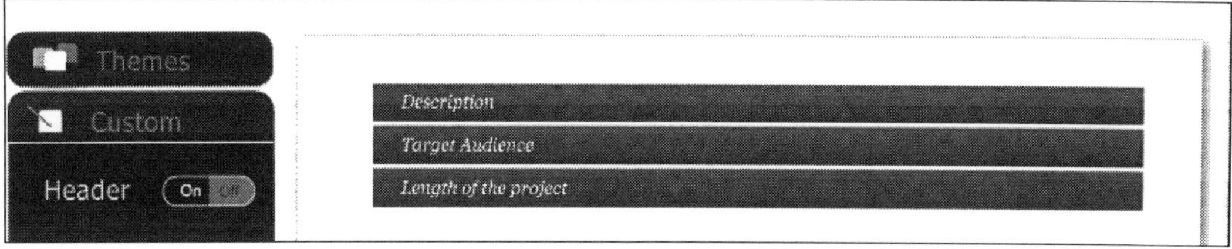

14. Add an appropriate descriptive text in each of the three panels.
15. Don't hesitate to explore the other options available and to further customize your accordion interaction. When done, click on the **OK** button.
16. Move and resize the Accordion so it integrates nicely into the slide.
17. If needed, click on the **Widget Properties** button situated in the **Animation** accordion of the **Properties** panel to re-open the **Configure Interaction** dialog and further customize your accordion.

This exercise concludes our exploration of the new Smart Learning Interactions of Captivate 6. There are some great tutorials and videos available on the Internet, if you want to have some more examples and insights on this new feature.

Here are some interesting links to get you started with the new Smart Learning Interactions. `http://tv.adobe.com/watch/new-in-adobe-captivate-6/smart-learning-interactions/` on Adobe TV.

One of the Sneak Peeks revealed just before the release of Captivate `http://blogs.adobe.com/captivate/2012/06/adobe-captivate-6-sneak-peek-4-interactions-actors.html`.
A Tutorial on the Smart Learning Interactions in the official Adobe Captivate YouTube channel `http://youtu.be/I2RYSOQUOkk`.

Summary

Thanks to the Advanced Actions and the Variables, we have been able to add a whole new level of interaction and interactivity to our projects. The good news is that we just briefly approached the tip of the iceberg in this chapter. The possibilities are virtually endless and your imagination is the ultimate limit to what can be achieved.

To implement these Advanced Actions and these Variables, Captivate takes advantage of its Flash roots and more specifically to one of the greatest additions to the Flash technology: a programming language called ActionScript. When publishing the project to HTML 5, Captivate translates these variables and Advanced Actions to JavaScript instead.

Advanced actions and Variables can be used to create some pieces of *Dynamic Text*, to turn the visibility of objects on and off, to control the movie, to access information about the movie, and much, much much more.

The Flash developers and the ActionScript programmers can also contribute to Captivate by creating Widgets. Widgets are extra-features that we can add to Captivate. A small selection of Widgets is provided with the standard Captivate license, but most Widgets can be downloaded from the Internet. Some Widgets are for free, while others are for sale. If you are an ActionScript developer, don't hesitate to write your own widgets and make them available to the community. The best Widgets are yet to be written.

Finally, we took a quick look at the Smart Learning Interactions of Captivate 6. These interactions work pretty much like the Widgets, but they are entirely compatible with both Flash and HTML 5, which makes them a tool of the future.

Meet the Community

CpGuru

Bio

Michael also known as Cpguru has been a part of the Adobe Captivate community since version 2 and early on started to experiment with pushing Captivate to the limit and expanding its functionality with custom Flash components. He is an active participant on the Adobe Captivate forums and a Community Champion on `http://captivate.adobe.com/`.

Michael runs the site `www.cpguru.com` where he provides tips and tricks on common issues and problems with Adobe Captivate and tutorials on how to achieve more advanced things with Adobe Captivate.

The site also has a number of free and commercial widgets for Adobe Captivate that can help you achieve more with your Adobe Captivate projects. Michael also provides freelance support and troubleshooting and develops custom Adobe Captivate widgets if you need to achieve something special in your projects.

Contact details

Website: `www.cpguru.com`

Twitter: `https://twitter.com/#!/cpguru_com`

Facebook: `http://www.facebook.com/pages/cpgurucom/228020020575087`

My personal note

I read quite a few articles on Michael's blog while writing this book, and when I contacted him about this *Meet the Community* section, he was one of the first individual to respond to my request.

You definitely want to bookmark his website when working with Captivate and to check out his free Captivate Widgets.

Index

Symbols

A

B

C

D

E

F

P

Q

R

S

T

X

Z

About Packt Publishing

Packt, pronounced 'packed', published its first book "*Mastering phpMyAdmin for Effective MySQL Management*" in April 2004 and subsequently continued to specialize in publishing highly focused books on specific technologies and solutions.

Our books and publications share the experiences of your fellow IT professionals in adapting and customizing today's systems, applications, and frameworks. Our solution based books give you the knowledge and power to customize the software and technologies you're using to get the job done. Packt books are more specific and less general than the IT books you have seen in the past. Our unique business model allows us to bring you more focused information, giving you more of what you need to know, and less of what you don't.

Packt is a modern, yet unique publishing company, which focuses on producing quality, cutting-edge books for communities of developers, administrators, and newbies alike. For more information, please visit our website: `www.packtpub.com`.

Writing for Packt

We welcome all inquiries from people who are interested in authoring. Book proposals should be sent to `author@packtpub.com`. If your book idea is still at an early stage and you would like to discuss it first before writing a formal book proposal, contact us; one of our commissioning editors will get in touch with you.

We're not just looking for published authors; if you have strong technical skills but no writing experience, our experienced editors can help you develop a writing career, or simply get some additional reward for your expertise.

Dreamweaver CS5.5 Mobile and Web Development with HTML5, CSS3, and jQuery

ISBN: 978-1-84969-158-1 Paperback: 284 pages

Harness the cutting edge features of Dreamweaver for mobile and web development

1. Create web pages in Dreamweaver using the latest technology and approach
2. Add multimedia and interactivity to your websites
3. Optimize your websites for a wide range of platforms and build mobile apps with Dreamweaver

---

Moodle 2 Administration

ISBN: 978-1-84951-604-4 Paperback: 420 pages

An administrator's guide to configuring, securing, customizing, and extending Moodle

1. A complete guide for planning, installing, optimizing, customizing, and configuring Moodle
2. Learn how to network and extend Moodle for your needs and integrate with other systems
3. A complete reference of all Moodle system settings

Please check **www.PacktPub.com** for information on our titles

Moodle 2.0 Course Conversion Beginner's Guide

ISBN: 978-1-84951-482-8 Paperback: 368 pages

A complete guide to successful learning using Moodle 2.0

1. Move your existing course notes, worksheets, and resources into Moodle quickly
2. No need to start from scratch! This book shows you the quickest way to start using Moodle and e-learning, by bringing your existing lesson materials into Moodle
3. Demonstrates quick ways to improve your course, taking advantage of multimedia and collaboration

---

WordPress for Education

ISBN: 978-1-84951-820-8 Paperback: 144 pages

Create interactive and engaging e-learning websites with WordPress

1. Develop effective e-learning websites that will engage your students
2. Extend the potential of a classroom website with WordPress plugins
3. Create an interactive social network and course management system to enhance student and instructor communication

Please check **www.PacktPub.com** for information on our titles

Made in the USA
Lexington, KY
17 May 2013